THE BLOOD
OF THE COLONY

THE BLOOD
OF THE COLONY

Wine *and the* Rise *and* Fall
of French Algeria

OWEN WHITE

HARVARD UNIVERSITY PRESS
Cambridge, Massachusetts
London, England   2021

Library of Congress Cataloging-in-Publication Data

Names: White, Owen (Associate professor of History), author.
Title: The blood of the colony : wine and the rise and fall
   of French Algeria / Owen White.
Description: Cambridge, Massachusetts : Harvard University Press, 2021. |
   Includes bibliographical references and index.
Identifiers: LCCN 2020017728 | ISBN 9780674248441 (cloth)
Subjects: LCSH: Wine industry—Algeria—History. | Wine and wine making—
   Algeria—History. | Decolonization—Algeria. | Algeria—History—1830–1962. |
   Algeria—Politics and government—1830–1962. | France—Colonies—Africa.
Classification: LCC HD9387.A4 W55 2021 | DDC 338.4/766320096509041—dc23
LC record available at https://lccn.loc.gov/2020017728

· *To Patricia* ·

Contents

Note on Place Names

Many towns and villages in Algeria changed their names after independence in 1962. Colonial-era names of places mentioned in the text are
listed below alongside their postindependence names.

Colonial	*Postindependence*
Aïn-el-Arba	Aïn El Arbaa
Aïn-Kial	Aïn Kihal
Aïn-Tédélès	Aïn Tédlès
Ameur-el-Aïn	Ahmar El Aïn
Bellecôte	Aïn Boudinar
Bellevue	Sour
Birkadem	Birkhadem
Bône	Annaba
Bougie	Béjaïa
Cassaigne	Sidi Ali
Castiglione	Bou Ismaïl
Courbet	Zemmouri
Descartes	Ben Badis
Djidjelli	Jijel
Dollfusville	Oued Chorfa
Dupleix	Damous
Er-Rahel	Hassi El Ghella
Fleurus	Hassiane Ettoual
Fondouk	Khemis El Khechna
Fontaine-du-Génie	Hadjret Ennous
Fort de l'Eau	Bordj El Kiffan
Gaston-Doumergue	Oued Berkèche
Jemmapes	Azzaba
Laferrière	Chaabat El Leham

Lambèse	Tazoult
Lamoricière	Ouled Mimoun
L'Arba	Larbaâ
Le Gué de Constantine	Djasr Kasentina
Les Abdellys	Sidi Abdelli
Lourmel	El Amria
Maison-Blanche	Dar El Beïda
Maison-Carrée	El Harrach
Marengo	Hadjout
Margueritte	Aïn Torki
Mercier-Lacombe	Sfisef
Mirabeau	Draâ Ben Khedda
Mondovi	Dréan
Montagnac	Remchi
Mouzaïaville	Mouzaïa
Novi	Sidi Ghiles
Orléansville	El Asnam (changed to Chlef in 1980)
Palestro	Lakhdaria
Palissy	Sidi Khaled
Philippeville	Skikda
Rio Salado	El Malah
Rivet	Meftah
Saint-Denis du Sig	Sig
Saint-Maur	Tamzoura
Sidi-Ferruch	Sidi Fredj

Note on Metric Conversion

1 kilometer = 0.62 miles

1 hectare = 2.47 acres; 100 hectares = 1 square kilometer = 0.38 square miles

1 hectoliter = 100 liters = 26.4 liquid gallons (US) or 22 imperial gallons (UK)

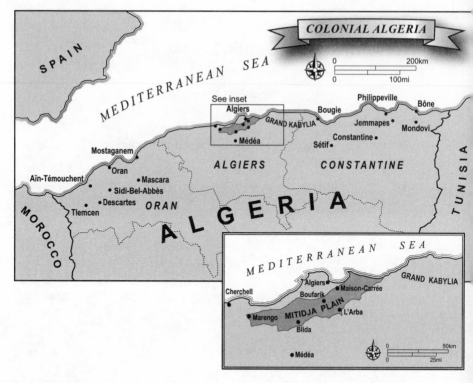

MAP 1 Colonial Algeria

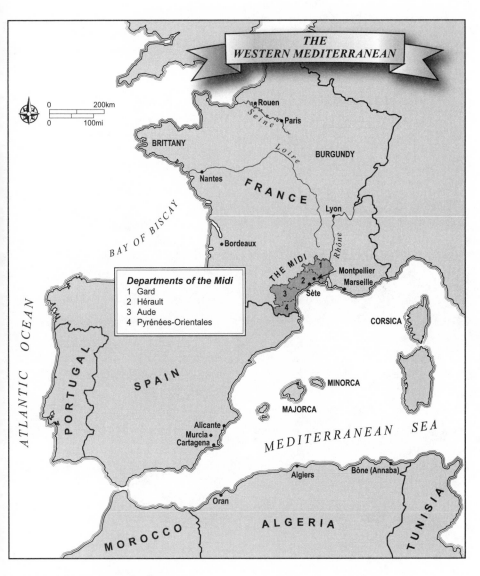

MAP 2 The Western Mediterranean

THE BLOOD
OF THE COLONY

Introduction

The Empire of Wine in Algeria

For most of the twentieth century, Algeria was the fourth-biggest wine producer in the world. By the 2010s, the three leading producers were the same as in 1900: France, Italy, and Spain. Algeria no longer placed anywhere near the top twenty.[1]

Underlying these basic facts is an extraordinary example of the capacity of modern European imperialists to transform lands in their own image. In the last decades of the nineteenth century, settlers from countries on the European side of the Mediterranean profited from the access to land created by France's conquest of Algeria to plant tens of thousands of hectares of grapevines. As the rows of vines lengthened, they gave new definition to the imperial edifice known as French Algeria. Wine became the colony's primary export, making fortunes for some while also drawing large numbers of Algerian Muslims into salaried labor. Some of those Algerian workers would eventually help bring French Algeria to a bloody end. Independent Algeria, a Muslim-majority country with a substantial wine industry, then had to decide how far it should undo the transformations the colonists had wrought.

Wine was so central to the economic life of French Algeria, the most important component of the world's second-largest empire, that it can be used to trace the rise and fall of the colony itself. That is exactly what this book sets out to do.

RISE AND FALL

To study a colonized territory in terms of its rise and fall is to risk embracing a cliché of writing about empire. Some historians criticize the rise-and-fall paradigm for reducing complex power dynamics to a simple parabola, as if empires were subject to the law of gravity.[2] As I researched the story of wine in Algeria from the start of the French conquest in 1830 through independence in 1962 and the half-century or so beyond, however, the arc of the production figures came to look very much like a rough measure of the strength of France's imperial influence.

The chronological structure of the following chapters should make the imperial trajectory clear. Despite the resources deployed in support of military invasion and European settlement in Algeria, the colony's early progress was halting and fragile. But it seemed clear to many that viticulture (the cultivation of grapevines) stood a very good chance of success on the slopes and plains that lay within about sixty kilometers of the Mediterranean. Settlers' wide-scale adoption of wine production later in the century placed the colony on a much firmer footing and went along with a doubling of the European population, from about 300,000 in 1870 to 600,000 in 1900. A new wave of vine planting after World War I coincided with what could be seen as the apogee of French Algeria around the time of its centenary in 1930. Though the wine industry maintained its importance thereafter, it faced increasing challenges from rural flight, labor protest, the hardships imposed by World War II, and, ultimately, the nationalist insurrection that catalyzed the end of French Algeria. After independence, wine was the most obvious vestige of the colonial economy until a concerted effort to reduce its prominence (and France's hold over Algeria) in the 1970s.

Within this overarching narrative we encounter individual tales of rise and fall, some of which fit Albert Camus's description of French Algeria as a land of "quick fortunes and spectacular collapses."[3] No one rose or fell further than Charles Debonno, a son of poor migrants from Malta who, by the turn of the twentieth century, produced wine on such a scale and using such modern techniques that it amazed French visitors, only to slide into bankruptcy and ruin as his debts got out of control. But, while the average colonist in Algeria was more of a risk-taker than the average farmer in metropolitan France and market fluctuations often hurt wine producers, focusing on booms and busts will not tell us the whole story. The profits earned by colonists with far fewer than Debonno's thousand hectares of vines helped sustain families across decades, and in that way sustained the wider project of colonization.

For Algerians, the subject of this book may suggest instead a fall followed by eventual recovery. The colonization of Algeria aimed, as the geographer Marc Côte has put it, "to people a land already peopled, to bring under cultivation a land already cultivated, to civilize a society that already had its own civilization."[4] Pursuit of those objectives entailed much violence. The French conquest and suppression of Algerian resistance was accompanied by widespread destruction of crops and followed by massive alienation of land from its previous owners or users.[5] At the moment vineyards in French Algeria reached their greatest extent, in the mid-1930s, about 400,000 hectares of arable land were devoted to a product that Muslim Algerians were not meant to consume. The vineyards required workers, but never enough or at salary levels able to satisfy the needs of Algerians when the lands that remained in their possession failed to provide enough food for their families. Nothing symbolized the French presence more than the colony's rows of vines, which at independence became more an economic and cultural problem for Algerians than a foundation for renewal. Inverting the rise-and-fall narrative for Algerians cannot capture the damaged inheritance of 130 years of colonization.

PEOPLE OF THE VINE

"We owe to wine a blessing far more precious than gold: the peopling of Algeria with Frenchmen," stated Pierre Berthault, a leading voice in colonial Algerian agriculture in the early 1930s. "It is thanks to the vine that wherever in Algeria there is a bell tower, a hamlet, a farm, there are also French hearts and minds."[6]

The image this statement conjures certainly contained a share of the truth. In village after village in the western department of Oran, for example, the view from the bell tower took in countless hectares of vines, which superficially made that part of Algeria look "French." More than other crops, too, viticulture helped to root settlers in the countryside. In turn this gave life to communities in which agricultural societies and *caves coopératives* (cooperative wineries) became features of everyday life just as much as the town hall, the school, the café, and the church.

In other respects the statement was incomplete or misleading. It offered no indication that the builders of the wine industry in French Algeria were frequently not of French origin. The author's romantic depiction of bell towers and hamlets obscured the fact that French Algerian wine was often a rather aggressively capitalist venture in which companies played a prominent role, quite unlike the small-scale, family-oriented production that was more typical of metropolitan France.[7] Nor did the statement acknowledge that the majority of the workers who tended the vines were Algerians, who, whatever their hearts and minds may have wished, lacked the rights of citizenship enjoyed by Frenchmen.

Colonial Algeria was, in fact, a very diverse place, which I have tried to capture in this study of its most important economic activity. In what follows we encounter vine-planting colonists with family origins in many different parts of France as well as other mostly Mediterranean lands. We meet seasonal migrants from Spain and Morocco, as well as captive workers from Italy and even Russia who had come to Algeria through the vagaries of war. We also learn how Arab and Berber day laborers gradually came to perform most manual tasks in Algeria's vineyards.

The interest of this book in the people who made the Algerian wine industry, however, extends well beyond the vineyard. We cover the industry's urban side and the employment it offered in wine-company offices, in barrel workshops, or at the docks in storage facilities or on the quays. We also see who acquired a stake in Algeria's wine industry in metropolitan France, from wealthy sulfur refiners in Marseille to dockworkers in ports of entry like Rouen.

My sources have not always allowed me to say as much as I would like about particular categories of people. Bank records and annual reports to shareholders, for example, provided me valuable information on wine-producing colonists, especially the better-off ones, but rarely commented on the people working in the fields. Women also proved elusive in my research. A few European women, often widowed, showed up as vineyard proprietors.[8] As for Algerian women, they seem to have been used more frequently in vineyard work after World War I, sometimes in tasks that involved fine motor skills like *ébourgeonnage*, a sort of tidying-up of the vine—though perhaps their greatest appeal to proprietors was that their pay levels were set lower than those of men.[9] We may catch

FIG. I.1 A mixture of Algerian and European women and youths packing table grapes at the Domaine de la Trappe near Algiers, ca. 1930. Reproduced from the author's collection.

occasional glimpses of women in photographs (see fig. I.1), but the subjects of this book are overwhelmingly male. Notwithstanding these deficiencies, I have done my best to add diverse new names to the historical record.

One of my aims in doing so is to contribute to a burgeoning social history of French Algeria, whose historiography seemed for a long time to be dominated by discussion of its demise rather than the decades during which its existence appeared relatively settled.[10] In places, I have been able to build on work done by Hildebert Isnard, whose doctoral dissertation on Algerian wine, completed in 1947, remains a remarkably useful piece of research.[11] In general, however, I emphasize the human element more than Isnard, a geographer with associations to the Annales school of historical writing.[12] Beyond that I also place particular stress on the importance of wine to the development of capitalism in colonial Algeria, how those who profited from it sought political influence, and the assistance European settlers received from a government dedicated to their success.

WINE AND THE ECONOMIC LIFE OF ALGERIA

Another way of putting this is to say that I hope to draw fresh attention to what we might call the economic life of French Algeria—and, since colonial wine production had an afterlife, to that of independent Algeria as well. Historians of economic life, to borrow William Sewell's definition, focus on "human participation in the production, exchange, and consumption of goods." To be consistent with this human emphasis, they need to be attentive to the ways that economic actions are "embedded" within society and shaped by "social ties, cultural assumptions, and political processes."[13]

As commodities go, few can be more socially embedded and surrounded with cultural assumptions than alcoholic drinks—and in imperial settings perhaps especially so. In his study of the colonial state's monopoly on alcohol production and distribution in French Indochina, Gerard Sasges shows how a regime avid for tax revenue managed to create a bureaucratic monster that sapped resources and generated intense hostility among local people, who much preferred the taste of their own alcohol.[14] In a different French territory on another continent, a governor of the Ivory Coast pursued a moralistic temperance campaign that deplored the consumption of gin from Germany and the Netherlands but simultaneously promoted imports of wine, on the basis that wine was a "hygienic drink" as well as "an eminently French product."[15] The administrations in these French territories both recognized alcohol as economically significant, yet their decisions were guided as much by cultural and political preferences as the rational maximization of revenue.

Wine in Algeria was subject to a variety of disputes over its rationality. Its expansion was resisted for decades by planners who believed the purpose of economic activity within an imperial territory was to complement rather than contend with metropolitan production—a view with a long history in imperial political economy (and a recurring theme in this book). Many vignerons in France, especially southern producers of cheap wine, naturally tended to support that argument, resulting in moments of intense opposition to French Algeria's winemakers and the customs union that allowed their output to enter France duty-free. Promoters of Algerian wine, by contrast, saw wide-scale viticulture as a logical deployment of the territory's assets. But Algeria's defenders were also led by their prejudices. Industry was best left to the colder regions of northern

Europe, argued Romuald Dejernon, the influential author of a manual for vignerons in Algeria in the early 1880s, and in any case indigenous Algerians were too in love with "the air, the sun, and freedom" to be suited to factory work.[16] Dejernon's implication was that French Algeria should evolve primarily as an agricultural colony and tap local populations for their labor in the fields, not seek to broaden the base of the territory's economic activity and thereby the types of employment it offered.

Views such as these relate closely to what subsequently happened. The rapid rise of wine production in Algeria near the end of the nineteenth century accelerated the emergence of an agrarian elite of European descent. This elite showed little interest in developing industry beyond that which serviced agriculture, and used its influence to maintain the status quo. Wine therefore helped set and sustain the contours of the relationship between Algeria and metropolitan France. The profits it generated paid for manufactured goods from the metropole, winning the colony valuable political allies against the hostile lobbying of southern French vignerons. Colonists sometimes wondered whether French Algeria might do better if less tied to the metropolitan market, but were mostly content to settle for comfortable dependence. Their comfort was finally disrupted as the Muslim majority challenged the fundamental inequality of colonial society and the fragility of colonization itself was revealed. But wine was still earning profits as Algerians gained their independence, ensuring that it had to remain an important if incongruous part of the economic life of the new state.

WHEN IS A COLONY NOT A COLONY?

Finding the right labels to attach to particular populations as well as the territory itself is one of the biggest challenges in writing about colonial Algeria. Algeria was first declared an integral part of France with the advent of the Second Republic in 1848 and divided into three administrative *départements* (Oran, Algiers, and Constantine).[17] Mentally, however, Algeria's French status was difficult for people in the metropole to digest. A comprehensive survey of French agriculture published in 1860 included Algeria only as an appendix, which perhaps worked as a metaphor: an inessential part of the body that might one day need to be removed.[18] (It is certainly true to say that historians have rarely incorporated Algeria into studies of French agriculture.[19]) But in 1870 the new Third Republic wasted no time in underlining its commitment to French Algeria's assimilation to the metropole: the civilian governor-general would henceforth answer to the minister of the interior in Paris. Other integrationist measures followed, not least in the economic realm; for example, goods traveling across the Mediterranean had to be transported in ships flying the French flag.[20] When nationalist insurrection began in 1954, the interior minister of the time, François Mitterrand, immediately gave parliament his unequivocal assurance that "Algeria is France."[21]

The legal structure that tied Algeria to metropolitan France must be taken seriously, but not so much that we overlook the arrangement's peculiarities. In its later years the territory's partisans liked to call Algeria a French province. But Brittany did not have a governor-general, nor Burgundy a bank to issue its own currency. Normandy did not have a special elected institution to vote on its budget. Provence did not operate a regime in which a minority were full French citizens while the majority were deemed subjects, holding French nationality but lacking the rights endowed by citizenship. All of those things were true in French Algeria. And dominating the territory were (at their greatest number) over 900,000 people of European descent, who owned the best land, made all the most consequential decisions, and whose opposition to political rights for Algerians appeared "biological," as the historian Charles-André Julien once put it.[22] In the eyes of metropolitan French and Algerians they were *colons* (colonists) until the colony of French Algeria ceased to exist.

That does not make the labeling problem any easier. The term *colon*, as the anthropologist Germaine Tillion noted during the Algerian War, strictly speaking accounted for fewer than 20,000 landowners of European descent and their families, for the majority of Algeria's European population lived in towns and cities and did not cultivate the land.[23] In the budget-approving institution mentioned above, the Délégations financières algériennes, voters chose two categories of European delegates: *colons* and *non-colons*.[24] The use of "colonist" is therefore questionable as a generic term for the Europeans of Algeria. "Settler" brings its own problems, for, like the word "immigrant," it loses its potency after one generation: people who are born and grow up in a place may reasonably think of themselves as "settled."

People of European descent born in Algeria often referred to themselves as *Algériens*. Algerians who write about the colonial era typically label them "Europeans." In this book I have taken the liberty of (I believe) coining a term that no one used at the time, "Euro-Algerians."[25] This has the advantage of capturing the identification of subsequent generations of "settlers" with the place of their birth—their sense of being settled—along with their families' varied geographical origins. Though it is often used by historians, I avoid *pied-noir*, a curiously inaccurate descriptor that emerged from some obscure source near the very end of French Algeria's existence. For my purposes, that term is meaningful in one sense only, as part of the postcolonial identity of those who once lived in Algeria (and who rejected another possible label, *rapatrié*, or "repatriate"). It is therefore in the final chapter alone, about the period since independence, that we will encounter *pieds-noirs*.[26]

As for the majority of the population of French Algeria—over eight million people by 1954—I do not use the term *indigènes*, partly following Tillion (who observed that "nobody in France calls me a 'native'"), and partly because the word itself was an element in their legal subordination, for example in the penal code known as the *indigénat*.[27] It should be understood that this majority was overwhelmingly Muslim, though I prefer not to define them by their faith, as in this book economic inequality rather than religious difference is of greatest significance. They became, and are, Algerians, who, unlike many of those now known as *pieds-noirs*, have little if any nostalgia for the place once called French Algeria. We begin with the invasion that brought this colony into being.

· 1 ·

Roots
Antiquity to 1870

Much about the French invasion was disorderly. There was the march on Algiers that lost its bearings in fog; there was also the unauthorized if predictable pillaging of the Casbah. Most of the highest-ranking officers would face criticism for their handling of the expedition. Everyone, however, agreed on one thing: the invasion force had come equipped to succeed. On June 14, 1830, the first French troops set foot on the low shoreline at Sidi-Ferruch, about twenty kilometers to the west of the city of Algiers, and there they began to offload several months of supplies. An aide to General de Bourmont, the expedition's commander, described the scene that unfolded at the beach. There were immense stockpiles of "cannonballs, shells, and bombs of every caliber"; tents, beds, mattresses, and blankets for a landing force over 37,000 strong; tools, building supplies, and medical equipment; "mountains" of fodder for the horses; as well as food for the men, casks of flour for making bread, and three "long, high walls" of barrels filled with wine.[1]

Reflecting on these events, one contemporary Algerian observer, a student in a religious institution, wrote that the French had been "vomit[ed] on our shore." Amid his disgust, however, this author sought explanations for the rapid defeat of the local ruler, the *dey* of Algiers. Clearly, there were military factors behind the inability of Algiers to resist the infidels: the scale of the French invasion party, which revealed itself "like locusts at their prime," and the terror inspired by their weapons; the Turkish troops who abandoned their positions; the *agha* (military commander) who "lost judgment" at a crucial moment. But this observer believed such explanations only went so far. There must also have been moral factors, other reasons for Allah in his wisdom to allow this calamity. Above all there was the "tyranny and injustice" of the rule of the *dey*, and the corruption of a Muslim polity in which "wine was honored and debauchery tolerated." In a statement that could be read either as history or as prophecy, the author added: "The place for license can last, but must inevitably perish." It was Allah who had brought the French to Algiers, but one day he would "chase away our corruptors" and restore order.[2]

Wine was already a culturally embedded presence at the outset of the French colonization of Algiers, meaning one thing to the French soldiers who "laughed and sang" on the shore at Sidi-Ferruch, and something very different to a pious Muslim trying to interpret (but not question) the will of Allah.[3] Yet the eventual outcome of the conquest, a territory called French Algeria, would become known not so much for the consumption of wine as for its production. Speculation about Algeria's wine-producing capacity began soon after the initial invasion. As the French added territory to the east around Bône and to the west around Oran, colonists would plant grapevines and begin to experiment with winemaking in a land that was known to have produced it in the distant past. Hopes for the new colony were high, and for some people wine represented part of the basis for that hope. In May 1831 a French merchant in Algiers wrote that it would only take "manpower and enlightened farmers" to produce an abundance of "cereals, wine, cotton, indigo, coffee, sugar, and in general all the transatlantic commodities that we are now obliged to seek in another hemisphere."[4]

The merchant's statement reinforces the historian Jennifer Sessions's argument that the colonization of Algeria was to some extent a side effect of developments in the Atlantic in the late eighteenth century, especially the slave revolt that lost France its prized colony of Saint-Domingue (Haiti), a key source for several of the "transatlantic commodities" to which the merchant alluded.[5] It also underlines that an economic rationale for conquest lay not far from the much better known political machinations of the unpopular Bourbon monarch Charles X. While merchants hoping to attract investment often do well to convey optimism, however, the optimism of this one was neither shared by all nor necessarily well placed. First, it was not clear where exactly the projected "enlightened farmers" would secure their manpower, as slavery was in retreat and other forms of coerced labor also subject to criticism. Second, though the merchant situated Algiers geographically in what he called "a hot latitude," it was by no means certain that the Algerian land and climate would cooperate in replacing the kinds of commodities formerly supplied by tropical Saint-Domingue. Lastly, there was no guarantee that the commodities whose success could be more reliably predicted would even be welcome in a metropole that produced those very same goods. If Algeria were to produce wine, in particular, it might well face opposition not only from French vignerons but also from imperial planners who did not believe it was the role of a colony to compete with the homeland.

While it was not inevitable that colonial Algeria should become a major wine producer, it would have been surprising had the new arrivals not attempted to produce it at all, for wine production was often a feature of new colonial ventures, and North Africa had an ancient history of viticulture. In the first four decades after the invasion of 1830 the topic of wine production was often contentious, and some influential figures actively tried to dissuade settlers from embracing it. By around 1870, however, many of the obstacles seemed to be lifting, and wine began to play a more central role in defining what "French Algeria" was going to be.

THE WINE FRONTIER

The common grapevine, *vitis vinifera,* is a crop that demands sustained, devoted care. It may be true that Paleolithic hunter-gatherers were the first to realize that grapes go through an interesting transformation when they ferment, but any serious production of wine required a settled population with time to experiment.[6] The spread of viticulture (or more properly viniculture, the cultivation of grapes to make wine) commonly followed when a population that had mastered the necessary technical skills uprooted itself from one location and moved to colonize another.

The diffusion of viniculture along western shores of the Mediterranean followed a series of such migrations from points further east. Among the carriers of the new culture were Phoenicians from the coast of present-day Lebanon and Syria. Toward the end of the ninth century BCE a group of Phoenicians traveled to northern Africa and founded the colony of Carthage in what is now Tunisia. Though the grapevine grew wild in northern Africa, it seems that these colonists were the first in the region to produce wine from domesticated grapes.[7] Other migrants from the eastern Mediterranean instead took their expertise to northern shores. Greeks from Phocaea in Asia Minor (modern Turkey) established a settlement at Massalia—Marseille—around 600 BCE. Archaeological evidence shows that, within a few decades, ships were carrying amphorae of Massalian wine to other Mediterranean ports.[8] In a sense this Greek colony gave birth to France's wine industry.

Wine production continued when these Mediterranean regions fell under Roman control. It is doubtful, though, that the Romans were specifically looking to their provinces in southern Gaul or northern Africa to produce an exportable quantity of wine. At times they may even have been concerned about the impact of provincial wine on producers within the Italian peninsula; a decree passed in the second century BCE, for example, forbade peasants in southern Gaul from planting new vineyards, "in order," as Cicero put it, "to increase the value of our own."[9] A much more important consideration was the need to supply grain to feed the Roman metropole, which strongly influenced the way imperial officials viewed agriculture in the provinces. In 92 CE the emperor Domitian issued an edict that ordered half of all the grapevines in the Roman provinces to be destroyed, "upon the occasion of a plentiful wine crop coinciding with a scarcity of grain."[10] This edict seems not to have been enforced, however, and wine continued to establish its importance both to the economy of southern Gaul and beyond.[11]

Grain was the chief Roman priority across the Mediterranean in northern Africa, but wine production also had its place.[12] Archaeological evidence from the coastal town of Cherchell, about ninety kilometers west of Algiers, is particularly compelling. Founded as the Carthaginian settlement of Iol in the fourth century BCE, the Romans renamed the town Caesarea and in the first century CE made it the capital of Mauretania Caesariensis, the eastern half of the province of Mauretania. Though the region was something of an imperial backwater, excavations of private homes and public buildings have revealed that a prosperous land-owning class flourished in the town from the late second century CE until the Vandal invasion of North Africa in the first half of the fifth century. Among the images on the mosaics with which these wealthy men chose to adorn their buildings were representations of Bacchus, the Roman god of wine, as well as scenes of viticulture in which field workers

FIG. 1.1 Mosaic from a house in Cherchell (ancient Caesarea) depicting the grape harvest, fourth or fifth century CE. The workers' red hair is a Berber trait. Wikimedia Commons.

tend vines and pick grapes (see fig. 1.1).[13] As in other parts of North Africa, estate sizes in the area were relatively large, and, for the owners of these estates, wine served as a marker of social distinction.[14]

Further to the east, yet still within what is now Algeria, the writings of Augustine of Hippo (354–430 CE) provide different kinds of insight into the place of wine in the everyday lives of the better-placed inhabitants of Roman North Africa. Augustine spent much of his childhood in Thagaste (now Souk Ahras) and eventually rose to the position of bishop of Hippo Regius (modern Annaba). In his *Confessions,* Augustine acknowledges no personal problem with wine in particular, though he does offer a general admission that "I struggle every day against uncontrolled desire in eating and drinking." Wine is nonetheless woven into the fabric of the life he describes. In a key "confession," we learn that it was close to his family's vineyard that Augustine and his teenage friends stole pears from a neighbor's tree, for no purpose other than the pleasure of "doing what was not allowed." Augustine also reveals that his mother, Monica, discovered "a weakness for wine" as a girl. Entrusted with going to the cask to fetch wine for her parents, Monica began by sneaking just "a tiny sip." On subsequent trips she drank progressively more, until eventually, as Augustine tells the story, she was "gulping down almost full cups" at each visit. Finally some harsh words from the enslaved girl who went with her to the cask shamed Monica out of this "foul addiction."[15]

Augustine's writings help to raise the question of wine's relationship to religion and the spread of Christianity in particular. As a young man, Augustine followed Manichean teachings and as such would have had to renounce wine, since the Manicheans considered it "a diabolical poison."[16] In converting to Christianity in 386 he joined a faith that by contrast vested wine and the vine with immense symbolic significance. In the Gospel of John, Jesus characterizes himself as the "true vine" that is tended by God; the lesson is that through Jesus the believer may connect to God's love.[17] (Augustine echoes this imagery in the *Confessions* when he puts his trust in God and Holy Scripture to protect "the tender vine of my heart."[18]) Most importantly, wine in the Eucharist is central to Christian observance, representing Jesus's blood and therefore his sacrifice. In the everyday world of the early Church in Africa, however, wine posed certain problems. As a bishop, Augustine struggled to prevent drunkenness at the shrines of martyrs, where libations were a traditional offering.[19] Christian institutions would go on to play an important role in advancing the wine frontier, including, as we shall see, within colonial Algeria. But although wine was permitted to followers of Christ, Augustine shows us that it represented something of a headache for those trying to enforce the religious and social norms of the Church.

Islam, when it emerged in the seventh century, took a different approach. Wine is not absent from the Quran; indeed it is said to flow in "rivers" in paradise.[20] If that image acknowledges the pleasure that wine can bring, for Muslims in this world the instructions are quite clear: the wine of the grape is an intoxicant, and therefore, like other forms of alcohol, it is forbidden. Some Islamic regimes have made the strict policing of this injunction central to their legitimacy. In the early eleventh century, for example, the Fatimid ruler al-Hakim commanded wine-producing grapevines to be uprooted in Palestine, while a few decades later the Almoravids of Morocco on their rise to power burned down the shops of wine merchants.[21] The periodic emergence of Islamic reform movements that publicly opposed alcohol serves paradoxically to underline the fact that drinking was a rather unexceptional feature of many Muslim societies.[22] Nevertheless, the seventh-century Arab invasions of North Africa as well as other Muslim conquests clearly reined in the wine frontier.[23] The contrast with the important vineyards of Christian monastic orders in medieval Europe is obvious.[24]

When Europeans opened an entirely new frontier and new possibilities in the Americas, wine quickly entered the calculations of colony builders. As governor of New Spain in 1524, the conquistador Hernán Cortés ordered Spanish land grantees to plant vines in the vicinity of the fallen Aztec capital, then being rebuilt as Mexico City—part of a broader effort to reproduce Iberian agricultural practices in the New World, but also simply to ensure that colonists would not go without a product deemed a necessity. Spanish attempts to produce wine in Mexico had mixed success, but the results were generally much better in southern territories like Peru, Chile, and Argentina. The ability of these colonies to provide for their own needs in wine rankled producers in Spain, who believed that supplying the settlers was their prerogative. In an apparent effort to placate this lobby and sustain Atlantic trade, in the late sixteenth century Philip II issued three separate prohibitions against the plantation of new vines in Spanish America.[25] The exemption of Catholic religious societies from these decrees represented a notable loophole. In 1598 the Society of Jesus—the Jesuits—began developing vineyards in the northern Mexican settlement of Parras (the name means "vines"). In turn these plantations contributed much to the Jesuits' ability to finance their operations in other parts of New Spain.[26]

French expertise in viticulture was already acknowledged in the early modern period and sought after in new areas of production. English attempts to produce wine in Virginia shortly after the first settlers arrived in the 1600s, for example, were fed by the hope that one day England's wine drinkers would not automatically benefit the treasuries of European rivals. But to reach that goal the colonists knew they would need some technical assistance. In 1619, therefore, the colony arranged to import eight "divers and skillfull vignerons" from France, as well as ten thousand vines from Europe. Upon arrival, the French experts recognized

Virginia's wine potential, but a major attack by Native Americans of the Powhatan Confederacy killed some of the vignerons and severely disrupted the project, and the colonists focused more of their attention on tobacco instead.[27] Later in the century, and further to the north, William Penn tested Pennsylvania's wine-producing capability with vines from Bordeaux and the help of French Protestant refugees.[28] French Protestant Huguenots, in fact, led several experiments on the wine frontier in different parts of the Atlantic World after fleeing persecution in their homeland in the 1680s. Huguenot efforts to produce wine in South Carolina largely failed, but those who headed to the Dutch Cape Colony in southern Africa fared better.[29]

The expansion of wine production around the Pacific Rim also gained from French assistance. British authorities hoping to develop wine in another new colony, Australia, transported two French prisoners of war there in 1800 under the assumption that they would give momentum to the endeavor. Of much greater importance, as it turned out, were the visits made to France in the early nineteenth century by wine advocates like John Macarthur and James Busby, who returned to Australia with practical knowledge and vine cuttings.[30] In another part of the Pacific, the aptly named Jean Louis Vignes traveled from the Bordeaux region to the Sandwich Islands (Hawai'i) in the 1820s as a lay auxiliary to a French missionary venture. After the missionary project failed, Vignes stayed and tried cultivating vines and sugarcane near Honolulu. Finally he gave up on the Sandwich Islands and around 1832 headed to California. Spanish Franciscans are generally credited with establishing the first vineyards in California around 1780, but viticulture had not developed much by the time Vignes arrived in Los Angeles. On a forty-hectare property by the Los Angeles River, roughly where Union Station stands today, Vignes planted vines that he imported specially from France, and in time the quality of his wine influenced other local producers to raise their standards.[31]

It could be argued that these examples of French contributions to global viticulture did not amount to very much. Even when successful, the cultivators were usually outliers operating more or less independently; individually ingenious, perhaps, but not part of a broader (or government-backed) trend. If French viticulture set an international standard early, only infrequently did French people themselves show the inclination to apply their expertise in new lands.

In the years around 1800, however, two French experiments with viticulture—part of a project for empire in the first case, a project for settlement in the second—in some ways presaged later developments in Algeria. The first experiment arose in the context of the invasion of Egypt led by Napoleon Bonaparte in 1798. In large part this expedition was undertaken with the aim of damaging British commerce, but beyond that there was also interest in the cash crops that Egypt might be able to supply France, such as sugar and cotton. Once installed in Cairo, Bonaparte founded the Egyptian Institute to study the country's environmental as well as its cultural attributes. The 151 scholars and experts who had accompanied Bonaparte and his troops were now asked to come up with solutions to a range of practical problems. A question raised at one early meeting of the institute hinted at concern for the French occupiers' supply of alcohol: "Is there a replacement in Egypt for hops to make beer?"[32] For this to be a fully French enterprise, though, there also had to be wine. In October 1798 Bonaparte constituted a commission whose charge was to "gather the most precise information on the means of cultivating the grapevine in this country."[33]

One of the scientists on the commission, Gaspard Monge, was confident that fifty years of French activity could make Egypt "a paradise on earth."[34] (Perhaps he pictured rivers of wine.) But time did not allow the French to test their theories about the vine in Egypt, or for that matter any number of other plans hatched at the institute. Instead the occupation foundered, and in August 1799 both Monge and Bonaparte were on their way back to France. If inconsequential in terms of the spread of viticulture, however, a precedent had been set: a French occupation force had shown itself willing to contemplate wine production in a predominantly Muslim land.

While the Egyptian venture shortly preceded Bonaparte's rise to power in France, another experiment with viticulture took shape as a consequence of his fall. In 1817 the US Congress authorized a land grant in the west of Alabama to a group of French expatriates. The group consisted mostly of exiled Bonaparte loyalists as well as French refugees who had come to the United States after the slave uprising in Saint-Domingue. The congressional grant specified that the land was to be used for the planting of vines and olive trees. Alabama was going to be tested for its Mediterranean qualities.

General Bertrand Clauzel was one of the grantees who tried hardest to make a success of the so-called Vine and Olive Colony. Clauzel, a veteran of Napoleonic campaigns in Saint-Domingue as well as Europe, established himself in Mobile, 150 kilometers or so to the south of the granted land, and from that base helped arrange for grapevines and olive seedlings to be shipped from France. The olive trees never stood a chance, and the vines failed to thrive. Cotton, as some of the settlers from Saint-Domingue soon discovered, grew much better. But Clauzel barely stayed long enough to find that out. In 1820 he was pardoned by the Bourbon monarchy, and at the first opportunity returned to France. Ten years later he was in Algeria as commander in chief of the army of Africa, seeking to apply the agricultural lessons he thought he had learned from his experiences in the Americas.[35] Through such men as Clauzel, French curiosity about agricultural adaptation in "hot latitudes" would persist in new places.[36]

In spite of French efforts in Egypt, Alabama, and elsewhere, by 1830 the country most closely associated with the production of wine had taken little direct role in advancing the global wine frontier. In part this was a consequence of location: almost without exception the few colonial territories France possessed in the 1820s, such as the sugar-producing islands of Martinique and Guadeloupe in the Caribbean, lay in regions inconducive to viticulture. But it was also partly a consequence of what metropolitan France already had: a fairly plentiful domestic supply of wine, and a lobby of alcohol producers that was always alert to potential new competitors. Rum manufacturers in Martinique and Guadeloupe knew about that lobby's influence all too well; it was one reason why by the 1820s most French Caribbean rum still did not leave the islands.[37]

The invasion of 1830, however, took France to a different type of territory. As the troops marched from Sidi-Ferruch toward Algiers they noticed grapes growing on land that reminded some of them of parts of France. Once they reached Algiers they found stores that offered plenty of goods for sale, but no wine or any other alcohol.[38] Over the next few months and years, French forces would enter other centers of indigenous grape production: to the south of Algiers around Médéa; to the west around Mostaganem, Mascara, and Tlemcen; toward the east around Dellys.[39] It was not hard to imagine producing wine in this country, which had seen viniculture in an earlier age. The contemporary local population, with very few exceptions, had chosen not to use their grapes for that purpose. The French would have to make their own choice.

COMPLEMENTARY COLONIZATION

When Alexis de Tocqueville visited Algeria for the first time in May 1841, he met a man he described as a "very well-informed colonist." The colonist, Monsieur Urtis, led Tocqueville to his property on the heights at Kouba, a short but steep journey south of what were then the limits of the city of Algiers.[40] Tocqueville told Urtis that he had heard that the soil along these heights, the Massif de la Bouzaréah, was unfavorable for cultivation, perhaps remembering the words of the Chamber of Deputies' African Commission of 1834, which had stated that on the massif "the absence of quality vegetation, and wasteland, are the rule."[41] Urtis dismissed any such idea. "That is a lie," he said. "The soil is very good." True, a settler might cast envious eyes further south to the Mitidja plain, where the soil was even better. But descending to the lowlands carried at least two big risks. For one thing, the plain remained highly vulnerable to attack by Arab raiders, as some settlers had fatally discovered in 1839. For another, the marshy environment led doctors to warn about its bad air, or "miasmas." The evacuation in 1839 of a fever-stricken settler village—Clauzelbourg, named after the general—was only one illustration of a serious local problem.[42] By 1841 there were reasons to believe that both of these problems could be remedied. Securing the Mitidja was a major priority of the new governor-general, General Bugeaud, while Urtis predicted that sanitation in the area would improve over time through drainage works, cultivation, and the planting of trees.[43] For now, though, Urtis calculated that it was safer to remain on the heights.

In any case, the potential rewards were already revealing themselves on Urtis's property at Kouba. "Everything grows here," he told Tocqueville, and showed him some examples: several thousand olive trees, mulberry trees on which he hoped to raise silkworms, and ground-growing crops like potatoes and onions. Then he gestured to a neighboring field in which he was testing a new form of cultivation: grapevines, which were "growing with tremendous vigor, like everything else." But Urtis was quick to play down his efforts in that part of his property.

He had not yet produced any wine, he said, and there was no guarantee it would be drinkable. Even if the wine were good, however, that might not be sufficient reason to expand its production, for "we must take care not to create troublesome competition with the vineyards of southern France."[44]

In his concern for wine producers in France, Urtis was deferring not only to metropolitan compatriots but also to a particular set of views about the utility of overseas colonies. One important way that a colony of the type that had become common after the European discovery of the Americas could fulfill its purpose, wrote the political economist François Véron de Forbonnais in his entry on the topic "Colony" in Diderot and d'Alembert's *Encyclopédie* (1753), was by "add[ing] to what is grown in the metropole." Echoing mercantile principles that Louis XIV's finance minister Jean-Baptiste Colbert had applied to French expansion in the seventeenth century, Véron de Forbonnais insisted that "it is trade that makes colonies flourish." But the terms of trade should always favor the metropole, as in the system known as the *Exclusif,* which excluded non-French merchants from French colonial markets. For such reasons, colonial commodities should "never [be] of the sort which will compete with those of the metropole."[45] Viewing colonies in terms of their economic complementarity with the metropole made it easier for a thinker like Véron de Forbonnais to accept the loss of French Canada in the Seven Years' War, whereas the prospect of losing tropical possessions in the Caribbean that supplied crops that did not grow in France was a more serious matter.[46]

Leaving aside the fact that the *Exclusif* was never watertight in practice, from the second half of the eighteenth century the system attracted influential critics. Among the most notable were the physiocrats, a group of French political economists who opposed monopolistic trade practices while also promoting the spread of metropolitan agriculture overseas.[47] After the invasion of Algeria, liberal French supporters of colonization, sometimes drawing on the ideas of Anglophone thinkers like Adam Smith, also challenged exclusionary colonial trade policies, which had revived under the Restoration monarchs.[48] In 1839, for example, the liberal political economist Adolphe Blanqui, a champion of Smith's work, spoke out after a visit to Algeria against customs restrictions in the new colony and argued that free trade was "the strongest ally of colonization."[49] Tocqueville similarly saw the success of colonization as a political necessity, and in support of that goal wrote in 1841 that the French government should "allow all Algerian products to enter France freely, especially those produced not by indigenous industry but by colonial industry."[50]

Urtis's remark about the vineyards of southern France, however, illustrates that thinking of the colonial economy as an adjunct to the broader imperial, metropole-dominated economy was a habit of mind that could even be found among the mental baggage of some early settlers. (Urtis also told Tocqueville that his olive trees would help to meet a demand that France's own production could not fully supply.) It seemed, as the historian Charles-André Julien aptly put it, that "the spirit of the *Exclusif*" continued to influence those with the power to shape France's new territory, even though a newer, nineteenth-century term for the relationship between metropole and colony, *pacte colonial,* implied greater reciprocity.[51] In essence, colonists would have a protected market for certain approved products, but in return would have to accept limits on their freedom to shape a colonial economy based on local productive capacity. It was impossible to predict, however, whether the majority of settlers—who might not even be of French origin—would be as solicitous of metropolitan concerns as Monsieur Urtis.

The problem of Algeria's complementarity with the metropole was also a matter of distance. The invasion in 1830 seems to have altered popular perceptions of the Mediterranean and led to its re-evaluation as a connective space between France and North Africa, rather than a barrier.[52] This mental "shrinking" of the Mediterranean, as Hélène Blais and Florence Deprest have shown, was reflected in maps that now depicted its northern and southern shores within the same frame.[53] But emphasizing Algeria's closeness to France also tended to draw attention to its difference from the Atlantic lands which, until that time, had provided French people with their primary mental image of a colony.[54] This narrowing sense of colonial space in turn made it easier for some to question how traditional ways of thinking about colonial economies could possibly apply when the colony lay more or less adjacent to the metropole. As one Algeria skeptic argued in 1838, the colonization of faraway lands might have entailed "the inconvenience of great distances," but these greater distances had gone along with greater prospects for an economically complementary colonization.[55] Once Algeria yielded to inspection after 1830, it became clear that much of the region most obviously conducive to settlement was ecologically comparable to the South of France. More-over, the agricultural products with which it was historically associated and which to varying degrees it still produced—grain, olives, grapevines—were also produced in France.

Grain was an early source of discussion. The notion that North Africa had been the "granary of Rome" was in French thoughts from the ear-liest days of the conquest.[56] The phrase was often invoked without much geographical precision; Algeria and North Africa were not synonymous, after all, and a substantial proportion of ancient North African grain ex-ports had actually come from Tunisia. It was a striking metaphor, how-ever, and enough to cause unease among French cereal producers.[57] A prominent early critic of Algerian colonization, Amédée Desjobert, tried to dismiss the "granary of Rome" idea as a "fable."[58] But writers of the 1830s and 1840s who (unlike Desjobert) went to Algeria and appraised the land for themselves did not entirely dispel the image. One author journeyed through Provence on his way to Algeria and concluded—perhaps hoping to attract settlers—that in terms of climate and fertility the latter was "infinitely preferable" to the former, and that even "barely cultivated" land produced "beautiful" cereal crops.[59] Others conceded that the image of abundance derived from antiquity was probably exag-gerated, yet still invariably expressed optimism for the land's potential.[60] While cereal production would clearly be essential to the colony's needs, however, what we might call "complementarian" thinking argued against developing Algeria too far as a "granary." As one governor-general of the colony put it in an analysis he titled *Cultures à encourager* (crops to encourage), "France has its own granary on its own soil, and unlike the Romans does not need to have one in Algeria."[61]

In that case, which crops *should* be encouraged? For one early advo-cate of colonization, taking a classical view on Algeria's possible worth, the question was best addressed by quantifying the value of products that France currently bought from foreign competitors. By that measure, he wrote, the greatest hopes should (in descending order) be vested in cotton, silk, vegetable oils, indigo, sugar, flax, tobacco, and citrus fruits.[62] The list of potentially beneficial crops only expanded with the expan-sion of colonization itself in the 1840s. Louis Moll, a professor at the Conservatoire royal des arts et métiers in Paris, spent a few months gath-ering information in Algeria in 1842 before publishing his book *Colo-nisation et agriculture de l'Algérie,* the most comprehensive effort yet undertaken to evaluate its agricultural capacity. Moll created the impression that almost anything could be grown in Algeria, as he divided more than fifty crops by type and then devoted a short chapter to each:

CEREAL CROPS AND STARCHES: Wheat, barley, rye, oats, maize, millet, sorghum, rice, buckwheat, broad beans, peas, beans, lentils, vetches.

ROOT CROPS: Potatoes, Jerusalem artichokes, beets, carrots, turnips, sweet potatoes, cabbages, eggplants, peppers.

FEED CROPS: Alfalfa, sainfoin, clover, wild chicory, vetchling.

CASH CROPS (*plantes commerciales*): Rape, sesame, groundnuts, flax, New Zealand flax, hemp, esparto grass (*alfa*), cotton, madder, indigo, sugarcane, tobacco, opium poppies.

CROP-BEARING TREES OR BUSHES: Olive trees, orange trees, lemon trees, mulberry trees, prickly pear (Barbary fig), fig trees, almond trees, grapevines, tea, hops, pistachio trees, banana trees, pomegranate trees, caper bushes, date palms, cactus, cork trees, sumac, bamboo.[63]

This was quite a menu for potential colonists, and Moll's book relentlessly reinforced its image of plenty. At the same time, Moll was at pains to consider the potential impact of Algerian agriculture on metropolitan producers, even if the number of people liable to be affected was small. He was worried, for example, that cultivating the madder plant in Algeria might have an unfortunate effect on production of that crop in southern France, so he encouraged settlers to try another dyeing plant, indigo, which would cause no such conflict.[64] When metropolitan production was not a concern, Moll gave free rein to his vision for the colony and wrapped his observations in their own blithely optimistic logic: so, we consume a lot of beer in Algeria; our hop supply comes mostly from foreign countries; hop growing "succeeds perfectly in Africa"; therefore, let us grow hops.[65]

A burst of agricultural experimentation had in fact recently taken place in a different French colony in another part of Africa. After France retook her possessions in Senegal from Britain in 1817, officials there envisaged the territory as an agricultural colony that might help rejuvenate an empire now lacking the sugar of Saint-Domingue and the cotton-growing potential of Louisiana. Especially under the governorship of

Baron Jacques-François Roger between 1822 and 1827, the administration encouraged and protected the production of cotton and indigo, and considered as well the possibility of growing sugarcane and coffee. (In a less complementary spirit, Roger also had grapevines planted in the colony's experimental garden.) Much effort went into developing cotton, in particular, but by the end of the 1820s the experiment had already failed; the cotton varieties imported for the purpose simply did not take to the Senegalese climate and soil.[66]

Only a few years later, in the 1830s and 1840s, it seemed that a similar kind of experiment was being repeated on a larger scale in Algeria. Merchant interests made known their preference for particular types of production; the president of the Société des colons de Lyon, for example, pointed out what a benefit it would be—not least to merchants in Lyon—to have a good supply of cotton and silk from a French territory.[67] Leading members of the military administration also paid close attention to questions of cultivation. General Clauzel told the Chamber of Deputies that his past experience in Saint-Domingue and the United States—where, as we saw, he was part of the Vine and Olive project in Alabama—gave him confidence in Algeria's ability to produce sugarcane, cotton, coffee, cocoa, and indigo.[68] As early as October 1830, in a practical step toward this goal, Clauzel authorized the creation of colonial Algeria's first model farm.[69] The ministry of war also took up the challenge, and over the next two decades supported the foundation of twenty-one experimental gardens. In these institutions horticultural technicians, foremost among them Auguste Hardy, tried to cultivate exotic plant species.[70] The work done in such gardens was fundamental to the developing field of acclimatization studies, which incubated in institutions like the Muséum d'histoire naturelle in Paris before reaching full bloom with the creation of the Société zoologique d'acclimatation in 1854.[71] All of the efforts to adapt plant species from one part of the world to life in another—olives in Alabama in the 1810s, cotton in Senegal in the 1820s, sugarcane in Algeria in the 1830s—now seemed to be summarized and given academic respectability in the word "acclimatization." Whatever the land had produced for people in antiquity, acclimatization advocates appeared to be saying, French techniques could now do better.

By 1840 the liberal Blanqui was already criticizing some of these experiments for fostering "illusions" in Algeria.[72] Judgment of the scientific pretensions of Hardy and his collaborators and the overconfident assertions of experts like Moll only hardened in later decades. Many of these schemes, commented one author, had been "folly," a culpable waste of time and resources.[73] Another author sarcastically regretted that it had not been possible to change North Africa's latitude by administrative decree and place it in the tropics.[74] It was not only "tropical" crops that failed to flourish in Algeria, though; we can now be fairly sure that anyone wishing to grow hops in the northern hemisphere is best advised to stay above the forty-eighth parallel. (Algiers is near the thirty-sixth.)

Acclimatization in the nineteenth century may look like the science of wishful thinking, and there was certainly a quixotic quality to the efforts of a colonist like Théodore Fortin d'Ivry, who in the 1840s appears to have tried planting virtually everything discussed in Moll's book on his domain at Reghaïa to the east of Algiers.[75] At the same time, much of the experimentation needs to be understood in the context of a global hunt for certain agricultural commodities in the nineteenth century. The supply of raw silk, for example, was a constant worry for producers in an important French industry, so it is no surprise that silk manufacturers were hopeful that Algeria, a place where mulberry trees grew well, could supplement southern French production. When Algeria failed to deliver, attention shifted to Syria, and then—amid a major epidemic of the silkworm disease called *pébrine*—to China and Japan.[76]

Nor were these schemes necessarily as far-fetched as hindsight sometimes suggested. The idea of cultivating sugarcane, later derided, appears less implausible with the knowledge that it grew in parts of Tunisia in the eighteenth and early nineteenth centuries.[77] In fact, another North African territory, Egypt, already offered a precedent for some of the crops attempted in Algeria. Muhammad Ali (ruled 1805 to 1848) oversaw the introduction of as many as 200 new crops into Egypt, and also revived its sugar industry, which had been an earlier object of interest for Napoleon.[78] In Senegal in the 1820s, Baron Roger's agricultural plans had drawn direct inspiration from Egypt, particularly the commercial development of long-staple cotton there after 1820 (instigated by a French textile engineer, Louis Alexis Jumel).[79] Three decades later, promoters of cotton in Algeria still took Muhammad Ali's Egypt as a model for what they hoped to achieve.[80] If it could be made to grow well in Algeria, however, cotton, most of which was then supplied by the United States, would fit perfectly within a complementary model of colonization.[81] Wine, a surer bet to succeed, was a much more problematic prospect.

SETTLEMENT AND THE WINE QUESTION

When General Thomas-Robert Bugeaud was appointed governor-general at the end of 1840, the French presence in Algeria was still limited to a handful of mostly coastal towns or cities and their surroundings. Early settlers in areas like the Mitidja plain felt beleaguered and insecure, and much of western and central Algeria was controlled by the leader known to many Algerians as "sultan of the Arabs," the emir Abdelkader.[82] The shape of French Algeria remained very much to be determined.

In Bugeaud's view, a strategy based on fortified enclaves was doomed to fail; that was one lesson he drew from the unsuccessful Napoleonic occupation of Spain after 1808, a campaign in which he had participated.[83] The call to Bugeaud to serve as governor signaled defeat for the advocates of an *occupation restreinte* (restricted occupation) for Algeria, and heralded instead the government's commitment to complete conquest followed by wide-scale colonization. France in 1840 felt diminished by the Rhine Crisis, but a maximal policy in Algeria provided the opportunity for a dose of grandeur.[84]

Bugeaud had completed two separate military deployments in Algeria in 1836 and 1837, and anyone familiar with his performance then might have predicted what his appointment to the governor-generalship was likely to entail. His considerable military ability won him many battles, but in the face of obstacles Bugeaud turned instinctively to overwhelming, vengeful force. In western Algeria in 1837 he had vowed to "scourge" the territory of recalcitrant tribes "like a river of fire."[85] That phrase provides a fair image of the all-out assault that, as governor-general, Bugeaud now launched in the Algerian countryside. The offensive used as one of its primary tactics so-called *razzias,* ultraviolent raids that targeted crops and other means of subsistence as much as they targeted human resisters.[86]

Bugeaud's campaigns meant, ironically, that the debate about what grew best in Algeria took place at the same time as widespread French destruction of local forms of cultivation. In 1843, for example, troops from the French garrison at Miliana carried out an extended *razzia* against inhabitants of the Ouarsenis Mountains. A leader of this *razzia,* Lieutenant-Colonel Elie Frédéric Forey, described the settlements his men encountered as comparable to villages he knew in France, well built and surrounded by gardens and "immense forests of olive trees." The troops, indeed, were "stupefied" by the beauty of these settlements, but orders were orders, and theirs were to leave "not a village, tree, or field standing." The French raiders set fire to ten large villages, took three thousand head of cattle, and "cut down or burned more than ten thousand olive trees, fig trees, etc." (The "etc." is chilling in itself.) After such ruination, these people would not give the French any more trouble, Forey concluded, and the governor-general could now "carry out his projects in complete tranquility."[87]

Bugeaud's main project for Algeria, beyond crushing resistance, was to promote European settlement, with particular emphasis on agricultural colonization—which, as an innovative farmer of the property he owned in southwestern France, was a special interest of his. Recruiters called attention to the quick progress of "pacification" under Bugeaud and projected an encouraging message. A pocket guide for migrants in 1843, for example, began with a section headed "Conquest and security of Algeria assured," and added, a bit prematurely, that "if the war by the sword is over, that by the plow is beginning."[88]

Finding migrants who would settle on the land, however, was much easier said than done. The first instinct of many new arrivals to Algeria was to cluster in towns (in which some observers found drinking establishments unhealthily prominent).[89] As for the land that the government turned over for colonization, much of it fell into the hands of speculators and sat undeveloped. Other settlers seemed not to realize the possibilities before them, or not to care; on the massif above Algiers, for example, some felled "superb" orange and almond trees for firewood.[90] Those more committed to agricultural colonization had to contend with a variety of dangers. Some of these might have been confronted successfully by farming "with gun in hand," as the saying went, but guns offered no protection against diseases like malaria.[91] Under these difficult conditions, many migrants succumbed to a destabilizing *mal du pays* (homesickness) and returned to Europe.[92] In 1847, the last year of Bugeaud's tenure as governor-general (and the year the resistance leader Abdelkader surrendered), Tocqueville wrote that "the real problem" in Algeria remained the need "to attract agricultural populations to the soil and to keep them there."[93] At that moment there were just over 100,000 Europeans in Algeria—a roughly even mix of French and non-French—but only about 15 percent were making their living from agriculture.[94]

Discussion over Algeria's agricultural potential was always concerned with this problem of attracting settlers to the land, and keeping them there with productive and remunerative forms of cultivation. The culture that colonial planners were most likely to discourage, however, was the culture of the vine, even though this was familiar to many migrants and offered the very image of rootedness. It was not that the "experts" denied the prospects for viticulture. Moll, the great promoter of colonial agriculture, believed not only that grapevines would grow well but also that there was a strong chance they would be able to produce good wine. (Thinking latitudinally, as always, he pointed to Madeira and Cyprus as possible comparators.) But Moll could not generate the same enthusiasm for Algerian wine that he felt for more speculative ventures like hops or tea. After all, he wrote, "France is not making so many sacrifices in Algeria to have more wine and increase the overabundance that is already causing our wine industry to sag."[95] Bugeaud, for all his support of agricultural colonization, was even blunter in his opposition. Reiterating the idea that Algeria should focus on products that were lacking in metropolitan France, he wrote in 1845 that "all of our departments fear the rivalry that our colony might produce." To that end, "an order should immediately prohibit the making of wine in Algeria."[96]

As it turned out, the government-general never issued such an order. Nevertheless, Bugeaud represented the prevailing official viewpoint for most of the first three decades of French rule in Algeria. Even as the Second Republic (1848–1852) pursued the "assimilationist" policies that included, most prominently, the decision to make the three provinces of Oran, Algiers, and Constantine departments of France, wine continued to be perceived as something of a special problem. In 1851, for example, a new law exempted Algerian agricultural produce from customs duty in France, but, to placate metropolitan vignerons, the law did not apply to wine.[97]

Despite the lack of official encouragement for wine production, some individual settlers, like the one Tocqueville met outside Algiers, decided to try their hand at viticulture. Perhaps some of them initially did so "out of curiosity," as Bugeaud put it, but from the 1850s in particular we gain a sense that the experimentation was more purposeful than that.[98] For one thing, the drive to conquer Algeria had opened some promising new lands to European cultivators. That was notably true in the West. In Abdelkader's former heartland in the town of Mascara, for example, the civilian administrator predicted in 1854 that "the industry that has the greatest future in Mascara is the wine industry. The nature of the soil, the configuration of the land, the climate—all is in its favor."[99]

If some saw clear potential, the challenges were also obvious. The fact that new vines took three years to yield any wine discouraged poorer colonists, especially at a time when credit for agricultural projects was hard to come by. Those who did decide to take the risk and plant vines then faced an array of problems. Some enemies of the vine confronted vignerons on both sides of the Mediterranean, like the fungal blight oidium, also known as powdery mildew, which ruined the crop in France in 1854 and was a problem in Algeria too that year. Other problems would have been new even to the most experienced French producers. Jackals and hyenas, for example, were attracted to the vines in numbers; in 1854 the mayor of Aïn el-Turck near Oran wrote that his community expected to produce some wine that year "if the jackals don't harvest the grapes before we do."[100] Visitations of locusts were brutally unpredictable and much more devastating. One settler described the "winged battalions" that descended upon his property to the west of Dellys during the terrible swarms of 1866. In two hours, he wrote, his fields of cereals and vegetables were leveled, his fruit trees defoliated, and his grapevines stripped to the roots by a seething mass whose frenziedly chomping mandibles produced an eerie sound "like the crackling of a fire."[101]

From year to year one never really knew what the biggest test was going to be. In 1857 Jérôme Bastide, a settler in Sidi-Bel-Abbès, directed his curses toward the jackals that damaged his grape harvest, but the following year his greatest enemy was much less exotic, if a little unexpected: a heavy frost in the middle of May.[102] One might have too little rain in spring, too much heat in summer, the sirocco wind blowing up from the Sahara to blast the vines just as they were flowering—or all three of these problems in the same year, as producers outside Algiers lamented in 1858.[103] There were, in short, all kinds of reasons for settlers to be cautious, and perhaps to limit their ambitions to not much more than a few bottles for the family table. At least then they would not have to pay for wine imported from France.

These early vignerons came from varied backgrounds and confronted the challenges with varying degrees of experience and expertise. Bastide, a French national who moved to Algeria from Spain in 1844, brought some genuine viticultural knowledge (as well as capital) to his endeavors in Sidi-Bel-Abbès.[104] In the Tlemcen area, according to one agricultural inspector, the only two growers who had managed to produce decent wine by 1857 were a Monsieur Sauvage, a notary from the Champagne region, and a Monsieur Ayme, a brewer from Provence. Naturally, both used techniques that were familiar to them from their home regions. The diverse origin of the vignerons was also reflected in the eclectic range of *cépages* (vine varieties) that they cultivated. Early colonists in western Oran planted vines from Languedoc, Burgundy, Bordeaux, and Spain, as well as testing varieties they found growing locally. The result was what one inspector called *un vin hétérogène:* a "heterogenous" wine as mixed as the colonists who had produced it.[105] Chaotic combinations of flavors failed to please the judges when colonists presented their wines for evaluation at the exhibition of the Société impériale et centrale d'horticulture in Paris in 1858. The task of awarding prizes at this contest was made still harder by the fact that most of the wine sent from Algeria acidified so much in transit as to be undrinkable. In the end the judges felt they could do little more than praise the "least bad" Algerian red, even though it "tasted strongly of the barrel."[106]

Alongside these small-scale individual experiments, Catholic religious societies were among those making serious efforts to develop Algerian wine. At the 1858 exhibition, in fact, the judges awarded a silver medal to the fortified wine entered by Father Brumauld, director of the Jesuits' agricultural orphanage at Boufarik on the Mitidja plain.[107] As in an earlier era, when Jesuits and other Christian groups had expanded the wine frontier in the Americas, nineteenth-century French missionaries helped to spread viticulture in many locations across the world. Marist priests planted vineyards in New Zealand around the middle of the century, and their wine was soon well known. Members of the Société des missions étrangères de Paris pulled off the feat of bringing wine production to Tibet in the 1860s. In that same decade, Jesuits at Ksara in the Bekaa Valley imported rootstock and personnel from their Algerian vineyards and helped lay the basis for Lebanon's modern wine industry.[108]

In Algeria, one of the most famous vineyards of the whole of the colonial period grew out of a Catholic project of colonization led by Trappist monks. Like other monastic orders in France, the Trappists had been forced to disband during the Revolution, but they revived early in the Bourbon Restoration and aspired once more to emulate the austere piety of the Cistercians in their twelfth-century heyday. Algeria represented an intriguing prospect for the Trappists, a chance to demonstrate that ideals derived from medieval example had their place in the emerging mission fields of the nineteenth-century world. Their opportunity came about following the intervention of a civilian, François de Corcelle, a liberal Catholic parliamentary deputy who traveled to Algeria in 1841 in the same group as Tocqueville. The abbey of La Grande-Trappe was in the constituency de Corcelle represented in Normandy, and his familiarity with the order sparked an idea that they could play a role in the colonization of Algeria. De Corcelle succeeded in persuading the minister of war, Marshal Soult, that the agricultural experience and "saintliness" of the Trappists would have a salutary effect on all around them, Europeans and Muslims alike; with less enthusiasm, Governor-General Bugeaud concurred. As a result, the Trappists received a grant of 1,020 hectares of uncultivated land at Staouëli, only a few kilometers from where the French forces had landed in 1830 and the site of an important early battle. (Cannonballs and shells from that engagement still littered the property.)[109]

The first Trappists arrived at Staouëli in 1843 and began clearing the land. In this task they received considerable assistance from the government-general. Military engineers and large numbers of convict laborers were sent to help dig up the deep-rooted dwarf palms that were a tenacious obstacle to early colonists, and to tackle drainage problems that contributed to an unhealthy and malarial environment. In return for this official aid, which extended over many years, the Trappists were periodically required to take part in the administration's experiments with different types of cultivation. Trials with mulberry trees and silkworms, madder, and cotton all took their turn at Staouëli.[110]

The monks' first attempt at viticulture, by contrast, was not imposed on them by the administration. They already had a hectare of vines by 1846, though the main intent of that plantation may have been to produce wine for sacramental purposes. The monastery's association with wine did not begin in earnest until after 1853, when the monks planted vines on a new extension to their property.[111] By 1865, when Emperor Napoleon III visited Staouëli during a tour of Algeria, the vineyard had grown to 50 hectares—much less than the 140 hectares the monks then devoted to cereal crops, but substantial for the time. (His majesty tried the wine and offered his approval.) As the emperor made his way around

FIG. 1.2 Trappist monks in their vineyard at Staouëli near Algiers, ca. 1900.
Reproduced from the author's collection.

the property, he inquired about a group of uniformly dressed Arabs and
learned that they were prisoners sent to Staouëli to be "initiated into agricultural work" while completing their punishment.[112] The heroism of
the monks of Staouëli, celebrated so often in the second half of the nineteenth century, was built to a large degree on the labor of such anony-
mous men. If the Trappists' work was exemplary, as their early advocate
de Corcelle had hoped, the lessons may have appeared most relevant to
the *grands colons* who pursued large-scale colonization projects in later
years and often made use of convict labor (fig. 1.2).

Christian missionary viticulture converged most obviously with the
drive to colonize in the person of Charles Lavigerie, the man some described around 1870 as *le plus grand colon*—the greatest colonist.
Lavigerie was appointed archbishop of Algiers in 1867 after several years
as bishop of Nancy, and brought to his new post a keen sense of both
history and destiny. Drawing inspiration from the early days of the
Church in France as well as Algeria's own Christian past, Lavigerie vowed
to "make the Algerian land the cradle of a great, generous, Christian
nation—another France, in a word."[113]

The circumstances Lavigerie encountered soon after his arrival certainly lent themselves to public displays of generosity. A combination of afflictions between 1866 and 1868—recurrent visitations of locusts, epidemics of cholera and typhus, and drought—led to widespread famine. In appeals to Christians in France for aid, Lavigerie evoked the pitiful spectacle of starving people forcing leaves or grass into their mouths, desperately trying to avoid the same fate as the corpses that lay by the roadside.[114] The death toll reached the hundreds of thousands.[115] Amid the massive disruption to traditional family life caused by these disasters, Lavigerie was especially interested in the children left orphaned or abandoned. The immediate aim of the missionary society he founded in 1868, the Société des missionnaires d'Afrique, whose members quickly became known as White Fathers after the color of the priests' robes, was to educate and provide for these orphans.[116]

In 1869 Lavigerie bought several hundred hectares of land close to the site of an old Turkish fortress known as the Maison-Carrée, by the river Harrach about fifteen kilometers southeast of Algiers. (The land had earlier belonged to General Clauzel.[117]) Here Lavigerie hoped to apply his understanding of early Christian Gaul, in which he believed abbeys had served a double role as custodians of ideas and agents of a sort of agricultural development program that had helped lay the foundations for the emergence of the French nation itself.[118] With such thoughts in mind, Lavigerie moved a few dozen of the older orphans to Maison-Carrée and set them to work clearing the land, just like "the monks of the earliest centuries of our history who cleared the land of Gaul."[119]

It was at this time, in 1869, that Lavigerie's workers planted the first vines at Maison-Carrée. Some of the vine stock came from Spain and the rest from the Médoc region outside Bordeaux, where Lavigerie had first begun to learn about viticulture some years earlier. (He still regularly drank a wine from the Médoc for its supposed medicinal powers.)[120] Lavigerie did not assume that one could approach the Algerian land in the same way that monks in centuries past had tackled the region around Paris. Anticipating that his vines might not cope well with the heat, he delegated two priests, one in Spain and one in Egypt, to study the question of vinification in hot countries. For Lavigerie, in fact, was an acclimatizer—a member of the Société zoologique d'acclimatation, and quite an enthusiastic one at that. The archbishop urged the society to make use of him for any agricultural experiments they wished to carry out in Algeria, and in reply the society's president promised to send some vine cuttings from the group's *jardin d'acclimatation*.[121]

Lavigerie is said to have helped in the fields during the first grape harvest at Maison-Carrée. By 1874, one hundred hectares of land adjacent to the White Fathers' motherhouse were already given over to grapevines as well as fruit trees.[122] These plantations would form part of Lavigerie's legacy, growing into a major business venture whose wines traveled far and wide. Though his project to revive the glories of the North African Church in antiquity did not succeed, Lavigerie, like the monks of Staouëli, played a leading role in restoring vineyards to Algeria on a scale not seen since the time of Saint Augustine.

SEARCHING FOR THE WEALTH OF A COLONY

In the first four decades of French rule in Algeria, much of what passed for agricultural policy seemed to follow the hope expressed in an aphorism attributed to the Comte de La Bourdonnais, who in the 1730s established France's Indian Ocean colony of Ile de France (Mauritius): "It only takes one crop to make the wealth of a nation." Over a century later, in the 1850s, the saying resonated so much with Algeria's governor-general, Jacques Louis Randon, that he revived it.[123] Planners stood by their vision of Algeria as an agricultural colony. As Europe became "less and less a farm and more and more a factory," wrote one, Algeria should have a great future as "the farm of France"—a new variant, perhaps, on the "granary of Rome."[124]

That image began to gain some substance as grain exports from the colony rose in the 1850s.[125] But no one thought that cereals would be the "one crop" to make French Algeria truly wealthy, and moreover it was not a culture particularly well suited to a project of settlement, as the temptation for landholders was always to turn production over to Algerian sharecroppers. The greater hopes continued to be placed instead in cash crops like tobacco and cotton—crops that held the promise of reducing Algeria's budget deficit without threatening metropolitan producers with unwelcome competition.[126] Both tobacco and cotton received official protection; in the 1850s, for example, the government-general itself purchased the cotton crop for the benefit of the small-scale cultivators—including some Algerians—who were encouraged to produce it.[127] That policy, however, tended to allow everyone to avoid the awkward question of how smallholders were expected to compete with international cotton producers who used slaves, if not with other forms of cultivation based on coercion as practiced in places like Dutch Java.[128] The labor question, in fact, did not pose itself urgently until the American Civil War, when finally the cotton industry in Algeria began to achieve significant volume. One cotton booster, anticipating further growth but doubtful that Algeria had the right sort of workforce to support it, reviewed the options before concluding that the government should import thousands of Chinese to labor in the cotton fields.[129] Instead of Chinese field hands, however, the crop continued to be grown by small proprietors, sharecroppers, and a few bigger plantation owners.

In May 1865 Napoleon III arrived in Algiers for a forty-day tour of the colony. Less than a month had passed since the surrender of General Robert E. Lee's Confederate Army, bringing the Civil War to a close and heralding the return of Southern cotton to the world market. That topic, however, does not seem to have come up as the emperor traveled in all three Algerian departments and observed cotton cultivation in each one. The promise Napoleon believed he saw was quickly found to be hollow. Price fluctuations after the Civil War and problems resulting from the Algerian climate, where winter temperatures often dropped significantly below the mean, combined to frustrate the hopes of the early 1860s. By the middle of the 1870s the Algerian cotton industry had unspooled to nearly nothing.[130]

For all the attention he gave cotton during his visit in 1865, Napoleon III was witnessing the stirrings of a more important agricultural development. In town after town the emperor learned that the culture of the vine was spreading. Having already sampled the wine made by the monks of Staouëli, he tasted the local vintage elsewhere too. He left the Mitidja plain with home-produced bottles proudly gifted him by colonists in Mouzaïaville and Marengo. In Miliana Napoleon asked his hosts about the vines that grew on the southern slopes of the Massif de Dahra. In the western town of Sidi-Bel-Abbès he had many questions for Jérôme Bastide, the colonist who in the 1850s had struggled with jackals and frost in his vineyards. Bastide's agricultural ventures were now well established, and the emperor accepted an invitation into his home to talk more about his "magnificent" vines and other crops.[131]

Not least significant was the fact that the government-general had since about 1860 dropped any opposition to viticulture in the colony. As one leading official put it, Algerian viticulture was *un fait fatal* (a fatal fact), something that should be allowed to take its course without concern for the desires and sensitivities of the metropolitan wine lobby.[132] Accompanying Napoleon III in 1865, the governor-general, Marshal MacMahon, declared in his brusque military manner that the "good colonists" of an area outside Algiers had decided to plant vines and they already made good wine. This was not a complicated policy statement, but rather a simple endorsement of what was increasingly seen as the new and natural order of things.[133]

At the time, it was hard to see this as an important development. In 1865 the Algerian *vignoble* consisted of only about 7,000 hectares, a mere fraction of the roughly 400,000 hectares then cultivated in the Midi region of southern France.[134] In July 1867 a liberal customs agreement allowed all of Algeria's products, including its wines, to enter the metropole duty free. But Algeria was still far short of providing for its own wine needs, and exports were not likely to be a priority for as long as that continued. With Algeria running a commercial deficit of ninety million francs in 1867, amid famine and other hardships, the wealth of the colony was hard to discern.[135]

The belief that Algeria's colonization should complement the metropolitan economy, however, was losing its dominance. The settlers who now planted grapevines were not thinking imperially; instead they were acting colonially. Even an acclimatization enthusiast like Lavigerie was most interested in adapting to Algerian conditions something that France already had. Colonial Algeria had tested and eliminated many agricultural options, but finally seemed ready to embrace a crop that had been there all along.

2

Phylloxera and the Making of the Algerian Vineyard

1870 to 1907

In the final decades of the nineteenth century there was significant move-ment on the global wine frontier. From the 1880s in particular, regions like California, South Australia, and Mendoza in Argentina established themselves as important centers of production. Population growth and immigration helped to expand internal markets in "New World" territo-ries, especially when new arrivals to countries like Argentina and Chile came from traditionally wine-drinking lands. In places where the local preference was for other alcoholic drinks, as in Australia, better tech-niques for producing and handling wine along with improved transpor-tation helped to make a long-distance export trade feasible. A consider-able amount of experimentation, ingenuity, and capital investment went into these developments. By the end of the nineteenth century, wine was a global industry on a scale never seen before.[1]

In the fin de siècle, however, no territory increased its production of wine more than Algeria. In 1870, vineyards in the colony occupied about 9,000 hectares and yielded 127,000 hectoliters. Three decades later, in 1900, the Algerian *vignoble* had grown to over 140,000 hectares, while that year's vintage comfortably exceeded 5 million hectoliters. Though in that same span of time Algeria's European population doubled in size to about 600,000, the colony no longer had to turn to the metropole to supply its everyday needs in wine: imports from France declined from around 500,000 hectoliters in 1870 to about 50,000 in 1900. (Better-quality wines, especially from Bordeaux, accounted for much of what continued to arrive.) With its 1900 output Algeria edged into fifth place on the list of the world's biggest producers, behind France, Italy, Spain, and Portugal, but a long way ahead of Chile, Argentina, the United States, and Australia. Algeria soon surpassed Portugal to achieve fourth place, then held onto that rank for much of the rest of the twentieth century.[2]

This development could not easily have been predicted. The historian of Germany David Blackbourn cites a saying among the agricultural colonists who migrated to the reclaimed marshlands of eighteenth-century Prussia: "The first generation meets with death, the second with privation, only the third with prosperity."[3] This formula might equally well have ended up applying to the fortunes of European settlers in Algeria. A great many of the first generation of settlers did indeed meet with death, be it from disease or, less frequently, as a consequence of local resistance. Mortality rates gradually improved after mid-century, but the hardships of the late 1860s as well as the failure of crops like cotton served as a reminder that colonization's economic fulfillment was still very far from guaranteed. Yet the development of the Algerian vineyard, especially from around 1880, allowed many members of the second generation to achieve prosperity ahead of the Prussian colonists' schedule. The problem then lay in determining whether theirs was a "surface prosperity," as some settlers worried in 1892, or whether wine could be relied upon to serve the longer-term aims of colonization.[4]

Though the primary focus of this chapter is on the emergence of a full-scale wine industry in Algeria, both driven and to a degree constrained by the vine pest phylloxera, it is also about the maturation of a settler community. Wine, through the wealth and the sense of rootedness it brought, helped people of varied European backgrounds develop confidence in their identity as "Algerians," as they liked to call themselves, who believed they belonged to (French) Algeria as much as Algeria belonged to them. (I mostly prefer to label them "Euro-Algerians.") After the hesitations of the first decades of colonization, wine set the colony on what seemed to be a firmer footing. Becoming French Algeria's most valuable export, the profits from its sale lubricated banks, helped to power a construction boom, and shaped and emboldened new political elites. Meanwhile, Algerians—that is, those the recent arrivals called the *indigènes*—struggled to remain in place.

PHYLLOXERA AND THE "SEDUCTION" OF THE COLONIST

Around the middle of the 1860s a few vignerons in France's lower Rhône Valley began to notice something inexplicably amiss in their vineyards. First there were discolored leaves, then dried-up grapes, then dead vines—and then the same process on neighboring plants. It was Jules-Emile Planchon, a professor of botany from the university at Montpellier, who in 1868 fingered the culprit as a colonist from across the sea. To blame was a species of plant louse from America that Planchon named *phylloxera vastatrix*: literally, "dry leaf devastator."[5] The tiny insects sucked the sap from vine roots, then sent what Planchon called "advance colonies" into nearby vines so that the invasion spread inexorably, like "a spot of oil" (*une tache d'huile*).[6] (Only a few years later the French generals Gallieni and Lyautey, expert colonists themselves, employed this oil-spot metaphor to describe a strategy for the Gallicization of newly conquered territories like northern Vietnam and Madagascar.[7]) In the late nineteenth century seemingly anything could turn into a colonial affair.

In disbelief at yet another assault on their vines—so soon after the oidium crisis of the 1850s—vignerons were often suspicious of both the experts' diagnosis and the possible remedies they advanced. In any case, as the phylloxera army began its march, the centers of infestation remained quite localized, and in many parts of the country French peasants could still reasonably hope not to be affected. So they continued to plant, and the French vineyard went on expanding right up until 1875. That year France recorded an output of eighty-three million hectoliters of wine, a figure both unprecedented and never attained since.[8] By then, though, spots of oil (to borrow the metaphor) had already spread extensively in southern departments like the Gard, the Vaucluse, and the Hérault, and been identified in regions like Bordeaux and the Charentais. In 1876 phylloxera began its attack on Burgundy. It became more and more clear that this new menace to an industry that may have supported as many as eight million people was going to have a major economic and social impact.[9]

It is difficult to pinpoint when phylloxera and its threat were first registered across the Mediterranean. None of the colonists who responded in 1868 to a major official survey of agriculture in Algeria mentioned it. That survey indicated that the vine was making modest progress in the colony, but the production figures still represented barely so much as a drop in the barrel compared with those of metropolitan France. Around the western town of Tlemcen, colonists believed they were close to satisfying local demand for wine, but as yet Algeria was not in a position to export. Several colonists expressed a desire to extend their vineyards, but recognized the obstacles to that ambition; one recurring complaint was the difficulty of securing credit for the costs involved in expansion. At the same time, many saw that the product itself needed to improve and admitted that conservation practices in the hot climate were insufficient.[10]

In the following decade, under the new Third Republic, the administration made 400,000 hectares (over 1,500 square miles) of land available for settlement by creating new "centers of colonization" or by expanding existing villages, assisted by legal sleights of hand like the 1873 Warnier Law, which provided a mechanism for taking apart native property holdings.[11] In town halls, prefectures, railway stations, and post offices across France, large posters aimed to catch the eye of potential new *colons* for the Algerian countryside, informing them of new settlements and giving them a sense of the opportunities in each.[12] "Land suited for the vine" became an increasingly common description on these posters over the course of the 1870s. Though hindsight permits the observation that the colonization service was not always good at identifying which lands were best "suited for the vine," it is clear that the administration was already nudging colonists toward viticulture in the early 1870s, and even more so after 1876, when phylloxera began its full-scale assault on the French vineyard. In 1877 Governor-General Chanzy asserted that "the question of the vine in Algeria is today completely resolved from the point of view of the scale this form of cultivation must take and the immense advantages it can procure for the country."[13] At Chanzy's invitation, a wine expert from the South of France, Romuald Dejernon, arrived in Algeria and began promoting the virtues of viticulture in public talks that were then often reprinted in newspapers and agricultural journals. An audience in Bône in eastern Algeria, for example, heard that France's wine-producing competitors in Europe were seizing the moment to capitalize on her misfortunes and capture her market share. "Faced with such a situation," Dejernon told his listeners, "the duty, even the patriotism of the Algerian [colonists] commands them to plant vines."[14]

At that moment French Algerian wine still covered barely half of the colony's demand. Due to phylloxera, however, in 1879 metropolitan

France failed to supply its own needs and became a net importer of wine.[15] That was roughly the tipping point, the moment after which Algerian colonists in ever-increasing numbers succumbed to the lure of the vine. The prominent political economist Paul Leroy-Beaulieu called this movement "the great seduction."[16]

The seduction was helped along its way by a changing financial environment. The Bank of Algeria, founded in 1851, had long endured criticism for what the Algiers Chamber of Commerce once lambasted as its "timid and parsimonious" policies. In a colony whose government placed so much emphasis on rural settlement, the bank's failure to fund agricultural projects stood out. The financial arm of a private company with close ties to Napoleon III's government, the Société générale algérienne, founded in 1865, promised to do more to support agricultural development but largely failed in that objective. Due to the shortcomings or statutory limitations of these institutions, many colonists instead had to run the gauntlet of the informal credit market, where interest rates typically ran to 25 or 30 percent.[17]

In 1880, though, as part of the deal to renew its status as the issuer of the colony's currency, the Bank of Algeria agreed to provide easier access to agricultural credit. At that moment, with phylloxera raging in France, the vine looked a good bet for the bank. Branch offices appeared in provincial towns like L'Arba, Médéa, Mascara, and Aïn-Témouchent— ten new branches opened for business in 1880 and 1881 alone—and began to issue loans at 7 percent interest to colonists who wished to create new vineyards or expand existing ones. Beginning in 1880, another credit-granting institution, the Crédit foncier et agricole d'Algérie, provided further support for this movement, albeit with a bit more circumspection: as enthusiasm for planting the vine spread, one official of the bank recalled that cotton and tobacco had inspired similar passion in the recent past.[18] The many colonists who took advantage of Algeria's new financial liquidity to plant vines, however, appeared undeterred by those inauspicious precedents.

Who were these colonial vignerons? One often-repeated idea is that, in the words of one historian, "hordes of southern vignerons fleeing the phylloxera" crossed the Mediterranean and created the Algerian vineyard.[19] The claim has a surface plausibility, but the evidence for it is weak. One example seems especially telling. In April 1878 the prefect of the Hérault, which before phylloxera had produced more wine than any other French department, contacted Governor-General Chanzy to see if Algeria might offer a new opportunity to families whose livelihoods had been ravaged by the pest. The governor-general responded quickly and with enthusiasm, telling the prefect that the peopling of Algeria with French settlers—especially from the French countryside—"is the constant goal of my efforts." Immediately Chanzy instructed the prefects of Algeria's three departments to identify land that would suit the skills of the projected new arrivals, and by June he was writing to the prefect of the Hérault with an offer to settle 166 families from his department in new colonial villages. Time passed, and then more time, and finally in September 1878 the prefect communicated his surprising response: far from finding 166 candidates for the available land concessions in Algeria, he had received a total of only 6 requests. The reason, he speculated, was that cultivators in the Hérault—which had already struggled with phylloxera for several years but was also (through its experts in Montpellier) at the center of efforts to fight back—were beginning to find hope in the chemical treatments being tried in some vineyards, as well as the experiments taking place to graft resistant American vines onto local ones.[20]

What this means is that when we read the journalist Paul Bourde, who traveled to Algeria in late 1879 and reported that people were saying "whole villages in the Hérault and the Midi departments" planned to move there to cultivate the vine on phylloxera-free French soil, we need to be clear that he was only relaying a rumor.[21] Certainly, some southern French vignerons made their way to Algeria, and some of these doubtless did so because of phylloxera. In the years following the creation in 1874 of the new settlement of Hammam-Bou-Hadjar to the southwest of Oran, for example, four or five dozen families arrived from the Hérault, the Gard, and the Vaucluse, in other words the core of phylloxera's early path.[22] The failed effort to recruit settlers from the Hérault in 1878, however, suggests that any such movement crested early. In effect the "whole villages" never came, while "hordes" is much too strong a word for the numbers that did arrive.

Broader migration patterns to Algeria also fail to demonstrate any strong correlation with the appearance of phylloxera in particular parts of France. The Midi department of the Aude, for example, a major wine producer, was hit relatively late by the blight, experiencing a vertiginous drop in production around 1884. Yet official statistics show that between

1881 and 1894 only 34 families moved from the Aude to new or expanded centers of colonization in Algeria. During the same period, for comparison, 776 families relocated to Algeria from the Ardèche, 670 from the Drôme, and 567 from the Hautes-Alpes. Those three southeastern departments contained a lot of rough terrain and together produced a fraction of the Aude's wine output; they were correspondingly much less affected by phylloxera, which cannot therefore explain the numbers that chose to leave. Poverty in geographically challenging environments certainly encouraged some rural French people to try their luck in Algeria, but the image of the ruined southern vigneron arriving to reshape the colony's agriculture is misleading.[23]

Instead, the story of the development of the Algerian vineyard revolves around a notably diverse group of people who more often than not were already in the colony. There were good reasons for this. Colonists of some years' experience were in a better position to take quick advantage of the opportunity presented by France's misfortune with phylloxera. They had adjusted to local conditions, knew how to access the equipment and manpower they needed, and were more likely to possess the wherewithal to sustain themselves for the three years it took newly planted vines to deliver a marketable product. Factors such as these help to explain why the Algerian vineyard expanded most rapidly around settlements that had existed for two, three, or four decades, or where settlers practiced *la colonisation libre*—the development of lands gained privately rather than via official programs.[24] In such places new arrivals were much less prominent than more experienced colonists or wealthy investors. In new settlements, by contrast, most colonists had to focus on clearing land for cultivation, and then typically gave priority to cereal crops. Some of the settlers from the Midi who moved to Hammam-Bou-Hadjar after its foundation in 1874 may well have had experience of viticulture, but as of 1884 the community still only cultivated 58 hectares of vines amid 800 hectares of wheat, barley, and other cereals. In focusing on those crops, they were fulfilling the emphasis the government itself had envisaged for the settlement. Only later did Hammam-Bou-Hadjar develop into a major center of wine production.[25]

It is, of course, easier to find information about the settlers who developed the bigger vineyards rather than those who planted a hectare or two, and this fact is reflected in the biographical sketches that follow. But the bigger planters were by no means always born to wealth, and indeed it is difficult to come up with a profile of a "typical" successful vigneron. Some of the most prominent were not even of French parentage. Family background in those cases did not prevent recognition of their role as colonizers, which was sometimes marked with rewards like the Legion of Honor. While urban politics in late nineteenth-century colonial Algeria was often characterized by divisive rhetoric about the threat to French "purity" posed by other European immigrants, some of the case studies below suggest that success in the countryside was the surest way to earn respect and acceptance regardless of social background.[26]

Charles Debonno, for example, was born in Algiers in 1846 to Maltese parents who had already struggled for a decade to make a living in the unhealthy environs of Boufarik on the Mitidja plain. It was in Boufarik that Debonno received his first lessons in agriculture from the Jesuits, who, as we have seen, were among the earliest notable cultivators of the vine in colonial Algeria. After a few years working as a grain purchaser for a miller, Debonno had earned enough by 1869 to buy a property in the Boufarik area, and he seems to have wasted no time in planting vines. An official from the Société générale algérienne bank was a witness at his wedding in 1871, hinting that Debonno already knew how to charm creditors. His rise to prominence, however, accelerated around 1879; that was when he began to buy up several large farms in the western Mitidja, facilitated by the Bank of Algeria, which had recently opened a lending branch in Boufarik. As early as 1884, three years after taking French nationality, Debonno was awarded the Legion of Honor for "exceptional services to colonization." At their greatest extent, his properties totaled as many as 3,000 hectares, on which he grew wheat, feed crops, and fruit trees as well as raising cattle. These livestock helped to fertilize the vineyards for which Debonno became best known. By the end of the century, he oversaw production across about a thousand hectares of vines.[27]

Though the scale of Debonno's endeavors was extraordinary, such rags-to-riches stories were not uncommon and the Mitidja plain seemed especially capable of delivering them. Rid of the security problems of the early days of colonization and with its problems of water management increasingly under control, this large swath of low-lying land induced expansive ambitions. Another settler of non-French parentage, Michel-Louis Pelegri, in some ways followed a similar path to Debonno. Born in 1838 on the island of Majorca, when he was aged eight his family crossed the Mediterranean and his father rented a modest piece of land outside Algiers; Michel-Louis spent much of his youth herding cattle. After working the lands of several colonists he eventually had the opportunity to grow feed crops and then, with the profits from that activity, to rent a large farm. By the end of the 1870s he had done well enough to buy property in several locations in the central and eastern Mitidja. Pelegri had therefore acquired the means to practice large-scale agriculture precisely at the vine's moment of opportunity. Basing himself in the village of Sidi Moussa, Pelegri soon cultivated several hundred hectares of vines, and at the time he became a French citizen in 1889 was already one of the most successful individual producers in the whole of Algeria.[28]

To outsiders, the spectacular successes of both Debonno and Pelegri may have appeared sudden. In fact, both had had a range of experiences in Algeria that acquainted them with the land and its possibilities before they decided to focus on the vine. Pelegri, whose family came from a wine-growing island, had already produced small amounts of wine before his big expansion. Debonno completed a course in viticulture at the school of agriculture in Montpellier before practicing it in Algeria.[29] Successful vignerons were then in a position to influence others, for example through the agricultural societies that began to emerge in increasing numbers at this time. In 1883 Debonno was elected president of one of these societies, the *comice agricole* (farmers' institute) of Boufarik, which awarded prizes to worthy local producers.[30]

Among those held up as examples to other vignerons during the boom of the 1880s were two French men who settled in Algeria within a year of each other. Claude Grellet followed an unusual (and unusually long) road to Algeria. In 1848, soon after the beginning of the gold rush, he traveled to California and built up a successful business importing French wine to San Francisco. Returning to his native Massif Central after sixteen years away, he no longer found the climate to his liking. Algiers, which had already established itself as a destination for winter visitors from Europe, seemed an attractive alternative, and Grellet evidently decided that this was as close as he was likely to get to a French California. He purchased a property at Kouba on the heights above the capital in 1867, and before long, having sold wine on one frontier, he began producing it on another (albeit by this time a much tamer frontier than the one he had worked in America). His vineyards became well known not for their size—140 hectares was big, but not in the same league as the properties of Debonno or Pelegri—but rather for their appearance and the quality of their wines, and Grellet's proximity to Algiers made it easy for those who wanted to visit him for advice.[31]

Arriving in Algeria around the same time was twenty-five-year-old Armand Arlès-Dufour. Like Grellet, he came with means, but in his case it was family wealth that bought him two very large properties on the western Mitidja plain: his father, François Barthélémy Arlès-Dufour, was a prominent businessman in Lyon and a leading proponent of Saint-Simonian thought, a nebulous ideology that aimed to advance the common good through innovative economic and social practices. For Armand Arlès-Dufour, the pursuit of Saint-Simonian ideals in Algeria involved much experimentation with new agricultural techniques and equipment: he was one of the first in the colony, for example, to use a steam-driven plow to clear his land of unwanted vegetation. In 1882 Hippolyte Lecq, one of Algeria's most influential agricultural experts, hailed Arlès-Dufour as a model colonist in part for the way his methods nurtured the long-term health of the soil and avoided what Lecq termed the "vampiric" system of agriculture that he felt too many colonists were practicing—an approach that was interested primarily in maximizing profits from exportable commodities. Arlès-Dufour's wine production, comparable in scale to that of Grellet, earned similar recognition for its quality as well as for the cooling techniques he developed in his cellars. Both men, like Debonno, were awarded the Legion of Honor, Arlès-Dufour in 1881 and Grellet in 1885.[32]

In all the cases cited so far, the owner of each property was closely involved with the development of the vineyard. This was the ideal for all those who had worried about maintaining a stable European agricultural population in Algeria. The culture itself seemed to foster stability; vines, wrote Léon Bastide in 1880, were a visible sign that an owner wished "to attach himself to the soil while surrounding himself with a certain well-being."[33] Bastide was a good example of the next step in this process: the establishment of successive generations on the land. Léon's father, Jérôme, as we have seen, had shown Napoleon III his vineyards outside the western Algerian town of Sidi-Bel-Abbès in 1865. Around that same time, Léon completed his studies in agriculture in Paris, then returned to Algeria to put what he had learned into practice. Jérôme

Bastide complemented his son's formal education by sharing some hard-earned local knowledge: experience had demonstrated, for example, that the Mourvèdre grape variety, which ripens late in the growing year, was well adapted to withstand the spring frosts that were common in Sidi-Bel-Abbès. (A late frost had ruined Jérôme's crop in 1858.) By the time of Jérôme's death in 1882, Léon was fully launched on a successful career. On his extensive property he raised cows and sheep and cultivated cereal crops and olive trees as well as substantial vineyards; he also popularized agricultural knowledge in books and pamphlets, and encouraged local producers as president of the farmers' institute in Sidi-Bel-Abbès. (He, too, received the Legion of Honor, as his father had before him.)[34] This kind of father-to-son succession was, of course, so much a part of the culture of the vine in France, and before long a second generation of wine producers was taking the lead in Algeria. One such was Claude Grellet's son Louis, who studied in Montpellier before returning to Kouba to oversee his father's vineyards.[35]

The vine-planting boom of the 1880s naturally also attracted investors who were not thinking of putting down roots in this manner. The eastern department of Constantine had an especially large number of absentee owners looking for a return on the vine, with a notable proportion of the capital flowing in from investors based in or near Lyon. Count du Sablon, a wealthy member of the *conseil général* (departmental assembly) of the Rhône who lived in a château in the Beaujolais region to the northwest of the city, in 1881 bought a property near the town of Bougie in coastal Constantine and helped spark a move to plant vines in that area. Two years later, a Lyonnais named Lucien Deyme bought a property on the plains south of Bône, which were in the process of becoming eastern Algeria's closest equivalent to the Mitidja. But these men differed from the speculators who had purchased lands sight unseen in the early decades of the colony and then failed to develop them. Du Sablon continued to enjoy the comforts of his château, but the viticultural experience he had gained in France shaped the development of his lands near Bougie, and it was vignerons from the Beaujolais and the nearby surroundings of Lyon and Mâcon who carried out much of the work. Deyme, for his part, entrusted the development of his eastern Algerian vineyards to others while he remained in Lyon and focused his efforts on ensuring that the wines from his property would find an outlet when they came to France. To that end, he set up a storage warehouse in Lyon and another in nearby Bourg-en-Bresse.[36]

Other vineyards began as corporate ventures. In 1878 the Compagnie algérienne, which had been conceded vast amounts of land by Napoleon III, decided to develop a large property to the west of Médéa in the department of Algiers via a subsidiary it created for the purpose, the Société viticole d'Amourah. Money bought expertise. The society was directed from Paris by Charles Dollfus-Galline, scion of a wealthy Mulhouse family of textile manufacturers with side interests in viticulture in the Gironde; a successful vigneron from Montpellier, Laurent Coste, relocated to Algeria to oversee the plantation; and a cellarman from Bordeaux followed Coste to supervise the winemaking process. By 1886 the vines already covered 370 hectares, and the community that developed next to it bore the name Dollfusville.[37]

For Jonathan Holden, another industrialist whose money came from textiles, an investment in Algeria became a family affair. Born in Bradford in Yorkshire, Holden moved to Reims to run his uncle's woolcombing factory, then later struck out on his own to become a leading figure in the economic life of the city. (And its cultural life, too: his donation on the occasion of Queen Victoria's golden jubilee built Reims's first public library.) In 1875 Holden bought a tract of land near Boufarik in the Mitidja and turned its management over to his son, John, and a nephew, John Cox. On the estate, Holden and Cox developed a vineyard of about a hundred hectares as well as a notable plantation of orange trees. This was an example of "abundant capital judiciously applied," observed the British consul in Algiers, Sir Robert Lambert Playfair, with patriotic approval. But in 1891 Playfair had the task of registering the death of John Holden at the age of thirty-seven. What may have begun as a simple business venture for Jonathan Holden—as well as a rare example of English participation in the colonization of Algeria— ended up acquiring unanticipated personal significance.[38]

With these examples we are perhaps already drifting too far from some basic truths about this moment in Algerian viticulture: most vineyards were far smaller than the properties discussed here, and for sure most colonists did not have anything like the resources of a du Sablon or a Holden. But the general impression created here is not false if it captures the idea that, in the 1880s, seemingly anyone who was in a position to plant vines did so. That opportunism, catalyzed by France's difficulties with phylloxera, had a certain gold-rush quality about it (as Claude Grellet might well have recognized). In these years fortune appeared to favor the brave, and cases like Debonno and Pelegri also appeared to show that the brave had a chance even when they were not of French origin. But most were not gambling for high stakes in the manner of a Debonno; one did not need a hundred hectares to hope the vine might improve the fortunes of one's family.

At Fort de l'Eau in the vicinity of Algiers, for example, a Minorcan community that had already been a presence for three decades or so was focused primarily on growing crops like potatoes, tomatoes, and artichokes for the market. In about 1880, members of this community began planting vines, and within a few years they had over fifty hectares in production between them. Cultivators with names common in the community like Sintès, Pons, and Alzuna looked more rooted than ever as the profits from the vine added to the income from gardening. In turn this may have helped to secure advantages for some individuals as Fort de l'Eau developed as a seaside bathing resort at the end of the century; already in 1893 a Pons ran a horse-drawn bus line to and from Algiers, and a Sintès owned a café near the beach.[39] Though Fort de l'Eau's periurban coastal location was somewhat unusual, the settlement nonetheless illustrates the way the vine helped improve the socioeconomic wellbeing of colonists from humble rural backgrounds.

The early 1880s was a moment of great activity and optimism among colonists. At the same time, the possibility that phylloxera might come to Algeria was a constant shadow. Some, it is true, chose to play down the risks or preached a kind of phylloxera denial: the Algerian vineyard was too new and its vegetation too lush to be hit, they said; Algeria was so spread out, argued others, that even if phylloxera were to appear it would not do much damage; nothing to fear, wrote a company seeking investors for a new plantation.[40] The administration was not nearly so sanguine about the danger.

THE INSURGENT: PHYLLOXERA IN ALGERIA

When Madame Jacquenot arrived at the port of Algiers in December 1884 she was surprised to be apprehended by customs officers. The problem in her luggage was a bundle of vine shoots and a few flowering plants. Jacquenot had declared these upon entry, but that didn't make what she had brought any more acceptable. The officers took the bundle away and burned it.[41]

This seemingly minor indiscretion was in fact very disturbing to the authorities. Details of the incident soon reached the desk of the minister of agriculture in Paris, Jules Méline, who in turn discussed it with the governor-general. The reason it came as such depressing news for top-ranking administrators was that it illustrated the fragility of the effort to keep phylloxera from crossing the Mediterranean. At the time of Jacquenot's voyage, Algeria was still officially phylloxera-free, and since 1880 a host of regulations had been in place to try to keep it that way. Only a few months earlier in 1884 a new decree had sought to make absolutely clear what one could not bring into the colony. (In effect all plant matter, soil, and fertilizer were barred from entry.) At the planning stage this decree was drafted and redrafted with an almost manic attention to detail: one amendment followed someone's observation that a particular French cheese, Saint-Marcellin, came wrapped in a vine leaf (not allowed). Yet, for all the efforts of the lawmakers, the message still did not seem fully to have sunk in. After Madame Jacquenot's mistake, placards that listed the restrictions went up in ports of embarkation and on board ships. Passengers now had even fewer excuses for ignorance of the rules or the potential punishments for breaking them, which could run to as much as fifteen months in jail and up to eight hundred francs in fines.[42] But the authorities knew that to keep phylloxera out of Algeria they would need as much luck as law.

The problem of identifying phylloxera if or when it should appear was another vexing topic. From 1883 there was an active phylloxera inspectorate, with a delegate to oversee each of Algeria's three departments and a local expert in every commune charged with the task of making annual visits to monitor the vineyards. Responsibility also fell on the shoulders of vineyard owners, who were required to inform their mayor if they noticed any sign of sickness in their vines.[43]

Even members of the French Senate legislative commission that played an important role in establishing this system seemed unsure that it would work. While serving on this commission, the senator for Oran, Rémy Jacques, particularly doubted that what he called "illiterate Spaniards" could be trusted to follow the rules, especially after some colonists, illiterate or not, had been caught bringing vine roots back from Spain.[44] (Phylloxera's presence in Spanish vineyards was first confirmed in 1875.) But the complexity of the problem certainly went beyond any particular fraction of colonial society. Many of the vignerons of 1880s Algeria were first-time growers who were already "improvising," as one phylloxera inspector put it, and might not be counted on to know when a vine was sickening; vines were subject to so many different types of malady that even experienced growers were sometimes unsure what was typical and what wasn't.[45] A vineyard was also a substantial investment—for some colonists perhaps even a first serious investment—and although the law of 1883 prescribed compensation for owners hit by phylloxera, the personal stakes involved meant that there was likely to be some wariness about reporting potential problems. In any case, many of the communal experts were overstretched and could scarcely be expected to inspect every single vine.[46] In short, there was considerable risk of an infestation going unnoticed.

In the summer of 1885 Algeria's luck ran out. On July 2, one of the communal inspectors, Onésime Havard, confirmed the presence of phylloxera in Mansourah, a village just outside the western Algerian city of Tlemcen. Havard, who had grown up in a farming family in the Aube department southeast of Paris but moved to Algeria in 1869, was responsible for checking vineyards in several centers of colonization in the Tlemcen area. A resident and vineyard owner in Mansourah himself, however, Havard first spotted the dreaded louse on the properties of three of his neighbors: Jean Mollier, originally from the Ardèche; Calixte Spenon, from the Vaucluse; and Fernando Alberto, from the Spanish region of Alicante.[47] Following his instructions, Havard first reported his discovery to the mayor. Then, once the news had worked its way up the administrative hierarchy, Governor-General Louis Tirman declared a two-kilometer "zone of protection" around the infested area. The regulations prescribed that all vines within this zone were to be treated and the phylloxerated vines destroyed.

Within a few days, the phylloxera delegate for the department of Oran, Louis Gastine, arrived at the site. Almost instantly there was a confrontation between local growers and the government's representatives. According to the law, Gastine now had full authority over the zone of protection. When a team working for him wanted to gain access to a property that adjoined one of the contaminated vineyards, however, Havard and the proprietor angrily tried to keep them out. Gastine complained immediately to his superiors and demanded that Havard be removed from his post. When that did not appear to be happening, Gastine tendered his own resignation, only to withdraw it a day or two later after the governor-general intervened and insisted that Havard be fired.[48]

Personal ties to the affected vignerons might help to explain why Havard reacted so strongly to the outsiders who descended on his community in 1885. (To give an idea of the way some of these people were involved in each other's lives, within the prior three years Havard had registered both Fernando Alberto's marriage and the death of his infant son at the town hall in Mansourah.) Havard appears to have cooled off fairly quickly, because by the end of the year he was again playing a leading role in the fight against phylloxera.[49] But the way he had been treated did not help the reputation of the government phylloxera service. A local weekly, *L'Insurgé* (The Insurgent), was unsparing in its mockery of the array of experts and officials who came to Mansourah after Havard's discovery. This included not just Gastine but also the head of the service for the whole of Algeria, Charles Nicolas, and the chief of the inspectorate in France, Georges Couanon. Such was *L'Insurgé*'s disdain for what it called these *pompiers sans pompes* (firemen without engines) and *budgétivores* (budget eaters) that the cartoon on the cover (fig. 2.1) appeared to identify more with the bug than with the pith-helmeted inspectors.[50] Phylloxera is depicted in much the same way that many settlers liked to see themselves, as a plucky "little guy" who outsmarts the government. Barefoot and irreverent, the louse is an insurgent spirit, and, after all, a colonist himself.

Around town, though, people were saying that it was one colonist's defiance of the law that had brought the pest to Mansourah. Jean Mollier, according to some, had boasted a few years previously about bringing vines from France; in one version of events he smuggled them into Algeria in two false-bottomed cases. The public prosecutor in Tlemcen found the truth of the matter hard to establish, and it is not clear that Mollier was ever called to account.[51] But the stories about him circulated widely, and the implication that phylloxera had been present for several years already was certainly sobering. Meanwhile, the authorities moved with a perhaps deliberate show of speed to compensate Fernando Alberto, who (despite his Spanish origins) was not under suspicion of importing the problem. Barely two weeks after phylloxera's presence was

FIG. 2.1 Phylloxera thumbs its nose at the government inspectors. In the background are the remains of the fourteenth-century Mansourah mosque, with its iconic minaret at right. *L'Insurgé,* 19 July 1885. 127 J 18, Archives Départementales des Bouches-du-Rhône, all rights reserved in the reproduction.

first announced, Alberto accepted an offer of nearly 4,000 francs in recompense for his one-and-a-half hectares of contaminated vines.[52]

The arrival of phylloxera clearly rattled the Euro-Algerian community around Tlemcen, where viticulture had been developing since the 1860s as a key part of the settler economy and was already a source of local pride. Once the community got over its initial shock, however, its vignerons— led by Onésime Havard—made Tlemcen something of a model for the government's argument that the best way to deal with phylloxera was via close surveillance followed by chemical treatment of any affected areas. In Sidi-Bel-Abbès, which in August 1885 became the second confirmed phylloxera host, the response was broadly similar.[53] The meetings of agricultural societies around this time were fractious affairs, found Louis Gastine, and vignerons often expressed their opinions "with great violence."[54] But the majority opinion of producers in the department of Oran, echoed also in the department of Algiers, quickly rallied behind a system in which vignerons would play a bigger role in monitoring vineyards, with the work to be paid for in part by a tax on growers of five francs per hectare of vines. These ideas were codified in a law of July 1886 that also supported the creation of local anti-phylloxera syndicates to organize the work of inspection. (Wine producers elected to the syndicate in the department of Algiers included Charles Debonno, Claude Grellet, and Armand Arlès-Dufour, with Havard and Léon Bastide among those chosen to represent Oran.)[55]

The system that evolved therefore set up the defense of the Algerian vineyard as a joint effort, with the growers taking the lead in surveillance and the state paying for and carrying out the necessary treatment as well as compensating owners for their losses. When this system functioned well, it greatly mitigated phylloxera's impact while giving colonists the confidence to keep planting (and banks to keep lending). In the eighteen years that followed the first discovery of the blight in Sidi-Bel-Abbès, for example, the phylloxera service destroyed about thirty-six hectares of vines in the district, while in the same period of time the local vineyard grew eightfold.[56]

A commitment to this system of defense did not necessarily signify positive feelings toward the administration. Consistent with a more general settler attitude that had been especially evident since the advent of civilian rule in Algeria in 1870, a prickly tone pervaded the journals of the anti-phylloxera syndicates, with the government-general variously criticized either for not placing enough trust in the growers' expertise or for failing to provide sufficient support.[57] This rather mixed message, that the administration was both too present and not present enough, was characteristic: the bold pioneers were always more dependent on the state than they cared to admit.

In a few places, however, the attitude to the administration over the question of phylloxera tipped into outright and sustained hostility. In those instances, colonial Algeria offered a parallel to metropolitan France, where vignerons blocked inspectors or teams sent to treat infested vines in numerous locations, including parts of the Var, Burgundy, the Loire Valley, and the Champagne region.[58] Though historians of the metropole have in some cases offered sociological explanations for such confrontations—having to do with factors like vineyard size or conflicts between richer and poorer growers—the reason why one community should object to treatment while others nearby did not can often remain obscure.

In Algeria one might feel similarly at a loss to come up with convincing reasons why the two most significant centers of opposition to the administration's policies should have been Philippeville, a port town in the department of Constantine, and Mascara, set among hills in an inland reach of the department of Oran. What is perhaps most important is that the objections in both places eventually found the same focus and achieved the same outcome: an end to the administration's attempt to deal with phylloxera solely by means of chemical treatments, and permission instead to introduce resistant American vines as an alternative solution.

The contest in France between those popularly categorized as the "chemists" and the "Americanists" is central to most histories of phylloxera. As is well known, the advocates of American vines ultimately prevailed, and their influence was already ascendant when phylloxera was identified in Algeria in 1885.[59] But, while some of the technical challenges involved in grafting French vines onto American rootstock had been worked out by that time, replanting was not guaranteed success. With phylloxera raging in the Charentais, for example, growers there despaired of finding American roots that would take to the region's chalky soil.[60] To the defenders of the Algerian vineyard it looked safer to offer ongoing support to the "chemists." By 1885 the standard chemical treatment of phylloxerated areas involved the injection of carbon disulfide

(CS_2) into the soil through a hollow metal *pal* (stake). The most commonly used injector was the one perfected by a chemist from Marseille, Gabriel Gastine—the older brother of Louis Gastine, phylloxera inspector for the department of Oran. The work crews called to Mansourah and Sidi-Bel-Abbès in the summer of 1885 all fumigated the soil using the *"pal* Gastine." (They also discovered one of its limitations: in Sidi-Bel-Abbès several injectors snapped in the dry, hard ground.[61]) Leading advocates of American vines in France were sometimes jeeringly labeled *marchands de plantes,* or "plant salesmen," for touting a remedy from which some of them stood to profit. But Louis Gastine's personal stake (literally) in the chemical treatment of phylloxera illustrates that there were vested interests on all sides of the debate.[62]

In contrast, many of the colonists in Philippeville whose vineyards were found contaminated by phylloxera in 1886 were neither wealthy nor well connected. The town was essentially a French creation built over— and, to a large degree, *with*—the ruins of the Roman settlement of Russicada.[63] More than a few of Philippeville's residents were of southern Italian (especially Neapolitan) or Maltese origin and, according to one inspector, lacked "any resources other than their patch of vines and their labor."[64] In a large vineyard, a mandatory treatment area extending twenty-five to thirty meters around infested vines was for most growers not worth the effort of contesting. But when the vineyards were small and close together, as was often the case in Philippeville, the extent of the phylloxera service's "zone of security" became a matter of real consequence— especially as the growers there complained that the government didn't pay them enough compensation for their destroyed vines. The service quickly began to feel the pressure. In 1887 they insisted on treating only up to ten meters around any contaminated vines, even as the bug continued to show up in an alarming number of new locations.

The anti-phylloxera syndicate in the neighboring department of Algiers, dominated by larger growers and committed to a strict interpretation of the rules, objected that this approach made it more likely that the problem would spread. That kind of support for the law was much more muted in the department of Constantine, where a departmental syndicate did not constitute itself until 1889, well behind the equivalent organizations in Algiers and Oran. In itself a symptom of the Constantine settler community's fractious politics, the delay left more room for anti-establishment views to take root.[65] Though at first the Constantine syndicate promised to back up the work of the head of Algeria's phyl-loxera service, Hippolyte Lecq, the situation failed to improve. In 1890, routinely facing "violent opposition" to his service, Lecq had to settle for a five-meter treatment radius. By early 1891, as local politicians ampli-fied a growing popular clamor in favor of the introduction of American vines—which had emerged as a kind of symbol of freedom for settlers to do things their own way—even the departmental anti-phylloxera syndicate was urging the administration to drop its chemical defense of Philippe-ville's vineyard.[66]

Over 600 kilometers away in the department of Oran, the conflict in Mascara unfolded rather differently. Formerly the center of Abdelkader's resistance to French expansion, by the late 1880s Mascara was a solidly established colonial town that was increasingly fulfilling its long-predicted role as a center of viticulture, with wines that had already gained a good reputation.[67] Mascara's initial encounter with phylloxera, how-ever, proved something of a local embarrassment. The presence of the louse was first brought to official notice in January 1889 by a vine pruner working on the property of a widowed furniture seller, Madame Ma-thieu, who owned a five-hectare vineyard about half a kilometer from the railway station. An investigation found that the local inspector for the department's anti-phylloxera syndicate, Paul Cuq, had known there was a problem in this vineyard since 1886. Since Cuq himself was skeptical that there was any phylloxera in Algeria, however, he had rejected it as an explanation for the damaged vines, and he failed to file the proper reports. The governor-general was hardly reassured by Lecq's conclusion that the inspector was merely incompetent, or his observation that Cuq was not the only phylloxera denier in the Oran syndicate.[68] The system of "expert" inspections did not emerge from this looking good.

For the time being, though, the affected growers in Mascara accepted the officially prescribed treatment of CS_2, and the enemy was kept rea-sonably well contained. Conflict with the authorities did not flare up until the summer of 1893, when inspectors discovered a new infestation in the district of Ras-el-Ma. The year had already been difficult due to a visitation of locusts and an ongoing fight against *altises* (flea beetles). Now, in June, with the fruit ripening on the vine, the sight of work crews with their fumigators was perhaps too much for growers to bear, and some became obstructive. When sections of the local press took the side of these vignerons, the situation became still more difficult for the phylloxera service. The department's anti-phylloxera syndicate was particularly infuriated by some newspapers' attempts to draw parallels with a struggle going on elsewhere at the same time: not in Philippeville, but rather in the Champagne region of France. That, objected the director of the syndicate to the mayor of Mascara, was a conflict between large and small proprietors in a place that hadn't been able to convene an effective syndicate of its own; the divisions that were helping to drive events in the Champagne, he implied, did not exist to the same degree in Mascara. In a general sense he was right—Mascara had no producers remotely in the league of the champagne magnate Gaston Chandon de Briailles of the firm Moët and Chandon—but once the opposition had gathered some momentum it did not stop. Blocking the inspectors became almost a local sport in Mascara, and resulted in the prosecution of dozens of people.[69]

The administration in Algeria had wanted to pursue a uniform defense of the colony's vineyard, avoiding the complicated patchwork of different remedies and *cordons sanitaires* that had emerged in response to the crisis in metropolitan France. Their commitment to fighting phylloxera by chemical means was matched by an equally strong commitment to excluding American vines. As it happened, there were a few Europeans in Algeria who owned American vines that they had planted on their properties before the protective laws were put in place. Some growers, among them Charles Debonno and Armand Arlès-Dufour, tried to persuade the authorities to let them expand those plantations or sell seedlings to fellow vignerons. The administration refused, arguing that although those vines might be resistant to phylloxera, they could easily conceal the pest. One of the biggest losers from this policy was the Société viticole d'Amourah in Dollfusville, which was ordered to incinerate several hectares of unauthorized American vines.[70]

As phylloxera spread, however, protestors chipped away at the administration's ability to sustain a unique policy for the whole of Algeria, and eventually the protective edifice began to crumble. Philippeville proved to be the first breach, as Governor-General Jules Cambon issued a decree in January 1892 authorizing seventy-nine colonists there to plant American vines on their properties. A third or more of the names listed in the decree belonged to people who were likely of Italian origin, alongside a handful of Maltese; some of these were perhaps among those who owned "a patch of vines and their labor" when phylloxera was first identified in 1886. But the list also featured some of Philippeville's biggest producers—who themselves were not all French in origin—and included the biggest of all, Count Landon de Longeville, whose château on his "Domaine des Lions" was one of the most notable buildings in the area, and whose wines were praised in 1892 for having "the bouquet and fortifying qualities of Médoc." The list suggests that while small growers may have given some initial impetus to the protests, the outcome resulted from a much broader effort.[71]

Before long, other settlements in Constantine gained the same privilege. In Jemmapes, to the southeast of Philippeville, growers founded a *syndicat viticole* in 1896 purely to pressure the administration into allowing them to reconstitute their vineyards with American vines, then stopped meeting after they got what they wanted.[72] The process was more drawn out in Mascara, but in 1898, with phylloxera spreading ever more rapidly and the prospect of defense looking increasingly costly as well as locally unpopular, the governor-general authorized American vines there too.[73] Soon afterward, in March 1899, a new law formalized the dual regime that had been emerging on the ground. Vignerons in a given area now had a set procedure for seeking permission to abandon the chemical system of defense in favor of *la libre culture*—the freedom to reconstitute their vineyards with plants of any provenance. (The petitioners had to represent over half of the vignerons in a district and two-thirds of the combined surface area of the local vineyard.) The administration pledged to continue to pay for chemical treatments in the communities that still wanted it, and to protect the areas that remained largely or entirely unaffected. In 1899 the untouched areas still included the whole of the department of Algiers.[74]

The vignerons of Philippeville, Mascara, and other communities now had to live with the wishes they had been granted. In Philippeville in particular, as phylloxera ran rampant across the remaining uncontaminated vines, some probably wondered whether they had pushed too hard too soon. A significant number still owed money for the vines they had planted when the local vineyard was first expanding, and they were not well placed now to undertake the cost of reconstitution. Those that did try American vines planted blindly, without the benefit of seeing which varieties were best adapted to the soil; some got lucky, but many did not. The situation was a little better in Mascara, more spread out than Philippeville and where some of the old French vines were still holding out against phylloxera. This bought some time and ensured a continued income as members of the community experimented with American vines.[75]

The failures in Philippeville were especially worrying to the government-general, since they touched upon its greatest fear: that if viticulture were to fail in Algeria it would seriously undermine the broader project of colonization. For this reason, despite having been (in a sense) chased out by the settlers of Philippeville, by 1895 the authorities were already promising to help subsidize their reconstitution effort. But there was a considerable variety of soils in the area, and if the settlers lacked the expertise to choose well among the American varieties that plant merchants were offering, then most government subsidies would amount to throwing good money after bad. Just before the passage of the law of March 1899, therefore, the administration decided to take more of a lead in educating Algeria's vignerons, and in that spirit called in France's foremost expert on American vines, Pierre Viala, to advise colonists on how best to proceed.[76] Though closely associated with the process of reconstitution, Viala, a professor of viticulture at the Institut national agronomique in Paris, took time on his travels to praise communities that had maintained the fight against phylloxera. In Tlemcen, where the struggle had first begun and continued in earnest, Viala congratulated the district's vignerons with particular warmth, reassuring them that in the long run "Your sacrifices will be less great than in those lands where reconstitution has become necessary."[77] That necessity was very likely to arrive in Tlemcen itself one day, Viala implied, but the longer a community could keep up the fight, and the longer growers could earn money from their French vines, the easier the transition would ultimately be.

That assessment seemed solidly founded. By the time of Viala's visit, phylloxera remained well contained in Tlemcen, with no more than 5 percent of its vineyards contaminated and the administration continuing to pay for the treatment of any new outbreaks. In the district of Philippeville, by contrast, vignerons were struggling, if not abandoning the culture altogether: from phylloxera's discovery in 1886 until 1902, the size of the *vignoble* in the region decreased from over 9,000 hectares to less than 4,000 hectares. Indeed, the contribution of the department of Constantine as a whole to Algeria's wine output declined substantially. In 1888, the department produced 30 percent of Algeria's wine; by 1897, that figure was down to 15 percent.[78] Though Constantine still had some major centers of production, most notably the plain of Bône, its viticulture did not develop in the same way as that of the departments of Algiers and Oran, and its agriculture would remain known primarily for cereal cultivation.[79]

This outcome was judged by Isnard, rather severely, as resulting primarily from the Constantine vignerons' "egoism, indiscipline, and miscalculations."[80] It is hard to disagree that they miscalculated: they were, after all, Algeria's most obvious losers from phylloxera. But the growers of a place like Tlemcen were not more virtuous than the growers of Philippeville for having guessed right. The expansion of the Algerian vineyard was based on a series of bets that inherently carried some risk. Phylloxera had already demonstrated its ability to sow confusion in metropolitan France, among scientists as much as among vignerons, and in the 1890s, as Kolleen Guy has pointed out, there were good reasons to doubt the efficacy of the chemical approach to the problem.[81] Some in Algeria responded to the bug with what proved to be questionable decisions, but only time and circumstances revealed which bets were good and which were bad.

That there was some opposition to the authorities of the type seen in places like Philippeville and Mascara is not surprising. More striking is that such instances were relatively rare. Vignerons in France had something of a reputation for "ferocious individualism."[82] Colonists in Algeria, meanwhile, were ready to tussle with the government at the slightest hint of a lack of support for their aims.[83] On that basis one might imagine wine-producing colonists to have been virtually ungovernable. Instead, Algeria's first engagement with phylloxera left the hardy settlers looking a little dependent. Their most common complaint was that they did not receive enough compensation from the government when their infested vines had to be destroyed. (No indigenous Algerians received compensation if their crops failed, and any such measure would have been resisted to the hilt by colonists.) The anti-phylloxera syndicates were not the first associations of rural European settlers in Algeria—there were already a few as early as 1850—but they did bring vignerons into a close working relationship with an administration that was doggedly backing their personal investments.[84] Almost invisible to the naked eye, phylloxera sapped the roots of an insurgent spirit as the French Republic came to the rescue.

MASTERS OF THE LAND?

In 1892 one of the principal builders of the Third Republic and its empire, Jules Ferry, toured Algeria for six weeks with members of a French Senate commission whose charge was to gather information on topics ranging from indigenous landholding to banking and public education. Taking in stride the cold shoulder he received from settler representatives, who saw the commission's agenda as sentimentally "indigenophile," Ferry was happy to express his admiration for what he felt colonists had achieved. Agricultural achievements seemed to capture his attention the most.[85] The Mitidja plain, he told his fellow commissioners, once they were back in Paris, was now "better cultivated than Normandy."[86] But if Algeria now had an "air of prosperity," and if colonists had found a "spirit of enterprise," he argued that the vine was most responsible.[87]

Ferry's prose bloomed as he contemplated the spectacle of viticulture. His official account of the commission's inquiry hailed the "audacity" of "these intrepid *viticulteurs*," who "ceaselessly push forward . . . these long lines of verdant vines that space and stretch out until they are lost to sight, in straight and weed-free furrows, covering the plains, climbing the hills, as if they are hastening to consecrate, by means of the most French of all crops, the peaceful and permanent seizure of the African land in the name of France." Other aspects of colonial Algeria could and (Ferry insisted) should be criticized, but only with a view to perfecting the French "colonizing genius" of which these vines in rows were the most potent symbol.[88]

In some ways Ferry's words offered a broadly accurate statement of how viticulture was transforming the Algerian land. In other respects, however, this was a myth-making piece of rhetoric that carried out the work of colonization as much as it described it. Years of violent resistance to the French conquest of places where "verdant vines" now grew, from Mascara to Bône by way of the Mitidja, were consigned to fading memory. As Ferry narrated it, colonization was a peaceful, organic, crop-driven process that advanced not so much as an "oil spot" but rather as an inexorable green wave. There was no place in this version of events for the participation of foreign nationals in the development of the colonial Algerian vineyard. This was a story of French heroism, and with an outcome so dramatic that Africa, startlingly, was ceasing to be Africa.

CLOS GRELLET

FIG. 2.2 Claude Grellet's vineyard in Kouba near Algiers, as depicted in 1890.
Reproduced from L. Berniard, *L'Algérie et ses vins. Deuxième partie: Alger* (Paris: G. Masson, 1890).

"Consecrated" by the (true) vine, as if part of a religious rite, the land
was now fully and authentically French and, in Ferry's vision, to be so
for all time, like eternal Rome.

An illustration of Claude Grellet's vineyard at Kouba (fig. 2.2), published in 1890 in a survey of wine production in the department of Algiers, provides a perfect visual match for Ferry's rhetoric. Here we see
vines "climbing the hills" in the Sahel of Algiers, whose "pleasant slopes,"
in the words of the book's author, L. Berniard, were "studded with white
villas drowned in an ocean of greenery," visible even to "astonished trav-
elers" arriving in the capital by boat.[89] The large white building in the
center of the picture may have the look of the lord of the manor's château; in fact it was Grellet's state-of-the-art wine production and storage
facility.[90] Alongside this picture it was superfluous for Berniard to praise
the meticulousness and rationality of Grellet's methods. The manicured
appearance of the vineyard and the "long lines of verdant vines" ex-

tending into the distance already shaped their own powerful narrative of colonial mastery.[91]

The vines that covered the plains were generally less picturesque than those of the slopes, yet in many ways offered an even more comprehensive portrait of colonization. A plan of the Ferme de Gazan (fig. 2.3), near Mondovi to the south of Bône, displays some features typical of vineyards in the plains. Formerly in the hands of the investor Lucien Deyme, from 1895 this 190-hectare property was controlled by a company, the Société agricole Lyonnaise du Nord de l'Afrique. (Deyme retained shares in this company and served as its administrator; he also continued to sell the company's wines via his storehouse in Lyon.) At the time this diagram was produced, in 1900, the company cultivated 140 hectares of vines. Water management was still a challenge on parts of the property, particularly in the riverside section labeled "Prairie de Gazan"; the plantation of eucalyptus trees, as seen at the top left of the plan, was intended to draw water from swampy ground. (Stands of eucalyptus became a common feature of low-lying areas like the Mitidja plain in the second half of the nineteenth century; for a time the tree was seen as one of Algeria's more successful experiments in acclimatizing an "exotic" species.) But in 1901 the company began planting on the "prairie," too, and drainage improved with the digging of a canal along the western and northern borders of the property.[92]

The rectangular divisions in the main part of the vineyard indicate the property's main grape varieties. The Sardinian variety Monica, labeled "Monique" near the center of the plan, was uncommon in the colony but testified to the presence of migrants from Sardinia in this part of eastern Algeria. The other varieties at the Ferme de Gazan were much more typical, and the predominant place in the vineyard of Carignan, whose color and strength enhanced its value as a *vin de coupage* (blending wine), was in line with trends in Algeria as a whole.[93] Producers of *vins des coteaux* (wines of the hills) like Grellet might aim to build a business on quality, but on the plains the main preoccupation was quantity.

The rigidly right-angled layout of the greater part of this vineyard was designed to maximize efficiency. Straight rows of vines were themselves largely an artifact of the later nineteenth century. Older vineyards in France were typically a leafy jumble, but modern methods called for easier access.[94] In 1884 the first major manual for vignerons in Algeria urged

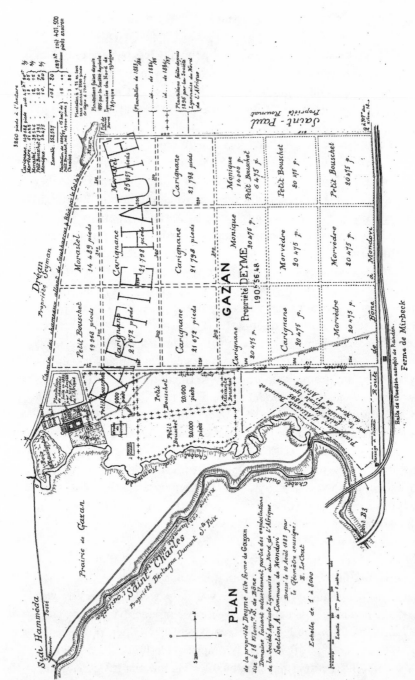

FIG. 2.3 Plan of the Ferme de Gazan in the commune of Mondovi, department of Constantine.
Reproduced from Comité départemental du Rhône, *Exposition Universelle de 1900: La colonisation lyonnaise* (Lyon: A. Rey, 1900).

colonists to plant in evenly spaced rows to facilitate tasks like pruning, harvesting, spreading fertilizer, and spraying the vines with sulfur to combat fungal parasites; this way, wrote the author, "everything gets done with order and economy."[95] After phylloxera, this kind of linear viticulture triumphed in France, too, as the old vines succumbed and grafted vines took their place. But properties in Algeria like the Ferme de Gazan already had the modern look before they underwent the process of reconstitution with American plants.

The plains of Algeria before the French conquest had been defined in part by the straggly paths taken by pastoralists and their livestock. In the early decades of French rule, large expanses like the plain of Bône continued to lack clear visual definition as most of those who obtained land concessions did little more than harvest naturally growing vegetation to sell as fodder. (Much of this was consumed by the military's horses.)[96] Over time, the picture changed. Colonial towns like Boufarik and Marengo in the Mitidja or Mondovi south of Bône were laid out in bounded rectangular grids. The roads built to connect them were also usually as straight as topography allowed. Increasingly, French colonization in Algeria entailed a "disciplined allocation of space," as the historical geographers Michael Heffernan and Keith Sutton put it.[97] The development of wide-scale viticulture in the late nineteenth century was central to that process. The "long lines of verdant vines" or "geometric vines" both colonized the land in a literal sense and served as shorthand metaphors for Algeria's transformation.[98] In French minds such phrases evoked order, economy, fixity, Frenchness, an almost Haussmannized landscape—in short, Ferry's "permanent seizure of the African land in the name of France."

If the illustration of Grellet's property and the plan of the Ferme de Gazan can both be taken to represent part of the narrative of French control over the Algerian land, though, they also embody one of its paradoxes. These plantations may have been rationally organized and successful, but would that guarantee the success of colonization? The depiction of Clos Grellet provides ample signs of settlement but no sign of settlers. The Ferme de Gazan, meanwhile, bears an odd resemblance in its layout to a post-Napoleonic French cemetery like the Cimetière de Montparnasse in Paris, and, with one solitary habitation indicated on the plan, looks as if it may have been similarly devoid of life.[99] Of course people worked on these properties. But if large estates like this were to become the norm, what kind of settler population would there be to root the French presence in the countryside?

For some of the settlers that Ferry and his commission met in 1892, the fragility of colonization was an imminent danger, not a problem for the distant future. Colonists claimed that theirs was only a "surface prosperity," and Ferry, rather in contrast to what he wrote in his published report, told the commission that he saw their point. First there was the insidious menace of phylloxera, which attacked at the roots while the surface continued—for a time, anyway—to look healthy. Concealed even from the view of expert inspectors, there was also the problem of the loans these growers had taken on to finance their vineyards.[100] It was hard to feel too masterful when one was mortgaged up to the neck and betting on a commodity as volatile as wine.

THE PERILS OF THE MARKET AND THE HONOR OF ALGERIAN WINE

Anyone who planted vines acquired a host of new adversaries. The preferred method for dealing with jackals was to bait them with strychnine-laced meat; in 1897 one rural policeman near Aïn-Témouchent killed sixty-two that way in less than a month.[101] For blackbirds, which were also attracted to grapes and could each ruin as much as five kilograms in a day, a manual for vignerons advised "just one remedy: the gun."[102] By the 1890s, some kind of treatment or deterrent procedure was available— if variable in their rates of success—for every one of the insect species that threatened the vine, be they beetles, caterpillars, crickets, locusts, or plant lice. The same went for plant pathogens like oidium or peronospora. Against certain forces of nature like the sirocco there was not a great deal one could do except afford as much shelter as possible, but some growers experimented with creating artificial clouds to counteract frost and, in the first decade of the twentieth century, hail insurance, long practiced among metropolitan producers, began to be taken more seriously in Algeria too.[103]

Once wine moved out of its production phase, however, the landscape of the market often looked just as hazardous and the enemies just as fierce. In September 1893, for example, with a simple, two-word phrase, the national French newspaper *Le Matin* threatened to do more harm to Algerian wine than all the jackals in North Africa.

"Poor stomachs!" The words appeared in a front-page article alleging widespread and potentially harmful contaminants in cheap wine.[104] The article was not only about Algeria; it also targeted adulteration and impurity in certain French wines. But this phrase, positioned at the beginning of a section headed "The Wines of Algeria," struck producers and merchants as a particularly low blow. A perfidious slander, cried one leading exporter in Algiers; defamation, proclaimed the city's chamber of commerce, rushing to defend the honor of Algeria's most economically important product.[105] The specific accusation in *Le Matin* was that Algerian wines contained high levels of the sugar alcohol *mannite* (mannitol). These wines were "sick," the newspaper claimed, and, since Bordeaux producers had been blending them with their own wines, the quality of the product offered the French consumer was seriously compromised.

This was not a new allegation. In the past it had gone along with a claim that Algerian producers adulterated their wines with alcohol from figs, which typically had a high mannitol content. The reason mannitol kept showing up in some Algerian wine was actually more innocent: it usually resulted from the fermentation of underripened grapes in overheated vats. The combined effects of a persistent sirocco and high summer temperatures in 1893 helped deliver that outcome to some producers, and earned the year's vintage a justly dubious reputation.[106]

The period from 1893 to 1907 was rife with incidents like the one provoked by *Le Matin* as well as several difficult years in the marketplace, especially 1893–1894, 1900–1902, and 1904–1907. Nevertheless it is important to keep the problems faced by Algeria's wine interests firmly in perspective. In metropolitan France the period culminated with huge and sometimes violent demonstrations in the Midi, as low prices drove many producers to ruin.[107] Colonial Algeria saw nothing remotely on that scale. Settlers at this time were very quick to use the word "crisis" in the face of difficulty, and it is true that market fluctuations claimed their share of victims, some of them prominent: the period is bookended, as we shall see, by the failure of two pioneers of Algerian viticulture. Historians should replicate the settlers' language of crisis sparingly, however, for the underlying trends, even as phylloxera worked its way through the departments of Oran and Constantine, continued to favor Algeria's vignerons.[108] (Whether that was good for colonial Algeria as a whole was another matter.) Instead the period is best seen as one of realignment, as France emerged from its struggles with phylloxera while European settlers in Algeria groped for a new definition of their relationship to the metropole and discovered just how far they could push the limits of debt.

The challenges in these years had to do partly with quality, partly with quantity, and partly a combination of the two. One problem was that, to a large extent, Algerian wine deserved its poor reputation. In 1879, just as production was beginning to pick up, the journalist Paul Bourde had sampled a number of *vins de table* as he traveled around the colony and observed that many of them had a *goût de terroir*. This was not the good kind of terroir, implying a distinctive flavor born of the local soil and climate. Instead, he meant the wine was earthy and rough.[109] By the 1890s this specific criticism was less common, but still most of the wines intended for consumption might charitably be described as unpretentious. A visitor to a community celebration after a christening wrote that everyone was drinking "this coarse Algerian wine that makes your teeth rattle."[110]

The bottles at the gathering quickly emptied, though, and perhaps that was all that mattered. A relative lack of social pretention was one of co-lonial Algeria's signature qualities, and it was reflected too in its wines. It was not that the land was incapable of delivering a higher-quality product. A few regions, like the Sahel of Algiers, were already known to make wines that did not require what the visitor at the christening de-scribed as a "hardened palate." Indeed the wines of one of the best-reputed vineyards in the colony even found their way into the Vatican cellars. In 1905 an aide to Pope Pius X placed an order for a fifty-liter barrel of Muscat from the vineyards Archbishop Lavigerie began on the White Fathers' property at Maison-Carrée. The aide explained that His Holiness planned to drink it as a restorative after morning mass, "with an egg."[111] But most Algerian wines were aimed squarely at the stom-achs of the poor in working-class cafés, or were developed as *vins de coupage* to boost the color and alcohol content of weaker French wines. That way many French consumers, including the better off, drank Alge-rian wine without being aware of the fact. In a speech in Paris, one oe-nological expert claimed that in an "excellent house" in the city he had been served a Beaujolais that was actually three-quarters Algerian.[112]

Though some producers grumbled about the way their wines were treated in metropolitan France—"like common Prussian spies," one put it—there was growing consciousness that perceptions of quality mattered.[113] This involved merchants too. The troubles of the Maison Joly et Pertus, an export firm in Algiers that went bankrupt in 1890, showed the kinds of things that could go wrong between the vineyard and the ultimate buyer: some of their wines spoiled, some were not of the advertised strength, while others came with too high a sugar content and were seized by customs at the docks in Marseille.[114] Attempted fraud may account for some of the difficulties this firm faced; a new measure in 1890 that required merchants to obtain a "certificate of origin" for the wines they were sending to France was one modest effort to tackle the problem of adulteration.[115] But it is more likely that the wines were just not good to begin with. The poor quality of the vintage in the hot year 1893 finally concentrated people's minds on finding reliable methods of cooling during the fermentation process. A system developed by a colonist in the Sahel of Algiers, Paul Brame, formerly a brewer in Lille, found success, and after around 1895 producers in Algeria widely practiced refrigeration, with a noticeable impact on quality.[116] In 1900 a leading wine merchant based in Algiers argued that vinification was now much more of a science in Algeria than it was in metropolitan France, where the climate was usually more favorable and technical knowledge was more a matter of family or local lore. That may have been a caricature, and in the Algerian case the most "scientific" producers were mainly the better-off ones. Yet the assertion reflected a newfound confidence that Algerian wine was at least as worthy as the ordinary wines of the metropole.[117]

France's output certainly had its own problems. As French growers replanted their vineyards after phylloxera, many focused on quantity rather than quality, aiming to pay down their debts as quickly as possible. The outcome in the Midi region in particular was what the historian Gaston Galtier called a *vignoble de masse* that produced cheap wine in large quantities for mass consumption.[118] The Aramon grape variety, which typically delivered a high yield but a product low in alcohol content, occupied more and more space in the vineyards of departments like the Hérault and came to emblematize the process as a whole. In 1899 the four Midi departments (the Hérault, the Aude, the Gard, and Pyrénées-Orientales) together accounted for over twenty-four million hectoliters of wine, fractionally more than half of France's total output.[119]

Algeria's wine interests, vignerons and traders alike, were indignant that same year when the chamber of commerce of Carcassonne in the

Aude—a department whose production in 1899 exceeded that of all Algeria—accused the colony of "inundating" France with adulterated wines. This charge carried a fair risk of hypocrisy: that year winemakers in France bought record quantities of sugar, strongly suggesting that many producers were flouting a recent prohibition on *piquettes* or "sugar wines."[120] (These wines, made by adding sugar and water to what was left in the vats after the first wine was drained off, had been tolerated at the height of the phylloxera crisis to help French vignerons maximize their production.) The chamber of commerce and the winegrowers' syndicate in Algiers offered a predictable rebuttal, and no one in authority on either side of the Mediterranean seems to have thought the matter worth taking further. But the accusation from Carcassonne that the colony practiced a *concurrence déloyale* (unfair competition) clearly stung.[121] Hadn't Algeria helped France when the metropolitan wine industry was down?

When metropolitan interests questioned Algerian wine, as the historian Charles-Robert Ageron pointed out, they fed what he termed the "autonomist current" that developed in colonial Algeria in the 1890s.[122] France, the idea typically ran, was reasserting the idea of the "colonial pact" that accepted colonial Algeria only insofar as it served the economic needs of the metropole. Driven by wounded feelings and nose-thumbing defiance, newspaper editorialists and writers like Félix Dessoliers argued that colonial Algeria needed to escape a harmful dependence on the metropole and find a greater level of economic autonomy.[123] Translated into social terms, this line of thought pointed toward the emerging ideology of "Latinité," which held that a Latino-Mediterranean mixture of French, Italian, Spanish, and (somewhat more problematically) Maltese immigrants was blending to form a new "race" in Algeria.[124] Among those left exposed by this bid to fabricate a distinct "Algérien" identity were Algeria's Jews, French citizens by virtue of the Crémieux Decree of 1870, who found themselves the target of some vicious attacks at the end of the century. In economic terms, however, "autonomism" seemed very largely assuaged by the creation in 1898 of a new elected body, the Délégations financières algériennes, which from 1901 had the power to approve the colony's budget, formerly voted on by parliament in Paris. Agricultural interests quickly found a dominant position in this institution, with the voice of wine producers especially prominent.[125]

In truth it made little sense for Algeria's wine producers to indulge antimetropolitan sentiment too much. The customs union of 1884 meant they did not have to worry greatly about the colony's limited internal market. Meanwhile, foreign competitors that had done even more than Algeria to fill France's production shortfall at the height of phylloxera now struggled against steep tariff increases, as the French vineyard recovered and the national government practiced a form of agricultural protectionism. Wine imports from Italy had already dwindled to insignificance by 1889, while those from Spain, strong if declining throughout much of the 1890s, slumped when tariffs almost doubled in 1901. Algeria, securely within the protectionist fence, went from supplying metropolitan France with a quarter of its wine imports in the early 1890s to supplying three-quarters in the early 1900s.[126] Business like that surely made the odd nasty comment easier to tolerate.

If the appetite of Algeria's wine interests for "autonomist" thinking was limited, settlers at least continued to honor the ideal of self-reliance. This was well illustrated in a burst of enthusiasm for seeking alternative markets in the first decade of the new century. Countries other than France had as yet shown little interest in Algerian wine, often doubting its quality.[127] But the governor-general for much of the decade, Charles Jonnart, pressed the issue as prices sank in the metropole. Turning the office of the government-general into something like a trade bureau, Jonnart eventually seemed to be making some headway, most notably in a contract with a London-based importer, James Leakey, to promote Algerian wine in the United Kingdom. As it turned out, Leakey was not the best partner; he failed to sell much wine and was insouciantly undiplomatic in his choice of marketing language. "Dietetic and ferruginous Algerian Burgundy and Chablis" may have sounded good to anemic city dwellers when they read the advertisement in the London *Times,* but to the keepers of the reputation of some of France's most prestigious appellations it sounded like poison. In 1905 commercial interests and political representatives from the Bordeaux region loudly protested a claim in Leakey's publicity that the wines of Algeria were "now principally absorbed by the Bordeaux market," which seemed to imply that wines labeled "Bordeaux" might not be Bordeaux at all. Jonnart agreed that Leakey should correct his error—at that time less than a tenth of Algerian wine imports entered France via Bordeaux—but he speculated that the Bordelais were also anxious to conceal their "considerable" use of blending wines from Algeria.[128]

Settlers in the colony enjoyed this controversy a great deal, and they rewarded the governor-general with a show of appreciation rare for a holder of that office; in late 1905 at least sixty-seven municipal councils in Algeria issued public statements of approval for Jonnart's efforts.[129] Other wine merchants angled for contracts similar to the one obtained by Leakey, while producers also explored their marketing options. Vignerons in Mascara, for example, organized a tour to promote their wines in Germany, Holland, Belgium, Switzerland, and England, helped by grants from the government-general as well as Mascara's local council and its agricultural society.[130] For a moment this felt like a kind of autonomy.

Jonnart insisted all along that his search for alternative outlets was primarily an attempt to cope with an ongoing depression in the metropolitan wine market.[131] The precise reasons for the slump were (and remain) difficult to pin down, but events came to a head in 1907, when Midi producers and wine industry workers, in despair after several years of selling their goods at or below cost, decided that fraudulent wines were the main cause of their misfortunes, and in a spring and summer of mass demonstrations dared the government to do something about it.[132] A leading historian of southern French viticulture has wondered why the Midi protests did not also target Algerian wines.[133] One possible reason is that they were not yet especially visible in the region. At the time, the Midi's biggest port, Cette, received about 10 percent of the wine that entered France from Algeria. The amount, while not insignificant, was still well short of what had until recently been supplied by Spain, and in any case some of it served the specific purpose of strengthening weak local wines.[134]

It was also the case, as a parliamentary inquiry into the 1907 crisis noted, that low prices hurt producers in Algeria too.[135] That was why so many Algerian municipalities expressed support for the southern French and their demands for effective antifraud legislation. Whereas demonstrators in the Midi tended to emphasize hunger and human misery in their protests, colonists had their own ways of posing the problem: the municipal council of Palissy near Sidi-Bel-Abbès, for example, argued that only swift action would prevent the "imminent complete and irremediable ruin of all that the French have brought to Algeria." If hunger was not a driving factor, the protests in Algeria were nonetheless serious in their intent. The organizers of a meeting in Mascara on June 2 urged wine producers to "stand up to defend your interests." Eight hundred people responded to the call and declared solidarity with their counterparts in the Midi. Though hardly comparable to the estimated 300,000 who turned out in Nîmes that same day, by the standards of small-town Algeria this was a substantial degree of public engagement.[136] In late June parliament passed a law that met many of the demands formulated by Algerian as well as French protesters. The new rules aimed to combat fraud through stricter controls on sugar in winemaking and required vignerons to declare after every harvest the size of their vineyard, their stocks, and their production for the year.[137] The agitation calmed and the crisis in France gradually subsided.

GETTING CAUGHT UP WITH CAPITAL

The events of 1907 in the South of France represented a genuine crisis, but that word is less justifiable in histories of colonial Algeria in the 1890s and 1900s. The colonists who planted vines discovered that a capital-intensive, export-reliant commodity like wine entailed what for many was an unaccustomed level of financial risk. But colonists themselves were a commodity in relatively short supply—indeed they were overvalued—and that fact limited their personal exposure. A ruined colonist could invariably find a situation somewhere else. By the end of the nineteenth century the insecurity and environmental challenges that early settlers had faced were no longer so acute, while the government, thoroughly invested in the success of viticulture given the revenue it brought and the central role it now played in peopling the countryside with Europeans, did not hesitate to put large sums of money into tackling problems like phylloxera or devise schemes to help growers through the depressed market of the early 1900s.[138] The real agricultural crises in fin-de-siècle Algeria were in rural indigenous society, on lands that colonization had not seen fit to claim. Lives there were lived on the narrowest of margins and beset still by occasional periods of famine, such as on the Chelif river plain to the west of Algiers in 1892–1893 or in the department of Constantine in 1909.[139]

Of course the difficult years for the wine market claimed their share of colonial livelihoods. Among the most prominent casualties was Armand

Arlès-Dufour, lauded in the early 1880s for his use of new agricultural methods and machinery and known for his impeccable Saint-Simonian pedigree. His love of expensive equipment in fact turned out to be a problem, as did his frequent absences in France or promoting his agricultural endeavors at exhibitions. When prices were good, the wines from his properties were usually sufficient to cover the interest on his debt. Toward the end of the 1880s, though, Arlès-Dufour's difficulties began to accumulate. In 1888, he had to step down from the board of directors of his biggest creditor, the Crédit foncier et agricole d'Algérie. In 1891, the bank placed his properties in the western Mitidja in sequestration, and, at the end of 1893, as wine prices dropped, he had to abandon his vineyards altogether, though the bank continued to provide him with an annual pension of 4,000 francs. His older brother Alphonse, who built a spa resort at Hammam Righa and also planted vineyards— he served his wines in the spa hotel—went bust a few years later.[140]

These years saw banks temporarily become vineyard owners in Algeria, as producers fell victim to market fluctuations, phylloxera, or bad business decisions. As of 1896, the Bank of Algeria administered twenty-two properties in the department of Constantine alone, testifying to that department's troubled relationship with viticulture, but for many colonists (and some subsequent historians) also standing as an indictment of the bank's own lending policies.[141] The most conspicuous failure was that of Charles Debonno, perhaps Algeria's biggest individual wine producer. To outward appearances, Debonno, of humble Maltese background, continued to be the master of viticulture in Boufarik and the Mitidja plain, with close to a thousand hectares of vines spread across several properties. A visitor from Burgundy in 1905 was stunned by the scale and modernity of Debonno's *chai* (wine storage facility) next to the station in Boufarik; of this "veritable factory" the visitor wrote that "I have rarely seen a French enterprise that gave such an 'American' impression."[142] Burgundy had nothing like it.

Beneath the surface, though, there were serious problems. In 1902, the Bank of Algeria was on the brink of expropriating Debonno's assets as his debt passed eight million francs, but backed down following a lobbying effort that involved Governor-General Révoil and the president of the Délégations financières algériennes, a fellow wine producer.[143] Wine prices then recovered, and Debonno was able for a time to keep to his repayment plan, but the market did not cooperate for long. In January 1907, the bank, which believed Debonno had consistently misled its officials about his true financial situation, finally resolved to cut its losses, taking control of his properties and putting them up for sale. Ruined, Debonno did not go quietly. He pleaded his case in the press—the influential *Dépêche algérienne* was notably sympathetic—and also gained support from several colonial agricultural societies, who saw his travails as a threat to colonists in general. In 1912, Debonno even brought the Bank of Algeria to court, seeking to void the sale of his former properties and claiming compensatory damages for what he called the bank's errors and fraudulent practices. After this legal effort failed, he seems to have moved to the new French protectorate of Morocco to help a friend develop an agricultural property. When news of Debonno's death in Casablanca reached Algiers in 1920, officials at the Bank of Algeria immediately went about cashing in the two life-insurance policies he had been forced to cede them two decades earlier. The 30,000-odd francs these policies yielded represented his last repayment.[144]

The main claim of Debonno's defenders was that he had been "strangled" unjustly by an institution whose main function was to help colonists.[145] But Debonno was not only a colonial pioneer, as his supporters portrayed him; with his multiple modernizing ventures, he had also been an emblematic figure in the emergence of a certain type of credit-fueled agricultural capitalism in Algeria. Many colonists evidently believed that capitalism should still be subservient to the needs of colonization, but viticulture on the scale Debonno practiced it was no game for innocents. The hard truth was that he had been caught out by a system his own ambitions had helped to feed.

The larger Algerian vineyards were now part of the ordinary run of capitalist activity, and the wealthy were always looking for good deals. Rising anticlericalism produced one sort of opportunity, as the economic enterprises of Catholic religious communities came increasingly under scrutiny. The White Fathers, for example, struggled to keep within secular rules on registration and taxation, and in 1899 decided to sell the vineyards next to their headquarters at Maison-Carrée to a group of businessmen—the Fathers always referred to them as "the capitalists"—who operated as the Société immobilière et agricole de l'Harrach.[146] The profits from the domain Archbishop Lavigerie created were henceforth divided among shareholders. The religious origins of the Algerian *vignoble* were further effaced in 1904, when the Trappists, fearful that

FIG. 2.4 Jean Combes, wine producer and mayor of Rio Salado, one of a string of towns to the southwest of Oran that rapidly embraced viticulture at the end of the nineteenth century. Reproduced from a copy of Joseph Sirat, *Le livre d'or de l'Oranie: Oran, 1897–1898,* held at the Centre de Documentation Historique sur l'Algérie, Aix-en-Provence.

they were about to be dispossessed, sold their vineyards at Staouëli to a wealthy family of Swiss Protestants, the Borgeauds. The monks then left Algeria for a new home in Italy.[147]

Other transactions were driven by more purely economic motives. During the market slump, the Compagnie Algérienne tired of the losses it was taking on its 400-hectare vineyard at Dollfusville and, in 1905, found two landowners from Dijon who were eager to buy.[148] As for Debonno's confiscated property, a large piece was picked up at a favorable price by Georges Chiris, director of an old family perfume company based in Grasse in the South of France and whose operations were global in scope. The primary interest of the Chiris family in Algeria, which had already owned land in Boufarik for decades, always appeared to be the plantations of geraniums and orange trees whose flowers went into the company's perfumes, but their massive vineyards of several hundred hectares were no less important as a secondary source of income.[149]

Debonno's dispossession in 1907 therefore did not signify anything in terms of the ongoing importance of viticulture or, for that matter, of agricultural capitalism. Indeed, Algeria now exported more wine than any other territory in the world—except that nearly all of these "exports," attempts to diversify notwithstanding, went to the country of which it technically formed a part.[150] The vine was becoming a monoculture in some parts of Algeria, simultaneously refashioning the land and shaping local identities. Across the three departments of Oran, Algiers, and Constantine, vineyard owners were also finding political influence. They were a vocal presence in the Délégations financières, the closest thing Algeria had to a parliament. That body's president from 1901 to 1913, Julien Bertrand, who had come to Charles Debonno's defense in 1902, was a major producer in the southern Mitidja plain.[151] Some were elected to the departments' deliberative councils. Others were chosen to be mayor (fig. 2.4.). In the town hall at Sidi Moussa there was Michel-Louis Pelegri, the Majorcan immigrant who owed his fortune to wine; in Sidi-Bel-Abbès there was Léon Bastide, whose vines represented one piece of a larger agricultural endeavor; in Bône in 1907 they were already completing a statue of the recently deceased Jérôme Bertagna, for whom vineyards were part of a portfolio of investments that he nurtured with his political influence.[152] From the late nineteenth century, South Africa had its so-called Randlords, whose wealth derived from gold and diamonds. Algeria, with an economy ever more invested in wine, now had its "vinelords."[153]

3

Companies and Cooperatives, Work and Wealth

1907 to 1930

The Great War offered Euro-Algerians plenty of opportunity to demonstrate their loyalty to France. Across Algeria's three departments, young men mobilized in 1914 and shipped out across the Mediterranean. Joseph Muriel, born to parents of Spanish origin in the port town of Arzew in the department of Oran, left his new wife, Marie, and his job with the phylloxera service near Algiers to fight with the Third Regiment of Zouaves. Lucien Camus, a cellar worker at a large vineyard on the plain of Bône in the department of Constantine, rejoined the same regiment of Zouaves that he had served in Morocco some years earlier. This time, however, Camus knew he had more to lose as he bade farewell to his wife, Catherine, and his two young sons: Lucien, aged three, and Albert, barely nine months. Henri Borgeaud, in contrast to Muriel and Camus, had a choice to make. Though born in Algiers in 1895, he retained the Swiss nationality of his father, Lucien, who was now firmly established in charge of the domain once owned by the Trappists at Staouëli. But Henri chose to renounce Swiss neutrality and instead applied to become a French national. In 1915 he, too, was heading for the front.

Of these three men in their twenties only one came back. Lucien Camus was badly wounded to the east of Paris in the first month of combat and died in a hospital in Brittany a few weeks later. Catherine Camus moved her family to Algiers, not far from where Lucien was born, and it is in that city that her son Albert's autobiographical novel *Le premier homme* (*The First Man*) largely takes place. Joseph Muriel was killed in May 1916 during the Battle of Verdun, on the peak known as Hill 304. For the remainder of the war his widow received half of her husband's salary from the phylloxera service. In more than one sense Henri Borgeaud had the greatest fortune of the three. He returned to join his father and other family members in their multifarious business ventures, and in time to become perhaps the quintessential vinelord.[1]

On the "home front" in Algeria, wine producers faced a variety of challenges during the war. Phylloxera had been discovered in the department of Algiers for the first time in 1907 and made quick progress thereafter. Fighting phylloxera, which one wine company official in 1916 called "an enemy even more tenacious and numerous" than the Germans, was made more difficult by the absence of key personnel like Joseph Muriel, who had led work crews treating infested properties right up until his departure for the front.[2] The scarcity of sulfur to combat vineyard pests was another problem, helping to explain the close scrutiny of traders like Henri Borgeaud's uncle, Jules, the Swiss consul in Algiers, who had to defend himself against an accusation of dealing sulfur-based products to German clients.[3] Labor was also in short supply, and shipping to northern ports like Rouen—the gateway to the Paris market—dropped precipitously during the hostilities.[4]

And yet, the period from the appearance of phylloxera in Algiers to around 1930 was on balance a good one for the Algerian wine industry. Bigger producers handled the problems they faced with a confidence underwritten by capital. The term "industry" itself felt more and more apt, as wine offered a variety of types of employment in urban as well as rural environments. The experience of the Camus family illustrates this well. Albert Camus may have moved from the countryside to the city as an infant, but in Algiers his brother, Lucien, found his first job as a messenger for the wine broker Jules Ricome, while his uncle, Etienne Sintès (Catherine's brother), crafted barrels in which wine crossed the Mediterranean.[5] Algerian wine had a more corporate look, as a growing number of producers chose to operate as companies, spreading the risk formerly undertaken by individuals like Charles Debonno. At the same time, *caves coopératives* (cooperative wineries) emerged as an alternative business model for smaller vignerons. For Euro-Algerians, wine was more than ever the lifeblood of the colony, and indigenous Algerians were increasingly caught in the flow.

PHYLLOXERA, WAR, AND RECONSTITUTION

The wine producers of the department of Algiers had been braced for phylloxera for a long time. Days after it was identified in Tlemcen in 1885, Charles Debonno traveled to the scene to gather information in his capacity as president of the agricultural society of Boufarik.[6] Growers in the department formed anti-phylloxera societies and paid the tax that supported regular inspections. But then the battle against the pest played out in the neighboring departments of Oran and Constantine, while Algiers, thanks to the administration's protective measures or through sheer dumb luck, remained uncontaminated for over twenty more years. Phylloxera finally showed up in the spring of 1907 in a cluster of communities just outside the city of Algiers.[7] The problem spread rapidly and soon reached the Mitidja. At the plain's eastern edge, the louse was found in 1908 in vineyards at Maison-Carrée, and likewise the following year at several points in the south and the west.[8]

Looking at Algerian viticulture as a whole, much had changed between the appearance of phylloxera in Oran in 1885 and Algiers in 1907. On the face of it, there was more of everything: 186,000 hectares of vines in 1907 compared to 70,000 in 1885; 7.8 million hectoliters of wine in 1907 versus 960,000 in 1885; and, along with those increases, a land-to-yield ratio that more than tripled with improved techniques and know-how. Algeria had more growers, too: about 16,100 in 1907 compared to 12,800 in 1885.[9]

These figures, however, conceal some important underlying trends. First, the number of growers had declined from its high, just short of 18,000, in 1901. By the outbreak of war, the figure stood closer to 12,000. This was accompanied by a tendency toward increased concentration of landholding and capital. Nowhere was this more evident than in the department of Algiers, and most of all in the Mitidja. Big estates had been a feature of the plain from the early decades of colonization, but, with the development of viticulture, its high-yielding land became an ever more precious commodity. In the mid-1880s, vineyards in the Mitidja had been fairly evenly divided between properties of less than ten hectares, those of eleven to fifty hectares, and those bigger than fifty hectares. But, by 1907, more than half of the *vignoble* in the Mitidja comprised properties larger than fifty hectares, while smaller vineyards of under ten hectares now covered less than a tenth of the total. The turnover of property was such that less than a third of the plain's vineyards in 1911 had the same owner as twenty years previously.[10]

This was, in short, a highly competitive environment. Those that survived, however, were often in a position to shape the development of viticulture well beyond the plain. There is no better example of this than the Germain family, whose influence—like that of other big producers—eventually radiated from the Mitidja to all three departments.

The Germain fortune by no means arrived in Algeria ready-made. The family's history in the Mitidja began with Jacques Germain, born in the wine-producing village of Saint-Sernin-du-Plain in Burgundy, who (according to family sources) came to Algeria to serve in the army and in 1835 decided to stay in the new colony with his wife, Jeanne, and his three-year-old son, Pierre.[11]

It was Pierre Germain who established the family and its wealth. As a young man, he helped his father clear a concession at Mouzaïaville in the western Mitidja. He then purchased several nearby tracts of swampy land that earlier concessionaries had failed to develop. The environment was hard, and he underwent a great deal of family misfortune. Within the space of two weeks in October 1857, for example, he registered the deaths of his wife, Françoise Cazes, their newborn daughter, and another child of theirs aged eighteen months. With his second wife, Catherine Lombard, Germain had sixteen further children, of whom seven died young in an area where malaria remained quite common.[12] But Germain persisted with drainage works on his property and increasingly shifted from wheat production to focus on the vine. Before long this gamble began to pay off, succeeding so well that at his death in 1905 he was able to leave what an official at the Bank of Algeria characterized as a "considerable inheritance" to his family.[13]

By then, several of Germain's sons—three of whom he baptized Pierre, presumably hoping that at least one would perpetuate the name (in fact all the Pierres lived long enough to marry)—were already vigorously pursuing their own careers in viticulture as well as property trading. The youngest Pierre, and ultimately the most successful, was known to his creditors to have a special flair for dealing in vineyards. On one occasion in 1910 this Pierre Germain bought a large property at Oued el Alleug, then sold it back to its former owners three months later for 75,000 francs less than he had originally paid. But Germain had bet that the proceeds from the property's wine harvest would turn him a profit, and so it proved. With prices strong that year, and with the wine broker Jules Ri-come a willing buyer, Germain came out of these transactions well over 100,000 francs to the good.[14] In 1913 he made his most important pur-chase when he acquired the Domaine du Kéroulis, a 1,050-hectare ex-panse near Aïn-Témouchent in the department of Oran. This, as we shall see, was a property worth keeping. By the end of 1919, when Pierre made the domain the basis for a share-issuing company, its value had already increased tenfold.[15]

Other family members were equally bold and (for the most part) suc-cessful. The second son, Auguste, who went by the last name Germain-Branthomme after marrying into a prominent family of lawyers in the town of Blida, was said by 1916 to own about 1,600 hectares of vines. Another, Jean Germain, earned a leading reputation as a winemaker but was also a skillful trader; in 1910 he bought 160,000 hectoliters of wine and sold all of it in France. The youngest of this generation of Germains, Maurice, apparently wished to do something different, and for a time considered moving to Argentina; in 1914 his share portfolio included in-vestments in such ventures as the Buenos Aires tramways and the Banco Francés del Río de la Plata. After returning from duty on the Western Front, however, he decided to sell his property in the Mitidja to the younger son of another vinelord of the plain, Michel-Louis Pelegri. Mau-rice then headed east, to create a large new domain on the plain of Bône.[16]

For major producers in the department of Algiers like the Germain family, phylloxera threatened at worst to dent their profits for a few years. Experience in France already suggested that the process of reconstitu-tion with resistant vines favored the richest.[17] The new vines also prom-ised higher yields that in the long run would help to offset their cost. There was no panic, therefore, when phylloxera was discovered in 1908 in the vineyards of the Société immobilière et agricole de l'Harrach (SIAH) at Maison-Carrée in the eastern Mitidja. Instead, the company's admin-istration developed a plan to reconstitute its primary vineyard over a pe-riod of years, and even to enlarge it by purchasing several neighboring properties. Recognizing that this expansion would require new produc-tion and storage facilities, in 1912 the company invested heavily in new buildings and new equipment.[18] For those who had the means, phylloxera represented an opportunity to get bigger, not a signal to scale back.

In Oran and Constantine, fighting phylloxera had involved a choice between reconstitution and a government-backed defense of the *vignoble* by chemical means. Once phylloxera appeared in Algiers, however, the government-general, encouraged by prominent growers, offered a new, more mixed approach. Via a decree issued in April 1910, communities could seek permission to begin reconstituting their vineyards, while the government promised to cover part of the cost of continued chemical treatment of affected properties. The goal now was not to beat phylloxera but rather to slow its spread, allowing growers to eke as much they could from their existing vines as they began to replant.[19]

The administration and its phylloxera service claimed that they wanted to protect small producers, not to subsidize those who could easily pay for their own treatment. For that reason, in 1912 Lucien Borgeaud was refused a subsidy toward the cost of 2,000 kilograms of carbon disulfide (CS_2) for use on his vines at the Domaine de la Trappe.[20] But plenty of wealthy vignerons still found the system working in their favor. In Sidi Moussa in the southern Mitidja, for example, the government-general paid three-quarters of the cost of applying CS_2 in the commune's vineyards in 1912, but later calculated that about nine-tenths of that money had gone to treating the properties of the two biggest owners.[21] In some places smaller growers even came to feel that more powerful vignerons were actively working against them. A group of small producers in Ameur-el-Aïn, also in the Mitidja, found it suspicious that they were not invited to a meeting of the local winegrowers' syndicate in 1913, especially as the meeting took place in a leading syndicate member's house rather than at the town hall. It turned out that some of the growers who had attended the meeting and signed a petition asking the government to apply the decree of April 1910 did not even belong to the syndicate, among them Jean Germain and a wealthy Germain-family ally, Gaston Averseng.[22]

Pressure to keep fighting the pest without compromise for as long as possible was now much more likely to come from small producers. This represented a change from the earliest days of phylloxera in Algeria, where the push to allow American vines in places like Philippeville did not obviously correlate with property size. Perhaps some lessons had been learned from cases like Saint-Cloud, an important viticultural center near Oran that in 1899 was one of the first communities to obtain permission to reconstitute its vines. Ten years later, the mayor of this community, Emile Jaeger, a grower himself, told vignerons from across Algeria (at a meeting called by the government phylloxera service) that in practice "only" the bigger proprietors had had the resources to reconstitute.[23]

Jaeger may have been exaggerating for effect, but the tendency he described was clear enough and it now played out in the department of Algiers as well. Bigger producers in the Mitidja and parts of the Sahel of Algiers found the 1910 decree a useful short-term expedient, but by 1916 or so many of these producers were well on their way to reconstituting their vineyards. Increasingly they began to complain about having to pay a tax to cover the cost of inspections and treatments that they no longer needed. For smaller producers, however, this was a moment of particular vulnerability, as the war unmanned many vineyards and the phylloxera service itself was stretched by the mobilization of workers like Joseph Muriel. When the war ended, some demobilized Euro-Algerians returned to regions like Médéa and the Sahel and found their vineyards effectively destroyed. By contrast, many of the big properties of the Mitidja were looking better than ever.[24]

This was certainly true of the vineyards of the Germain family. Members of the family placed huge orders with nurseries for phylloxera-resistant rootlings, cuttings, and grafted vines. In November 1917, for example, Auguste Germain-Branthomme requested 3.5 million *boutures* (cuttings) that he planned to use in replanting 300 hectares across three of his vineyards the following year. The plants all came from Spain from a preferred Germain supplier, Jaime Sabaté, a father-and-son business with a large nursery at Vilafranca del Penedès in Catalonia.[25] In 1921 the government-general outlawed the importation of non-French vines, but by then the younger Jaime Sabaté had already moved to Algeria, where he built up an extensive operation of nurseries as well as vineyards.[26] Over the next decade Sabaté not only supplied a great many vignerons as they reconstituted their vines but also became ever more closely involved in various Germain-family ventures as a shareholder and as a board member.[27] For "plant merchants" like the Sabaté family, there was a lot of money to be made from Algeria in these years.

The SIAH at Maison-Carrée also pressed ahead with its reconstitution plan, despite all the challenges posed by the war. These challenges included the military requisition of a quarter of the Algerian wine harvest for the benefit of the troops at the front; increased costs for transportation, labor, and pesticides; and, of specific relevance to the SIAH, the loss of an important German client for the company's most lucrative

FIG. 3.1 The reconstituted vineyard of the Société immobilière et agricole de l'Harrach at Maison-Carrée, pictured in the 1920s. The buildings operated by the company, at right, stand directly adjacent to the headquarters of the White Fathers. Photo Library of the Société des Missionnaires d'Afrique, Rome.

product, communion wine.[28] Yet in spite of all these problems, and all the expense of replanting, strong prices enabled the company to make a profit, and usually a healthy one, in every year of the war. In 1921, the annual report to shareholders boasted that the company now had "one of the most beautiful vineyards in the colony."[29] (See fig. 3.1.)

WAR AND THE HORIZON OF CAPITAL

War troubled the horizon of the Algerian wine producer through its immediate impact on shipping, so crucial due to the territory's limited internal market. By far the most important port of entry for Algerian wine before the war—receiving over half of the territory's exports—was Rouen, which allowed the easiest access not only to the Paris market but also to much of the northern half of France. In the early months of the war, however, the port of Rouen was a staging post for the British army, and, with priority given to coal in the space that remained, it became hard for ships carrying Algerian wine to find a berth.[30] Mediterranean ports increasingly picked up traffic that would otherwise have headed north, and the situation in Rouen did improve somewhat in the spring of 1915. Yet several problems persisted. Barrels that traveled to France were often slow to return to Algeria, if they returned at all, while a reduced fleet for commercial uses drove up the cost of freight. A hectoliter of wine that had cost two francs to ship just before the war cost more than ten times that much by the end of 1916.[31] With the military liable to commandeer ships for their own purposes at a moment's notice, and German submarines sinking others, the frequent outcome in Algeria was barrel-packed quays and wine that had to be distilled in order to leave any room in the cellars for the new harvest.[32]

Unused to such a lack of control, early in 1917 a group of wealthy producers—described in the newspaper L'Echo d'Alger as "the elite of commerce and agriculture"—began to talk about how to alleviate these circumstances.[33] One outcome of their discussions was a new organization called the Union des viticulteurs d'Algérie. Though the name implied broad participation across the three departments, in reality the group consisted initially of fewer than forty members, all rooted in the department of Algiers and closely connected to institutions like the Délégations financières algériennes and the Algiers chamber of commerce. The founders included four Germain brothers as well as other wealthy and influential figures like Lucien Borgeaud, Julien Bertrand, and Jules Ricome, men whose goods crossed the sea but whose capital stayed (as we shall see) largely in North Africa. This convocation of vinelords was focused primarily on acquiring a fleet of three or four ships to expedite the sale of its members' wine, and by early August the group was already in advanced negotiations for the purchase of a Greek steamer. Within weeks, however, the conditions for the transport of wine abruptly improved, as more ships were made available to commerce. Just as suddenly, the group stopped looking for ships to buy, thanked the government-general for supporting its aims, and vowed to reactivate if conditions deteriorated again.[34]

As short-lived as the Union des viticulteurs proved to be, it stands as a useful marker of how far Algerian viticulture had come and where it appeared to be heading. The need to reconstitute in the face of phylloxera and the difficulties posed by the war did nothing to daunt these highly capitalized wine producers. Some bullish discussion of the need to build an "Algerian fleet" to counterbalance the influence of shipping companies whose interests lay firmly in the metropole carried echoes of the "autonomist" talk of the 1890s.[35] Yet autonomism remained primarily a pose that was sometimes convenient to strike during periods of negotiation. In the end these men knew that their main product tied them to the mainland market, and with sons or brothers serving at the front, there was no question of letting go of the French part of their French Algerian identity. Their commitment to succeeding on their own terms and the scale of their ambitions, however, were already making them look increasingly singular among French wine producers.

THE COOPERATIVE MOVEMENT

The big producers never hesitated to assert their interests, but equally they never claimed to represent a model for the whole colony. Topics like rural credit and fears of European flight from the land often came up for debate at meetings of the Délégations financières, where representatives like Julien Bertrand contemplated what was best for fellow vignerons who owned considerably fewer hectares than themselves. For the government-general, charged with the management of colonization as a whole, the fate of the smaller Euro-Algerian producers was a persistent concern, even as the administration tried to satisfy the demands of the richest and most influential.

Attempts to help colonists with smaller landholdings and counterbalance the trend toward concentration of land and wealth were already under way by the beginning of the century. This was seen in 1901 with the passage of a law that enabled the constitution of *caisses régionales de crédit agricole mutuel,* cooperative lending institutions—capitalized partly with revenue diverted from the Bank of Algeria—that offered mostly short-term credit to rural borrowers and in turn helped to create and direct smaller *caisses locales.* Within a decade these institutions had spread widely and reshaped the financial landscape for colonists with small and medium-sized properties.[36] But the *caisses régionales* did more than just assist smaller vignerons in securing loans to carry out their yearly operations; they also helped lay the foundations for one of the most important developments in the Algerian wine industry in the early twentieth century, the creation of *caves coopératives.*

Despite some promising experiments in places like the Rhineland and parts of Italy, French and Euro-Algerian vignerons alike initially showed little inclination to turn wine production into a cooperative venture.[37] It is surely not a coincidence that communities in the South of France finally began to embrace the idea in the first decade of the new century, when low prices and questions over quality placed many livelihoods in jeopardy. Pooling resources to buy equipment and expertise offered the prospect of a more marketable product as well as lower labor costs.[38]

In France, most of the earliest *caves coopératives,* in departments like the Hérault and the Var, were located on or near the main circuits of viticultural exchange; the famous cooperative winery at Maraussan, for example, built in 1905, was only a few kilometers from the great wine hub of Béziers.[39] By comparison, the first such institution in Algeria was much more remote. In the village of Dupleix, along the Dahra coast about fifty kilometers to the west of Cherchell, Euro-Algerian colonists had quickly embraced viticulture after the settlement was founded in 1896. In a community of only forty households, within a few years thirty-one settlers already tended vineyards. Since most lacked the resources to build cellars, however, these were not strictly speaking wine producers so much as grape growers. After the harvest these growers had to travel twelve kilometers from Dupleix to sell their grapes, and they were not in a strong position to reject the low prices offered by buyers for produce that was generally of low quality.

For Roger Marès, a leading figure in Algerian agriculture and then head of the phylloxera service, Dupleix represented a perfect testing ground for the *cave coopérative* idea. Backed by Governor-General Jonnart, Marès nudged the settlers toward founding a cooperative society and helped them draw up its statutes. Twenty-eight of the thirty-one growers in the village, owning a total of seventy-five hectares of vines between them, opted to join the cooperative. The members paid a quarter of the cost toward building and wine-making equipment, while the government-general covered half. (The government subsidy for later cooperatives was usually closer to a quarter of the total.) The remaining funds came in the form of a loan from the *caisse régionale* in Algiers. The building work was complete in time for the 1905 grape harvest. A professor of oenology from the school of agriculture in Maison-Carrée, J. Foussat, was seconded to guide the colonists in the process of vinification, and in that first year the winery produced 3,000 hectoliters. Buyers came in with initial offers higher than the average for wines in the region, yet the cooperative felt confident enough to hold out for more.[40]

The experiment in Dupleix was an immediate success, helping to stabilize a struggling settler community and demonstrating how a cooperative could strengthen the hand of small producers in relation to buyers. Nearby communities took note, and by 1909 four other coastal villages in the vicinity had founded cooperatives of their own; some growers even abandoned their own private *caves* to join.[41] The new cooperatives were in many ways good for buyers, too: centralized production offered a better guarantee of quality and simplified the logistics of doing business in a comparatively isolated region. No sooner had each new cooperative opened than leading Algiers *courtiers* (wine brokers) like Gabriel Simian and Jules Ricome were buying up much of their output. Simian, for example, acting mainly for a merchant based in Oran, in 1909 purchased 5,000 hectoliters from the winery at Dupleix and 12,000 hectoliters from the cooperative a bit further up the coast at Fontaine-du-Génie (see fig. 3.2).[42]

Despite these promising beginnings, the cooperative movement spread fitfully, hampered in part by the war and its disruption of the ordinary workings of credit.[43] In the 1920s, however, with the government-general continuing to offer its support, *caves coopératives* became an increasingly familiar sight in Euro-Algerian communities, their buildings often occupying prominent positions alongside main roads or railways.[44] The same decade also saw the development of other types of cooperatives for distilling alcohol or for processing and selling commodities like cotton, tobacco, and olive oil.[45]

This wave of mutualism in Algeria mirrored a similar movement in the metropole. There, the emergence of cooperative institutions was tied in some regions to the influence of left-wing syndicalism. (The socialist politician Jean Jaurès described the wine of the cooperative at Maraussan as "the wine of the social revolution."[46]) In other regions, by contrast, the impetus came more from socially conscious Catholics, who tended to hold a conservative view of the peasantry as the bedrock of social order and regarded cooperatives both as a way to check rural flight and as an antidote to harmful individualism.[47]

FIG. 3.2 The coastal community of Fontaine-du-Génie, with its distinctive circular *cave coopérative*, built in 1908. Reproduced from the author's collection.

If it is difficult to generalize about the ideological underpinnings for the development of mutualism in France, doing so for Algeria is in many ways even harder, given that most Euro-Algerian communities were diverse in personal background and distinct political traditions had had little time to take root. (One study of mutualism in 1929 argued that cooperatives took longer to develop in the department of Oran because its many settlers of Spanish origin were hostile to associations, though this explanation is belied by the significant number of Spanish settlers involved in early cooperatives near Algiers.[48]) It is certainly the case, however, that some of the movement's champions in Algeria were devoted, and wealthy, Catholics. One of the most notable was Gaston Averseng, a third-generation colonist in the Mitidja. The Averseng family fortune came from *crin végétal*, shredded plant fibers used to make mats and brooms and as stuffing for mattresses and seating—a productive use for the ubiquitous dwarf palm—but Gaston Averseng also owned over 300 hectares of vines and was deeply involved in some of the Germain family's most lucrative ventures. At the same time, he was a committed supporter both of Catholic charitable causes and of cooperatives. As mayor of El-Affroun in the western Mitidja from 1919, in close collaboration with the town's agricultural credit institution, Averseng oversaw the creation of cooperatives of every sort, including a large community winery. When the governor-general, Pierre Bordes, came to El-Affroun in 1930 to award Averseng the Legion of Honor, the event turned into a celebration of rural mutualism and its benefits for the cause of colonization.[49]

There is little doubt that cooperatives, backed with subsidies from the government-general, worked well for many smaller wine producers, and in some places probably did help to keep settlers on the land. That was particularly true in areas less populated by Euro-Algerians, like the small community near Djidjelli in the department of Constantine that thanked the administration for supporting its wine cooperative in a region "little known to capitalists."[50] Examples such as this underline the fact that the "cooperation" that went into these cooperatives was as much between producers and the government as it was among producers themselves.

By 1931 the mutualist movement in viticulture had succeeded to the extent that there were 128 cooperative wineries across Algeria's three departments, concentrated especially in Algiers and Oran. (In metropolitan France only the department of the Var had more *caves coopératives* than the department of Algiers.) Even so, it is important to recognize that there was a good deal of variation among the Algerian cooperatives. At one end of the spectrum there was the winery at Castiglione, in the Sahel of Algiers, about a third of whose 112 members in 1931 cultivated at most a hectare of vines.[51] Quite different was the cooperative at Hammam-Bou-Hadjar in the department of Oran, housed in a building painted with the slogan "L'union fait la force et le bon vin" (Unity gives strength and good wine). In this wine-wealthy community—reputedly "the richest *commune* in France" in the 1930s—the *cave coopérative* and its considerable personnel produced 48,000 hectoliters of wine in 1933 with the grapes of just twenty-three members.[52] In cases like that of Hammam-Bou-Hadjar and other wineries that emerged in the 1920s— mostly good years for Euro-Algerian wine producers—"cooperation" looks like another form of concentration of wealth.

The mutualist movement was beneficial to the consolidation of the rural Euro-Algerian population at a time when actual colonization had tapered off. *Caves coopératives* provided even small vignerons with access to the trappings of industrial wine production, while bigger producers looked benignly on a movement that could only improve the image of Algerian viticulture and the overall quality of its wines. But if cooperatives represented an aspect of the rationalization of agricultural colonization, the question of labor was often more difficult for Algeria's wine producers to handle. To assess this we need to take a longer perspective.

WORKING IN THE VINES

No sooner had viticulture begun to spread rapidly in Algeria than producers were searching for ways to improve their profit margins. One key challenge, wrote Léon Bastide in 1878, was to reduce the cost of labor with the help of better agricultural equipment while at the same time increasing output through the most rational production techniques.[53] Naturally the bigger producers were best placed to take up this challenge. The Société de viticulture algérienne, for example, a company that in 1881 began to develop a large property in the southern Mitidja, proudly reported back to its shareholders on the steam-powered equipment it had used to clear the land, as well as the benefits realized by planting rows of vines more widely than was typical in the Midi. The configuration of the new plantation allowed enough room for a team of four horses to pass through with a plow specially designed to break up the hard soil between the vines—a preliminary to the process of soil-turning known as *piochage*—and in this way only one man was needed for a task that had previously required eight. The company told its investors that it would continue to try "to reduce manpower and to replace manual labor and above all [more expensive] European labor with animal power." In much the same way, Bastide wrote of the desirability of substituting human labor with what he called *instruments:* agricultural implements, animals, and machines.[54]

For producers whose vineyards exceeded the scale of what could be handled by a family, labor—its availability, its cost, its management—was a constant preoccupation. New "instruments" did indeed emerge over time to aid the process of production, yet still for efficiency-minded vignerons, labor was a problem that seemed to defy attempts at rationalization. The difficulty arose in part from the seasonal nature of the work. The largest and most advanced vineyards in Algeria were not comparable to, say, the big rubber plantations of Southeast Asia, in which the tropical climate allowed year-round production.[55] Instead, labor was needed in spurts, reaching a crescendo at the annual grape harvest in August or September and then dropping substantially between October and the spring.[56] This favored the short-term migration of workers for particular tasks, and meant that even while viticulture was considered to be a *culture industrielle*, the vineyard could never be run like a factory. In years in which the labor supply appeared insufficient or overly demanding in terms of pay, producers were quick to perceive a "crisis," much as they did in the face of any downturn in the wine market. Yet, at the same time, they developed several weapons to shape the labor market toward their own interests.

Wine producers, like other agricultural proprietors, made their employment decisions on the basis of a combination of factors. Cost and availability were central considerations, of course, but the reputation of certain categories of worker also came into play. In the first decades of French rule, for example, praised by notable early colonists like Baron Augustin de Vialar, Minorcans (known as *Mahonnais*) were widely preferred for a variety of agricultural tasks in the region around Algiers.[57] As such, familiarity weighed into employers' calculations as well as cost. When the minister of war offered to facilitate a new stream of low-cost migrant labor from the region around Lucca in Tuscany ahead of the wheat harvest in 1857, the prefect of Algiers found that most proprietors didn't like contracting for workers they knew nothing about, and they rejected the idea.[58] But colonists were not always in a position to be selective. In less-trafficked regions in particular they might even need to employ members of the so-called *armée roulante*, literally "the rolling army": itinerant bands of men (including ex-soldiers), mostly but not exclusively European and claiming a variety of types of work experience, who roamed in search of jobs by the task and in avoidance of the gendarmes who were charged with preventing vagabondage. It seemed to some observers that when members of this "army" found work, the main beneficiaries were the keepers of roadside bars; not surprisingly their appearance in a community was a cause of unease.[59]

Amid the options available, it is clear that proprietors hiring hands for basic agricultural tasks accorded no privilege to French workers. The first big expansion of the Algerian *vignoble* from the 1870s took place when there was a relatively abundant supply of seasonal rural labor from wine-producing southeastern Spanish provinces like Alicante and Murcia, arriving by steamship and concentrating especially in the departments of Oran and Algiers. These temporary migrants offered their labor more cheaply than French workers, and with the peseta weak, they found

Algeria an attractive destination in which to earn francs for a few weeks or months.[60] Many others chose to stay on, like a group that Charles Debonno used to clear land for one of his new vineyards in the early 1880s and then helped to settle on the property. A visiting French parliamentarian admired these Spaniards' efforts but regretted that Debonno had not employed French workers instead.[61] In the minds of most proprietors, though, the cost differential left little room for such sentiment. It was perhaps especially naïve to expect a preferential policy toward French workers from an Algeria-born colonist of Maltese extraction like Debonno.

What of the possibility of using Algerian workers? On the eve of the expansion of viticulture, one European viewpoint held that colonization was good for Algerians because it would guarantee them plenty of agricultural work. The mayor of L'Arba in the Mitidja wrote with enthusiasm to that effect in 1868, adding, with an ostensibly egalitarian flourish, that the growth of colonization would "ensure the mixture of races."[62] In reality there were no such guarantees, not least because Algerians—both Arab and Berber alike—displayed little inclination to "mix" so long as they could sustain themselves through their own resources.

But those resources were becoming ever more precarious. The structure of local society was modified out of recognition by Napoleon III's *sénatus-consulte* of 1863, which chopped up tribal authority and allowed collectively held land to transfer to the public domain and therefore the colonial grasp.[63] The drought, locusts, disease, and famine of the late 1860s hit a society already under intense pressure. The failure of the Kabyle insurrection led by Mohammed el-Mokrani in 1871 then demonstrated that if French power did not like collectively held land, it did endorse collective punishment. The massive land sequestration and fines that followed the uprising had a devastating impact on eastern Algerians; a Kabyle song commemorated 1871 as "the year of our ruin."[64]

It is natural to assume that all of this upheaval ensured that rural Algerians would now seek wages from Euro-Algerian colonists.[65] The example of viticulture suggests, however, that this was a gradual process, and moreover was not actively encouraged by many colonists. Certainly, there were exceptions, among them Archbishop Lavigerie, whose vineyards in Maison-Carrée made use of Kabyle workers on a permanent or semi-permanent basis starting as early as 1869. But that was part of a philanthropic-evangelical project—Lavigerie hoped to bring the Kabyles "back" to Christianity—and it stood out because it was so unusual.[66] It remained more common for colonists to look elsewhere for their workers. In the western half of Algeria the stream of Spanish labor in the second half of the nineteenth century lessened the need for European wine producers to cultivate an Algerian workforce. Migrants from Morocco offered another alternative, long before the 1912 division of that territory into French and Spanish protectorates. When phylloxera was discovered in the summer of 1885 in Sidi-Bel-Abbès, about a hundred kilometers from the Moroccan border, Louis Gastine of the government's phylloxera service was easily able to find a crew of Moroccan workers to carry out the necessary chemical treatments. Gastine considered this a much better option than using members of the Foreign Legion, who were based in Sidi-Bel-Abbès but scared local proprietors, while Moroccans were judged to be workers on a par with the Spanish and cost about the same.[67] Eastern Algeria was not so well supplied with inexpensive labor from the outside, but to some extent Italian migrants performed similar roles, as did Maltese migrants who concentrated particularly around the town of Bône.[68] The Ferme de Gazan on the plain of Bône developed its vineyard with laborers from Sardinia, Tuscany, Calabria, and Sicily, as well as temporary migrants from Kabylia.[69]

The evidence for a significant Algerian, and especially Arab, presence in the vineyards is therefore patchy until the 1890s.[70] It was in that decade that Algerians, driven by economic necessity and squeezed by colonial restrictions, seem increasingly to have offered their labor to Euro-Algerian vignerons. A group of notables from the area around Jemmapes in the department of Constantine, for example, told the Senate's commission on Algeria in 1892 that local people's forest rights had been so curtailed that "only those who work in the vines can still earn a living."[71] The 1893 slump in wine prices then encouraged proprietors to reduce the number of European workers they employed and fill some longer-term jobs with Algerians instead.[72] Concern rose in official circles about the condition of the Algerian rural population and led some to criticize the impact of temporary Spanish migrants on the labor market. The French consul in the port of Cartagena in Murcia, for instance, argued in 1897 that Spanish migration had now outlived its usefulness and that Algeria should reserve manual labor for its "French and indigenous" inhabitants.[73] Efforts to tighten visa requirements appear not to have had much effect, however, and the flow of Spanish migrants only dwindled as the peseta appreciated in value in the first decade of the new century.[74]

In consequence of these various factors, around 1900 vineyard employment began to settle into a pattern that would remain broadly familiar for the rest of the colonial period. The leading technical and overseeing roles were filled by Euro-Algerians who were paid by the month, assisted by a certain number of Algerians. The basic manual tasks were carried out mostly by Arab or Berber day laborers whose remuneration varied according to the work they performed; a day spraying fungicides, for example, earned more than a day hoeing the soil around the vines.[75] Short-term migrants from the mountains of Kabylia offered supplementary labor at key times of the year, especially in the departments of Algiers and Constantine, while in the department of Oran in particular Moroccans coming mostly from the Rif and some eastern parts of Morocco fulfilled the same function.[76] Temporary Spanish migrants remained associated with one job in particular, that of the winter *taille* (pruning) of the vines. In 1913 the government-general backed an effort to give Algerians the skills to replace them, but if this program had some success, the substitution was far from rapid or complete: in the early 1930s over 2,000 Spanish *tailleurs* still traveled each year to the department of Oran alone.[77]

Certain specialized tasks aside, the judgment of some prominent figures from around the turn of the century was that colonization, and viticulture in particular, offered more economic benefit to Algerians than anything they could have procured for themselves. In his massive evaluation of "official" colonization since 1871, the administration's director of colonization, Henri de Peyerimhoff, conceded in 1906 that there was now what he termed an "indigenous proletariat" that gave some cause for concern, but overall he believed European commercial agriculture could resolve the problem through its capacity to provide employment.[78] Surveying the colonial settlement of Gouraya to the west of Cherchell, for example, built on lands confiscated from a Berber tribal grouping as punishment for their support of el-Mokrani's rebellion, de Peyerimhoff discovered viticulture doing well and argued that the indigenous population "have found, in the salaries from the *vignoble* and the economic advantages brought by the European colonial center, substantial compensation for the lands that their participation in the insurrection lost them."[79]

Such an assessment starkly contrasts the view expressed by a Berber from a village located just fifty kilometers across the Dahra Mountains from Gouraya. Mohamed ben el-Hadj Ahmed Yacoub was considered the ringleader of an uprising that took place over the space of a few hours on April 26, 1901 in the small colonial settlement of Margueritte. There, Yacoub worked as a day laborer in the vineyards that had come to dominate the lands expropriated from his tribe twenty years earlier. One vineyard owner, Pierre Gariot, was among the seven people killed in the uprising; another, Marc Jenoudet, the biggest landowner and wine producer in the village, was captured and might have had his throat cut like Gariot if he had not pronounced the *shahada,* the Muslim profession of faith; while the Algiers wine broker Jules Ricome, who also had vineyards in Margueritte, apparently avoided the rebels only by exiting through the back window of his house, which was later ransacked.[80]

De Peyerimhoff's survey of Margueritte, conducted before the uprising, had called it a "flourishing" colonial settlement thanks to viticulture. He acknowledged what the local Algerians had lost, but, as in the case of Gouraya, suggested that salaried work offered "a certain measure" of redress.[81] When Yacoub was brought to trial in Montpellier in late 1902 with about a hundred other alleged insurgents, however, he defended himself in more precise economic terms. "We have been stripped of our lands," he testified, "some taken by M. Jenoudet, the rest by various *colons,* and we have been obliged to work to live. . . . Our lands formerly allowed us to live, [but] today we are obliged to live on a salary of 1 franc or 1 franc 50 [per day]. What can a man do with such a salary, when he has a numerous family to feed, to clothe, and to support in all its other needs?"[82]

The events in Margueritte spawned no immediate imitations, and it would take years for a voice like that of Yacoub to be heard so publicly again. Agricultural salaries, moreover, would not be regulated until the 1930s, and it was difficult for Algerian workers to negotiate higher rates unless there was a clear shortage of labor at a moment of great need for the proprietor. The grape harvest in particular sometimes provided such a moment. In regions like the Mitidja and the Sahel of Algiers, for example, late summer saw the arrival of large numbers of Kabyles to assist with the *vendange.*[83] Their appearance was an annual relief to vineyard owners, but these migrants knew their value: on some large estates in 1899, at the height of the *vendange,* Kabyle crews abruptly stopped working and demanded more money, having realized that manpower was in short supply.[84]

One method through which bigger proprietors tried to insulate themselves from such demands was by using convict labor. The value of convicts as agricultural workers was a matter of debate among administrators, but there was no official objection to private interests paying for prison labor. Wine producers in Algeria appear to have perceived convicts as a useful commodity for two reasons: first, for their contribution to the workforce at times of special need, and, second, for helping to tamp down indigenous wage demands. Convicts were therefore not an uncommon sight in larger vineyards. Lavigerie used them as early as 1871, while around the turn of the century producers in the Sahel or the Mitidja paid for the services of men from military penitentiaries like those at Douéra and Koléa near Algiers. Further south, the agricultural penal colony at Berrouaghia was itself a significant wine producer, with a large vineyard labored by the institution's military and civilian inmates.[85]

The use of convict labor remained relatively widespread into the 1920s and 1930s and was especially sought after at the *vendange*. In 1921—a year in which famine drove many southern Algerians toward the cities of the North—the SIAH at Maison-Carrée employed 555 workers to pick and transport the grape harvest. Of these, 180 were inmates from the local prison, watched by a guard detachment that included several Algerian *tirailleurs,* who stood in the fields with their guns. The cost of this went largely to the prison administration, though as an incentive to work each man was daily given a small bonus of twenty-five centimes as well as a ration of tobacco and wine. (The wine allowance signals that these convicts were French or other non-Muslims.) At the same time, the director of the vineyard noted that the "abundance" of labor that year had allowed the company to pay less to the Algerian civilian workers than those it had hired at the previous *vendange*.[86]

It is true that the war and the year or two that followed it had presented some challenges in terms of labor recruitment, but even then a particular category of convict had helped to fill the gap. In the summer of 1917 a mutinous spirit among soldiers serving with the Russian Expeditionary Force in France culminated in a major uprising at the military camp of La Courtine in the central department of the Creuse. Inspired by the February Revolution and the formation of soviets in their homeland, thousands of the men demanded repatriation and barricaded themselves in the camp. After breaking the siege, however, the French military decided to send the most refractory of the rebels—the so-called *irréductibles*, who refused either to fight or to work in France—not back to Russia, but rather to Algeria. By January 1918 there were about 4,500 Russian soldiers in the colony, a figure that soon doubled with the arrival of yet more recalcitrant Russian troops who had been serving with the Armée française d'Orient in the Balkans.[87] Organized into forced-labor brigades, over the next two years many of these soldiers found themselves detached to work in vineyards. There they carried out a variety of mostly unskilled tasks, though on at least one property some were taught how to prune the vines in winter.[88]

If the vineyard owners were not generally impressed with these workers—they needed too much surveillance, one complained[89]—the soldiers' own letters, intercepted by French censors in Algiers, show that the lack of regard was more than mutual. The work itself was difficult; one wrote, "I work for a local bourgeois. 148 of us, in all. We work in the vineyards. The workday is ten hours." (For this they were fed and paid twenty-five centimes.) He continued, "The work is very hard . . . especially when we spray the vines with vitriol. One careless instant and you have the sulfur in your eyes. It blinds you for a while. . . . My head hurts from it. I work until I am exhausted." This kind of experience led some of the Russian rebels to contemplate the lives of those for whom this work was both familiar and necessary. "Here, we are not the only ones who suffer," wrote another. "The French also pay the Arabs low wages and punish them cruelly, just as we were punished under the old [Tsarist] regime."

For these Russian soldiers, who until recently had been fighting to defend what they had considered a country with a rich revolutionary and egalitarian tradition, colonial Algeria was an affront to France's ideals. As one put it, "The local people live under the benevolent French republic worse than we did under Nicholas II. To the French, the local people are nothing more than working cattle, which they drive with sticks."[90] The last group of detainees was repatriated in 1920, with the overwhelming majority choosing to be sent to parts of Russia that were now under Bolshevik control. Their radical voices left no evident mark on Algeria at the time, but were a foretaste of struggles to come.

As landowners in Russia underwent a moment of reckoning, we have already seen that the war did no serious harm to the Algerian vinelords. A postwar trend for a greater number of Algerians to seek work in France produced an unwelcome surprise for some wine producers, who found that the Kabyle workers they were accustomed to using were no longer available in the same numbers.[91] The annual reports of major vineyards in the 1920s reveal persistent grumbling about the scarcity or shortcomings of workers, especially in the East, yet their bottom lines remained generally healthy and the employers' dissatisfaction arose mainly from minor slippages of control. For all their complaints about Algerian labor's "demands" or "pretentions" in this time, the bigger vignerons in all three Algerian departments remained adept at finding workers at profit-maintaining levels. In the West, managers at Pierre Germain's huge Domaine du Kéroulis could easily "knock at the doors of Morocco to find a sufficient labor force at relatively cheap prices," as the company reassured its investors in 1922.[92] On the plain of Bône in the East, another large vineyard, the Domaine du Chapeau de Gendarme in Mondovi, maintained a barrack building that accommodated up to 200 prisoners who were brought some 250 kilometers from the penitentiary at Lambèse (see fig. 3.3). By the late 1920s the facility at the vineyard had become so dirty and dilapidated that the penitentiary threatened to stop sending its prisoners until the domain built a new one. The company complied because, as it confided to its shareholders in 1931, the use of these convicts was "indispensable for us to moderate the demands of indigenous labor."[93] In the meantime, this company and others like it were increasingly able to fulfill the aim of replacing the labor of humans with that of machines.[94]

The view that officials like Henri de Peyerimhoff expressed around 1900 about the ability of commercial agriculture in general and viticulture in particular to create "compensatory" employment for Algerians was thus revealed to be hopelessly optimistic. The way wine producers ran their businesses, coupled with the seasonality of the work itself, did not guarantee a stable existence for any but a minority of Algerians.[95] For Euro-Algerians as well as some metropolitan investors, though, the wine industry continued to offer much in terms of both employment and profit.

FIG. 3.3 Convict workers boarding trucks at the Domaine du Chapeau de Gendarme, early 1930s. Reproduced from *Vignobles et vins d'Algérie: Etude spéciale de Grands Crus et Vins de France, octobre 1934* (Lyon: Publications Pierre Argence, 1934).

WORKING FOR THE VINES

When the writer Louis Bertrand looked back on the time he had spent in Algeria in the 1890s, he characterized one place in particular as "the kingdom of wine." What he had in mind was not some hazy plain of vine-yards, but rather Belcourt, a rough-edged district of Algiers close to the port. On the surface this may have seemed an unusual choice, for the neighborhood's only grapevines grew within the state-run experimental garden, the Jardin d'essai. Instead of vines, however, Bertrand was thinking of the many people of French, Spanish, and Italian descent who made their living in Belcourt's barrel workshops or wine storehouses, or by equipping the horses or repairing or driving the carts that transported the barrels from vineyards to the docks (see fig. 3.4).[96]

The horses and carts soon gave way to trucks, but wine was still cen-tral to the economic life of Belcourt when Albert Camus grew up there in the 1910s and 1920s, as his brother Lucien and his uncle Etienne could both personally testify. The census of 1921 prompted French talk of a "crisis of rural settlement" in Algeria as the population of European

FIG. 3.4 Carts loaded with wine from the Domaine d'Oulid-Adda in Maison-Carrée, 1890s. Photo Library of the Société des Missionnaires d'Afrique, Rome.

colonial centers in the countryside stagnated or lost numbers to the cities, especially in the departments of Constantine and Algiers.[97] Yet even as cities like Algiers increasingly spread outward, many urbanized Euro-Algerians retained a connection to the agricultural hinterlands through the work that they did, and no more so than in servicing colonial viticulture. If Bertrand had made his observations in the 1920s, he would have found that the "kingdom of wine" itself now sprawled to encompass other communities alongside or close to the Bay of Algiers. Here the "industrial" side of the Algerian wine industry was particularly evident, though the work to be found was not only of the blue-collar variety.

Just to the east of Belcourt in the suburb of Hussein-Dey, for example, a working-class population that was heavily Spanish or Italian in origin found work at barrel companies like Francalfûts or in businesses like Etablissements A. Blachère et ses fils, a foundry and machine manufacturer that specialized in supplying wineries with the pumps and other equipment they needed (fig. 3.5).[98] Slightly inland at Le Ruisseau there was a *bouchonnerie* (bottle-cork factory) owned by a member of the Borgeaud family, Alfred. (He had acquired a 3,000-hectare cork forest

FIG. 3.5 The urban face of Algerian wine. In this late 1920s advertisement for the barrel company Francalfûts, rows of factory workshops appear as a sort of industrial equivalent to rows of vines in the countryside. Reproduced from the author's collection.

at Souk Ahras in the department of Constantine.)[99] A few kilometers further south, workers refined Sicilian sulfur for use in pesticides in a factory belonging to one of Alfred Borgeaud's brothers, Jules, alongside the
railway tracks at Le Gué de Constantine.[100]

Along with these manual trades (including transportation), wine also
produced a great deal of white-collar work. In government, the fight
against phylloxera as well as various forms of regulation generated vast
amounts of paperwork.[101] In the private sector, wine traders and brokers
needed clerks to fill orders and maintain their accounts, as did wine companies and many individual producers.

For Euro-Algerians like Michel Roig, this kind of work represented
an opportunity for social mobility. Roig was born in 1895 at the eastern
end of the Bay of Algiers in Fort de l'Eau, to parents who had emi-
grated from Ibiza and (like so many others from the Balearic Islands in
that community) worked in market gardening. Though his parents
were illiterate—neither could sign their name when they married—his
mother ensured that Michel began receiving instruction at a young
age from a locally based congregation of nuns, who set him up well to
succeed when he was old enough to enter the *école communale*. At the
age of sixteen, Roig was hired to work in the offices of the SIAH in
nearby Maison-Carrée. Within three years, he was in charge of shipping the company's products (including much communion wine),
while at the same time studying for a diploma in business. Returning
from three years' military service in 1920—he was wounded in one
shoulder and also gassed—Roig was appointed to be the SIAH's chief
of accounts (fig. 3.6). He held that job until his death in 1956, while at
the same time taking part in a variety of Catholic charitable works and
also serving for two decades on Maison-Carrée's municipal council.[102]
For a child of poor migrants this was a solid career indeed, but many
other Euro-Algerians could have told of similar paths away from fields
and into offices.

These examples, drawn from around the Bay of Algiers, of course had
analogues in other locations in Algeria: there were barrel workshops in
Oran and Bône, a sulfur refinery in Arzew, an important manufacturer
of machinery for wine production in Boufarik, cork factories in several
towns in the department of Constantine (Bône, Bougie, Djidjelli), and
so on—all of them hiring hands for the factory floor as well as administrators like Roig.[103] Together, businesses such as these represented a not

FIG. 3.6 White-collar wine: working in the offices of the Société immobilière et agricole de l'Harrach at Maison-Carrée, 1920s. Michel Roig is standing by the desk in the center. Photo Library of the Société des Missionnaires d'Afrique, Rome.

insubstantial proportion of Algeria's industrial sector in the early decades of the century. Other than mineral extraction, indeed, there was little else in the colony that qualified as "industrial" that did not link in some way to agricultural production.[104] Relatively paltry though this industrial base was, it created pockets of development that served both to draw Algerian migrants toward the cities and provide new opportunities for the owners of adjacent lands. In 1919, for example, the colonist Charles Pourcher sold his domain at Le Ruisseau to what he called a "rich industrialist" from Nîmes who wanted room to expand operations from the factory he had recently established next door, which included a wine distillery. Though at first reluctant to sell a property that he had occupied for thirty-eight years (and on which his vineyards had produced prize-winning wines), with the money he received Pourcher was able to buy a villa in nearby Kouba with a "superb" view of Algiers and the bay.[105] Around Algiers after the Great War the repurposing of land formerly used for viticulture to residential or industrial uses would become increasingly common, as the city extended further and further into the hinterland.

The fact that Pourcher's property sold to a southern French buyer signals that outside capital continued to seek profits from Algerian viticulture. The sulfur industry provides an especially good example. Algeria had no sulfur of its own, so the products that workers applied to the vines to counteract oidium, mildew, and various insect pests were largely manufactured using sulfur mined in Sicily or, starting around the turn of the century, drawn from underground deposits in Louisiana. (A smaller supply was mined near Apt in the South of France.) The few refineries in Algeria, however, lacked the capacity to treat enough crude sulfur to meet the insatiable demands of the colony's vines. Instead, the bulk of the profit went to refiners who were mostly located in French ports, especially Marseille and Sète, and often collaborated to form cartels.[106]

Marcel Roubaud was the director of one of the biggest sulfur consortiums, the Marseille-based Raffineries de soufre réunies (RSR). At the same time he served on the board of the Compagnie des vignobles de la Méditerranée (CVM), owner of a large vineyard at Monville on the plain of Bône. This connection was clearly beneficial to the company, which in 1910 thanked Roubaud for his help with the supply of sulfur products.[107] Soon Roubaud became president of the CVM alongside a powerful roster of fellow board members, all based in the metropole, including, in 1920, France's minister of finance, Frédéric François-Marsal. While remaining an important force in the economic life of Marseille—Marcel's son Jean took over as director of the RSR, which in the 1930s achieved a virtual monopoly of the sulfur business—the Roubaud family maintained its connection to Algerian wine until independence through the CVM and by acquiring the Hussein-Dey barrel company Francalfûts (run by Marcel's grandson Guy Roubaud).[108] The vine and its needs made this family very wealthy, but the profits from its investment in Algerian viticulture largely flowed north across the Mediterranean.

WEALTH AND INFLUENCE

The Algerian wine industry attracted two particularly important types of investor. The Roubauds were representative of the external investors, who owned properties or wine-related companies in Algeria and served on company boards but continued to be based in France; they were never "colonists." In a trend dating back to the nineteenth century, the department of Constantine seems especially to have attracted external investment toward large-scale viticulture, perhaps a result of the relative paucity of European settlement there. (Vineyards in the more densely settled department of Oran were much more likely to be owned by Euro-Algerians.) But there were notable external investors in other areas too, like the Grasse perfume magnate Georges Chiris with his large vineyards at Boufarik in the Mitidja.[109]

More significant, though, were what we might call (thinking spatially) lateral investors: Euro-Algerians who became rich thanks to viticulture or other local economic ventures, but whose capital mostly stayed in North Africa. Often the revenue generated by wine in the Mitidja and parts of the Sahel of Algiers was reinvested "laterally" in viticulture in the departments of Oran and Constantine. In the West, the Société des domaines du Kéroulis, with its thousand-plus hectares of vines near Aïn-Témouchent, was developed in the 1920s into a highly profitable fiefdom of the Germain family, assisted by allies like Gaston Averseng.[110] In the East, the Mitidja producer Julien Bertrand founded the Société du domaine du Chapeau de Gendarme in 1910 to revive a large vineyard on the plain of Bône whose past owners had had to cede the property to the Bank of Algeria. Soon the company was thriving, and by the 1920s its board was dominated by notable figures from around Algiers like the wine producer and mayor of Boufarik, Amédée Froger, and the owner of the Domaine de la Trappe at Staouëli, Lucien Borgeaud, who succeeded Bertrand as company president.[111] Members of the Borgeaud family like Lucien and his son Henri, in fact, represented virtually the paragon of the lateral investor, for, as an official at the Bank of Algeria noted, their extensive share portfolios were made up almost entirely of North African investments—albeit often in Borgeaud-controlled companies.[112]

These wealthy Euro-Algerians naturally expected to achieve a commensurate level of political influence. As the detailed research of Jacques Bouveresse has shown, the elective body the Délégations financières algériennes was so dominated by agricultural interests as to represent a sort of "agrarian assembly," with wine producers like Bertrand and Froger especially prominent voices.[113] Such voices were amplified by a sympathetic press. Two of the figures whose financial backing was instrumental in the founding of the important daily newspaper *L'Echo d'Alger* in 1912, for example, were one of the Germain brothers, Michel, and Jean Manent, from a wine-producing family of Minorcan origin in the southern Mitidja. (Both were married to daughters of the vinelord Michel-Louis Pelegri.)[114] From 1927 the *Echo* was owned by Jacques Duroux, reputedly the richest man in Algeria between the wars. With the profits from his large flour-milling company in Maison-Carrée, his hometown, Duroux had developed two vineyards of several hundred hectares in the eastern Mitidja. As vice-president of the Union des viticulteurs during the Great War, Duroux was frustrated in that group's effort to buy ships on behalf of the colony's wealthiest producers, but in 1923 he was able to cofound a new shipping company, the Cargos algériens, much of whose business came from transporting wine. Between 1921 and 1938 Duroux represented the department of Algiers in the French Senate, where he had ample opportunity to serve on commissions with the power to shape policies of relevance to the Algerian economy.[115]

The structure of power in Algeria was too diffuse for these wealthy Euro-Algerians to constitute a political oligarchy. But the governor-general between 1925 and 1927, the socialist Maurice Viollette, had no doubt that Algeria's agricultural elite—with wine producers foremost among them—qualified as an "economic oligarchy."[116] As we have seen, the government-general understood that there was a danger in concentration of property, hence its active support of the cooperative movement. At the same time, however, it was beholden to the needs and demands of the big producers. As governor-general, Viollette himself had assisted a scheme to channel water to the Domaine du Kéroulis from a source twenty kilometers distant.[117] In 1929 the Société anonyme des domaines du Kéroulis was the twentieth most profitable company in the entire French Empire, on a list made up largely of banks, trading companies, and mining concerns.[118] In its annual report that year, the company announced that the most recent *vendange* had yielded 109,975 hectoliters of wine, of which by March 1929 it had already sold over 95 percent.[119] An article in the journal *L'Afrique du Nord illustrée* celebrated the modernity of the company's central domain with its 1,200 hectares of vines, its new winery with the capacity to hold 105,000 hectoliters, and its "imposing battery" of tractors. The journal asserted that if such *grandes exploitations* were an exception in metropolitan agriculture, in Algeria they were the necessary motor of colonial development and were also good (in ways unelaborated) for the well-being of the *"indigènes."* But as the photographs depicting one or two people amid vast plains, factory-like interiors, and rows of machines might have suggested to some readers, this agro-capitalism represented a very different type of colonization from the model based on small freeholders that the Third Republic had idealized more or less since the 1870s.[120]

The 1910s and 1920s represented an inflection point in the history of Algerian wine in another way, too, as members of the generation that had propelled the first big expansion of the *vignoble* both experienced a period of triumph and began to die out. The manner of their passing was sometimes telling in itself. Michel-Louis Pelegri, whose impoverished family had migrated from Majorca in 1846 when he was a boy, died in 1917 after his chauffeur-driven limousine caught fire near his downtown apartment in Algiers.[121] Julien Bertrand, a Burgundian who had arrived with the army in 1870 and stayed to become one of Algeria's most influential figures in viticulture, agriculture, and financial affairs, died in 1925 after a fall at his villa overlooking the Bay of Algiers.[122] The trappings of viticultural wealth were now often to be seen in luxurious urban residences, not only in the cities but also in smaller communities in wine-producing regions: to the west of Oran, for example, the town of Rio Salado had a neighborhood known as the *quartier des millionnaires* from as early as the 1910s. Some put their money toward expensive new pursuits; around 1930 aviation became a passion for many members of the Germain family.[123] As a younger generation took over, the typical vinelord now spent much of his time in urban comfort, supervising by telephone and visiting properties by car as necessary.[124] Yet the likes of Henri Borgeaud and Robert Germain (who took control of the Société des domaines du Kéroulis when his father Pierre died in 1933) were still as committed as their fathers to their vineyards and the businesses they fed.

The approach of the centenary of French Algeria in 1930 occasioned celebration and some reflection among Euro-Algerians. A large monument dedicated to the "French genius for colonization" went up in Boufarik, the town in the Mitidja that had served as a nodal point for the expansion of viticulture.[125] Meanwhile, one of colonial Algeria's leading scholars of the time, Augustin Bernard, offered the judgment that the development of the *vignoble* had been "the most important economic fact in the modern history of Algeria."[126] The decade that was just about to begin would test the solidity of that statement.

4

Algeria and the Midi

The 1930s (I)

For advocates of European settlement, the physical resemblance of coastal Algeria to the region that faced it across the Mediterranean had long been considered an advantage, a factor likely to mitigate feelings of *dépayse-ment* or homesickness among any southern French who chose to relocate to North Africa. In 1906, the director of colonization in Algeria, Henri de Peyerimhoff, argued that in geographical terms there was "much more difference between Flanders and Provence than between the south of France and the north of Africa." In his view, the way colonization and cultivation had developed in Algeria in the second half of the nineteenth century had only served to emphasize the similarity of the lands around the Mediterranean, so that now "the vigneron of the Aude can feel at home in the Mitidja or the plain of Bône."[1]

Of much greater importance, however, were the feelings of the mass of southern French vignerons who had no intention of moving. For them, Algeria's proximity and purported similarity were as likely to represent a threat—and most threatening of all were the plains that produced large amounts of the kind of cheap wine that was also the mainstay of southern departments like the Aude. Fears that Algeria could develop into a competitor for French producers had existed since the early days of colonization, when the authorities in Algeria had expressed misgivings about promoting viticulture in the colony and, as we saw, Governor Bugeaud had even threatened to ban it. In the event, serious antagonism did not emerge until the twentieth century. It flickered into life among Midi producers in the aftermath of the vigneron revolt of 1907, then smoldered until a new expansion of the Algerian vineyard combined with the challenging economic environment of the 1930s to produce a crisis that legislators would struggle to manage.

The conflicts described in this chapter arose from a striking example of a relatively rare phenomenon in the history of nineteenth- and twentieth-century colonialism: a colonized territory competing with an established form of production in the imperial metropole. The jute industry provides one of the better-known exceptions from British imperial history. For several decades in the nineteenth century, mills in the Scottish city of Dundee had spun and woven much of the world's jute sacking and burlap cloth—the pre-eminent packing material of the age— only to be outcompeted by factories in Calcutta by the century's end.[2] The comparability of this to the Midi-Algeria wine dispute is limited, however, since Dundee's factories were only in the business of finishing a raw good that grew best in the monsoon climate of the Bengal delta (and in chilly Scotland not at all). Rice production in Japanese-ruled Korea and Taiwan offers a more promising comparison, not least because of the physical proximity and climatic similarity of these imperial possessions to their metropole. In this case, high rice prices in 1918—brought on by inadequate supply—prompted serious rioting in Japanese cities. In its response, the government chose to take the side of metropolitan consumers, by reducing the protection afforded Japanese rice and more strongly encouraging colonial output. By the early 1930s, when Taiwan and Korea supplied a third of the rice consumed in Japan and the Depression and a big harvest in 1933 worsened conditions still further for domestic producers, the government was buying up much of the crop to prevent the market from collapsing.[3]

This Japanese example of increased supply from a colonized territory, superabundant harvests, and sinking prices echoes some of the themes that feature in this chapter, but there are some differences worth underlining as well. Whatever anyone claimed about the importance of wine to the French diet, it was not a staple like rice in Japan, which influenced the relative weight given to the needs of consumers and producers in each context. The identity of the colonial producers was also different. In Algeria, of course, the vast majority of vignerons were French citizens with full rights and representation. In Korea and Taiwan, by contrast, the rice was grown by local farmers rather than Japanese settlers. The subordination of these colonized producers is illustrated by the fact that the colonial administration compelled Koreans to replace rice in their own diet with imported Manchurian sorghum, and Taiwanese to use sweet potatoes in theirs. In that way the authorities maximized the amount of rice available to send to Japan after the 1918 riots.[4]

The stakes in what some in the press labeled the "wine war" (*la guerre du vin*) were rather different. Livelihoods were on the line, certainly, but the conflict also involved a strong cultural dimension that revolved in large part around French Algeria's ambiguous status. Almost at the same time as colonial Algeria celebrated its centenary, a well-organized lobby in France was forcefully questioning a fundamental element of the Algerian economy and even, in somewhat daring terms, aspects of the legitimacy of French Algeria itself. The Euro-Algerian population responded with all the strength it could muster, either through its political representatives or via public protests that at their peak mobilized tens of thousands of people. These conflicts were not only about Algeria's relationship to the metropole; some at the time interpreted the central problem in terms of a struggle between small- or medium-scale producers and large-scale agricultural capitalism. A longer-term perspective allows us to see the "wine war" of the 1930s as a crisis of imperial complementarity that had been brewing for decades. It also highlights what French Algeria had failed to become in a century of colonization.

COMPETITION VERSUS COMPLEMENTARITY

The Algerian wine industry had developed far enough by the 1890s to earn an occasional blast of criticism from strongholds of metropolitan production like the Aude. As we saw earlier, however, Euro-Algerian vignerons backed their southern French counterparts during the market slump of the 1900s, as both sides of the Mediterranean eventually focused on adulterated wines as the common enemy.

That Algeria remained apparently exempt from the Midi's diagnosis of the troubles afflicting French viticulture when that crisis climaxed in revolt in 1907 may have owed something to the influence of Marcellin Albert. A café owner and small-scale wine producer from the village of Argeliers in the Aude, Albert became for several months the heroic mouthpiece of the Midi's cause through the committee of viticultural defense that he helped to found and by addressing huge crowds at a series of spring and summer rallies.[5] It is not clear whether Algerian wine's contribution to the overburdened wine market in 1907 came up as a topic of discussion in Albert's committee, but it is true to say that he was a loyal supporter of French Algeria: he had served in the Algerian *tirailleurs* there in 1870, and his brother Pierre-Etienne settled in Oran a few years later.[6] Albert's supporters in the Midi deserted him rapidly in late June 1907 when he was compromised by a private meeting with Prime Minister Georges Clemenceau (who had sent in troops to control the protests), but his popularity in Algeria endured long after his fall from grace at home.[7]

Because of Albert's sudden loss of influence, his voice was not present to temper the message of a new organization formed in September 1907 in the immediate aftermath of the revolt. The Confédération générale des vignerons du Midi (CGV) was led by Ernest Ferroul, mayor of Narbonne and a former ally of Albert, who helped to weld the association into an influential amalgam of not just large and small wine producers but workers and employees in all aspects of the industry, including its commercial side. Very soon after its creation, the CGV began publicly to criticize Algeria as part of the organization's effort to shape a wine market more favorable to the Midi.[8] By late 1908 Euro-Algerian wine interests were already becoming accustomed to having to rebut charges of unfair competition, fraudulent production, or the idea that the Algerian vineyard was a "huge mistake."[9] The CGV's harsh tone led Euro-Algerians to rue Marcellin Albert's lost influence all the more. When Albert made a tour of Algeria in 1910, he received a rapturous welcome wherever he went, tinged with nostalgia for a time when the Midi and the colony had fought for the same cause, and, in the words of the mayor of the town of Marengo in the Mitidja, "the prejudices of our French brothers against Algerians" were not so evident.[10]

The prosperity of Algerian viticulture seemed to goad the CGV's "prejudices," even in the generally stronger wine market of the early 1910s. In late 1911, for example, facing lower prices than the previous year, the CGV—with the support of viticultural associations in some other parts of the country—began advocating a limit of seven million hectoliters on the amount of Algerian wine that could enter France duty-free; anything beyond that would be taxed as a foreign import. Such talk of a *contingentement* (quota) for Algerian wine sparked alarm among Euro-Algerians, fearful that the customs union was under threat.[11] To mount an organized defense, in the spring of 1912 colonial growers founded the Confédération des vignerons des trois départements d'Algérie (CVA). (The impetus for this development came largely from producers in the department of Algiers like the Mitidja vinelord Julien Bertrand.) By the end of the year, the CVA was already trying to fulfill its mission to protect Algerian wine by sending prominent members to speak at the meetings of French viticultural societies.[12]

In 1914 Algeria produced its biggest wine harvest yet, crossing the ten-million hectoliter threshold for the first time. In other circumstances this might have fed metropolitan antagonism, but the outbreak of war rendered any talk of competition moot, as French nationals in Algeria mobilized. Soon Algerian wine itself was pressed into service—a quarter of the colony's production in 1915, more as hostilities continued—for consumption in the trenches.[13] The rough comfort provided by the cheap wine the soldiers dubbed *le pinard* was much romanticized during the war and in the years that followed, and Algeria had certainly made a loyal contribution on that front.[14]

The war heightened the metropole's awareness of the empire in general, particularly through the participation of troops from the colonies. In economic terms, however, that awareness was accompanied by a sense that France's possessions were capable of contributing more. Even before the fighting ended in 1918 there was increasing discussion of the untapped resource potential of colonial territories and the prospect of articulating some sort of coherent imperial economic plan.[15] Questions of imperial value were voiced most prominently after the war by the former governor-general of French Indochina, Albert Sarraut. As colonial minister between 1920 and 1924, Sarraut urged greater state investment in the development, or *mise en valeur*, of the empire, and envisaged an economic system in which different regions would specialize in a few key products for the benefit of the whole.[16] The French state ultimately remained true to its traditional reluctance to put serious money into colonial development, which after all was a potentially boundless long-term expense, at a time when the main priority of most metropolitan citizens was stabilization and reconstruction at home.[17] But ideas like those of Sarraut found empire-wide influence nonetheless as a kind of ethos of exploitation.

Part of what Sarraut and others did was to encourage a revival in a more holistic conception of the French imperial economy—an outlook

that had been a habit of mind in earlier periods but had become less pronounced as the empire grew ever wider and more complex. For the administration in Algeria in the 1920s, this outlook manifested itself most
obviously in support for what it called *cultures complémentaires:* crops
that would complement those produced in the metropole.[18] That this
theme so strongly echoed a debate that had been equally current in the
1830s points to the stasis at the heart of the French approach to Algeria.
Large-scale Algerian viticulture was one of the biggest differences from
that earlier time, however, and it would inevitably be drawn into any new
discussion of imperial complementarity.

Complementarity proved to be a key theme during the visit made to
Algeria in 1923 by forty legislators from the Chamber of Deputies' *groupe
viticole,* a lobby whose stated objective was to defend French and Algerian viticulture. Leading the delegation was the group's president, Edouard Barthe, a socialist deputy for the Hérault and a native of the CGV
stronghold of Béziers.[19] With such origins Barthe was naturally the object of some suspicion in Algeria, but on this occasion he reassured members of the CVA that "with respect to your wines, the misunderstand-
ings of the past have disappeared." Circumstances were favorable to that
sort of message, for the extent of Algeria's vineyard and its production
statistics were almost identical in 1923 to what they had been at the start
of the war, while wine itself still exuded a patriotic glow: in an address
to the visitors the governor-general of Algeria, Théodore Steeg, called it
"the soul of our nation" and hailed the "glorious *pinard* of the years of
anguish." (This comment earned Steeg prolonged applause.) But beyond
the unifying rhetoric, both Barthe and Steeg were hoping to shape the
behavior of the colony's wine producers. Speaking at a banquet organized
by the CVA, Barthe argued that "the special qualities of your soil and
your climate mark you out for giving the mother country the foodstuffs
and produce that she cannot cultivate herself and that she is obliged to
get from foreign countries." The best course of action for all, he continued, was to "direct your labor toward crops that complement those
of the metropole. In that way you will strengthen your position and that
of France." At the same event Governor-General Steeg presented a similar argument that colonial Algeria should aspire to "complete" French
agricultural production.[20]

What exactly did these advocates of complementary production envisage? For Barthe—just as for some supporters of colonization as far

back as the 1830s—the question was most easily answered by listing the agricultural produce that France had imported from other countries in the previous year; this could then guide landowners in Algeria who were willing to develop substitutes.[21] Eventually, the promoters of Algerian complementarity attached particular hopes to fruit trees; vegetables such as potatoes, green beans, and tomatoes; and—evoking certain nineteenth-century projects—*plantes industrielles* like cotton and tobacco.[22] As for viticulture, Algeria's vignerons were urged to give more priority to deeply colored wines of high alcohol content that blended well with weaker metropolitan counterparts, as well as expanding their production of fortified wines, examples of which had impressed some members of the parliamentary group as they toured the colony.[23]

The imperial thinking offered by the advocates of complementarity was underpinned by two important assumptions. One held that Algeria was, in its essence, *un pays agricole,* a land fit primarily for agriculture (see fig. 4.1).[24] In the metropole, the postwar period saw a revival in idealized visions of rural society. The image of the peasant soldier stood central to French myths about how the conflict had been won, while the association that some drew between factory workers and revolutionary disorder tightened with the growth of communism. Yet, at the same time, the war underlined the fundamental significance of French industry and fostered its further development, while rural out-migration continued apace.[25] In Algeria, by contrast, the impulse toward industrial development appeared as weak as ever. The territory offered up well over two million tons of iron ore each year, for example, as well as notable quantities of zinc and lead, but continued to have no metallurgical industry worthy of the name.[26] A cement factory that the French manufacturer Lafarge took over and expanded at Rivet in the eastern Mitidja in the early 1920s represented a rare instance in which a local natural resource (in this case lime and clay) was turned into a finished good in Algeria itself.[27] Maintaining Algeria as a supplier of raw materials suited metropolitan industrialists perfectly well, while the territory's emphasis on agriculture aligned with both the administration's concern to protect colonization in the countryside and the economic inclinations of Euro-Algerian notables.

Majority French and Euro-Algerian opinion seemed to accept Algeria's essential characterization as an agricultural land, but another (unstated) implication of the advocacy of complementary colonization—that

FIG. 4.1 Produced for the 1930 centenary, this poster projected an agricultural essence for the colony. Archives Nationales d'Outre-Mer, 9Fi 64.

Algeria was a subsidiary addition to the metropole—was more conten-tious. Edouard Barthe's audience had received him warmly in 1923 and applauded his assertion that Algeria was the work of "the most authentic peasants" from all corners of France.[28] Leaving aside the fact that viti-culture in particular had developed with a great deal of input from "peas-ants" of non-French origin, this viewpoint nonetheless conformed to how most Euro-Algerians liked to see themselves. But if their French-ness was not in question, why then should any of them be asked to "com-plement" or "complete" the production of other Frenchmen? The deci-sions Euro-Algerians now made about what to cultivate on their land—and especially whether to rein in their enthusiasm for viticulture—would provide their response to that question.

PLANTATION FEVER

Euro-Algerians always felt a certain anxiety about their French status, and this naturally made them susceptible to the flattery of skilled met-ropolitan politicians like Barthe. At the same time, however, they were vigilant about potential threats to their economic rights as citizens. The war had not banished their reasons to be mistrustful. In 1925, a year in which Algeria produced a new record of over twelve million hectoliters of wine, leading figures in the CGV once again raised the possibility of setting a seven-million-hectoliter limit on the amount that could freely enter the metropole.[29] Not all metropolitan vignerons felt so threatened by Algerian production as to support calls for a quota, but the Midi had enough influence and enough votes to carry a motion to that end when France's associations of wine producers met for their annual congress in 1926.[30] From this point on the conflict gathered momentum.

Algeria's producers, with the backing of the governor-general, argued for the maintenance of the customs union, and in the short term there didn't seem to be any serious prospect that legislators in Paris would re-vise that long-standing arrangement.[31] But a strain of opinion seemed to be developing in a way that was unnerving to Euro-Algerian landholders. In 1928, for example, one of the deputies who had toured Algeria five years earlier, Charles Guilhaumon from the Hérault, condemned the "stupid lack of foresight" that had led to the development of the Algerian vineyard. Euro-Algerians, he believed, should instead be directed to emphasize "complementary" cereals, vegetables, citrus fruits, and cotton.[32]

Such exhortations rang increasingly hollow as the crops envisaged either failed to take off or producers encountered economic obstacles. In the late 1920s, for example, the cultivation of citrus fruits, which struck many as a natural fit for the colony, remained limited to a few areas, and the marketplace was challenging for new growers.[33] Meanwhile, wheat farmers in Algeria faced growing competition from producers in the neighboring protectorate of Morocco. In that recent addition to the French Empire, the planting of wheat—especially by European settlers—was central to the local administration's development program (and conformed to Sarraut's encouragement of North African cereal crops as a substitute for foreign imports). By 1929, though, increased metropolitan output combined with North African production to create a glutted market.[34] This did not say much for imperial planning.

The difficulty of developing remunerative new forms of production and the declining fortunes of cereal cultivators only enhanced the appeal of the vine, the crop that seemed above all others to promise the best return on investment. The ideal of diversified production did not disappear, but hopeful talk of *cultures complémentaires* was effectively swept aside in a new wave of vine planting in Algeria.

Statistics for the period 1928–1932 underline just how dramatic this expansion was (see table 4.1). In those years, Algeria's share of the combined amount of wine produced in France and the colony went from 15.4 to 24.9 percent. The biggest jump came in the department of Oran, which eclipsed the Hérault to become France's leading wine-producing department, both by output and by extent of vines. Yet in 1932 the number of declared producers in Algeria (15,538) still totaled little more than 1 percent of the number of vignerons in the metropole (1,489,849).[35]

A few had seen this plantation fever coming. In November 1928, Albert Dromigny, a vigneron who represented colonists from the Sahel of Algiers at the Délégations financières, worried about the "equilibrium" of Algerian agriculture, as he saw thousands of hectares of land being cleared for vines. Much of this was land formerly devoted to cereals; on some of it had even grown orchards of fruit trees.[36] But the vine, on which so many Euro-Algerians had gambled before, was now seen as the safer bet. Creditors seemed to agree.[37]

TABLE 4.1. Extent of Wine Cultivation in Selected Departments in France and Algeria: Hectares in Production, 1928–1932

	1928	1932		1928	1932
Aude	114,336	124,595	Algiers	80,849	114,846
Gironde	134,714	130,910	Constantine	15,346	23,921
Hérault	181,426	191,016	Oran	115,141	213,185
France total	1,373,410	1,412,796	Algeria total	211,336	351,952

Source: ANOM, BA, série continue 455, Ministère des finances, Direction générale des contributions indirectes: Relevé, par département, présentant des renseignements d'ordre statistique sur la répartition des superficies plantées en vigne en 1928 et en 1932.

Metropolitan opponents were quick to spot the trend, and equally quick to try to stop it. In March 1929, two prominent Midi deputies presented bills to parliament. One, from Léon Castel of the Aude—another who had visited Algeria with the *groupe viticole* in 1923—sought to require official approval for any new plantations. A second bill, from Charles Caffort of the Hérault, took more explicit aim at Algeria by proposing a quota of eight million hectoliters on the amount of wine its producers could send duty-free to the metropole.[38] Caffort's bill in particular had a populist appeal, and many municipal councils, not only in the Midi but also departments like the Gironde, issued statements of support that identified Algeria as a threat to metropolitan viticulture.[39]

Algeria's defenders emphasized one idea above all others in their response: that Algeria was an integral part of France, and as such could not be subjected to differential treatment. At times the argument was made in emotional terms, evoking the contribution made by Euro-Algerians to the defense of the *mère patrie* in the Great War, or, via a different family metaphor, urging French citizens on the two sides of the Mediterranean to avoid a "fratricidal struggle."[40] (In a particularly ominous vein, a parliamentary deputy for Oran warned that metropolitan France should take care not to alienate Euro-Algerians in the manner that Britain had once alienated "her nationals in America."[41]) At other times, the appeal was to reason, assuming and encouraging a view of Algeria as a French region like any other. One author tried to draw an analogy between Algeria and the province of Alsace. Textile manufacturers in Normandy had not demanded the closure of cotton mills in Alsace when it was returned to France after the Great War; why, then, should Midi wine producers seek to impose limits on French Algeria?[42] Amid their protestations of Frenchness and calls to economic rationality, however, Euro-Algerians often held a markedly protectionist outlook of their own, not only toward "foreign" wines but even toward agricultural produce from the neighboring French protectorate of Morocco.[43] In that case, Euro-Algerians believed that quotas were just and needed to be upheld.

If Euro-Algerians insisted on their inviolable Frenchness, popular perceptions of Algeria could easily undermine that idea. Attempts to promote Algerian wine around this time often traded on the ambiguity of the territory's status. It is not clear that the patrons of working-class cafés in France always knew the provenance of the wine they were served; much Algerian wine simply blended in—often literally—with the stock available to metropolitan drinkers. A remark by the narrator in George Orwell's *Down and Out in Paris and London* about "the coarse African wine" that "still tasted good" at the end of a night out with fellow hotel workers in Paris, however, suggests that some level of awareness existed by the late 1920s.[44] At the same time, merchants trying to capture the attention of discriminating consumers frequently drew upon the standard visual rhetoric of Orientalism. Bottle labels signaled wine's Algerian origin with images of pointed arches, domes, oases, and palm trees, as well as white-robed Muslims, some of them even in the act of prayer (see fig. 4.2). The star and crescent on the label of the well-known brand Royal-Kebir, marketed as the "doyen" of Algerian fine wines, was more discreet but served the same purpose. Such images, often the work of designers in France, may have had some commercial appeal, but only by amplifying a sense of Algeria's difference from the metropole.[45]

The political and commercial establishment nonetheless remained generally warm in its embrace of French Algeria—itself a brand, so to speak, that had now reached a certain level of maturity. The exhibition held in Oran to mark the centenary in 1930, visited by President Gaston Doumergue and other notables, saw prominent metropolitan food and drink companies displaying their wares alongside those of their Euro-Algerian counterparts in the event's cavernous "Palais de l'Alimentation." This was "proof," proclaimed the official book of the exhibition, of "the solid bonds that link us economically to the mother country," as well as "the futility of any attempt to treat us as second-tier Frenchmen."[46]

FIG. 4.2 Wine label, late 1920s. Reproduced from the author's collection.

A metropolitan public was presented with a similar message in the following year. Millions of visitors to the Exposition Coloniale in Paris witnessed the fountain of wine that formed a centerpiece to the exhibition's Algeria pavilion, and had the chance to sample the product itself at tasting stations organized by the CVA.[47] One visitor, the author Louis Bertrand of the Académie Française, could recall drinking wine so unrefined in Algiers in the 1890s that it had "set my head on fire."[48] But at the exhibition in 1931 he toured the Algeria pavilion and toasted "the triumph of Bacchus."[49] Even at this moment of "triumph," however, lawmakers were debating whether Algeria's wine industry needed to be reined in for the good of the Republic.

FIXING LIMITS

Prompted by a big harvest in 1929 that caused the price of wine from regions like the Midi and Bordeaux to drop below cost, the government urged the formulation of a plan to regulate viticulture. Just as in 1907, there was room to debate where the principal problem lay. A surface reading of market conditions suggested "overproduction," but some argued that the emphasis should instead be on "underconsumption" and a marketplace burdened by too many wines of inferior quality. Rather than try to pinpoint the relative culpability of supply or demand, parliamentary committees generally agreed that both were awry and that viticulture now faced a "crisis" necessitating government intervention for the good of all.[50]

There was broad consensus that Algeria, though not the only cause of this situation, was certainly a major contributor to it. But the debates that led up to the law of July 4, 1931—the first major piece of legislation in what came to be called the *statut viticole*—mostly treated Algeria in relatively temperate fashion. Edouard Barthe from the Hérault remained the leading figure on the wine question in the Chamber of Deputies, presiding over its Commission des boissons, the permanent committee that guided discussion of the proposed legislation. On the one hand, Barthe's presence may have reassured Midi producers that their concerns would be represented, while on the other, he perhaps helped to silence some of the more radical voices, which extended even to a fringe that suggested France should get rid of Algeria.[51] An idea more commonly advanced by some in the Midi, of setting a quota on Algerian wine, did not emerge as a serious proposition among legislators at this time.

That the debate never acquired an overtly anti-Algerian cast also owed something to André Tardieu, who as prime minister in 1930 first set the legislative process in motion and then as minister of agriculture in 1931 was a key influence in its passage. Tardieu, a political "fixer" on the center-right, forcefully scotched any talk of a quota; such a measure would "separate France in two," he argued, with consequences that he was certain would prove "catastrophic."[52] In the impeccably republican wording of the sponsor of the bill in the Chamber of Deputies, Henri Labroue, French viticulture was "one and indivisible."[53]

The debate centered not on a rogue colony, therefore, but rather on producers who were judged to have gone too far. As Tardieu summarized it, the low-yielding "good plantation" (often on the hillside) was increasingly overwhelmed by the high-yielding "bad plantation" (often on the plain and associated with a lower-quality product).[54] The problem was not Algeria as such; it just happened that there was a concentration of what Barthe dubbed "wine factories" there.[55] The egregious success—or, to the bill's sponsors, the excess—of one Algerian vineyard drew particular attention: Pierre Germain's thousand-plus-hectare Domaine du Kéroulis near Aïn-Témouchent, which Labroue claimed was offering investors an 80 percent profit on their outlay. Indeed, the Société des domaines du Kéroulis had just informed its shareholders of another successful year, reporting a production total of 75,000 hectoliters of wine with an average alcohol content of more than 12 percent. Since much of this wine was destined to be blended with weaker wines, however, the company regarded itself not as an overproducing menace, but rather an "indispensable additive for the metropolitan *vignoble*."[56]

The widespread use of Algerian wines as *vins de coupage* offered the colony's deputies one line of defense against some of their parliamentary adversaries. Objecting to Labroue's characterization of Algerian wine as poor-quality "*vinasse*," the Algiers deputy André Mallarmé pointed to the department Labroue represented, the Gironde, and asked why Bordeaux winemakers had been willing for so long to add Algerian wine to their own product.[57] But the colony's association with large-scale production was difficult to shake. Even one of Algeria's own deputies, Emile Morinaud from the department of Constantine, a vineyard owner himself, openly criticized the "big firms and multimillionaires" that he believed were driving down prices and harming small- and medium-scale producers.[58]

While for many metropolitan parliamentarians the key objective was to limit "big viticulture," for most of the contingent from Algeria it was not that simple. Much of the debate revolved around a proposal to prohibit any new planting for ten years, with an exception that would allow growers whose vineyards did not exceed ten hectares and 500 hectoliters of production to plant an additional ten hectares. This ten-hectare exception seemed to crystallize the moral economy at play in the debate, while simultaneously exposing what made Algeria different. For some conservative politicians in the metropole, to set limits on what people could do with their lands was an example of government over-reach and a threat to property rights.[59] But the bill's supporters noted that ten hectares was considerably larger than the average vineyard of the vast majority of French cultivators. A deputy from Burgundy, a region that generally did not see itself as being in competition with Algeria, pointed out that in the metropole you had to be rich to plant as much as ten hectares. With that in mind he considered the proposed exception to be quite generous, even as he expressed "solidarity" with Algeria.[60] For most of the deputies from Algeria, by contrast, to set limits on the size of plantations was above all to hinder colonization. In the understanding of colonists in Algeria, in fact, ten hectares was barely enough. Mallarmé warned that, if passed, the bill "would break France's colonial spirit."[61]

After much debate, including a marathon session in the Chamber of Deputies that ended at 5:30 in the morning, the bill did pass. The new law introduced a complicated structure of taxes on yields, calibrated so that higher production earned higher penalties. It installed a mechanism allowing the government to block the release of wines to the market if the annual harvest threatened to exceed the average level of consumption of the previous three years. (Both of these two measures exempted most growers who produced less than 400 hectoliters.) A further provision stipulated that a national harvest of more than 65 million hectoliters would trigger a mandatory distillation order to prevent the surplus from reaching the market. Finally, parliament also passed into law the plantation limit and its ten-hectare exception.[62] Immediately after the bill was voted in the Chamber, Barthe acknowledged that it was "imperfect."[63] The imperfections would soon become apparent.

BACKFIRE AND BACKLASH

For the colonists of the recently founded official settlement of Gaston-Doumergue, the law of July 4, 1931, was tantamount to a betrayal. This new village near Aïn-Témouchent in the department of Oran, named in honor of the sitting president of the Republic, occupied land that the government had deemed especially suitable for viticulture and had priced accordingly. Aggrieved and fearful for their investment, the colonists of Gaston-Doumergue petitioned lawmakers, the governor-general, and President Doumergue himself for an exemption from the limit on new plantations of vines. But the possibility of allowing an exception for recent settlements had already been raised and rejected by the Chamber in the debates leading up to the law. The citizens of Gaston-Doumergue had been busy planting since purchasing their lands in 1928, so they—along with others in a similar position—would need to make the best of what they already had.[64] Only a few kilometers away, the Domaine du Kéroulis would also have to "make do" with its thousand-plus hectares.

Though some colonists felt victimized by the law, many responded in a manner that would have been familiar to the phylloxera inspectors of earlier decades: by searching for ways to get around it. One tactic saw several large plantations subdivided into smaller ones, as big producers tried to minimize their exposure to the new taxes on yields, which were scaled according to a property's total production.[65] Another popular maneuver attributed new plantations—often the maximum ten hectares—to family members with no vineyards previously to their names. The joke at the time went that, after July 1931, Euro-Algerians planted "in the name of the Father, the Son, and the Holy Spirit."[66]

There is evidence, too, that colonists encouraged and at times may even have directly helped Algerians to plant vines, especially on neighboring properties, with the expectation that in most cases Euro-Algerians would be the ones to turn the grapes into wine.[67] With that said, Algerians had not been immune to the "plantation fever" that took hold in the 1920s. Some of the Algerians who embraced viticulture were notables like the Benchiha family, savvy businessmen who were influential in the Aïn-Témouchent region. (Their demands for compensation for lands coveted by the colonial administration had delayed the founding of Gaston-Doumergue.)[68] But the potential for profit from viticulture compared with cereal cultivation around 1930 also lured less well-off Algerians into taking a chance on a new form of production, perhaps lending support to the historian Ahmed Henni's contention that the interwar years saw the emergence of a "Muslim peasant middle class." Any such development is difficult to measure and was certainly small in scale, but the idea appears to carry weight for parts of the department of Oran and most of all the area around Mostaganem, where the production of grapevines by Algerians increased from 1,038 hectares in 1929 to 4,900 hectares in 1933.[69]

One way or another, therefore, the forward momentum of the Algerian *vignoble* may have slowed but certainly did not stop after July 1931. And, as more and more of the vines planted in the three years or so before that date became productive, Algeria's overall output kept increasing: from 13.5 million hectoliters in 1930, to 15.8 million in 1931, to 18.3 million in 1932. Lawmakers in 1931 had taken a shot at controlling supply; in December 1931 the government also aimed to boost demand by creating a new promotional body, the Comité de propagande du vin.[70] But by 1932 these measures already looked inadequate to southern French producers, and, as wine exporters and consumers alike were increasingly affected by the global Depression, the general outlook seemed grim.[71]

The year 1932 was a miserable one for Midi viticulture. Severe mildew in the spring was followed in late summer by downpours and flooded plains. The outcome was a great deal of wine that was low in quality and alcohol content. By contrast, Algeria had a good harvest, and its blending wines were soon commanding healthy prices to "doctor" the Midi's ailing vintage. That there was a degree of truth to the claim made by some colonists that Algerian wine had helped to rescue the French harvest only enhanced feelings of anger and humiliation in the Midi. Producers there were realistic enough to accept a bad year, but they feared that Algerian output now represented a perennial obstacle to the kinds of prices they needed to survive.[72]

Even before the 1932 harvest was in, there was a strong sense among metropolitan producers that the July 1931 law would need to be revised, and, more particularly, that more of Algeria's output should be prevented from reaching the market when metropolitan production was high. This feeling was not contained to the Midi. At the annual meeting of viticultural federations in Avignon in April 1932, the Euro-Algerian contingent found few allies against a motion from the Narbonne CGV proposing to allow no more than 10 million hectoliters of Algerian wine to enter the metropole duty-free in years when France's total production reached 65 million hectoliters. The word that proponents used for this management of the market was *aménagement*, a kind of rebalancing, but for Euro-Algerians this was simply a euphemism for a *contingentement* or quota.[73]

Through 1932 and the first half of 1933 the anti-Algeria rhetoric proliferated, emboldened by the support of a parliamentary commission on viticulture for an *aménagement* that would treat surplus Algerian production separately from that of the metropole. Newspapers like the conservative Montpellier daily *L'Eclair* issued a steady stream of articles with titles like "The Algerian Danger." Many of these were written by a columnist known as Ribalte, who played up the image of Algeria as a disruptive outsider in relation to French viticulture, if not the economy as a whole; in July 1932 he stated that Euro-Algerians were now "alone" in wanting the economic assimilation of the colony to the metropole.[74] Pamphlets and brochures that claimed to represent the views of all of France's viticultural associations similarly called Algeria's purpose and value as a colony into question. One tract resurrected General Bugeaud's century-old admonition that Algeria should only cultivate agricultural products the metropole lacked, and concluded with a warning to present-day metropolitan citizens that the colony was "preparing your ruin."[75] Another asserted that wine production in Algeria was typified by "la grande exploitation industrialisée"—large plantations run like factories—whose owners were guilty of "a veritable DUMPING" on the metropolitan market.[76]

As lawmakers began working in early 1933 toward modifying the July 1931 law, the tensions increased further. At a special hearing of the Commission des boissons in March that was attended by leaders of viticultural associations from France and Algeria, Ernest Brousse, representing vignerons from the area around Montpellier and Lodève in the Hérault, accused Algeria's colonists of trying to "kill" a million small- and medium-size French producers.[77] Two months later, Brousse addressed a large meeting in Montpellier during which ninety-nine municipal councils from the region publicly offered their resignations in protest at what they perceived to be the government's "hostility" toward Midi viticulture. Evoking the spirit of 1907, Brousse told the crowd that it was better to revolt than suffer dishonor.[78]

At the same time, Euro-Algerians were also in a state of agitation. The arguments marshaled by the colony's wine interests, often in pamphlets and brochures of their own, were by now quite familiar, revolving first and foremost around the idea that anything resembling a quota for a product from Algeria called into question the customs union and, beyond that, the territory's French status.[79] They made sure to point out that by 1932, in the context of rising tariff walls across the world, Algeria had become the biggest single destination of metropolitan-made goods. Euro-Algerians found various ways to communicate the idea that the economic balance between the metropole and Algeria still tipped in favor of the former, with Algeria's agricultural produce a complement to France's manufactured goods. The message, in effect, was that a version of the colonial pact still operated, and, moreover, that it worked.

The response in Algeria at this time was distinguished most of all by the number of people who turned out for meetings that were designed as much to support the customs union as to defend Algerian viticulture. As many as 3,000 came to the municipal theater in Oran in January 1933, picking up flyers like the one pictured in figure 4.3, with loudspeakers set up outside to broadcast the meeting to those unable to get in.[80] By June, in the days before parliament met to vote, the meetings had grown considerably larger. In the East, perhaps 5,000 people rallied on the Cours Bertagna in Bône. A reported 25,000 turned out in Algiers, where participants made their way after the speeches to the war memorial to pay their respects to those who had "fought so their Algerian brothers could remain French," as the *Echo d'Alger* put it.[81] But the most vocal defense was in the West. In April and May the town of Sidi-Bel-Abbès, with the support of the government-general, staged an eighteen-day "Foire du Vin" (wine fair) that celebrated the coming of age of Algerian wine after "sixty years of apprenticeship" to the metropole.[82] Then, in June, maybe 50,000 people—what one newspaper dubbed a "levée en masse"—demonstrated in Oran, whose Euro-Algerian population at the time was only about 125,000, against the "fratricidal laws" up for discussion in Paris. During the proceedings, three airplanes from local aviation clubs flew overhead and dropped leaflets that read: "Citizens of Oran. No quota. All stand up to protest the tyranny of the Midi. We are and want to remain French."[83]

Just before the vote in parliament, posters that were presumably the work of the Midi lobby went up around Paris urging lawmakers to put

FIG. 4.3 "Benefits of the Metropole-Algeria customs union."
Brochure distributed in 1932–1933, with Algeria's contribution
depicted on the right-hand scale. Archives Nationales d'Outre-Mer,
Gouvernement-général de l'Algérie, 10 55.

"Métropole d'abord" (Metropole first).[84] Most ignored the advice. The proposal to treat surplus Algerian wine differently from surplus metropolitan wine—what Euro-Algerians had perceived as a quota—was comfortably defeated by deputies who chose to follow a formula laid down by André Tardieu in 1931, that parliament should legislate only in a "framework of national unity" wherein Algeria was integral to the nation.[85] The law that passed on July 8, 1933 instead fixed the terms under which wine would be blocked from the market when the combined total of production and stocks from France and Algeria reached 70 million hectoliters. Responding to concerns about abuse of the ten-hectare exception, lawmakers also restricted any new vine plantings to three hectares for growers who did not already cultivate that much.[86]

ALLIES AND ANTAGONISTS

This new law represented a largely satisfactory outcome for French Algeria, where the rallies of June 1933 created an appearance of unity as urban centers came out in defense of the colony's predominantly agricultural economy. A close reading of the events of 1932–1933, however, reveals the importance of trans-Mediterranean alliances to the success of the colonial Algerian lobby, as well as some emerging fault lines and fractures that had the potential to define the territory in new ways.

Though the critique of Algerian wine offered by many Midi producers had found some supporters in a variety of French centers of viticulture, Euro-Algerians could generally count on the backing of metropolitan commercial interests. Nowhere was this truer than in the port cities through which Algerian wine entered France. Leading figures in the CVA were predictably well received when they toured Atlantic and Channel ports in search of support in early 1933. Equally telling, though, was the suspicion in which Sète, the primary port in the Midi, was held by the Midi's own vignerons. When producers from the Hérault rallied in Montpellier in May 1933, the port's very name elicited hostility and a comment from one protester that Sète should "go and join up with the Oranais," given that so much western Algerian wine entered France via that route.[87] Yet support for French Algeria was by no means confined to coastal locations, for anyone with goods to sell could recognize its importance as a market. Chambers of commerce in towns far inland like Nevers and Châlons-sur-Marne were unequivocal in rejecting any prospect of a quota, while the chamber in Grenoble worried what consequences an attack on the customs union might have on local manufacturers who sold products like paper, cement, and lingerie to clients in Algeria.[88] In short, it was not true to claim that Euro-Algerians were "alone" in defending economic assimilation.

At the same time, just as metropolitan views on Algerian viticulture were diverse, it is important to recognize varieties of opinion within Algeria. In the department of Constantine, where cereal cultivation was of prime importance and wine played little role in the economies of urban centers like Sétif and the city of Constantine, some felt that speculation on the vine in the departments of Algiers and Oran had unnecessarily caused problems for all. In 1931, in fact, the two deputies for Constantine, Emile Morinaud and Gaston Thomson, chose a different path from their Euro-Algerian colleagues and voted in favor of measures like the ban on planting all but ten hectares. The fear of quotas in 1933 brought Algeria's parliamentarians onto the same side again, but a feeling persisted in Constantine that its interests as a department might sometimes be better served if decoupled from those of Algiers and Oran.[89]

The united front was also called into question by smaller producers. In March 1932, 2,000 vignerons in the Hérault founded a Ligue des petits et moyens viticulteurs (League of small and medium wine producers) to stand up to *la culture industrielle,* or "industrial cultivation"; they named Edouard Barthe as their honorary president.[90] Following this lead, and prompted by what they felt was inadequate representation of their interests in the debates leading up to the law of July 1931, a group of over 300 smaller producers in the department of Algiers constituted their own association, the Ligue des moyens et petits viticulteurs du département d'Alger, arguing that the voices of "11,174 small and medium wine producers" in Algeria had been "stifled" by "600 magnates of the vine."[91] ("Small" was defined here as owning up to ten hectares of vines, and "medium" from ten to fifty—a figure that would have struck many metropolitan vignerons as rather on the large side.) Similar leagues formed later in the departments of Oran and Constantine.

These new leagues, as Jean-Marc Bagnol has pointed out, offered a new way of viewing the conflict "in terms of categories of producers" rather than different regions or *vignobles.*[92] Their creation was a welcome development for Barthe, since they helped give credence to his argument that he was not taking sides in a struggle between France and Algeria, but rather was defending agricultural artisans against agricultural capitalism. He could also be seen to be upholding a view with ongoing currency on the political left that represented small freeholders as one of the foundations of social stability.[93] Very soon the president of the new league of small and medium wine producers of Algiers, Auguste Gimbert, was invited to address committees Barthe chaired in Paris, such as the Commission des boissons.[94]

In one regard, the valorization of small-scale production appeared to dovetail with a widely held opinion that, as the agriculture minister Henri Queuille put it, too many producers on both sides of the Mediterranean had "sacrificed quality for quantity."[95] This view rested on a somewhat shaky assumed correlation between quality and scale; plenty of small producers made bad wine, after all, while big vineyards like the Domaine du Kéroulis often had the means to maintain good standards. (It is worth mentioning here that fine wines designated as *appellations d'origine* were exempted from the laws of the *statut viticole*, which focused instead on *vins ordinaires*.[96]) Discussions about the need to improve quality certainly increased around this time, however, and extended to Algeria as well as metropolitan regions. In 1934, for example, the *conseil général* of the department of Constantine issued a statement urging the government to promote *une politique de qualité*—"a policy of quality."[97] That idea, as we shall see, would resurface in debates over Algerian wine into the twenty-first century.

The wine debates of the early 1930s also touched upon more fundamental questions of land and labor. The rhetoric of Algeria's small and medium wine producers shared much in common with that of metropolitan counterparts like the vignerons of the Loire basin, who in 1933 called for resisting the "progressive and rapid disappearance of the familial, artisanal wine producer." Such people, these vignerons claimed, represented "the basis of life itself in our regions."[98] It was not uncommon for rural French people to voice such elemental fears in the 1930s, but in Algeria they were sharpened by concern for the fate of the colony. Thus the small and medium producers of Algiers accused local "magnates of the vine" of "killing" family-centered colonization with their vast domains (and companies).[99] Algeria's "parliament," the Délégations financières algériennes, remained under the influence of an agrarian elite, but in the 1930s a spokesperson for small and medium wine producers, Henri

Baretaud from Cherchell, voiced some of the most forceful warnings that body had yet heard about the long-term viability of the project of colonization if capitalist agriculture continued to dominate.[100]

Perhaps most alarming of all to French Algeria's defenders were accusations from the Midi concerning the use of labor on bigger vineyards. A common contention of the Midi lobby was that wine producers in Algeria unfairly benefited from their employment of, as one grower in the Hérault put it, "water-drinking Arabs working for poverty wages," while growers in the Midi had to pay their workforce much more (and give them a wine allowance, too).[101] In responding to this charge, as well as the broader suggestion that the cost of producing wine in Algeria was lower than in the metropole, colonial Algerian interests fell back on denigrating the workers at their disposal. Algerian laborers were less than a third as productive as French workers, asserted Edouard Kruger, a leading voice of wine producers in Oran, and moreover they lacked the intelligence of metropolitan workers, whose mentalities had been "shaped by long centuries of civilization." In a similar vein, others claimed that paying Algerians more had the perverse effect of reducing their effort further. An unpersuaded Léon Blum, serving in 1933 as the socialist deputy for Narbonne, noted that the stance of the Algeria lobby appeared to be that one had to pay Algerian workers low wages for their own good. Blum was not alone in finding such arguments self-serving.[102]

Midi wine advocates grew especially irritated whenever Euro-Algerian politicians and officials invoked higher principles in support of their position. In a heated debate before the Commission des boissons in March 1933, a deputy for Algiers, Jean-Marie Guastavino, protested that Algeria should not be treated differently from the metropole since the Declaration of the Rights of Man and the Citizen applied in Algeria as well. In response, a representative of producers from the Montpellier region, Marcel Pomier-Layrargues, snapped: "The day you apply the Declaration of the Rights of Man to the *indigènes,* then we can discuss the problem in the terms you propose."[103] The remark evidently startled some in the audience—the minute-taker at the meeting recorded that it was followed by "exclamations"—but if it represented a breach in acceptable metropolitan discourse about Algeria, it was not unique. Just after the passage of the law of July 8, 1933, a long-time antagonist of Algeria, Gustave Coste, the president of the CGV, published an angry open letter in *L'Eclair* of Montpellier, lambasting Algeria's "profiteers," who were trying to "hide the re-establishment of slavery while hypocritically draping themselves in the tricolor flag."[104]

It is unclear how much the likes of Coste and Pomier-Layrargues truly cared about the condition of Algerian workers; their ultimate concern was a group of wine producers in their own region, not agricultural workers in another. But that does not make any less striking their willingness effectively to disown French Algeria in established metropolitan venues like the Commission des boissons and *L'Eclair,* and to condemn a left-leaning Euro-Algerian politician like Guastavino for being on the wrong side of universal republican principle. For Coste and Pomier-Layrargues, the question was not merely to ascertain Algeria's value to France; one also had to question French Algeria's values. Euro-Algerians had enough metropolitan defenders in the 1930s to deflect the charges leveled against them, but the way elements of the Midi lobby depicted French Algeria as operating beyond French norms planted the seed of a more complete disavowal in the future.

THE TIDE CRESTS

Despite the efforts of lawmakers, the wine market soon looked more out of control than ever. In 1934 the harvest in Algeria yielded 22 million hectoliters, a figure never to be surpassed. Added to an extraordinary 75 million hectoliters in the metropole (of which 30 million was contributed by the Midi), plus unsold stocks, France's total for the year exceeded 100 million. Prices entered a tailspin, and were still on their way down in 1935 when the new *vendange* yielded almost as much as the previous one.[105] There could be little argument that this was what overproduction looked like. Algeria's wine producers had led something of a charmed life until as late as 1933, even as cultivators of cereal crops battled a severe slump. Now it was viticulture's turn to suffer. Banks called in loans, especially hurting those who were still paying off the cost of recent plantations. The government-general, ever concerned to shore up European settlement in the countryside, offered colonists ways to restructure their debts, but meanwhile the colony's own budget slipped into the red. The movement to build cooperative wineries, which had continued into the early 1930s—six new ones opened in 1933—ground to a sudden halt.[106] The many built over the preceding decade would come to seem fixed in

FIG. 4.4 The former community winery at Lourmel (now El Amria), to the west of Oran. In 2013, when this picture was taken, the facility was being used by a private wine-production company. Photograph by the author.

time as much by their Art Deco–influenced details as by the dates on their facades (see fig. 4.4).

Parliament and the government kept looking for ways to steady the market by adjusting the levels at which output would be temporarily blocked from sale or distilled. For a time in 1934 and 1935 Algerian interests rose up against a proposal to mandate the *arrachage* (uprooting) of some percentage of the vines in France and Algeria. Barthe appeared to favor a plan that would especially target vines planted after 1928, in other words roughly the moment at which "plantation fever" gripped Algeria. Instead, the government's decree-law of July 30, 1935 deferred the prospect of compulsory *arrachage* and offered indemnities for growers who agreed to remove vines voluntarily.[107] But ultimately it was two much smaller harvests, in 1936 and 1937, that helped more than any legislation to stabilize the situation. Viticulture would continue to operate under a slew of complex new regulations, in addition to remaining subject, as it always had, to the whims of both nature and the market. The Algerian *vignoble*, meanwhile, with all planting now effectively outlawed, had finally (in 1935) found its furthest limit, at 399,513 hectares. It would never reach 400,000.[108]

Algeria's large producers had been the bogeymen in the debates of the 1930s, but in the end the legislation that was passed did not seem to reduce their strength. The fortunes of members of the Germain family and the Société des domaines du Kéroulis in particular illustrate this well. The company, from 1933 under the direction of Robert Germain after the death of his father Pierre, was not at all happy with the "planned economy" enacted by legislators, which they believed violated "the most elementary principles of law and natural economy." Under what its directors perceived as "draconian" new laws, the company had to distill about 40 percent of its massive 1934 harvest of 103,350 hectoliters—and yet, even accounting for the losses this entailed, it still reported a profit for the year. In 1936 the company voluntarily uprooted 135 hectares of its vineyard at Kéroulis, but in 1938, to compensate, bought a neighboring property with excellent soil and 210 hectares of vines already planted.[109] With the resources the company had at its disposal, it was more than able to adapt quickly to the strictures imposed by law. Other big producers seemed to manage similarly well.[110] The only member of the Germain family who went bankrupt in the 1930s was Michel Germain, whose interests lay primarily in urban property; two of his wine-wealthy brothers helped him tackle his debts.[111]

The years of superabundance did cause many in Algeria to consider new strategies, or to revive old ones. As in the market slump of the 1900s, there was fresh interest in the possibility of developing sales beyond the metropole. But, just as before, these hopes proved largely illusory. The repeal of Prohibition in the United States in 1933, for example, did not magically deliver a receptive new market, while the idea of a trans-Saharan railway, which tantalized some in the 1930s (as it had for decades) as a potential path to consumers in France's colonies in West and Equatorial Africa, failed again to materialize.[112] The SIAH at Maison-Carrée, with its niche product of communion wine, remained a rarity in Algeria in the extent to which it depended on foreign clients.[113] The vast majority of producers stuck to the French market, where competition from foreign producers like Spain had been virtually eliminated by protective tariffs.[114]

In view of the glut of 1934–1935 it is not surprising that the mid-1930s saw another revival in talk of "complementary cultures."[115] This time the results in Algeria were slightly more substantial. Voluntary uprooting after 1935 provided some growers with a good occasion to diversify their production. The Domaine de Sidi-Salem in the eastern Mitidja, for example, tore up twenty-six hectares of vines and planted citrus-fruit trees instead under the expert guidance of Gustave Pelegri, the younger son of the late vinelord Michel-Louis Pelegri.[116] (Around the same time, in Boufarik in another part of the Mitidja, an entrepreneur began to develop and commercialize a new product named Orangina.[117]) State investment in dams expanded possibilities for irrigated plantations of orange trees in places like the Chelif river plain in the west of the department of Algiers. By 1938 Algeria's production of oranges, mandarins, and clementines had increased by nearly 40 percent from a decade earlier.[118] In January of that year a promotional agency of the government-general, the Office algérien d'action économique et touristique (OFALAC), staged an exhibition in Paris called "Algeria, French California," emphasizing the colony's ability to supply fresh fruits and vegetables.[119] Once again, however, those best placed to profit from this mini-boom were established names like Borgeaud and Germain—the kinds of people whose vineyards were big enough that uprooting parts of them would not disturb the core business.

Had the *statut viticole* and the quarrel with southern French wine producers changed anything? Debating the topic of viticulture in the 1930s had certainly inspired some lofty oratory from politicians like Eugène Rouart, a senator for the Haute-Garonne, for whom wine had "profoundly influenced French spirituality and helped greatly to define our race."[120] Posing the problem in such terms might easily have excluded French Algeria. Indeed, some from the Midi attempted to do just that, not by branding Euro-Algerians as racial outsiders but by depicting them as hostile to the French spirit. This disrupted the cozily inclusive narrative that had pervaded the celebrations for the centenary of French Algeria perhaps, but lawmakers and consumers alike largely rejected the idea that the territory was a menace to the metropole. If its production did not complement that of the Midi and a few other viticultural regions, many parts of France—especially in the northern half of the country—actively welcomed Algeria's wine. In the late 1930s, for example, the president of the chamber of commerce in Brest, in non-wine-producing western Brittany, claimed that "nearly all" the wine drunk in his region came from Algeria, while a socialist deputy in nearby Lorient commented on its appeal to Breton drinkers.[121] There was no sense that the claims of Midi wine producers needed to be supported simply because they were metropolitan in origin. Though some had raised the question as to whether Algeria should become a sort of British-style dominion along the lines of Canada or Australia, for the time being most metropolitans seemed to consider Algeria to be acceptably French.[122]

French Algeria also appeared to be locked more than ever into its function as an agricultural producer and a consumer of metropolitan manufactures. The idea of a "colonial pact" had influential critics, some of whom aired their views at an imperial economic conference held in 1934–1935.[123] Yet the specter of a "quota" on wine had rallied Euro-Algerians to the customs union that underpinned the territory's acute economic dependence on the metropole. The status quo was equally untroubled by the *statut viticole*. The voice of the smaller producers, many of whom favored measures that bigger producers opposed, such as compulsory uprooting of vines, failed to have a significant bearing on policy.[124] It did not take long for big producers to realize that the laws passed in the 1930s did not strike at their dominance. Rather, the end to new plantations seemed to fix everyone in place. But if the system looked static, beneath the surface Algeria was changing in ways that would begin to show up in the vineyards themselves.

5

Labor Questions

The 1930s (II)

In 1935, Jean Mélia, an administrator and author born in Algiers, published a book in which he worried that "we are at a decisive turning point in our political history in Algeria."[1] Many scholars since then have echoed the idea that the 1930s was a pivotal decade, with certain moments standing out as particularly crucial. The Euro-Algerian sociologist Jacques Berque, for example, writing as colonial Algeria was coming to an end, looked back on the years 1934–1935 as "a watershed, a logical crux."[2] Others have placed more emphasis on 1936, with Charles-Robert Ageron claiming "all historians affirm" that year was "decisive" for Algerians.[3]

The title Mélia chose for his book, *Le triste sort des indigènes musulmans d'Algérie* (The unhappy lot of the indigenous Muslims of Algeria), told a large part of the story. The Depression exacerbated the "unhappy lot" of Algerians and fed anxiety among Euro-Algerians like Mélia about the potential lure of communism or an emergent Muslim Algerian nationalism. The election in 1936 of a leftist government, the Popular Front coalition, then allowed new political forces more space to express themselves. One boldly radical strain was represented by Messali Hadj and his left-wing nationalist movement, the Etoile nord-africaine (North African Star), which had proselytized for a decade among North African migrant workers in France before finally gaining permission from the Popular Front to organize in Algeria.[4] Also radical, though with a different emphasis, were the Islamic reformers of the Association des ulama musulmans algériens (Association of Algerian Muslim Ulama), who introduced into public discourse the idea that Algeria was—or could be—a Muslim nation.[5]

Contrary to what some Euro-Algerians believed, the Popular Front was not trying to kill colonial Algeria. In December 1936, hoping to shore up the support of influential local elites a few months after a Muslim Congress had met in Algiers and formulated an extensive "Charter of Demands," the prime minister Léon Blum and the reformist ex-governor-general Maurice Viollette proposed to extend French citizenship to a select few Algerians without requiring them to give up their personal status as Muslims. The number of individuals likely to be eligible was small—fewer than 25,000 from a Muslim population of more than 6 million—but the hostility of influential Euro-Algerians to the idea made clear that they were not willing to be turned onto a path of assimilationist reform.[6] The Blum-Viollette plan failed, leaving Muslim Algerians and Euro-Algerians to continue what Mahfoud Kaddache has characterized as their "political double life."[7] In many ways the 1930s would come to seem pivotal not so much because of what changed in Algerian politics as because of what didn't. Euro-Algerians had once again revealed their reflexive opposition to reform, but in the long term denying the substance of Algerian political aspirations would not suffice to contain them.[8]

What did these developments mean for workers in Algeria's wine industry? Historians might treat the 1930s as a time of portents, but at the time the future did not look at all clear to either Algerian or Euro-Algerian workers. Vineyard workers, especially Algerians employed for seasonal tasks, knew that the pay they received did not go far toward meeting their needs in a time of economic hardship, and they viewed the spread of new agricultural machinery with a wary eye. Modernization was also causing concern in port cities, where for years Algerian wine had reliably generated work for Euro-Algerians and Algerians alike at docks and in barrel workshops.[9] Experiments with the transportation of wine in specially designed steel containers after 1934 threatened to upend the livelihood of anyone who depended on building, repairing, or handling the much more labor-intensive barrels. That meant workers not only in Algerian ports but also around the docks in French cities like Rouen and Sète. The responses of rural and urban workers to these problems seem to have aimed more often to preserve what felt familiar in wine-related work, rather than push for radical changes in workers' basic conditions.

The picture that emerges from a study of wine-related labor in 1930s Algeria is complex. Efficiency-minded employers were open to innovative production and distribution techniques, but also explored new strategies to stabilize their workforces. The decade saw the first sustained agitation among rural workers from political forces on the radical left, but to some degree also the radical right. At the same time, workers who made a living from the wine industry in urban settings did not appear to give much consideration to the condition of wine workers in the countryside.

This chapter focuses on the three most prominent wine-related labor conflicts of the 1930s. The first of these—the strikes that accompanied the earliest use of "wine tankers" in 1935—involved a mixture of Euro-Algerians and Algerians and took place in an urban environment (though many of the Algerians who took part were likely recent arrivals from the countryside). The participants in the other two conflicts, which involved violence on some large estates in 1936, primarily on the Mitidja plain, and a series of attacks and labor stoppages on vineyards in the department of Oran in 1937, were mostly Algerian agricultural workers, but with some organizational contribution from Euro-Algerian leftists. When set against the background of a developing Muslim nationalist movement, the vineyard conflicts in particular may appear anti-colonial in nature. While the protests may have proved formative for their participants and served as precedents for future action, however, I argue that their immediate intent was to improve conditions for workers, and as such they should not be incorporated uncritically into a narrative of anticolonial resistance.[10] Together, these conflicts suggest that the agricultural capitalism practiced by Algeria's big wine producers was increasingly troubling a fragile social order, and that to view the period in which they occurred as a time of portents is not a serious abuse of hindsight.

TOWARD "WELFARE VITICULTURE"?

In studying a place like colonial Algeria there is a natural temptation to assume that any sort of conflict between rural Algerians and Euro-Algerians was on some level "anti-colonial." The historian who makes that assumption, though, may simply be echoing the hopes of Algerians or the fears of Euro-Algerians from the time that he or she is studying. Rural bandits could acquire the status of anti-French heroes in the eyes of Algerians, regardless of whether they were consciously challenging authority. French officials might treat fires in forested areas as overt acts of resistance, however hard it was to establish the intent (let alone the identity) of suspected arsonists.[11] But attacks that unambiguously targeted colonial authority in rural Algeria between el-Mokrani's failed rebellion of 1871 and the 1930s were in reality rather few. Aside from an insurrection in the south of the department of Constantine in the context of recruitment for the Great War, the event that most obviously qualifies as "anti-colonial" was the quickly suppressed uprising in the small and relatively isolated colonial village of Margueritte in 1901.[12] Alarming though this was to Euro-Algerians, it failed to spark similar outbreaks in other colonial settlements, and the extent of its violence was atypical.

It was certainly true that at particular moments Algerians acted in ways that left Euro-Algerian colonists fearful for their security. The early 1890s was one of those times, as statistics suggest an increase in Algerian attacks on Euro-Algerians or their property. This included, as wine producers around Jemmapes in the department of Constantine complained, the theft of grapes from vineyards.[13] Vignerons around Mostaganem in the West experienced similar problems in the mid-1910s, alleging that armed gangs stole from their vines just before each year's harvest.[14]

Such actions may not qualify as "anti-colonial," whereas certain non-physical forms of opposition probably do. Periodically the authorities would identify among Algerians a kind of millenarian rumormongering that questioned colonialism and predicted the imminent fall of French rule. Around the time of the events in Margueritte, for example, Algerians in the surrounding region reported sightings of a celestial Arab horseman over the Dahra Mountains, and claimed this as a sign that the colonial order was coming to an end. In the same area in 1903 the word went around that the *roumis* (Europeans) would not harvest the grape crop that year. Rumors like these could be unsettling, as the British found in India in the same period, but Algerians had been predicting the ultimate demise of French Algeria from as early as 1830. The 1903 grape harvest, one French observer complacently recorded, was gathered as normal, in spite of what he called "the apostles of Muslim fanaticism."[15]

While the isolated instances of Algerian violence toward settlers attracted a good deal of attention in the Euro-Algerian press, Euro-Algerian violence toward vineyard workers was certainly underreported. A French drive against abuses of power in the 1890s brought one notable case to light. In 1897 the Mitidja vinelord Michel-Louis Pelegri was found guilty of "violence toward and illegal detention of natives," earning him a sentence of six days in jail (suspended) and a 200-franc fine. Investigation revealed that, as mayor of the settler village of Sidi Moussa, Pelegri had been abusing the power he held to issue the permits that migrant Algerians then needed to travel within the colony. Particularly around the time of the grape harvest, he would withhold these permits as a way of intimidating migrant workers who might want to dispute their salaries. Those Algerians who dared to stand up to him often found themselves locked up. The evidence against Pelegri led to his removal from office as mayor. At another time, however, what he had done might well have gone unpunished; according to the governor-general, indeed, he had been behaving this way for several years. Moreover, Euro-Algerian opinion does not seem to have been troubled by Pelegri's conduct: within three months the colonists of Sidi Moussa re-elected him to the local town hall, and his career continued to flourish.[16] In 1909 the popular journal *L'Afrique du Nord illustrée* produced a laudatory profile of Pelegri's viticultural operations, and noted that as well as still serving as mayor he was president of the bank in the nearby town of L'Arba.[17]

Though Pelegri's style of worker management undoubtedly persisted at some vineyards, after the Great War more wine producers explored subtler techniques. These producers' objectives closely matched those of employers in many other places at that time: to secure a stable workforce when labor was in relatively short supply, without simply relying on higher pay to outmaneuver their competitors. One possible solution was offered by what some historians have labeled "welfare capitalism."[18] In metropolitan France, for example, this term might apply to a number of businesses around Marseille in the 1910s and 1920s that sought to minimize the turnover of their predominantly non-French labor force by building worker housing and offering other forms of social support, such as educational facilities for the workers' children.[19] Similar methods were being tried in diverse colonial settings, too, like rubber plantations in British Malaya or copper mines in the Belgian Congo.[20] In tropical environments employers began to take public health especially seriously and looked for ways to reduce employee mortality rates.[21] Even hardened anti-colonialists on rubber estates in southern Vietnam conceded that the material condition of workers improved there from the late 1920s.[22]

In many ways the "welfare capitalism" of the early twentieth century was part of a longer tradition of corporate paternalism (and its associated goal of maintaining control over the workforce). Indeed, one of the agricultural estates considered by some to be among the most progressive in Algeria, the Domaine de Lismara near Tlemcen, was run by descendants of a pioneer of worker housing in France, the Alsatian textile manufacturer Jean Dollfus. In 1853, Dollfus had co-founded a society that not only built houses for workers in the town of Mulhouse but also provided them with facilities like a dispensary and a grocery store.[23] In 1930, a survey of colonization in the department of Oran praised two members of a new generation of Dollfuses, the brothers Jean and Louis, for the organization of their 1,200-hectare estate (and its 250-hectare vineyard):

> This enterprise constitutes a model of rational exploitation as it must be conceived at the present moment, when the scarcity and high cost of labor and the progressive Americanization of the economy oblige us to account for all our operations, to organize production on an industrial plan, and, in short, to rid ourselves of the agricultural producer's habitual negligence, which contact with the Arab tends to reinforce. The Domaine de Lismara offers an example of what one might call financial philanthropy, a system that improves the living conditions of those who work the land in order to increase the yield. A workers' village, with a cooperative bakery and grocery, a school, and a cinema, allows agricultural workers to live the modern life while encouraging them to attach themselves to the domain that they are helping enrich.[24]

To varying degrees—and with varying degrees of enthusiasm—this model was followed by other large estates, becoming especially visible in the late 1920s when parts of Algeria experienced labor supply problems.[25] In the West, the Domaine du Kéroulis broke ground in 1927 for a school for the children of its salaried workers.[26] At Maison-Carrée in the department of Algiers, Father François Clément, the member of the White Fathers who oversaw production at the SIAH's central vineyard, argued that good housing and family benefits were essential to maintaining a stable workforce—a concern made doubly important for him by the fact that many of the vineyard's permanent workers were

FIG. 5.1 Workers of Maltese origin and their children at the Domaine de Daroussa near Bône, late 1920s. Reproduced from the author's collection.

Algerian Christians.[27] In the East, the Société des fermes françaises de Tunisie, which operated a vineyard of over 500 hectares on the plain of Bône, built small but solid homes with tile roofs for some of its year-round workforce, many of them Maltese in origin (see figs. 5.1 and 5.2).[28] The company that ran the nearby Domaine du Chapeau de Gendarme also had the retention of European personnel in mind in 1930 when it replaced its run-down estate housing with brand-new construction. The company evinced much less concern for its nonspecialized Algerian workers, some of whom rented rooms for themselves and their families in the adjacent settlement of Mondovi.[29] Many more Algerian vineyard workers occupied flimsy structures that were not likely to be depicted on any promotional postcards—colonists referred to them as "rabbit hutches" (*niches à lapins*)—or lived in informal villages of tents or *gourbis* (shacks usually constructed from thatch and dried earth).[30] Accommodation therefore made manifest the hierarchy within the vineyard, as different dwellings connoted different degrees of permanence or expendability for the people who worked there.

FIG. 5.2 Housing for workers at the Domaine de Daroussa. The caption on the reverse of the postcard specified that each house was intended for "two Maltese families." Reproduced from the author's collection.

Presiding over these domains were men like Lucien Borgeaud, who offered a large *méchoui* (sheep barbecue) to estate employees at his Domaine de la Trappe at the end of each agricultural year, and Pierre Germain at the Domaine du Kéroulis, who, according to a eulogy after his death in 1933, considered his organization "like a big family."[31] (In the view of critics of the big producers, such gestures and attitudes fit a pattern of "feudal" behavior.[32]) These wine producers' sense of themselves as benevolent employers may have been sincere, but, at the same time, the rationale for the enterprises they ran was not to create as many good-paying jobs as possible. Borgeaud, for example, made extensive use of convict labor at La Trappe.[33] All, too, were interested in the wage-saving possibilities represented by new machines. The SIAH bought one of the first tractors designed for viticultural work (a vehicle that straddled the vines) in 1926, and two years later also owned two tractors manufactured by the American company Deering. An inventory carried out in 1939 revealed that there were 1,334 tractors in the department of Oran alone, with particular concentrations in wine-producing areas.[34]

One could not argue with the benefits such machines offered land-owners, but for those who had to come to depend on agricultural work they seemed an obvious threat. In 1934 a trade-union publication in neighboring Tunisia printed a poem in Arabic with the lines: "A beautiful 'tractor' made by America / Is the cause of our poverty and our ruin."[35] The author was exercising some poetic license in placing so much of the blame on machines, and it is true that many viticultural tasks, from pruning to grape harvesting, were more resistant to mechanization than in other branches of agriculture, such as cereal production. The fear he articulated was nonetheless real and widespread. Ironically, however, the perception that modernization imperiled the ability of workers to make a living wage from wine first led to open conflict not in the countryside, but rather in an urban setting.

"MACHINES OF FAMINE": THE FIRST WINE TANKERS

Wine barrels at the docks were among French Algeria's defining sights (see fig. 5.3). In ports like Algiers, Oran, Mostaganem, and Bône, six-hectoliter-capacity wooden barrels known as *demi-muids* occupied seeming hectares of quayside. More wine for export meant more activity in barrel workshops; the "plantation fever" of the late 1920s, indeed, helped drive an increase in imports of wood to make barrel staves from places like the United States, Russia, Italy, and Romania. Hauling barrels to port was lucrative business for the owners of motorized trucks, which definitively superseded horse-drawn carts after the Great War. And, at the quays, manipulating wine's bulky containers, weighing 750 kilograms (1,653 pounds) when full, meant work for hundreds of men. In 1933, wine accounted for 68 percent of the tonnage of French Algeria's exports, and most of that came in the shape of a barrel.[36]

Just as tractors promised to make agricultural production more efficient, however, new technologies emerged to streamline the transportation of wine. The key innovation was the use of coated steel *citernes*, tanks that could hold wine without harming its composition. Beginning in the 1920s there were already *wagons-citernes* to transport wine by rail and tanker trucks, or *camions-citernes*, for the road. The year 1931 saw the first use of *chalands-citernes*, barge tankers that were soon helping to improve one of the most crucial links in Algerian wine's supply chain,

615 ALGER. — Les quais — Expédition des vins

J. Geiser, phot.-Alger.

FIG. 5.3 Wine barrels at the docks in Algiers, 1916. Reproduced from the author's collection.

along the river Seine between Rouen and Paris.[37] It was only a matter of time before shipping companies began to look at using the same technology for longer journeys. Pumping wine from one tank to the next would reduce labor costs, speed the transportation process, and potentially lower prices to the consumer. Those whose work revolved around barrels, however, were not likely to welcome these new efficiencies.

This proved to be equally true in French ports as in Algerian ones. As we have seen, wine producers in the Midi were generally hostile to the expansion of Algerian viticulture in the 1920s and 1930s, but workers in Sète—the Midi's main port, second only to Rouen as a point of entry for Algerian wine, and a major center of barrel manufacturing—took a different view: for them, wine from elsewhere meant work. That was why dockworkers there reacted so swiftly in March 1934 when a local merchant tried to use a *bateau-citerne*—a wine tanker—to bring 3,500 hectoliters of Tunisian wine to the port. So credible seemed the workers' warnings that they would use "any means" to prevent the ship from unloading that its operator eventually decided to avoid the port altogether.[38] Sète's barrel handlers thus revealed their stake in Algeria's wine industry (as well as

Tunisia's much smaller one), and the fight over the use of wine tankers would unite port workers in France with their counterparts in North Africa.

The battle over wine tankers was only fully joined, however, when a ship named the *Bacchus* berthed in Algiers on January 14, 1935, ready to transport wine for the first time to its receiving port of Rouen. The moment of the ship's arrival in Algiers was less than auspicious. One indicator of the economic downturn the city was experiencing can be taken from its construction sector: in the month the *Bacchus* appeared, only 1,780 workers were actively employed in building projects, compared with nearly 8,000 in 1930.[39] The stream of Algerian migrants to France had decreased significantly in the early 1930s as the Depression began to bite in the metropole, too, but Algeria's cities continued to attract internal migrants hoping to escape hardship in the countryside, and shanty towns had begun to sprout up around Algiers.[40] The docks were an obvious place to seek work, but the supply of labor far exceeded demand. In Oran in February 1935, according to one source, only about 1,000 dockworkers out of 3,500 or 4,000 could find work. At the same time, a soup kitchen for Muslims in the city was serving 400 people a day.[41]

Such conditions help explain why posters around the docks in Algiers in early January 1935 referred to the *Bacchus* as a "machine of famine" and urged workers to rally against it. The threat the ship posed was easy to grasp. Filling its tanks to their combined capacity of 18,000 hectoliters would require the labor of no more than eighteen men for sixteen hours. To load the equivalent amount of wine in barrels—about 3,000 of them—would have employed at least seventy-five men over two days.[42]

The hostility toward the *Bacchus* in Algiers was shared in Rouen, but the protests that developed in the two ports each presented their own characteristics. The dockworkers in Rouen were more fully politicized and unionized than their counterparts in Algiers, but a united response to the *Bacchus* was hampered by factional feuding between partisans of the reform-minded Confédération générale du travail (CGT) and the communist-aligned Confédération générale du travail unitaire (CGTU). A meeting to decide on strategy before the ship first arrived in Rouen degenerated into a noisy bout of name-calling and even a fistfight. The dockworkers in Algiers had their own divisions: for example, the CGT there was almost entirely Euro-Algerian in composition, while Algerians were much less likely to be members of any union. Yet it was the workers in Algiers whose protests proved by far the more effective. This owed much to the organizational ability of three delegates from the dock-workers' union in Sète, who traveled to Algiers in February 1935 ahead of the third voyage of the *Bacchus*. Under their guidance, port workers went on strike—workers in Sète staged a sympathy strike at the same time—and an estimated 2,000 people, perhaps as many as 90 percent of them Algerian, came down to the quays to confront the "machine of famine" itself. Some of the demonstrators split open wine barrels or rolled them into the water, while a few succeeded in getting past police to the side of the ship, where they cut the pumps through which wine was flowing from tanker trucks into the *Bacchus*'s special steel containers.[43]

Though the organizers from Sète do not appear to have planned the violence, it had an effect: by the time the ship finally reached Rouen, the wine-trading house Nicolas had already committed to no longer make use of wine tankers for any of its imports.[44] At the same time, interested politicians were doing what they could to assist the movement. Lucien Salette, a deputy in the National Assembly from Sète, helped publicize the fact that the company that owned the *Bacchus*, the Société d'armement fluvial et maritime (known as SOFLUMAR), was a French offshoot of the Rotterdam-based shipping firm Van Ommeren, and that two-thirds of its shares were in Dutch hands. If the ship did not already seem threatening enough, it was now associated with foreign capital.[45] And, in June 1935, with the port at Algiers shut down for six days by another strike as the *Bacchus* prepared for its fourth voyage, it was another politician from Sète, Mario Roustan, senator for the Hérault, who took advantage of a brief spell as minister of the merchant marine to help bring the conflict to an end. The companies that owned and operated the *Bacchus* announced that they would lay up the ship indefinitely, leaving protesters in Algiers, Rouen, Sète, and other ports to return to the quays and their barrel workshops in triumph.[46]

Throughout this protest, the workers had enjoyed the sympathy of some who would ordinarily have been on the side of entrepreneurial innovation: the chambers of commerce in Sète, Algiers, and (less strongly) Rouen all stated the view that the wine tanker was a good idea that had arrived at a bad moment, and that their use should be delayed until the economy improved. (The chamber in Marseille, hoping that *bateaux-citernes* might help their city capture business from rival ports that were better set up for barrel traffic, dissented.)[47] But even some of the workers' strongest defenders sensed that any success was likely to be temporary. A motion from the municipal council in the Algiers suburb of Hussein-Dey, home to many barrel workshops, cautioned that "the *bateau-citerne* will have the last word."[48] It would take no more than a decade or so for that prediction to come true.

Though the wine-tanker protests of 1935, probably the biggest industrial conflict in Algeria in that year, felt very necessary to their participants— the majority of them Algerian, as the police who monitored meetings and demonstrations observed—in some ways they also look like a (tacit) defense of the prevailing order. One of the delegates from Sète who came to Algiers to help organize the movement, François Cavallier, condemned the *bateau-citerne* as part of a "vast plan" of capitalist exploitation.[49] But, in practice, the protesters trained their hostility quite narrowly on the capitalism of the ship owners and operators; the movement never discussed the wine industry as a whole, or the place of agricultural workers within it. The port labor stoppages were of the type Leon Trotsky termed "defensive strikes," aimed at protecting a living wage.[50] They did not in any way challenge the agricultural colonialism that defined French Algeria and structured its economic relations with the metropole. Rather than offering clear portents of class or nationalist struggles to come, the wine-tanker protests do more to illustrate a kind of social ferment stoked by hardship and demographic trends. Soon that ferment would begin to manifest itself in the vineyards.

POLITICIZING THE AGRICULTURAL WORKER

The number of attendees at the rallies held in June 1933 to defend the free movement of wine to the metropole would not have been so large without Algerian participation. In recognition of that fact, and to support an appearance of French Algerian unity, the Euro-Algerian organizers of these demonstrations typically allotted a few minutes at the podium to an Algerian notable who claimed to represent the "Algerian" point of view. In Oran it was the Bachagha Abdelkader Benchiha, a major landowner (and wine producer) in the Aïn-Témouchent region as well as a member of the department's chamber of agriculture, who took the occasion to back the protests on behalf of "indigenous Algerians," ever grateful to France for "the inestimable benefits of her genius and her civilization."[51] In Bône in the same month it was Mahmoud Benyacoub, an Algerian representative to the Délégations financières, who proclaimed that the *"indigènes"* formed a "steadfast bloc" of support against any measures to treat Algeria separately from the metropole, and favored remaining part of "maternal, strong, and just France."[52]

For the Algerians in the crowd, Benyacoub's high-flown allusions to the Declaration of the Rights of Man presumably resonated much less than his statement that "viticulture gives work to 500,000 of our working families and we want to safeguard their salaries." (His estimate was probably too high; other sources put the number of agricultural workers earning from the vine in the 1930s somewhere between 250,000 and 350,000.[53]) What attendees did not hear at these mixed meetings was the kind of anguish voiced in 1932 by a group of Algerian agricultural workers in the Mascara region, who after the end of the growing year complained to a newspaper of the "starvation salaries that millionaire *viticulteurs* paid us," and added—in language reminiscent of that used by Mohamed ben el-Hadj Ahmed Yacoub, the leader of the 1901 Margueritte uprising—"What do you want a worker who often has to support a large family to do?"[54]

This crystallized a central problem. Between 1921 and 1936 the Algerian Muslim population increased by about a quarter, to 6.2 million. (The increase in the number of Euro-Algerians across the same span of time was less than 12 percent, to around 950,000.)[55] Just as the surplus of births over deaths progressively widened, however, by the early 1930s rural salaries were entering a period of volatility. A study of the western part of Oran noted that between 1931 and 1932, agricultural workers' daily pay slumped by anything between a quarter and a half.[56] The downward trend had first appeared in cereal-growing areas, but, as the workers' letter from Mascara illustrates, it was soon evident in wine-producing regions as well.

This was the same time that the wine lobby in the Midi was needling producers in Algeria about the low salaries they paid their workers, especially in comparison to those offered in France. French Algeria's own lobby defended itself against the accusation that this gave its wines an unfair advantage on the metropolitan market by pointing to the cost of shipping and other charges they had to cover to bring their product to the French consumer. But their defense on the question of the salaries they paid often seemed to boil down to the claim that Algerian workers got what they deserved.[57] Any sense of accumulating economic hardship in the countryside was hard to discern in the pages of a prominent Euro-Algerian newspaper like *L'Echo d'Alger*, owned by the wealthy grain miller, vineyard owner, and senator for Algiers Jacques Duroux. In the Senate in 1935, in fact, Duroux suggested with blithe assurance that the population increase was a measure of the "general well-being" that France had developed in Algeria.[58] Early the next year, though, albeit buried in a periodic agricultural report, even his newspaper had to acknowledge that rural salaries had "cruelly" descended.[59]

For some of the political forces at work in the 1930s, this represented an opportunity. In metropolitan France during the Depression, an unprecedented array of political groups competed for peasant support. The success in some rural parts of France of two of the more radical options—the far-right "Greenshirts" of Henri Dorgères at one end of the spectrum, and the communists at the other—can perhaps be explained as a consequence of what Laird Boswell has described as the French state's "immobility and lack of interest in rural areas."[60] Though one cannot exactly argue that Algeria's government-general showed a lack of interest in rural areas, leaders of the same two radical movements were hopeful they could make some inroads among peasants and agricultural workers in the colony, too.

The Front paysan (FP, Peasant Front) burst into life in Algeria's three departments in the summer of 1935. The movement was inspired by, but not directly affiliated with, Dorgères's "committees of peasant defense" in the metropole, which were loudly hostile to the Third Republic (and its taxes), pro-authoritarian and corporatist in ideology, and found particular support in parts of the North and West of France.[61] In Algeria, the movement took a similar anti-government message into rural communities suffering the sting of price decreases for agricultural commodities. Bankruptcy sales offered one opportunity to confront allegedly rapacious authority. On one occasion, for example, thirty landowners in the Aïn-Témouchent region showed up at the public auction of the grape crop from a thirty-two-hectare vineyard belonging to a widow, Madame Valero; it may have been their intimidating presence that discouraged anyone from bidding.[62] Among the favorite targets of FP orators were Jewish millers or traders in agricultural commodities, who they portrayed as "complicit" with hated government officials.[63]

This openly anti-Semitic movement also made some effort to cultivate the sympathies of rural Algerians. The FP's founder and leader, Marcel Pitollet, asserted that the "native question" in Algeria was first and foremost a question of "native destitution."[64] It is not clear how many Algerians paid the twelve-franc membership fee to join the FP, but a good number seem to have been curious about this group that spoke so boldly about rural misery, and Algerians often represented up to half of the audience at the FP's meetings. In September 1935, in the town of Saint-Denis du Sig, to the north of Mascara, an estimated 250 Algerians (in a crowd of 600) heard the FP's most vitriolic speaker, René Alibert, denounce French parliamentarians as "cowards, thieves, cretins," then condemn the taxes Algerians had to pay. "The day will come," Alibert warned, "when the *indigènes*, no longer able to pay or eat, will revolt."[65]

It should be stressed that this was not a prophecy that the virulently pro-French-Algerian FP wanted to see come true, but in any case the movement lost impetus almost as quickly as it had begun. The group's inability to rally significant numbers of wine producers probably contributed to its failure in Algeria.[66] The dominance of big producers in Algeria potentially left some room for the insurgent FP, but the leagues of small and medium wine producers that began to appear in 1932 were openly suspicious of the group and its rabble-rousing methods, including the idea of involving Algerians in anti-government protest.[67] Nor did the FP gain much traction by stirring up fear that parliament would enact compulsory uprooting of recently planted vines. In one speech in September 1935, Pitollet imagined confronting government agents "with gunshots at our vineyard," but this seemed overwrought given that the authorities had just instituted a policy of voluntary and compensated uprooting.[68] (The leagues of small and medium growers, for their part, were actually in favor of forcing big producers to uproot vines without compensation.[69]) Finally, there was the problem of what the FP's spiritual leader in the metropole, Dorgères, thought about the Midi-Algeria wine rivalry. For months Dorgères's position on the topic remained unclear, but when he went to Montpellier in November 1935 and announced his support for the Midi vignerons, it was hard for the FP leadership to find a positive gloss.[70] Several key members quit the organization, and the movement, which had managed to attract perhaps 12,000 adherents in the second half of 1935, soon fizzled.[71]

It was with much greater stealth that communists announced themselves in the Algerian countryside. This was partly a consequence of their initial instinct to concentrate on workers in urban settings; partly a function of the practical difficulty of organizing in rural locations; and partly a result of the repression periodically carried out by the authorities, with particular force around the time of the centenary of French Algeria in 1930. By the end of that year, the few communists who remained active in Algeria frequently divided among themselves (or with metropolitan communists) over questions of strategy, and several of the leading figures in the movement had already experienced jail or exile.[72]

When communists in Algeria began to pay more attention to the countryside in the early 1930s, they attracted some of the same curiosity that later drew Algerians to the Front paysan's meetings, but with an edge provided by their promise of fundamental change and their denunciations of colonial injustice. A dawning sense of colonial injustice, indeed, was central to the radicalization of Euro-Algerians as well as Algerians who found their way to the communist movement. Nicolas Zannettacci, the son of poor colonists from Corsica in the department of Constantine, never forgot how, as a young boy, he heard a *colon* casually discuss finding two Algerians in his vineyard and imprisoning them in his wine cellar, where they died from asphyxiation. (Zannettacci grew up to be a perennial leading light in the communist movement in Algeria; he himself was imprisoned around the time of the centenary.)[73] For Ali Mira, who would play a key role in organizing agricultural workers in the 1930s, a pivotal moment came when he was employed as a clerk in a notary's office and learned about some of the practices used by colonists in their expropriation of land from Algerians.[74]

Mira's hometown of Blida, in fact, served as one of the anchor points for an attempt to spread communist influence among Algerian peasants on the Mitidja plain in 1932 and 1933. The campaign focused especially on peasant grievances over expropriation, and worried the authorities enough that activists in turn began to fear the possibility of a new wave of repression. That did not deter the leader of the French Communist Party, Maurice Thorez, who had recently stated that Algeria was ready for an "anti-imperialist and agrarian revolution," from visiting the Mitidja in May 1933. Outside the town hall at L'Arba—true vinelord territory—Thorez told about 200 Algerians that his visit had helped him to understand their plight better, and promised to speak up for rural workers back in parliament.[75] He stayed true to his word. Returning to Paris in time for the debates about whether to impose a quota on Algerian wine, Thorez took the opportunity to demand that vineyard workers in Algeria should receive the same salaries and union rights as those in the metropole.[76]

The communists' official policy at that moment was resolutely hostile to collaboration with other leftists. The party's section in Oran, for example, mocked socialists for taking part in the demonstrations against a possible wine quota, arguing that the low salaries colonists paid their workers was the most important problem and predicting that the "*crise viticole*" would eventually "get worked out between the metropolitan and Algerian producers of cheap wine on the backs of the peasant masses on both shores [of the Mediterranean]."[77] But this uncompromising stance relaxed as the threat of fascism in Europe drew parties of the left into joint action. In May 1935, communists presented themselves for election to municipal office in Algeria as part of the new Popular Front coalition.[78]

By 1936 the communists' presence in the Algerian countryside remained fragile and highly localized, while on the political right support for the erratic and unstable Front paysan had already crested. Yet, in concentrating on problems particular to the countryside, both movements had helped spread an insurgent mood among some rural Algerians. To this picture must be added other political developments, like the statement issued by the association of ulama in April 1936 that "the Algerian Muslim nation . . . is not France."[79] All of this made 1936 a turbulent summer.

VIOLENCE IN THE VINES

In June 1936, a thirty-one-year-old colonist named Charles Jauvion went on trial for murder. Jauvion told the court that in August the previous year he had found four Algerians gathering grapes on his property at Voltaire, about 150 kilometers southwest of Algiers. He shouted at them to stop, he said, but they ran away, so Jauvion fired what he claimed he intended to be a warning shot in their direction. Instead, a bullet hit one of the four in the head and killed him. An Algerian witness told the court that he had seen only one person cross Jauvion's property, not to steal but to access a water source; but a rural policeman said footprints around the vines backed up the claim that "several *indigènes*" had been there. A jury made up of Jauvion's citizen peers spent very little time deliberating before deciding to acquit.[80]

Stories like this were not uncommon in Algeria, though usually it was vineyard guards who fired the shots and ended up in the *faits divers* of the newspaper.[81] If the violence of this event was unexceptional, however, the trial took place at an exceptional time. The French general election of May 1936 brought the anti-fascist Popular Front coalition of radical republicans, socialists, and communists to power. The prospect of working with a government more amenable to colonial reform prompted Algerian political figures to think about cooperating with each other in new ways. Prominent ulama led by Abdelhamid Ben Badis joined forces with the reformist notables of the Fédération des élus, headed by Dr. Mohamed Salah Bendjelloul, who pursued the goal of greater assimilation to France as a path to equality for Algerians. Out of this collaboration emerged the Muslim Congress, which met for the first time in Algiers in early June.[82] In addition to these political developments, however, the election of the Popular Front touched off large-scale activity among workers. A massive strike wave in metropolitan France involved up to two million.[83] Similar activity in Algeria mobilized tens of thousands.[84]

These labor conflicts in Algeria, just as in the metropole, were initially concentrated largely in towns and cities. Among those striking for higher pay and better conditions, indeed, were urban employees in trades associated with the wine industry: barrel workers, *cavistes* in the wine storehouses near the docks, cork-factory workers. (The bottle-cork factory owned by Alfred Borgeaud just outside Algiers was among those affected.)[85] The *Echo d'Alger* reported these urban conflicts, which involved substantial numbers of Euro-Algerians, without evident alarm; the newspaper's owner Jacques Duroux, after all, identified with the republican Radical Party, and the paper had (albeit hesitantly) pronounced in favor of the Popular Front. (The more conservative *Dépêche algérienne* was strongly opposed from the start.)[86] But the disturbances that began to occur on farms and vineyards in early June represented something that seemed new and potentially very threatening to the colonial order. Euro-

Algerians may have accepted the violence that colonists like Charles Jauvion were ready to use as part of the fabric of life in rural French Algeria, but armed Algerian agricultural workers were an entirely different matter.

Some of the few historians who have written about these rural conflicts have labeled them "anti-colonialist," implying that they were opposed to the colonial system as a whole.[87] Though that description surely fits the views of some of the participants, I would argue that it is more accurate to see the protests in general as "anti-colonist," meaning opposed to specific employers and their practices. The fact that parts of rural France saw similar worker-employer confrontations at the same time is one reason to view the disturbances in Algeria primarily as a challenge to agricultural capitalism. If one also incorporates a study of vineyard conflicts in 1937 alongside those of 1936, one finds a varied series of events whose common denominator was an intense fear among rural Algerians about their ability to make a living. In that sense, the events do not seem so different from those brought on by the appearance of the *Bacchus* in 1935.

1936

On June 13, 1936, at a time of year normally marked by the cereal harvest and the treatment of vines with copper sulfate, a group of Euro-Algerian landowners met at the town hall in Sidi Moussa in the central Mitidja to discuss a troubling series of events. Bands of men armed with sticks had been entering private agricultural properties and telling employees to stop working under threat of violence. One attack that very morning had been repelled with gunfire. The colonists telegrammed the prefect of Algiers to demand immediate strong security for their properties and those who worked on them, adding that they would not be held responsible if they felt the need to take "grave" measures in their defense.[88]

The prefect, Charles Bourrat, did not hesitate to take action. With other communities in the vicinity of Algiers experiencing similar problems, Bourrat authorized the formation of a rapid-reaction force of thirty platoons of *gardes mobiles* (riot police) who would head to trouble spots as quickly as possible by motorcycle and sidecar. He also sent reinforcements from the city to back up gendarme brigades in the rural interior.[89] Algiers' policing of the conflict over wine tankers in the previous year had in some ways been relatively light; in Rouen the riot police were deployed at the first arrival of the *Bacchus,* but in Algiers not until its fourth voyage.[90] In 1936, however, there was a strong sense among the forces of order that one could no longer run the risk of underpolicing, not only because of the threat of insurgency but also because one could not be sure what colonists might do if they did not feel protected.[91]

Confrontations like those at Sidi Moussa occurred at estates across the Mitidja and a few in the Sahel of Algiers, affecting several of the vinelords we have encountered. Groups of young men, often carrying vine stakes or heavy sticks, were arrested at Lucien Borgeaud's Domaine de la Trappe and at a large vineyard in Birkadem operated by a Germain-family-controlled company. Trouble also reached Rouïba in the eastern Mitidja, where Jacques Duroux had a 600-hectare vineyard, just as the senator himself was meeting with the governor-general in Paris to discuss the unfolding situation. But there were also fifteen arrests at Fort-de-l'Eau, where most of the properties were much smaller in scale.[92]

Amid the turmoil came appeals for order from Algerian notables like Dr. Bendjelloul, president of the new Muslim Congress, who tried to assure agricultural workers that he would promote their interests. A similar call came from Ahmed Si Salah, president of the Kabyle section at the Délégations financières, who urged faith in the Popular Front government and warned Algerians not to follow "bad shepherds."[93] Precisely who the "shepherds" were—or the extent to which the events were being directed at all—is hard to pin down. Prefect Bourrat believed the fault lay with a group of Kabyles returning from the metropole, while the arrest of a militant trade unionist belonging to the CGT at the Germain property in Birkadem provided some support for the theories of Euro-Algerians who blamed communist agitators.[94] But overall responsibility was not established with any more certainty than a vague allegation that "elements foreign to the agricultural profession," as the colonists of Sidi Moussa put it, were providing the muscle in the confrontations. The clearest thing, as the incidents became less frequent after about a week of agitation, was that they had injected new urgency into discussion of the problem of agricultural salaries. Within days there was a heated debate on that topic in a session of the Délégations financières, during which an Algerian delegate, Dr. Abdennour Tamzali, accused a Euro-Algerian delegate of representing the interests of no more than "sixty big landowners."[95]

As unprecedented as all of this appeared to inhabitants of French Algeria, it is important to set the events in a broader context. Beginning in May, metropolitan France had entered a period of significant and sustained rural unrest that would see thousands of agricultural workers go out on strike. Concentrated in areas where agricultural capitalism was at its strongest—notably the region around Paris and other parts of northern France—the rural strike wave's targets were often large-scale producers of wheat and sugar beet. Like Euro-Algerian colonists, these producers blamed outsiders for instigating trouble, and they were similarly unnerved: Gordon Wright goes so far as to argue that the strikes "produced a kind of small-scale repetition of the Great Fear of 1789."[96] The question of how far the rural strikes in the metropole were either "spontaneous" or sparked by outside agitators is as difficult to resolve for the metropole as it is for Algeria, but it is clear that in at least some locations in France communist organizers actively participated, while they also supported a drive for rural workers to join agricultural federations affiliated to the CGT.[97] Across the Mediterranean, likewise, we find activists like the communist Ali Mira from Blida urging Algerian agricultural workers to unionize; on July 3, for example, 300 came to hear him speak at Marengo in the western Mitidja.[98] If the fears of Euro-Algerian agricultural producers resembled those of metropolitan agro-capitalists, it was because they faced some very similar circumstances.

The so-called Matignon Accords of June 1936, the Popular Front's signature achievement for workers—prescribing higher salaries and regulating union rights, and supplemented by legislation mandating the forty-hour working week—did not apply to agricultural labor.[99] That anomaly provided the context for further rural conflict in France as the summer progressed, and proved difficult to resolve. Yet Blum's government was serious about improving conditions for agricultural workers, including those in Algeria. By July the minister for agriculture, Georges Monnet, was already pushing prefects in Algeria to find ways to help agricultural employers and workers make collective agreements about salary levels.[100] A facilitating structure was set in place by decree at the beginning of August. Algeria's departments were divided into different agricultural regions, in each of which a commission composed of representatives of agricultural employers and workers as well as administrative officials would meet to agree on minimum salaries for particular jobs.[101]

The grape harvest of 1936 provided an early test of this new structure. Just before the *vendange* was due to start in the region around Oran, local leaders of the CGT, such as Nicolas Zannettacci, joined by representatives of the department's federation of agricultural workers, revealed their salary demands for the cutters and porters and others who would soon be needed in large numbers in the vineyards. When the salary commission met soon afterward, it recommended a 40 percent increase on the average salaries of the previous year—very close to what the workers' representatives had proposed before the talks began.[102] In areas where union organization was less strong than in the Oran region, however, salary commissions set the minimums at less robust levels. The Médéa region in the department of Algiers, for example, was known for a better quality of wine—some liked to call it Algeria's Burgundy—but male cutters at the *vendange* of 1936 could expect only 5 francs 40 for a day's work, while women, who, along with under-sixteens, were categorized as "workers of reduced capacity," would get just half of that amount.[103] At that time the price of a kilo (2.2 pounds) of bread was 2 francs 15, and a kilo of couscous about half a franc more than that.[104]

In view of the disturbances earlier in the year, many Euro-Algerians feared trouble at the *vendange,* and security forces—including regular troops—were on high alert. Ultimately, the period passed with few notable incidents.[105] Though the fixing of salaries in advance was very likely one of the reasons that spared Euro-Algerians serious conflict, some producers still chose to show their disdain for the new system by underpaying the minimums that had been set by administrative decree. In the Mascara region, for example, an act of coordinated disobedience by vineyard owners landed dozens in court for underpaying workers at the *vendange*. One offender, Jacques Manuel, who owned a seventy-hectare vineyard, was assessed seventy-five separate fines. Each of the plaintiffs received five francs in damages, but most had still not received the balance for their work in the vines.[106] These employers' unwillingness to pay helped set the tone for further conflict in the following year.

1937

On April 1, 1937, three colonists in Bellevue, not far inland from Mostaganem, woke to find that hundreds of vines on their properties had been cut down in the night. Over the following six weeks or so, many more colonists in the same region would experience the same unwelcome surprise. Some of the attackers used sticks or their hands to do the damage; others, as on the 180-hectare vineyard of the mayor of Aïn-Tédélès, Gabriel Bonfils, severed the vines neatly with pruning shears. In the vineyard of another mayor, Alphonse Sabrié in Pont-du-Chéliff, entire rows were down.[107] The Mostaganem region, as we have seen, was not unfamiliar with the theft of grapes around harvest time. But this was not the time of the *vendange,* so the attacks could not be put down to mere banditry.

Investigators struggled to identify the agents of these actions, though the imprint of shoes as well as espadrilles in the soil, as in the Sabrié vineyard, led them to speculate that the attackers came from the outside but were guided by insiders who knew the property.[108] That interpretation fit the view of Euro-Algerians about who was to blame for the confrontations that occurred at many vineyards in the department of Oran that April and May: it had to be the work of "Stalin's lackeys" (*les valets de Staline*), as a writer in the newspaper *Oran-Matin* put it, who were taking advantage of "the complicity or the weakness of our rulers" to spread disorder among rural Algerians in ways that menaced the colony's very future.[109]

There is enough evidence to suggest that communists did have a hand in at least some of the disturbances, and moreover that they hoped to build support from them. But there was a lot more to these events than the claim that they were all caused by maleficent "outsiders," as two examples make clear.

The deadliest encounter took place at a medium-sized vineyard at Les Abdellys, near Tlemcen. Agricultural workers at two farms in the community stopped work early in the morning of April 12, demanding higher salaries. A crowd of Algerian workers, some carrying heavy sticks (*matraques*), then proceeded to the nearby vineyard of René Alvernhe, the president of the local *cave coopérative.* In the fracas that ensued, Alvernhe shot one of the protesters in the stomach and killed him. Several of Alvernhe's workers were hurt, too; one of them, Abdelkader Belahcene, sustained a fractured skull from which he later died in hospital.[110] Belahcene's funeral three days later provided the second act to this drama. Police estimated that a thousand people followed the cortège around the streets of Tlemcen before a succession of speakers at the cemetery—among them the leader of the local branch of the Algerian

Communist Party, Mohamed Badsi—condemned the tactics of "colonists who refuse workers their due and thereby foil the efforts of the government." Greatly disturbed by these events was a pillar of Tlemcen's Euro-Algerian establishment, Léon Havard, whose father, Onésime, had identified Algeria's first case of phylloxera there five decades earlier. Havard claimed that agitators had gone around the *cafés maures* in town urging patrons to come and watch the funeral of a Muslim "assassinated by a colonist," even though Belahcene had not wanted to strike and was clubbed by a protester, not the vineyard owner, Alvernhe.[111]

Another series of confrontations, around the village of Bellecôte near Mostaganem, began in the same month with a similar charge of insufficient payment, but eventually revealed an additional grievance. A group of union members in the area, some of them armed, encouraged workers at three estates to stop working on April 2, and emphasized their point by detaching the sulfur sprayers the workers had been using to treat the vines. The estate workers stayed out for over two weeks, backed by the local chapter of the CGT, which at one point delivered a truckload of semolina as relief for the strikers and their families. But official inquiries found a particular complaint to be the use of *main-d'oeuvre étrangère*, or "foreign" labor—a term applied loosely, it would seem, not only to Moroccans but also to migrants from other parts of Algeria. On one of the striking estates in Bellecôte an investigation by the gendarmerie identified 40 of its 140 workers as "Sahraoui"—"Saharans," who had come in search of work from southern Algeria (and perhaps southern Morocco as well).[112]

Agricultural employers' strategic use of migrant workers to depress wages was something the CGT and communists condemned. When issuing their demands for vineyard workers' salaries back in August 1936, indeed, the CGT's officers in Oran had stated very clearly—in capital letters—that "PRIORITY MUST BE GIVEN TO THE LOCAL WORKFORCE."[113] A few days later, local people came to two estates close to Mostaganem and attacked Algerian migrants who had traveled from an inland region for the *vendange*. In one case a group of workers were beaten as they lay sleeping on a threshing floor.[114] Though there is no proof that these attacks were inspired by anything anyone from the CGT had said—and perhaps there was no connection—they foreshadowed what many migrant workers went through in the department of Oran in 1937. In that year Moroccans bore the brunt. At Gaston-

Doumergue, local people pelted Moroccan migrants with stones; around Aïn-Témouchent and Aïn-Kial and out to Laferrière, where subsequent inquiries strongly suggested some degree of CGT coordination, over 500 people marched to demand (as a police report put it) "the expulsion of Moroccan workers and work for themselves"; at a large vineyard in Saint-Maur, two dozen Moroccans were lured out of their temporary lodgings and beaten.[115]

As in 1936, there were parallels here to events in the metropole, as well as some differences. In France, in contrast to Algeria, some immigrant agricultural workers—especially Poles—played prominent roles in the strikes of 1936 and 1937. Many French-born workers nonetheless believed that nonunionized outsiders undermined their cause, and, as John Bulaitis has noted, opposition increased as the promise of the Popular Front began to fade. In the spring of 1937, protests took place against immigration at several hiring fairs.[116]

It is not hard to see why this kind of suspicion existed in either place. During one of the highest-profile agricultural confrontations in the Paris region in 1936, at Tremblay-lès-Gonesse, employers had tried to break a strike using what a report called "mainly African" labor.[117] (The report did not specify whether these were North Africans, though this seems likely.) In the previous year, and in a different setting, 150 Moroccan workers had been brought to the port of Algiers to load and unload cargo during one of the strikes against the *Bacchus*.[118] Sometimes the estate guards who were so quick to use their shotguns were Moroccan. The rough treatment of Moroccan migrants in parts of rural Algeria in 1937 in some ways brought out resentments that went back decades.[119]

The migrants themselves, however, did not see themselves as tools of employers. Rather, the journeys they made from French or Spanish Morocco to the estates of Algeria were driven more by necessity than by choice. A series of droughts and poor harvests in eastern and southern Morocco culminated in severe food shortages in 1937. In May of that year Governor-General Georges Le Beau identified this hardship as the main cause of what he called the "overabundance" of migrant labor in the department of Oran. But Le Beau could not ignore the social impact this was having on the territory under his control.[120] In August, with the grape harvest getting under way, further confrontations—one of them at the Domaine du Kéroulis—prompted Le Beau to do something that members of the CGT in Oran had also been calling for: close the border to any new entries from Morocco.[121] For the local CGT this perhaps represented a small victory against colonial capitalism. To colonists it represented little more than a minor inconvenience.

MOUTHS TO FEED

The events of the years 1936 and 1937 had forced Euro-Algerians in the countryside to envisage some disturbing possibilities. In 1936 colonists had even been issued instructions on how to communicate distress to aerial surveillance patrols. White sheets draped on the roof would mean "occupants of the farm consider themselves in danger and request help"; a triangle of three small fires in the main courtyard would signal "occupants of the farm in danger and request immediate intervention."[122] It is not clear that anyone put these signals to use in that year, but colonists did see and hear much to make the scenarios possible to imagine. The manager of an estate near Mostaganem was told by a protester, "You are the owners here, but soon we will chase you out and the Arabs will be the owners of your lands." At the funeral of Abdelkader Belahcene in Tlemcen, a speaker at the cemetery urged Algerians to seek "the restitution of your lands, stolen by the French."[123] I have argued that the rural disturbances of 1936 and 1937 are best seen as labor disputes; they opposed colonists' employment practices, but did not directly challenge the colonial system. Colonists, though, could easily see what they might portend.

While Euro-Algerians in 1936 and 1937 tended to blame violence amid the vines on ill-intentioned "outsiders," much of the violence ended up being directed not at them, but rather toward the "outsiders" they so often employed. That seems to have come about in part through the role of communists and union organizers, who prioritized the protection of "local" labor. In joining the Popular Front, the communists had adopted a policy of national defense to counteract the radical right, and at the same time the party officially retreated from the anti-colonial views it had until recently promoted. The rural disturbances of 1936 and 1937 barely concealed the ongoing anti-colonial instincts of communists in Algeria; the party line was one thing, but, as Allison Drew has pointed out, it was constantly contested by communists on the ground.[124] Even so, there was something incongruous about how this movement ended up targeting another group of colonial subjects who were failing to thrive under French (or Spanish) colonialism in a neighboring territory. The intent was to hurt colonial capitalists, but it was impoverished outsiders who suffered the most painful blows.

Just as France in 1938 saw the "bosses' revenge," as the Popular Front failed and its gains began to be rolled back, in the same year it seemed clear that the colonists in Algeria had regained full confidence and control.[125] Politically, many Euro-Algerians were convinced that the Blum-Viollette bill, in raising the prospect of electoral rights for some Algerians, had helped to spread a "pernicious spirit" among them.[126] Faced with implacable opposition from Euro-Algerian interests, the bill finally died in the Senate in 1938.[127] Economically, representatives of agricultural workers appeared to have lost the bargaining power they had wielded on salary commissions in 1936. The salary commission for the Tlemcen region that met in September 1938, for example, featured two men who had taken very different positions on the funeral of Abdelkader Belahcene the previous year—the communist Mohamed Badsi and the colonist Léon Havard. This time Havard and the employers won the day, blocking any increase in agricultural salaries.[128] Meanwhile, Badsi continued to accuse colonists of maneuvering to employ migrant workers on the cheap. With the border re-opened in 1938, Moroccans now entered on a quota system. But the rules for employers, like the border checkpoints themselves, did not seem difficult to get around.[129]

In the late 1930s, too, colonists continued to invest in "labor-saving" machines.[130] Once again, the impact of machines was not only felt in the countryside. In 1939 a new and even bigger wine tanker called the *Sahel* appeared in Algiers, igniting a new round of strikes. Barrel workers seemed to recognize that the fate of their industry now hung in the balance; one striking employee in a barrel workshop in Hussein-Dey, Vincent Nacher, characterized the conflict with wine tankers as "a matter of life or death."[131] Only France's declaration of war on Germany in September 1939 stayed the execution.

Some of the underlying trends in Algeria troubled those who oversaw its economy. In typically paternalistic language Governor-General Le Beau observed in 1939, "Each year I have 130,000 more mouths to feed in a country where we already have difficulty employing everyone."[132] For now, though, the colonists—and the *gros colons* in particular—still looked in charge.

· 6 ·

Wine in the Wars
1940 to 1962

Wine was one of the reasons Edouard Barthe felt optimistic when France declared war on Germany in September 1939. As French troops awaited a possible German offensive and winter approached, Barthe, the *député du vin* who had done so much to shape the *statut viticole* earlier in the decade, helped organize a campaign to fortify the soldiers at the Maginot Line with mulled wine. In the Chamber of Deputies he proclaimed that wine, "the pride of France, is a symbol of strength; it is associated with warlike virtues."[1] Just as in World War I, Barthe believed that *le pinard* would help the French prevail against beer-drinking Germans.

A few months later, this socialist defender of the Republic was trying to adjust to some unpalatable new realities. In the summer of 1940, Barthe wrote a series of letters to Marshal Philippe Pétain, the man to whom—against his better judgment—he had recently voted to grant full powers as head of the French state. Urging Pétain to take account of the plight of winegrowers after France's shocking defeat, Barthe pointed out that the biggest areas of production lay in the part of France left unoccupied by the Germans—especially Barthe's own Midi—and in Algeria, whose governor-general now reported to Pétain in Vichy. The biggest centers of consumption, however, lay in what was now German-occupied territory, and the obstacles to distributing the forthcoming harvest looked daunting indeed. In this new situation Barthe encouraged Pétain to negotiate to allow wine rations to be sent to French prisoners of war in Germany (among whom were some of the 215,000 men who had been mobilized in Algeria). But as Barthe failed to receive a response to his letters, he must have reflected on how quickly his influence had evaporated.[2]

The shock of France's defeat in 1940 was felt no less strongly in Algeria. Many Euro-Algerians seemed nonetheless to draw satisfaction from the demise of the Third Republic, however instrumental it had been in securing and underwriting their well-being over the preceding decades. The *Echo d'Alger,* which only four years earlier had endorsed the Popular Front and its defense of the Republic, now embraced Marshal Pétain and his authoritarian regime's promise of "regeneration."[3] The salary commissions that employers so disliked stopped convening, and antagonistic advocates for agricultural labor like the Tlemcen communist Mohamed Badsi were interned.[4] At Maison-Carrée in 1941, end-of-year celebrations held by the company that operated the vineyards first established by Archbishop Lavigerie were marked with a popular new song of praise: "Maréchal, nous voilà."[5]

There was a feeling, in short, that what Pétain was offering would restore some things to the way they should be, particularly in terms of controlling Algerians. But while certain ideological features of the Vichy regime held some appeal for Euro-Algerians, the economics of the war years were barely workable for export-dependent Algeria. Martin Thomas has observed that economic disruption to the empire during World War II often bore political consequences down the line, and this was certainly true in Algeria.[6] A focus on the wine industry illustrates how wartime hardship among Algerians fed postwar turbulence. The years from 1945 to 1954, in fact, would turn out to form their own "interwar" period that echoed aspects of the 1920s and 1930s, but during which labor protests became ever more overtly hostile to the colonial order. When a nationalist insurrection began in 1954, vineyards were immediately on the frontline.

This chapter begins with Vichy and ends with the agreement to end the Algerian War in another spa town, Evian. The wine kept flowing amid the intense conflicts of this period, even as the pool of colonists seemed to be draining away. Though we may take the year 1962 to mark the official end of French Algeria, the vines that stood as such a powerful symbol of the transformation wrought by colonization would in their own way prove as difficult to uproot as the people who had planted them.

VICHY ALGERIA

Regardless of the potential consequences of France's defeat for Algerian wine, prominent figures in the industry quickly offered the new regime their support. As had long been the case, their public influence was often exerted from town halls. Some of Algeria's Vichy-era mayors had already behaved in ways that suggested they would be receptive to Pétain's brand of right-wing authoritarianism. The mayor of Sidi-Bel-Abbès, for example, Lucien Bellat, who owned over 300 hectares of vineyards, paid a visit to General Francisco Franco during the Spanish Civil War and helped earn his town a reputation as a "Little Berlin," not least through his anti-Semitism.[7] The case of the mayor of El-Affroun in the Mitidja plain, Gaston Averseng, was more ambiguous. A substantial wine producer and associate of the Germain family, Averseng was widely honored for his advocacy of agricultural cooperatives; in 1930, at the ceremony to award him the Legion of Honor for his work in that field, he was described as "the perfect republican." But Averseng's social Catholicism made him difficult to pin down politically. Still promoting cooperatives as mayor in 1942, he nonetheless gave a speech describing Pétain as "our savior."[8] For Léon Havard, who replaced a leftist as mayor of Tlemcen in 1940, it was perhaps the memory of the Popular Front that did most to shape his attitude to Vichy; as we have seen, he had tangled with communists on the agricultural salary commissions of the late 1930s.[9]

Whatever their ideological preferences, Euro-Algerian wine producers had to accept some new limits on their activity as the government-general recognized that the colony would now need to be more reliant on its own resources. A law of August 1940 stipulated that all properties with over five hectares of vines had to devote 10 percent of the surface area to food crops—vegetables, potatoes, cereals—though the order failed to deliver the intended results.[10] As for wine, shortages of the chemical products used to control vineyard pests had a clear impact on the colony's output, and yields were soon in decline. This would presumably have been a greater concern if transporting wine to France had not simultaneously become so difficult. Everything that required fuel was at a premium. Insecurity in the Mediterranean drove up insurance costs, and barrels were in short supply.[11] Ports in southern France like Marseille initially saw an opportunity to pick up business from ports in the now-occupied North or West, but quickly found that moving Algerian wine onward via rail stretched their logistical capacities and caused bottle-necks.[12] Whereas in 1939 roughly 90 percent of Algeria's wine harvest was transported to France, by 1942 that percentage had fallen to less than half.[13]

The local market could not absorb what remained in Algeria, but the new administration had a plan for what to do with some of the surplus: distill the wine to pure alcohol for use as much-needed fuel. From the defeat in 1940 until the end of 1941, for example, 420,000 hectoliters of Algerian wine was turned to that purpose.[14] Though the government paid market rates in compensation, the policy revealed the persistence of old sensitivities. Some producers feared that their competitors in the Midi would profit at their expense, while others worried that sending so much to the distillery would over time have an impact on the quality and the reputation of Algeria's output.[15]

Treating wine as an industrial product in a way reflected what emerged as another interest of the Vichy regime in Algeria: the prospect of developing the territory's industrial base. Significant impetus for this project came from General Maxime Weygand, who was assigned to North Africa as Pétain's representative in October 1940 only months after serving as commander of French forces in the hour of their defeat. Weygand found several compelling reasons to prioritize industry at this moment: the need to sustain Algeria at a time when it could not easily be provisioned from outside, the desire to support the metropole, and the recognition that the expanding Algerian population desperately needed new sources of employment. Abnormal circumstances allowed more leeway to break with past orthodoxies and disregard familiar voices of opposition. When the president of Marseille's chamber of commerce insisted that it was not a good idea for Algeria to industrialize—and that "complementarity" should remain the guiding economic principle—his words were greeted more with irritation than respect.[16] Though the timing for new economic programs was hardly auspicious, government backing helped to advance plans for new factories in industries such as metallurgy and glass manufacturing.[17]

The urgent need for Algeria's landowners to produce enough food for the colony—seen at this moment as a duty—also pushed the Vichy administration to broach the question of land reform. Weygand was no radical, to say the least, and he was as likely to condemn what he perceived as the insolent attitude of Algerians toward authority as to worry about their poverty.[18] But his critique of underproducing large estates, or what he termed *latifundia,* and his support for a scheme that would have reallocated some irrigable land from big properties to poorer Euro-Algerians and Algerians, made him sound a bit like his socialist predecessor as governor-general, Maurice Viollette.[19]

Euro-Algerian agrarian interests predictably opposed the plan to redistribute land, but in general big wine producers could not object much to the Vichy administration's impact on their economic well-being. Those with property close to Algiers particularly anticipated the value their lands might accrue with greater industrial development.[20] The core business also seemed to be holding up better than might have been expected. In April 1942 the Domaine du Chapeau de Gendarme could even report to its shareholders "one of our best years," in spite of "the difficulties of the hour."[21]

An allusion in the same report to the tattered clothing of the company's Algerian employees, however, indirectly highlighted the fact that Algerians were not faring nearly so well. A poor cereal harvest in 1940 strained already-stretched family resources.[22] Agricultural salaries bore less and less relationship to the cost of living. Many Algerians who had owned some livestock before the war sold it. Consumer goods like cloth and espadrilles were increasingly unaffordable; one fellah told a government researcher that he ploughed barefoot not through choice, but rather to conserve his fraying footwear a little longer. Some turned to illegal means to get by. Theft of foodstuffs doubled around Algiers in the first months of 1941 compared to the same period in 1940. Around Oran in the winter of 1942, vineyard owners complained of intruders cutting vines that they then sold on the black market for fuel. Algerians also made use of the black market to sell their allowance of rationed goods, especially sugar.[23] Administrators generally accepted that these trends and incidents resulted from harsh circumstances, and there were fitful efforts to address specific shortages: in May 1942, for example, a textile drive in France encouraged donations of all types of fabric, including torn curtains, to be sent to North Africa.[24]

Undernourishment, of course, was liable to have an impact on output. Father Bernard Perruche, the priest who oversaw the vineyard operated by the SIAH at Mirabeau in Kabylia, recognized in June 1941 that "You cannot ask an empty stomach to do a steady job."[25] But other Euro-Algerian proprietors were unwilling to scale down their expectations, instead portraying Algerian laborers as slackers and complaining about administrative interference with salary levels.[26] Having met with colonists in the Tizi-Ouzou area in the summer of 1942, Perruche observed that most were determined to keep agricultural salaries as low as possible. This, he felt, betrayed a "selfishness [*égoïsme*] that lacks a certain foresight," adding that "it isn't the worker we need to exploit, but the land."[27]

Some Algerians tried to improve their condition by looking beyond the colonists for alternate opportunities. Starting at the end of June 1942, hundreds, and eventually several thousand, Algerians signed up to travel to occupied France to work for the Nazis' construction conglomerate, the Organisation Todt. Colonists and the administration in Algeria did what they could to prevent the news of this program from reaching the countryside, and then to find ways of disqualifying applicants. But Algerians' response to the call—for work that promised better pay than was on offer from private French companies in the unoccupied South, and certainly from franc-pinching colonists in the Algerian countryside—seemed born of a combination of economic necessity and a lack of regard for the defeated French.[28] In these times of hunger, wine itself attracted hostility. Two producers from the Mostaganem region reported being told by a group of Algerians, "We sowed and harvested [cereal crops] because we eat bread; we don't drink wine, [so] let the French take care of their grapes themselves."[29] Attitudes like these were not tied to any particular political faction, but are suggestive of the way hardship could drive anti-colonialism.

"LIBERATED" ALGERIA

The flow of Algerians to work for the Germans was abruptly halted after November 8, 1942, with Operation Torch and the landing of American and British troops in Algeria and Morocco. The success of this operation in turn placed the flow of wine to France in doubt, as within days German and Italian troops reacted to the Allies' strengthened position in the Mediterranean by occupying southern France. For Algerians the arrival of Allied forces offered some hope of new employment opportunities, though by December it was already evident that the Americans' spending power was driving up the cost of living.[30]

One group with special cause for relief at the Allied intervention was Algeria's Jewish population. In October 1940 the Vichy regime abrogated the Crémieux Decree that in 1870 had bestowed French citizenship on Algerian Jews. The regime also enacted a slew of measures to exclude Jews from most public employment and professions.[31] Relatively few Algerian Jews were involved in agriculture, so their participation in the wine industry was often on the side of commerce and distribution, from small-scale operators like Moïse Lascar in the southerly settlement of Saïda to somewhat bigger players like Albert Benassouli in Oran.[32] For Jewish wine producers, like members of the Monsonégo family around Aïn-Tédélès near Mostaganem, or Emile Moatti, a respected promoter of the wines of the Mount Zaccar region, a November 1941 decree that aimed to confiscate Jewish property was a dire threat.[33] Two particular targets of the Office for Economic Aryanization that was created to fulfill this decree were Elie and Adolphe Douïeb. Originally cloth merchants based in Algiers, the Douïeb brothers owned several large vineyards in the Mitidja plain and had only a few years previously been praised for contributing to the "grandeur" of French Algeria.[34] When the administration solicited bids for these properties, covetous Euro-Algerians typically offered well below their market value, as seen in the bid submitted by Raymond Laquière, a prominent lawyer and conservative politician in Algiers, for the 171-hectare Domaine Ben d'Ali Ali at L'Arba.[35]

The Allies' arrival saved the Douïebs and others from being stripped of their property, though in triggering the German occupation of southern France put Jews elsewhere at greater risk. (One of them was Fédia Cassin, a leading importer of Algerian wine in Marseille, who went into hiding in the central department of the Creuse.[36]) November 1942 did not, in fact, bring a clean break with the preceding regime in Algeria. For several months, prominent defenders of Pétain remained in leading positions, and the last anti-Semitic legislation was not revoked until October 1943. At that point the Crémieux Decree was restored, along with Algerian Jews' French citizenship.[37]

The Allied invasion, what it suggested about France's ability to maintain control in North Africa (or its empire more generally), and French demands for Muslim support in liberating the metropole did embolden some Algerians to advance their claims to a new political and economic order. Most notable was the Manifesto of the Algerian People issued by Ferhat Abbas. Characterized as an assimilationist before the war, Abbas was allowed to retain his freedom by the Vichy regime while the more overtly radical nationalist Messali Hadj was sentenced to forced labor. Abbas's manifesto of February 1943, however, illustrated the evolution of someone once regarded as an elite moderate into a frustrated advocate of Algerian self-determination. The manifesto took special note of the rural economy, calling for "the condemnation and abolition of colonization," "the suppression of feudal property through comprehensive agrarian reform," and "the right to well-being of the immense agricultural proletariat." But the new regime, which from the summer of 1943 was dominated by General Charles de Gaulle and his supporters, showed little inclination to address any of the manifesto's demands, and in September the governor-general, Georges Catroux, had Abbas arrested.[38]

The 1943 wine harvest of 6.5 million hectoliters was Algeria's smallest in over twenty years, as bad weather, shortages of essential materials like copper sulfate, a proliferation of pests, and the mobilization of men took their toll. Even the Domaine du Kéroulis reported its worst year ever.[39] At least the lower output offset the fact that the French market was now all but inaccessible. Other French colonies in Africa received more Algerian wine than usual, as merchants sought alternative outlets.[40]

The extended military presence in Algeria was not always welcome for producers. Lands were requisitioned and vines sometimes uprooted to make room for landing strips or supply depots; military authorities found wineries (like the *cave coopérative* at Tipasa) to be useful places to house troops; and the SIAH at Maison-Carrée complained about groups of American and British soldiers strolling through their vines with baskets to steal grapes just before the *vendange* was about to begin.[41] But these troops also represented new customers. Villagers in Fleurus near Oran sold their surplus wine to Americans from a nearby base at the rate of a dollar per bottle, with some entrepreneurs marketing "luxury" wines for twice that amount.[42] The drunkenness that often ensued did not go unnoticed by the higher-ups. A set of instructions for British servicemen heading to France in 1944 warned, "If you get the chance to drink wine, learn to 'take it.' The failure of some British troops to do so was the one point made against our men in France in 1939–40 and again in North Africa."[43]

Adding to the foreign presence in wartime Algeria were Italian and to a lesser extent German prisoners of war, who arrived by the hundreds after the surrender of Axis forces in Tunisia in May 1943.[44] Even more than the Russian detainees who were set to work in Algeria in World War I, the Italians were quickly deemed particularly suited for agriculture and placed at the disposal of wine producers. Within weeks an administrator was praising them as hard-working and "economical," which was only too true: their daily salary was fixed at ten francs (with a half-liter ration of wine), a figure low enough, in the administrator's words, to "reduce considerably the exaggerated claims [*prétentions*] of the *indigènes*."[45] Once again, labor from elsewhere was being used to keep Algerians in line.

Italian prisoners of war remained in demand among producers through 1945, as the condition of Algerian agricultural workers appeared progressively to worsen. From 1943 to 1945 the grape harvest happened to overlap with the month of Ramadan. In those years, Father Perruche found that by the afternoon fasting workers at the vineyard he directed in Mirabeau were "tortured by thirst," and children, who did not fast, proved indispensable as vine cutters.[46] But hunger was not limited to that month of the year. Monthly agricultural reports from early 1945 noted critical food shortages from east to west, to a degree that was impairing productivity. "The state of poverty," observed one report, was becoming "more and more evident," as seen, for example, in rural workers' clothing, and thefts of produce were widespread again.[47] Observers in different parts of Algeria tried to capture what seemed like a new mood. In March 1945 the director of the SIAH identified a "troubling state of mind" among his Algerian employees in Maison-Carrée, while further east an administrator in the department of Constantine found agricultural workers around Bougie in similarly militant spirit.[48] That same month in the West, the governor-general was confronted in Oran and Tlemcen by several thousand women protesting about insufficient bread rations and high food prices.[49]

Compared to previous moments of hardship, Euro-Algerian anxiety at this moment was heightened by the development of oppositional Algerian politics. On the back of his manifesto, and spurning a French measure to expand the Muslim electorate as well as other liberalizing reforms, Ferhat Abbas had begun a movement he called the Amis du Manifeste et de la Liberté (AML, Friends of the Manifesto and of Freedom), which quickly gained significant popular backing. When the AML held a congress in March 1945, the movement largely fell under the sway of supporters of Messali Hadj's banned pro-independence party, the Parti du Peuple Algérien, which was forming itself into clandestine cells as well as helping to coordinate public confrontations like the women's food protest.[50] Though by then the metropole was almost entirely liberated, French Algeria was clearly following its own trajectory.

THE OTHER *ENTRE-DEUX-GUERRES*

The term *l'entre-deux-guerres* is uncontroversial for historians of metropolitan France, and empire specialists also find it useful to refer to a discrete "interwar" period.[51] If one considers the phrase from the vantage point of some of France's overseas possessions, though, it looks much less clear-cut. Vietnam's World War II, for example, soon blurred into a protracted new conflict in which France fought to cling onto its prized territory in Southeast Asia against a revolutionary nationalist movement.[52]

Algeria did not follow Vietnam down the path of war; not yet. But Ferhat Abbas's hometown of Sétif, in the cereal-growing high plains of the department of Constantine, was transformed into a battle zone by the events of May 8, 1945. On the day Europe marked the defeat of the Third Reich, drawing crowds out on the streets in Algeria as in France, an attempt by the forces of order to smother a nationalist demonstration in Sétif degenerated into murderous violence. By eleven o'clock in the morning, twenty-one Euro-Algerians lay dead, including the town's socialist mayor. News from Sétif reached other parts of Constantine through the day, inspiring some Algerians to imitation—usually in less deadly fashion, as in Bône, where a crowd threw stones at the sub-prefect—but also prompting officials to police more aggressively and colonists to arm themselves. The repression and reprisals that followed over the coming days and weeks ran the gamut from brutal vigilantism to heavy firepower, including aerial bombardment; one general considered these operations to amount to a "veritable war." The official death toll of Euro-Algerians in Sétif, Guelma, Kherrata, and the other communities affected by the violence was 102. The number of Algerians killed has proved impossible to pin down, but was certainly in the thousands.[53]

In some ways what happened in May 1945 was the kind of violence many Euro-Algerians had feared might transpire during the rural disturbances of 1936–1937. The events in 1945 did indeed have a strong rural dimension. This was even true in the ostensibly urban environment of Sétif: the town had recently grown rapidly with the arrival of migrants from the impoverished countryside, and some of the violence was committed by country dwellers who were there on May 8 for the weekly market. The aftershocks then rippled through small communities in the region, with authority figures like estate managers or forest guards often the targets of what took on the appearance of a predominantly rural insurrection. The forces of repression devoted much of their focus and firepower to *douars* (Algerian villages) in the vicinity of centers of colonization that had been attacked.[54] The repression turned many Algerians onto an actively anti-colonial path.[55]

These events in the department of Constantine were, naturally, monitored closely in other parts of Algeria, both by Euro-Algerians and by officials who envisaged how they might handle similar circumstances. In the *arrondissement* of Oran, for example, authorities quickly carried out an inventory of the weapons at the disposal of 781 isolated farms in the region, and concluded that there were not nearly enough.[56] But the violence did not spread in any serious fashion beyond Constantine, and, by the end of June, French forces considered the insurrection (if that is what it should be termed) to have been suppressed. As a result, 1945 represented the beginning of what could be called Algeria's other interwar period. It would last until 1954, and would share many features with the earlier *entre-deux-guerres*—urban growth, increased use of machines in the countryside, periodic labor conflict—but this time against the background of a much more fully developed nationalist movement and anti-colonial successes in other parts of the world.

In many other ways, of course, French Algeria was attempting in 1945 to return to what had been normal up to 1939. That meant getting the wine industry back on track. Two challenges were particularly pressing: first, to get Algerian wine out of packed cellars and across the Mediterranean to undersupplied French consumers; and second, to reconstitute vines that were often old or deteriorated.[57] At the same time, some saw this as a moment of opportunity for French Algeria. The German occupiers in France had helped themselves to the country's fine wines and commandeered some of what was left for fuel or even anti-freeze for their vehicles.[58] Algeria's *vignoble* may not have been in the best condition, but it was doing better than that of the metropole, which on top of everything else was suffering from a major outbreak of the viral disease *court-noué* (fanleaf degeneration). Evoking the time when the Algerian vineyard first expanded, the popular author Paul Reboux wrote in 1945 that Euro-Algerians "must tell themselves that the Fatherland is once again calling them."[59]

France was struggling to return to normality in other ways too. In Marseille, the wine trader Fédia Cassin came out of hiding to resume direction of the Société d'approvisionnements vinicoles (known as SAPVIN, with three subsidiaries in Algeria); as the new president of the Marseille Consistory, he also did everything he could to aid the recovery of the city's Jewish community. (Cassin's younger brother René, with broader concerns in mind, was soon at work on the drafting committee for a Universal Declaration of Human Rights.)[60] But Marseille's port had been damaged, as had that of Rouen, the prewar leader in Algerian wine imports. It was the southern port of Sète, with the advantage of its relative proximity to Algeria, that did most to satisfy demand as wine headed to the metropole by whatever means available.[61]

The exigencies of the moment ensured the final victory of the wine tanker. Thousands of barrels had gone astray or been destroyed in the war, leaving the stock available in Algeria at less than half the prewar figure. Barrel companies worked as fast as possible to reduce the shortfall, but shipping companies were now ready to offer a more "modern" solution to government authorities charged with re-provisioning the metropole. This time there was enough available work that protests against wine tankers in places like Sète did not amount to much. So quickly did *bateaux-citernes* enter into service after the war that within five years they already transported up to 80 percent of Algeria's annual wine exports. Soon barrel manufacturers themselves were diverting their capital to where the new profits lay. In 1949 two Algiers-based barrel companies, Francalfûts and Lassallas, teamed up to buy a wine tanker, which by the end of the following year had made forty voyages to ports in the Mediterranean, the Atlantic, and the English Channel.[62] But what had been a reliable source of labor for working-class communities like the Algiers neighborhood of Belcourt—the urban location the writer Louis Bertrand had once called "the kingdom of wine"—declined as a result.[63]

The shift to wine tankers paralleled the increasing mechanization of agriculture after the war. This trend received a boost from the Marshall Plan, which, beginning in 1948, contributed $17,226,700 over the span of four years toward the purchase of agricultural machines or machine parts in Algeria. In 1949, for example, the department of Oran took delivery of 140 new Ferguson tractors.[64] More and more of the horses and other animals that had been a common sight around vineyards were switched out for machines that could do the same work two or three times more cheaply. The SIAH at Maison-Carrée had sold all but a few of its horses by the end of 1952.[65] The same company can be used to illustrate the fact that not all the mechanization of this period affected work done outdoors. In 1948 the cellars installed a machine to wash bottles and another to stick on labels, and, with a few further upgrades, the whole process of bottling, from putting the wine in to corking, labeling, and sealing, was soon being done by machine at the rate of a thousand bottles per hour.[66]

"Mechanization" in agriculture was not necessarily an inexorable, one-way track; environmental conditions could obstruct the progress of shiny new machines, as was discovered in other French-ruled parts of Africa at the same time.[67] In Algerian viticulture, it remained more difficult to work vineyards with machines on the slopes than down on the plains. But, if the land allowed it, the trends were such that by the early 1950s a medium-powered tractor was an economically viable proposition even for a wine producer with a modest (by French Algerian standards) property of ten to fifteen hectares.[68] Machines provided significant help in the process of restoring Algeria's *vignoble* to its prewar health.[69]

Producers were aware of the impact that one or two new machines could have on their employment needs. At Aïn-el-Arba in the department of Oran, for example, two brothers, Henri and Louis Bourde, cultivated both cereals and vines on their properties. Before they bought a combine harvester, the laborers they employed would have more or less continuous work through the summer, as threshing often continued up until the time of the grape harvest. A machine like their harvester, which by the early 1950s could cut, thresh, and bundle up to fifteen hectares of cereal a day with the aid of four or five men rather than a crew of a hundred, forced many to look elsewhere for work during the middle months of the year.[70] In Mohammed Dib's novel *L'incendie* (The fire, 1954), about agricultural laborers in Dib's home region of Tlemcen, the symbolism of a scene in which a worker is mangled to death by a threshing machine is impossible to miss.[71]

These trends sustained the concerns expressed by the likes of General Weygand during the war that Algeria's growing population required additional forms of employment. The end of the war brought renewed calls for industrialization, which one economist claimed had long been blocked in Algeria by the "covert but powerful interventions" of vested interests wanting to preserve the status quo.[72] The plans and directives of industry's new advocates, however, did little to break long-established patterns, which tended to be kept in place by investment-deterring factors like high energy and transport costs and the local budget's lack of capacity to carry through significant improvements to infrastructure.[73] The few high-profile projects that came to fruition after the war offered no panacea. The company Lesieur opened an "ultra-modern" vegetable-oil-processing and soap-making factory in Algiers in 1948, for example—a project that had been anticipated for several years—but it was so modern as to require only 150 workers, not enough to make much of an impression on employment statistics.[74] In any case, such jobs may well have been more likely to go to Euro-Algerians shifting from foundering industries like barrel making than to needy rural migrants.

Developments like the Lesieur factory, as wine producers around urban centers knew, could still have an impact on property markets. La Mitidja, a Germain-family company spun off from the Société des domaines du Kéroulis, knew it had a good thing in the old Ferme Modèle (Model Farm), the property at Birkadem just outside Algiers that General Clauzel had earmarked in 1830 to test crops for their ability to grow in the Algerian climate. As of 1948 the property was still largely used for agriculture, with over half of its 300 hectares covered with vines. But its location next to the railway line and a major road now made it a prime spot for industrial development. The company closely monitored land values in the surrounding area and waited for the right moment to sell or turn the land to nonagricultural purposes.[75]

An expanding housing market offered further opportunities. In Maison-Carrée, the SIAH was similarly hoping to profit from Algiers's "ineluctable" sprawl; it had already sold some land to the city for a new cemetery before the war.[76] In the late 1940s the company set aside seventy-two hectares to become what it called the "Lotissement Lavigerie"—a mixed residential and industrial development bearing the name of the man who had established the vineyards whose profits made such projects possible. What Archbishop Lavigerie himself would have made of the promotional materials that marketed middle-class comfort on the Bay of Algiers is hard to say (see fig. 6.1); but, with the great majority of the company's shares still in the White Fathers' hands and the profits being

FIG. 6.1 "Life will be sweeter if you build at the Lotissement Lavigerie."
Promotional flyer, 1950. Archives Générales de la Société des Missionnaires d'Afrique, Durrieu 551,
by permission.

used to fund Catholic missions in sub-Saharan Africa, perhaps the project would have satisfied his entrepreneurial instincts.[77]

These were not the only types of investment that wealthy Euro-Algerians were pursuing. The standard narrative of colonial Algeria's eventual unraveling has tended to focus on a mass exodus at independence in 1962. Much less appreciated is that there had been a low-profile, smaller-scale outflow of Euro-Algerians even before the war of independence began—a sort of pre-exodus. One of the more striking departures was that of Paulin Borgeaud, son of the importer-exporter and industrialist Jules Borgeaud and cousin of Henri Borgeaud of the Domaine de la Trappe. As early as 1923 Paulin Borgeaud left Algeria for Paris to start a private bank, the Banque Borgeaud & Cie; later he would claim that he and a few of his friends had already begun to doubt France's long-term grip on Algeria and the wisdom of continued investment there, though he remained closely linked via the bank to Borgeaud family affairs.[78] Another scion of a notable Euro-Algerian family to seek an alternate path was Jean Duroux, whose father, Jacques, had been so prominent in Algeria's politics and business in the 1920s and 1930s, not least as owner of the *Echo d'Alger*. When his father was incapacitated by illness in 1941, Jean turned the newspaper over to his brother-in-law, Alain de Sérigny (who took its politics further to the right).[79] After Jacques Duroux died in 1944, Jean began selling off his father's business empire piece by piece. That way another big wine producer, Joseph Torrès, who had worked for decades in the Duroux family's flour-milling business and was a cousin by marriage, was able to buy Duroux's 550-hectare vineyard at Maison-Blanche in the eastern Mitidja.[80] Jean Duroux himself decamped to Canada.

Other leading names in Algerian viticulture looked for new investments within the wine business, or at least in agriculture. It is possible that the limitations placed on the expansion of vineyards in the early 1930s encouraged some wealthy Euro-Algerian producers to increase their stake in urban property, but rural property in France represented another option.[81] In 1935, for example, Pierre Sénéclauze—son of the Oran wine merchant Théodore Sénéclauze, whose business was well known through its abundant advertising (see fig. 6.2)—bought a storied vineyard in the Médoc region near Bordeaux, the Château de Marquis de Terme. (Contacts in the Bordeaux wine trade apparently alerted Sénéclauze to the fact that some notable properties were on the market at

FIG. 6.2 "Wine, essence of joy and health." An example of the Sénéclauze marketing machine, ca. 1950. Reproduced from the author's collection.

a difficult moment for the region.)[82] Members of the Germain family also turned to southwest France for new opportunities, and, being Germains, they looked for big properties in underpriced areas. Having already purchased a property by the Garonne near Toulouse in the 1930s, in 1941 Robert Germain took over the 300-plus-hectare Domaine de Nolet at Aucamville—château included—where he concentrated on fruit production. Though remaining in charge of the Domaines du Kéroulis and La Mitidja and maintaining his primary residence in Algiers, his new domains allowed him to envisage a future that was not definitively tied to Algeria.[83] In 1947 one of Robert's cousins, Roger Germain, did relocate to France, to direct a 400-hectare domain that his father, Maurice, had bought near Condom.[84] Finally, representing the next generation, Claude Bertagna—whose great-uncle Jérôme and grandfather Dominique had established massive vineyards on the plain of Bône that remained in the family's hands—headed instead to Burgundy. There, in 1950, he began reviving a prestigious vineyard in the village of Vougeot, a place synonymous with the Cistercians who had produced wine there for centuries until the Revolution.[85] These wealthy colonists promised to bring their brand of capitalist agriculture to the metropole.

THE LOGIC OF DESCARTES

This picture of Euro-Algerian vinelords fixing up run-down châteaux in France could hardly contrast more with the housing situation among poor Algerians after World War II. In Sidi-Bel-Abbès, for example, a suburb that had first taken root in the 1920s on a piece of land owned by the Sénéclauze wine company devolved after the war into a rapidly mushrooming shanty town, inhabited mostly by migrants from the countryside. Known as the Cité Sénéclauze, this was not a place to evoke the joy and health of the company's publicity. Water for its 6,000-plus residents was available only via a few public fountains, and the neighborhood's high mortality rate stemmed from diseases like tuberculosis that were effectively absent from better-off districts. By the late 1940s conditions were bad enough that the municipality opened proceedings against Sénéclauze and its beneficiaries to force them to cover some of the cost of a basic sewer network and other utilities.[86]

Uprooted rural migrants in urban settlements like these represented a population that political groups hoped to reach; indeed, communists were active in the Cité Sénéclauze, though without much success.[87] Efforts to organize agricultural workers, meanwhile, remained transitory and geographically patchy. Even so, in the period after World War II there were several moments of confrontation in wine-producing areas that approached the intensity of the events of 1936 and 1937, including, in the village of Descartes in 1951, a direct attack on a state building that showed how a labor dispute might develop in unexpected ways.

Historians of Algerian labor have naturally tended to insert the disputes from this period into the prehistory of the war of independence. Overtly political objectives, however, were hard to discern in the demands made by or on behalf of vineyard workers. When workers at the SIAH's vineyards outside Algiers threatened to strike ahead of the grape harvest in 1947, for example, company officials felt sure the threat must be related to the debates then taking place about a new Statute for Algeria. (Passed by parliament in September 1947, this instituted a new, 120-seat Algerian Assembly, half of whose seats were to be elected by citizens with French civil status—the Euro-Algerian population, primarily—and the remainder by the far more numerous Muslim citizens of "local status.")[88] But SIAH workers were under the influence of trade unionists from the CGT, whose communist allies had taken a much less strong position in these debates than Algerian nationalists like members of Messali Hadj's new party, the Mouvement pour la triomphe des libertés démocratiques (MTLD). The strike threat amounted to nothing, and when the employers sat down with SIAH workers' representatives and delegates from the CGT they negotiated over a standard range of concerns related to working conditions and benefits.[89]

Wine producers at the time tolerated such negotiations as an unavoidable feature of doing business, but the wealthier ones had several weapons at their disposal to keep the balance in their favor. It was surely no coincidence that, in 1949, after lamenting an increase in labor costs over the previous year, the Société des domaines du Kéroulis chose to build up its inventory of machines; the company's three new *moto-sulfateurs* (motorized sulfur-sprayers), for example, would help to reduce the payroll at certain moments of the year.[90] Robert Germain's opinion of the demands of labor is also suggested by the way the other company he presided over, La Mitidja s.a., sold a property it owned near Lourmel in the department of Oran not long after workers there had gone on strike.[91]

The events that unfolded in Descartes in 1951, however, were of a type to dispel any complacency. Descartes was a place of many large vineyards in an area whose lands were virtually monopolized by Euro-Algerians. Perhaps not coincidentally it also lay within one of the more vigorous circuits of rural communist activity, about fifty kilometers from Tlemcen to the west and Sidi-Bel-Abbès to the northeast.[92] In 1936, several vineyard owners in the area had been fined for underpaying their workers the mandatory salary minimums, and similar complaints arose a year later. In 1938, the Tlemcen communist Mohamed Badsi also tried to stir action against Descartes producers' use of cheaper Moroccan laborers. One proprietor, Edouard Ravel, who owned a 400-hectare vineyard, was accused in all of these complaints.[93]

At the grape harvest in 1951, amid what one administrator called an "effervescent" atmosphere among rural workers in this part of western Algeria, Descartes became a site of open conflict.[94] On September 13, two representatives of the CGT came to the village urging *vendangeurs* to withhold their labor and demand higher salaries. Two others who carried this message into the vineyards were arrested and brought to the gendarmerie for questioning. By the evening, a crowd of as many as 800 protesters gathered outside the gendarmerie to demand the men's release, some throwing cobblestones at the shuttered windows of the gatehouse.

A group succeeded in breaking down the gate into the courtyard and then tried to force their way into the main building, aiming to free the detainees. The gendarmes on duty were able to repel the attackers using two dozen tear-gas grenades, but order was only restored with the arrival of reinforcements from Tlemcen and Sidi-Bel-Abbès.[95]

Wine producers in Descartes hastily agreed to increase the harvesters' daily pay, just as they did in several other locations in the area under similar (if less violent) pressure. In the end, twelve stood trial for their alleged role in the disturbances. The four who were then given prison sentences became "the Descartes four," their cause championed in public protests and in the pages of the communist-linked newspaper *Alger ré-publicain*. Several months later, two of the four—the communist organizer Boumédiène Boumédiène from Lamoricière, and Medjoub Berrahou from Tlemcen, a member of the Algerian Communist Party's central committee—were being transported by train to serve out their time in the prison at Berrouaghia in the department of Algiers.[96] As the train passed through a poor part of Oran, the faubourg Victor-Hugo, its progress was interrupted by a group of women affiliated with a communist-led women's group, the Union des femmes d'Algérie (UFA, Union of Women of Algeria), who approached the tracks chanting "free Berrahou!" Descriptions of the extent of the disruption this caused vary according to the source: communist and UFA publicity claimed that "women lying on the tracks stopped the Algiers train," whereas a police report stated that the train only had to slow down as a "small group of Algerian women, French and Muslim" came toward the rails but then backed off.[97]

Two Algerian labor historians have labeled the events at Descartes "pre-insurrectionary."[98] To what extent is that characterization accurate? The ferocity and directness of the attack on the gendarmerie certainly made it alarming for Euro-Algerian landowners. Moreover, they could not pin the disturbances only on "outsiders," for, despite the contribution of a few individuals like Berrahou, most of those arrested came from the immediate area, hinting at a deeper well of anger among rural Algerians. On the other hand, the initial protest was driven by the most basic of demands, an increase in pay for people doing short-term work at the grape harvest. It is also worth keeping in mind that communists in Algeria were popularly perceived in terms of their stance on labor, not the national question; the inconsistency of their past position on colonialism still counted against them in the eyes of many Algerians, as did their image as a largely European and non-Muslim movement.[99] What happened at Descartes still looks first and foremost like a labor dispute.

The disturbances and their aftermath were nonetheless of a moment in which challenges to empire were becoming more and more common. The women's train protest claimed inspiration from the actions of a young communist in the metropole, Raymonde Dien, who went to prison in 1950 after she was found guilty of blocking a train carrying military matériel through the city of Tours en route to the war in Indochina. Members of the UFA in Oran, indeed, had already taken part in demonstrations at the local docks, aiming to disrupt the traffic of ships heading for Vietnam.[100] Other anti-colonial struggles also reverberated in Algeria. Nativist hostility against Moroccan workers of the type that CGT organizers had tried to use to their advantage in 1937 and 1938 was not as much in evidence in the early 1950s. The authorities remained concerned about the social impact of Moroccan migrant workers in western Algeria, but with Morocco's independence movement advancing swiftly, their concern now also embraced the possibility that migrants— or migrants who had decided to stay on—might be nationalist militants. That fear appeared to be borne out by the role played by Moroccans in a strike by agricultural workers at the time of the grape harvest of 1952 in Er-Rahel, to the west of Oran.[101]

However one assesses the objectives of striking vineyard workers in the department of Oran in 1951 and 1952, it is easy to see why hindsight makes this moment look "pre-insurrectionary." The beginning of the actual insurrection at the end of 1954 would see attacks on gendarmeries and the discovery of a bomb factory in a *douar* outside Er-Rahel.[102] And by 1955, the Descartes agitator Medjoub Berrahou would be organizing an armed *maquis* guerrilla unit in the mountains around Tlemcen.[103] Algeria's other *entre-deux-guerres* was coming to an end.

THE FRONT LINES

On October 19, 1954, France's minister of the interior, François Mitterrand, sat down for dinner in Algiers as a guest of the Algerian Assembly. This was the menu:

La Chorba (soup with cracked wheat and vegetables)
Le Bourak (filled savory pastry)
Le Méchoui des Hauts-Plateaux (sheep barbecue)
Le Couscous Ould Soltan (couscous)
Les Halaouïat d'El-Djezaïr (sweet pastries)
La Grappe d'Or du Sahel (fresh local grapes)[104]

Mitterrand was visiting Algeria after an earthquake caused serious damage to Orléansville and its surrounding region in the west of the department of Algiers. Previous interior ministers hosted by the Assembly had been treated to French-style cuisine, but the menu this time seemed to be trying to communicate something. Perhaps it was intended to convince Mitterrand that the Assembly was an institution that served all inhabitants of French Algeria equally, rather than what many believed it to be: a sham stacked in favor of Euro-Algerians and an unrepresentative selection of Algerian "moderates," through elections that were manipulated with the help of the administration.[105] The wine list for the meal was more typical of such receptions: a white from Henri Borgeaud's Domaine de la Trappe, a 1949 red Médéa, and, because there were some things that even French Algeria's winemakers couldn't do, Pol Roger Brut champagne.

Mitterrand was regarded with suspicion by Euro-Algerian members of the Assembly. Hadn't he been at the conference in Geneva in May at which France gave up Indochina? Was he truly committed to ensuring that French Algeria was not similarly undone? Mitterrand's hosts were nevertheless eager to reassure him that nothing was fundamentally wrong in Algeria. Neighboring Morocco and Tunisia might be effectively in a state of insurrection, but Algeria, in the words of Assembly president Raymond Laquière, "is calm and will remain so."[106]

Publicly, Mitterrand echoed Laquière—on whom he had just bestowed the Legion of Honor—and pronounced himself "optimistic" as he returned to Paris on October 23.[107] Privately, however, Mitterrand knew better. Even before his visit he had met with Ferhat Abbas, who tried to explain that Euro-Algerians' refusal to countenance change put French Algeria at risk as countervailing forces brewed below. Then, in Algiers, Mitterrand had been briefed at length by Jean Vaujour, Algeria's director of security. Vaujour relayed intelligence about a group based in the

Casbah of Algiers, and voiced his suspicions of an attack in the coming weeks.[108]

On October 31, a Sunday, Vaujour drove out to the Sahel of Algiers with his family. The *vendange* was over and the vines were in their fall colors of gold, ocher, and brown. Vaujour noted how they were "aligned in perfect rows" on "Germain properties" that sloped into the distance. But, while his description unconsciously echoed the observations of Jules Ferry in 1892, in which parallel lines of vines represented "the peaceful and permanent seizure of the African land in the name of France," Vaujour could not feel confident on that day that either peace or permanence was guaranteed.[109]

Not far away, in another part of the Sahel, Henri Borgeaud had reason to feel good. Politically, his sway still appeared strong: since 1946 a senator for Algiers, he was president in Paris of a center-right political coalition, the Rassemblement des gauches républicaines, while influencing the department of Algiers and its finances through more local institutions like the *conseil général*. He continued to be a nodal figure in French Algeria's business networks, with leading roles at companies like the cigarette maker Bastos, the cement manufacturer Lafarge, and the car dealer Vinson. But his roots remained in Staouëli at the Domaine de la Trappe, over which he had had full control since the death of his father Lucien in 1948. October 1954 was a notable month for the domain: first, because Borgeaud had the occasion to show Mitterrand around the property, and second, because it marked fifty years since the Borgeaud family's purchase of the estate from the Trappists.[110] This anniversary was celebrated on October 30, Borgeaud later recalled, with a "massive couscous" and the award of certificates to a hundred Muslim estate workers, who, he said, he "embraced one by one."[111]

The attacks that took place in thirty locations across Algeria less than two days later, in the early hours of November 1, 1954, did not square with Borgeaud's cozily paternalist imagining of intercommunal relations. He quickly wrote an editorial for the newspaper he owned, *La Dépêche quotidienne*, denouncing the "handful of agitators" he believed to be responsible and insisting that "the evil must be sought where it is to be found and the ringleaders routed out wherever they are."[112]

The authors of the events announced themselves as a new group called the Front de libération nationale (FLN, National Liberation Front), which issued a call to arms in pursuit of national independence. Their numbers were not immediately clear, and the mixed success of their opening salvo suggested that their strength for the time being was greatest in the Aurès Mountains of the department of Constantine and in Kabylia, rather than more westerly regions. But assaults on five gendarmeries, two police stations, and two barracks made a powerful first statement, as did a dozen dead.[113] On November 12, Mitterrand affirmed in the Chamber of Deputies that "Algeria is France" ("*L'Algérie, c'est la France*"), and, before the end of the month, he returned to monitor the efforts to keep it so.[114]

Several of the attacks of November 1 had taken place amid (if not necessarily on) the vines. For one thing, vines provided good cover. The three men who bombed the citrus-fruit cooperative at Boufarik in the Mitidja gathered first in a neighboring vineyard. (More than any other attack this one caught the attention of big wine producers in the Algiers region like Borgeaud, who had an important sideline in oranges.) A few kilometers up the road to Algiers, the target was a facility to process paper-making *alfa* (esparto grass), stacks of which produced a dramatic impression when they went up in flames. The capture of suspects in that case led investigators to find three incendiary bombs hidden in a vineyard.[115]

The wine producers most directly involved in the night's events, however, were much further to the west. Hostility dating back years seems to have factored into the decision to attack two estates not far to the east of Mostaganem, one owned by Salomon Monsonégo, the other by Edmé de Jeanson, an especially disliked *colon*. A witness to the incident at the Monsonégo property, Laurent François—a wine producer himself—drove to the village of Cassaigne to raise the alarm, but arrived at just the wrong moment: he was shot dead outside the gendarmerie by one of a group of insurgents planning to enter the building to look for guns.[116]

François thus became one of the first casualties of a struggle that was to last over seven years and end with Algerian independence.[117] Algeria's vines, as well as those who owned them or worked on them, were very much on the front lines of this conflict as it unfolded. Producers—or the guards or the estate managers they employed—would wake to find that as many as ten hectares of vines had been cut down under cover of darkness by groups numbering ten, twenty, or thirty people. Sometimes several properties would be hit on the same night. Around Philippeville on the night of June 17–18, 1955, for example, unknown attackers cut

thousands of fruit trees as well as vines, and across nine separate properties set fire to piles of fodder, wood, and manure; a Citroën truck; and a
Renault 4CV.[118] In 1956, attacks of this type became much more
common, reaching into parts of the department of Oran that were relatively densely populated with Euro-Algerians and until then had been
largely unaffected.[119]

The general strategy behind these attacks was not difficult to discern,
since it resembled some of the actions taken by French forces during the
conquest of Algeria a bit more than a century previously. Indeed, Ferhat
Abbas—who in 1956 completed his transition away from assimilationism
by joining the FLN—evoked these nineteenth-century actions in a book
he wrote during the war. Abbas quoted at length General Armand de
Saint-Arnaud, who matter-of-factly recorded destroying swaths of land
and property, including thousands upon thousands of olive and fruit
trees. Of his campaign in Petite Kabylie in 1851, Saint-Arnaud wrote,
"I left behind me a vast fire. All the villages, about two hundred of them,
were burned, all the gardens laid to waste, the olive trees cut."[120] But
now the threat was to French villages of colonization or the farms around
them. The insurgents in the 1950s lacked the capacity for destruction
on the scale wreaked by Saint-Arnaud, but attacks on vines and other
crops undermined Euro-Algerians' sense of security while chipping away
at what remained one of the bases of the colonial economy. In response,
French forces sometimes reacquainted themselves with their old tactics,
pillaging suspect villages and destroying allotments and trees, in addition to deploying twentieth-century techniques such as aerial bombardment and napalm.[121]

The big producers could cope with the loss of a few hectares. On the
plain of Bône, the Compagnie des vignobles de la Méditerranée, a company dominated by wealthy metropolitan investors, reported that it had
had 6.5 hectares of vines chopped down one night in July 1956. But that
was a small piece of a viticultural enterprise that covered nearly 600 hectares. The company collected the compensation offered by the state and
continued much as before.[122] For smaller proprietors, though, the loss
of a few hectares bit much more deeply. Some individuals were hit multiple times. About forty kilometers inland from Philippeville, for example,
Jean Emeric maintained fifteen hectares of vines outside Jemmapes, by
late 1955 a dangerous area.[123] Between September 1956 and August 1958
Emeric claimed compensation for four separate attacks that affected ap-

proximately thirteen hectares of these vines as well as many fruit trees. (Assessors counted 18,369 felled vines after a June 1958 attack.) Emeric also filed a claim after saboteurs on the railway line that ran alongside one of his properties caused a goods train to derail and land amid his vines. In that instance neither the railway company nor the military authorities whose vehicles drove back and forth across the property to deal with the problem accepted any responsibility for the ensuing damage. Emeric, who described himself as "just a small farmer," spent much time in these years pursuing the amount of compensation he felt reflected what these various losses represented, in order, as he put it, "to support our families and to hang on."[124]

"Hanging on" entailed considerable physical risk for the likes of Emeric, who was personally attacked in January 1956, and for the people who worked on their properties. Vineyard guards were a particular target, not least because they carried guns that insurgents were eager to get their hands on (see fig. 6.3). One guard, Mohamed ben Ahmed Zalani, told gendarmes in October 1956 that four armed men had taken the gun from his shack, tied him and the night watchman up, then set fire to farm buildings and the residence of the owner, Jean Camilliéri. This was not the first attack that Zalani had experienced on this property, which lay a few kilometers from Jemmapes; only two months previously he had raised the alarm when he realized Camilliéri's winery was burning down. There were no human victims in either of these two attacks, but the fire in October did kill fifteen head of cattle, among them a cow named République.[125]

It was rare for investigators to discover who carried out such attacks, but one exception points to the cultural tensions that made vineyards or wine facilities a natural target for some Algerians. In June 1955, police found a packet of letters at the scene of one of a pair of vine-cutting incidents to the west of Orléansville. The letters led them to M'hamed Gueridi, who lived in a nearby *zawiya*, a Sufi religious complex that housed a school. Implicating five students from the same institution as his accomplices, Gueridi admitted to directing the attacks and stated that his goal was to "create a climate of insecurity" that would hasten the departure of the colonists from Algeria. The students told police that they were regular readers of *El Bassair* (*al-Baṣā'ir*), the Arabic-language newspaper of the reformist ulama movement. Despite the clumsy execution of the plan, the local administrator worried that "the war of

FIG. 6.3 A vineyard guard in his watchtower, location unknown, 1951. Reproduced from the author's collection.

'Liberation' risks becoming a 'holy' war [*guerre 'sainte'*]." On that basis, he proposed closing the most "suspect" Islamic schools.[126]

This case from early in the war stands out in part because of the identity of the perpetrators; later attacks were presumed to be the work of the FLN. Yet it also suggests that attacks on vines could appeal to a variety of people for a variety of reasons. As we have seen, cultural condemnation of wine had formed part of the initial Algerian analysis of the French conquest. But in the early twentieth century alcohol use became an increasing moral concern for some Muslim notables (as well as a low-level public health concern for French authorities), especially as military service and labor migration to France were said to have spread alcoholism among Algerians.[127] For this reason French temperance measures aimed at Algerians found support among some Muslim leaders. When the controlling and moralistic Vichy regime prohibited the sale of alcohol to Muslims in Algeria in October 1941—with fines for vendors who broke the ban—the measure won praise from religious leaders like the mufti of Orléansville.[128]

Another letter of thanks for this 1941 decree came from the *djemâa* (village assembly) of Palestro, a traditional source of authority in a region between the Mitidja plain and Kabylia. Less than fifteen years later, the vineyards around Palestro came under ferocious assault as part of an FLN campaign in the area that also claimed the lives of several colonists. The acts of sabotage were so extensive—four-fifths of Gilbert Pembroke's twenty-six hectares were destroyed, for example—and the climate of insecurity was so great, that many colonists effectively abandoned their properties.[129] The connection between a letter praising a measure against drinking in 1941 and violent attacks on vineyards in 1956 may appear tenuous. What the example does show, however, is that by targeting vines, the FLN could lay claim to a pre-existing moral authority. Values drawn from the reformist ulama—of the type espoused by M'hamed Gueridi—also led the FLN to enforce bans on alcohol consumption and smoking among Algerians, which in turn increased their everyday control over Algerian society.[130] FLN placards placed near colonists' properties with such slogans as, "If you work, you will be killed," had the same intent.[131]

Locating and retaining workers naturally became a challenge in these conditions. In the fall of 1956, for example, wine producers in Novi, near Cherchell, had to begin the grape harvest without the workers they had come to expect annually from nearby mountain communities. Instead, the mountains now harbored an active *maquis,* which threatened colonists and claimed the life of the president of Novi's *cave coopérative* in a knife attack on the winery's grounds.[132] Producers in the West also began to experience serious problems with their regular workers. It was already evident to some that foot-dragging had reduced productivity, but in early 1957 many Algerian vineyard laborers simply walked off the job and did not return for weeks, if at all. One producer, Marcel Petit, who ran a fifty-hectare vineyard at Montagnac near Tlemcen, informed his local prefect in April 1957 that he was functioning with four workers instead of his usual twenty. Two weeks later he wrote again to report that the vineyard had been attacked and his new estate manager shot dead, while "all my [Algerian] workers joined the other side."[133]

Yet, helped by a variety of protective measures, viticulture did not break down. The authorities ensured that the biggest properties were well defended; at the Domaine du Chapeau de Gendarme, for example, there was a permanent military presence from early in the war.[134] One way or another, indeed, French troops were often made aware of the centrality of wine to colonial Algeria's economy. Members of the 117th Infantry Regiment who were posted to Fondouk in the eastern Mitidja paraded in front of the *cave coopérative* in the village and assisted at the grape harvest.[135] In places lacking that level of protection, wine producers sometimes hired deterrent groups of former Foreign Legionaries.[136]

Security measures were in constant evolution. Around Aïn-Témouchent in 1955, the authorities ensured that enough weapons were available to more isolated farms and devoted particular attention to those who still spent the night at their properties. By mid-1957 colonists in the area had to join a self-defense syndicate, paid for in part by a tax calibrated to property size.[137] Some colonists in this area, as in others that used a similar system, apparently balked at the financial contribution they had to make for their protection, rather as an earlier generation had objected to mandatory measures to combat phylloxera.[138] The syndicates, however, did help to keep some properties functioning that otherwise would have been abandoned, and military authorities noted that defended properties were rarely attacked.[139]

Under these protections, estates like the Domaine du Kéroulis came to look rather like prison camps, with multiple guard towers and long coils of barbed wire. They had up-to-date radio and signaling systems, and, in the case of Kéroulis, a permanent squad of ex-legionaries to enhance security. The problem then was how to find the necessary workers, for the labor market in that part of western Algeria had fundamentally changed. Most of the Moroccans in the region had returned home, and the border over which so many seasonal migrants had crossed in previous years was now a genuine barrier.[140] (Morocco gained its independence in April 1956.) Nor could the domain rely on nearby *douars* that had historically supplied workers. Instead, the labor had to be brought in from further afield. Beginning in 1957, much of the local rural Algerian population had been concentrated in camps known as *camps de regroupement,* an extreme way to isolate them from rebel recruiters. (The official rationale was that it was for the Algerians' protection.) It was from these camps in places like Aïn-Témouchent and Laferrière that the Domaine du Kéroulis now drew many of its workers; two or three hundred were trucked in every day in protected convoys. As extraordinary as the circumstances were, and as much as danger persisted on the estate, the defense provisions ensured that the vineyard was able to keep posting massive production figures.[141]

Meanwhile, of course, large numbers of French troops—as many as 450,000 by 1957—were carrying out the work of "pacification" across Algeria.[142] In a number of well-documented instances, wine-production facilities became part of the apparatus of repression, as Algerian suspects were confined in empty wine vats with sometimes fatal results. One night in March 1957, at Aïn Isser to the east of Tlemcen, members of the Seventh Infantry Regiment forced 101 Algerians into four vats, each with an air capacity of roughly thirty cubic meters—or so it appeared. In fact, two of the four vats were smaller on the inside. It was in these two vats the next morning that the guards discovered a total of forty-one corpses. The following month, twenty-three Algerians died in a vat on a vineyard at Mercier-Lacombe to the east of Sidi-Bel-Abbès; this time sulfur dioxide poisoning was a factor in the deaths. (SO_2 is used to clean winery equipment.) Following another mass suffocation at Mouzaïaville in the western Mitidja—this time killing twenty-one—army commander General Jacques Allard forbade the use of wine vats as holding facilities, "despite the advantages they present in terms of guarding prisoners."[143] Their use, however, remained part of the Algerian memory of the war, as seen in a documentary titled *Les cuves de la mort* (The vats of death), shown on Algerian television in 2010.[144] The documentary explicitly compared the suffocation of Algerians in these vats to the notorious *enfumades* of the era of conquest, in which the likes of General Saint-Arnaud killed hundreds of Algerians by lighting fires in the mouths of the caves in which they had taken refuge. From destroyed crops to deaths from asphyxiation, so much about the war of independence evoked the brutal Franco-Algerian conflict of the previous century.

THE HOLLOWING

In August 1957 unknown attackers set fire to Jean Camilliéri's vineyard near Jemmapes. It was highly unusual for vines to be destroyed by fire, rather than cutting, but the inspector sent to assess the damage for compensation purposes had an explanation: the fire had spread because the vineyard—with no workers to maintain it—was overrun with weeds. All

Camilliéri could now do for his property was rely on a military escort to let him carry out the most essential tasks of pruning and applying fungicides. Nor was fire the only hazard of the neglect forced by the FLN's campaign. The section of Camilliéri's vineyard that escaped the fire would not yield a harvest either, because the untended grapes had been eaten by wild animals, mostly boar. As it happened, grapes and wild boar were both emblazoned on the coat of arms that colonists in Jemmapes had concocted for their community, but in real life wine producers wanted to keep those two symbols apart. In breaking down the boundary between them, the FLN was trying to return the vines to nature.[145]

Jean Camilliéri himself had long since retreated the six kilometers from his rural property to the comparative safety of Jemmapes, by then a town of close to 10,000 people. The movement from the countryside to towns and cities was a general phenomenon during the war. Between November 1954 and November 1960, the non-Muslim population of the fifty-five biggest towns in Algeria increased from 760,000 to 853,000. That meant that in 1960 less than 15 percent of Euro-Algerians lived in the countryside.[146] But this migration, and the evident reasons for it, should not obscure the fact that the war hastened a process that was already underway. To understand how rural colonial Algeria reached the point it did by the late 1950s, we need to reflect briefly on some settlement trends and also the theme of inheritance.

Euro-Algerian rural flight had been a source of anxiety to some for decades. The settlement advocate Jules Saurin lamented as early as 1920 that "the rural [European] populations of Algeria are disappearing with frightening rapidity." Certainly there was some exaggeration in Saurin's language, but in the coming years census data confirmed a general trend.[147] The cooperative movement helped to stanch the flow, but ambitious schemes to redivide large properties, like one in which a 360-hectare estate at Mouzaïaville was redistributed among nine colonists deemed worthy of assistance, did not catch on.[148]

The settling of Algeria's final new *villages de colonisation* at the end of the 1920s—right around the centenary—marked the definitive end of what some perceived as the "pioneering" era in French Algeria. The limitations the *statut viticole* placed on vine planting in the early 1930s ended the years of plantation fever, and, argued Hildebert Isnard in the 1940s, helped make wine producers more conservative in their investments and colonization less dynamic. "The pioneers turned into bour-geois," observed Isnard, with what seems like regret.[149]

Part of what being "bourgeois" implied was a desire to pass wealth and property down to the next generation. It is helpful, indeed, to con-ceive of colonial Algeria in terms of succeeding generations. The popular author Paul Reboux did just that in 1945 in his book *L'Algérie et ses vins.* The period from 1835 to 1870, wrote Reboux, could be thought of as the era of the grandfathers. From 1870 to 1905 was the era of the fathers; next, from 1905 to 1940, came the turn of the sons; and in 1940 began the time of the grandsons.[150]

Basic though Reboux's scheme was, it has the merit of forcing us to think about the importance of inheritance in the life of the colony. Some families saw an orderly progression from one generation to the next. The wealth of Gaston Averseng, for example, was founded on the business his grandfather, an early settler, had created in 1847 to process *crin vé-gétal* (plant fibers), but, through viticulture and fruit production, Gaston was able to expand the family's riches. In 1936 he drew up a succession plan in which his four sons would each inherit a different piece of his portfolio of properties. Upon his death in 1950 the plan went into full effect, leaving the four with just over a thousand hectares of vineyards between them in either the western Mitidja or near Tlemcen, as well as multiple additional assets.[151] Other notable families from the early gen-erations, however, did not persist. Jérôme Bastide and his son Léon, as we saw, were central to the development of colonial agriculture and viti-culture in and around Sidi-Bel-Abbès. But by the 1950s the family's pres-ence was vestigial, seen, for example, in a street name, Boulevard Bas-tide, which ran alongside where their vineyard had once grown at Clos Bastide.[152]

Rural colonial Algeria—that is, the part inhabited by a significant con-centration of Euro-Algerians—was in many ways subject to the same trends as the metropole, where the part of the population engaged in agriculture was declining after World War II at the rate of 1 or 2 percent every year.[153] Young people in French Algeria were often no different from their counterparts in the metropole in exploring alternate paths from their parents. The vinelord Michel-Louis Pelegri's son Michel fol-lowed his father into viticulture, but Michel's son, Jean, became a writer instead. In his elegiac autobiographical novel *Les oliviers de la justice* (The

Olive Trees of Justice, 1959), Jean Pelegri has his narrator reflect on the way the sons of original colonists inherited wealth, and with it a different set of attitudes toward the colony: "Few among them were capable of laboring the land with love as their fathers had done. . . . The country-side often bored them."[154] In an accusatory study of the French prosecution of the war, another writer, Jules Roy, who grew up in the same part of the Mitidja as Pelegri but likewise no longer lived in Algeria, hinted at a kind of late-imperial decadence in a slighting reference to "the great-grandsons of *colons*, who drive to the Lycée Bugeaud [a high school in Algiers] in their Mercedes."[155]

Roy's book, written near the end of the war, gave voice to some of the bitterness that was then percolating among Euro-Algerians. Roy's colonist brother and sister-in-law held big landowners most to blame, claiming that they had "invested their money in Switzerland. They've bought property in France, and they don't live on the land any more."[156] We have seen that there was some truth to this accusation, as some big landowners—such as members of the Germain and Bertagna families—purchased property in the metropole even before 1954. The hunt for attractive deals in France continued during the war. In 1956, for example, Marc Perrin, whose family's roots in western Algeria stretched back to the 1840s, bought Château Carbonnieux, a centuries-old wine estate in the Graves region outside Bordeaux.[157] For several years the classified section of the newspaper *L'Echo d'Oran* tempted the well-off with advertisements for vineyards or other agricultural properties in France, mostly in the South or West of the country. But in March 1956 editor Pierre Laffont announced that the newspaper would no longer carry ads for overseas properties, arguing that they undermined morale. Those who left Algeria in its moment of crisis, wrote Laffont, were effectively "deserters."[158]

The influence and decisions of big landowners, however, represented only part of the explanation for a gradual hollowing of rural colonial life. More than other forms of agricultural production, viticulture had always been said to tie colonists to the land. But in the final decades of French Algeria, as may be seen in wine harvest declarations before the insurrection began, absenteeism among wine producers helped to drive a surge in *métayage* (sharecropping). Inheritance patterns surely had something to do with this trend. For example, sometimes a subdivided property did not provide individuals with enough incentive to remain. In Fleurus, a village near Oran whose economy revolved around wine, Laurent Knecht divided his twenty-eight hectares of vines among five people, leaving plots that would have been too small on their own to sustain a family. By 1951 a sharecropper was working the five hectares inherited by Knecht's son Emile.[159] Those who were willing to work the land of others sometimes did well in this period; in Fleurus, Joseph Sévilla oversaw several vineyards for other villagers while maintaining ten hectares of his own. In broader perspective, though, the incidence of sharecropping tended to serve as an index of community decline that was also reflected in population size. The number of Euro-Algerians in Fleurus is a case in point, as it dwindled from 710 in 1945 to 480 in January 1962.[160]

Nowhere was the hollowing more evident than in eastern Algeria, including those parts of the region where there was still significant wine production. This is clear from the evidence provided by compensation claims filed after vineyards were attacked during the war for independence. The claims were often filed by sharecroppers working for absentee owners who were living in big towns like Constantine, if not in France: two separate claimants from the small village of Lannoy near Jemmapes were living in Grenoble when their losses occurred.[161] While some examples of absenteeism were certainly a consequence of local violence during the war, recurrent terms like *veuve* (widow) or *héritiers* (heirs) in prewar lists of vineyard owners around places like Jemmapes often represent clues that many proprietors were already nonresident.[162] This, coupled with a significant population disparity—Algerians outnumbered Euro-Algerians in the *Constantinois* by about eighteen to one—gave rise to proposals to cede the East to Muslims while preserving a space for Euro-Algerians in the West, where the demographic imbalance was less great. By the late 1950s, however, such schemes were easily outrun by events.[163]

THE FUTURE AND THE END

The big Euro-Algerian wine producers were not unaccustomed to having a negative image in France. In the early 1950s, protesters on the streets of Narbonne and other wine towns in the Midi once more shouted slogans hostile to Algerian wine, as consumption failed to keep pace with production and prices slumped. Amid a sense of crisis in 1953, the government revisited some of the corrective methods applied in the old *statut viticole* by decreeing a new *code du vin,* which set the terms for blocking a proportion of the French and Algerian wine harvest from the market and distilling the excess.[164] Some talk again penetrated Algeria about the need to reduce output in favor of a *politique de qualité,* but there was not much sign that producers there intended to do things differently.[165]

Amid French reconstruction and planning after World War II, however, the big wine producers' influence on Algeria's overall economy attracted sharp new critics.[166] An article in the left-leaning journal *Esprit* in 1952 argued that an ossified, self-serving economic elite in North Africa worked against France's greater interests.[167] In that same year, the well-known journalist Claude Bourdet echoed this critique as he singled out the supposedly baleful influence of one figure in particular: Henri Borgeaud, senator for Algiers and "grand master of Algerian viticulture," who brought "one of the most reactionary currents of the Maghreb" into the heart of republican French politics.[168]

In January 1955, only a few weeks into the war, this idea entered the mainstream with full force as the popular center-left weekly magazine *L'Express* featured on its cover a close-up photograph of Borgeaud beside the headline "The Masters of Algeria." Inside, the article suggested that rather than "Algeria is France," it would be more apt to say "Algeria is *their* France"—"they" being cosseted colonists with "feudal" attitudes, who were "leading us, with them, and for them, toward new dramas."[169] As the FLN's initial actions developed into the full drama of war and more and more French men were called into armed service, others joined the finger-pointing. Before the general election held in January 1956 the French Communist Party's manifesto in the wine-producing department of the Rhône fulminated, "The sons of the vine growers are being sent to their death in order to defend the interests of the large Algerian wine producers who compete with the metropolitan wines."[170]

Though these criticisms might have been dismissed as the opinions of natural enemies, it soon became clear that Borgeaud's influence was waning. New men in the administration sought new approaches; Jacques Soustelle, appointed governor-general in January 1955, favored policies that would integrate Algerians into the French nation, for example by making effective the promise of the 1947 Statute to offer equal political representation.[171] The old agro-capitalist elite suffered a blow in December 1956 with the assassination of Amédée Froger, vineyard owner, mayor of Boufarik, president of the association of mayors of Algeria, and one of the fiercest advocates of settler power. Froger had deep roots in viticulture—his father Virgile had been a phylloxera inspector during Amédée's early childhood in Philippeville in the 1880s—and close ties to the Borgeaud family: he was married to one of Henri Borgeaud's cousins, and served with him on the board of directors of the Domaine du Chapeau de Gendarme.[172] The mob violence that killed at least eight Algerians and wounded many more in retribution for Froger's death (and a bomb that went off at the cemetery on the day of his funeral) reaffirmed the lengths to which Euro-Algerians would go to preserve a long-established status quo, while obscuring the way Froger had helped sustain the structural inequalities that fed the revolt.

Algerian wine and its advocates looked in some respects increasingly passé. The discovery of significant oil as well as natural gas deposits in the Sahara in 1956 heralded a new source of liquid wealth.[173] In Europe, the European Economic Community that came into being with the Treaty of Rome in March 1957 promised integration for Algeria's agricultural goods, but with it the ominous prospect of new competition from cheap Italian wines that tariffs had virtually excluded from the French market before.[174] In Algeria, official discourse equated modernity primarily with industry. The language of a Gaumont newsreel report from 1958 on the opening of the French vehicle manufacturer Berliet's new truck-assembly plant east of Algiers at Rouïba—a place that had generated big profits in the past for wine producers like Jacques Duroux—was telling: "Where only sparse vineyards grew before," read the announcer, "the most modern industrial plant in Africa is born."[175] Berliet's venture may in fact have been a long-term bet on French companies' ability to do business in an independent Africa, rather than a show of confidence in French Algeria. Either way, it seemed to fit the spirit of the time. The Constantine Plan, announced by Charles de Gaulle in October 1958, promised to modernize as well as equalize Algeria's economy through investment in industry and energy, spending on infrastructure, and re-distribution of land.[176]

De Gaulle had returned to power in May of that year after the government in Paris proved incapable of squaring its objectives with those of Euro-Algerians and the army. Henri Borgeaud did not know what to make of the new regime, but offered de Gaulle his loyal assistance anyway.

De Gaulle made no attempt to conceal his lack of interest.[177] Borgeaud chose not to stand for election to the Senate of the new Fifth Republic.

It may look as if an old order was in eclipse, yet the Algerian wine industry continued to generate profit and optimism, and not only among the territory's putative "masters." In 1958, twenty-three-year-old Paul Bosc became the head of the *cave coopérative* in his birthplace of Marengo in the western Mitidja, which he considered "the best job in town," paying more than the municipality's chief financial officer.[178] In the same year, a brand-new *cave coopérative* opened at Laferrière near Aïn-Témouchent.[179] Half a million troops in Algeria created new levels of internal demand; a decree of September 1958 required all producers with an output greater than a hundred hectoliters to set aside 14 percent of the total to satisfy the army's needs (with compensation, of course).[180] Wine traders still saw a future in exports; in 1959, André Vigna opened a large new storage facility at Chalon-sur-Saône in Burgundy, where it would bottle brands from Algeria like Sidi Brahim.[181] Now transported mostly in tankers (see fig. 6.4), Algerian wine continued to represent an important element of maritime traffic into French ports as far north as Dunkirk.[182] The shipping company Schiaffino—whose director Laurent Schiaffino was re-elected as a senator for Algiers in 1959—was busier than ever. In Brittany, wine drinkers downed what they colloquially called "un Schiaffino," or several: the daughter of a sailor in Brest said of the company's tankers that "our fathers would drink straight from the pipe"—a joke that pointed to an unfortunate social reality.[183] In 1960, wine represented 53 percent of the value of Algeria's exports.[184]

There is little sign that the business of the best-connected wine-producing concerns suffered much during the war, though some did seek new sources of profit. The way the SIAH handled its assets is especially interesting. First, the company was able to sell its most troublesome property, at Mirabeau in Kabylia, where the security situation was so bad that by 1956 over a quarter of the ninety-nine hectares of vines at the estate had been destroyed. The buyer was the state, for 130 million francs, under the terms of a new program called the Caisse d'accession à la propriété et à l'exploitation rurale (known as CAPER), which aimed to redistribute big estates to small Algerian farmers. Internally the SIAH had discussed selling the property for years, so the transaction seemed like good business.[185] The more lucrative deals, however, involved the company's properties in and around Maison-Carrée. Archbishop

FIG. 6.4 Loading a wine tanker at the port of Algiers.
From *La vigne et le vin en Algérie. Edité à l'occasion du IXème Congrès International de la Vigne et du Vin, 6–15 octobre 1959, Alger* (Algiers: Baconnier, 1959), used by permission of the Centre de Documentation Historique sur l'Algérie, Aix-en-Provence.

Lavigerie's lands, at the junction of the eastern and southern approaches to the city of Algiers, were more desirable than ever in light of the Constantine Plan for development, proximity to the airport at Maison-Blanche, and even the discovery of oil and gas: in December 1958 the company sold a property with a 142-hectare vineyard to a division of the Compagnie française des pétroles, which planned to install a refinery.[186] By 1961 the SIAH still owned 221 hectares of vines, but acknowledged that its business was now founded more on commercial property than on agriculture. Indeed, the company had moved its headquarters to Paris, where it owned several buildings in high-value locations like the Esplanade des Invalides.[187]

Other well-capitalized, well-protected wine producers also thrived. In 1959 the Domaine du Kéroulis reported a wine harvest of 109,979 hectoliters, its biggest ever, from over 1,300 hectares of vines.[188] Enterprises like this were still looking to expand: the Compagnie des vignobles de la Méditerranée in 1959 bought a 118-hectare property adjacent to one of its own on the plain of Bône, and envisaged planting new vines on it. What seemed to vex such businesses most was not so much the war as the limitations the government placed on when they could release their product to the market.[189]

Optimism in these quarters was not unreasonable. The year 1959 did not only yield the sixth-largest wine harvest in French Algeria's history; it also represented a low point for the FLN's forces within Algeria, as severe French "pacification" operations brought results. The Constantine Plan also began with vigor and serious financial backing. The FLN's weakness in Algeria, however, did nothing to clarify the territory's political future. The independence movement could regroup outside Algerian borders and also work diplomatic channels to advance the cause. De Gaulle boasted in September 1959 that Algeria had made progress toward a better future in the fifteen months since his return to power. But by offering the inhabitants of Algeria the prospect of self-determination—which the United Nations was poised to recognize as their right—he laid out a clear political path to independence.[190]

Euro-Algerian hostility to this prospect led to much of the violence that marked the years 1960 to 1962, alongside a gradual recovery of the FLN's forces. In January 1961, voters in France approved a broadly worded referendum for the government to ready Algeria for self-determination. Large numbers abstained from the same vote in Algeria, but de Gaulle believed he now had a mandate for action. This led eventually to the Evian Accords of March 1962, and independence in July. The 1961 referendum, however, triggered hardliners to form a Euro-Algerian terrorist group, the Organisation armée secrète (OAS, Secret Armed Organization). It was already widely believed that some Euro-Algerian agricultural producers paid protection money to the FLN.[191] By the spring of 1961, the OAS was making similar demands.[192] Asked just after the war whether he had paid either or both organizations, Henri Borgeaud implied that he had paid the OAS—"who didn't?"—but was evasive as to whether he had also paid the FLN.[193]

Yet there remained the protection offered by the army, and this was what enabled some wine producers to keep investing in their properties virtually throughout the war.[194] In 1960, Jules Roy traveled to Mondovi, birthplace of his recently deceased friend Albert Camus and still home to the Domaine du Chapeau de Gendarme. There he found tanks at the gates, defending the vines to the end.[195]

"Seize the countryside," Lieutenant-General Bugeaud had urged in 1838, when the French presence was still largely limited to a few protected enclaves.[196] After Bugeaud's army slashed through Algerian resistance and cleared new paths to settlement, viticulture eventually emerged to help colonists establish some of their sturdiest rural roots. Over a century later, however, Algeria had failed to become anything other than a colonial society. Though wine continued to flow, the FLN's war hastened the hollowing of the colonial countryside and its reversion to a patchwork of guarded enclaves. The principal beneficiaries of the army's protection were often nonresident investors. By 1962, wine was still fundamental to the colonial economy, but the decline of rural settlement, the true blood of the colony, left French Algeria anemic at the last.

Pulling Up Roots
Since 1962

When Egyptian president Gamal Abdel Nasser visited Algeria in May 1963, he toured the Domaine de la Trappe, a destination familiar to visiting dignitaries dating back to Napoleon III. The estate had just gone through a rapid and radical upheaval. Only a few weeks previously, Henri Borgeaud had still been in charge, traveling regularly to the property from his apartment by the old port in Algiers. About a third of his 220 European workers remained in their jobs. That all changed at the end of March, when the Algerian government, declaring that the domain was now the property of the nation, took control with what was surely an excess of armed personnel. (Properties in the Mitidja plain belonging to the Germain and Averseng families were seized at the same time, and, in the East, the Domaine du Chapeau de Gendarme a few days later.) At La Trappe, Borgeaud and his wife, Denise, were allowed two hours to gather some belongings. So departed the last of the vinelords.[1]

By the time Nasser arrived, the newly nationalized property bore a new name, the Domaine Amar Bouchaoui, honoring a young man who had grown up on the estate but left early in the war of independence to join the *maquis*. Dead at the age of twenty-two, his name now served as a reminder of the sacrifices made to bring French Algeria to an end.[2] Perhaps of greatest interest to the man who had nationalized the Suez Canal, however, would have been the structure of management introduced after Borgeaud's eviction. The Domaine Amar Bouchaoui was to be part of Algeria's experiment with worker-managed farms, a system called *autogestion*. The same principles of self-management were applied in industry too.[3]

At independence Algeria still had the fourth-biggest wine industry in the world.[4] As the vines' former owners attempted to plant new roots in France or elsewhere, Algerians had to work out their relationship with a crop that covered some of the best land yet whose product had to find outlets abroad—France most of all. "French Algeria" might be dead as a political entity, but wine made many Algerians feel their independence was not yet complete.

SELF-MANAGEMENT

In some ways self-management emerged naturally out of the chaotic departure of the majority of the Euro-Algerian population in 1962. Between January and the end of August of that year, as many as 580,000 left Algeria.[5] One of them was Albert Malleval, who in June walked away with his family from their domain of over 300 hectares of wheat and vines at Damiette, just outside Médéa. The 150 workers on the estate kept working under the guidance of their Algerian foreman. In August, the Provisional Executive Council of the new Algerian state issued a decree that allowed local authorities to take over agricultural or industrial enterprises deemed to be abandoned (referred to as *biens vacants*) and find managers to run them until, in theory, the owners returned. Under those conditions the workers at Damiette brought in the estate's grape harvest. Then, in October, with Ahmed Ben Bella newly installed as Algeria's prime minister, the government authorized the formation of management committees (*comités de gestion*) on vacant agricultural properties. One such committee was elected at the Malleval property, where, next to a sign on the estate's mansion that read "Domaine Malleval 1914," someone wrote "Ferme Collective Malleval Bien Vacant 1962" (Malleval Collective Farm, Vacant Property 1962).[6]

The apparent spontaneity of some of these developments should not obscure the fact that other countries already provided models for a system based on workers' councils. In Algeria the most influential proved to be the Yugoslavian model, in which workers were permitted the primary responsibility of decision-making through a combination of assemblies and elected councils, while a director served as a link to the state.[7] This, in essence, was the system codified by the government in a series of decrees issued in March 1963. The second of the *décrets de mars,* for example, stipulated, "Vacant industrial and mining enterprises as well as agricultural concerns are to manage their own affairs through the following bodies: a) The workers' general assembly, b) The workers' council, c) The management committee, d) The director."[8] A number of large properties that were objectively speaking not "vacant," such as Borgeaud's La Trappe, were then selectively nationalized in the following days. These seizures were retrospectively justified by a novel interpretation of "vacant property" that encompassed "domains whose current ownership is an insult to the Algerian revolution." The government also took steps to prevent better-off Algerians from speculating on formerly "colonial" land.[9]

Euro-Algerians still maintained about a million hectares of agricultural land. Among them was Louis Jourdan, who continued to hold three properties, all with Algerian managers, most notably a 350-hectare estate in the western Mitidja of which vines covered about 200 hectares. But Jourdan's 1963 grape harvest was his last. On October 1, Ben Bella—now Algeria's president—pronounced the nationalization of all remaining lands belonging to "colonists." "This is a historic moment," Ben Bella told a large crowd in Algiers, "that restores to our country its most fundamental right: the land." The former owners were to be permitted to sell their recent harvest, but would not be offered any compensation. Jourdan chose this moment to leave Algeria. Further east, at the SIAH's remaining holdings, Brother Gallus of the White Fathers oversaw the production of one last batch of communion wine before he, too, departed for France in June 1964.[10]

Guided by a government body formed in March 1963, the Office national de la réforme agraire (ONRA, National Office of Agrarian Reform), self-managed farms were often constituted from several colonial-era properties. One massive vine-and-cereal-growing *domaine d'autogestion* at Zemmouri to the east of Algiers was pieced together from as many as thirty-two colonial farms.[11] Sometimes the rationale for such combinations was to help ensure greater crop variety. At the core of the Domaine Bouglouf Braïek, a few kilometers outside Skikda, for instance, was a 677-hectare estate that had belonged before independence to Léopold Morel, the owner of the newspaper *La Dépêche de Constantine.* To this were joined adjacent farms less dominated by the vine, forming a self-managed domain of over a thousand hectares.[12]

The names adopted by these farms underlined the change that had taken place. The communities in which they stood were themselves often newly named: in the colonial era Zemmouri had been Courbet, for example, while Skikda was the former Philippeville. At the level of the farm, the Domaine de la Trappe was far from the only estate to adopt the name of a former worker designated a martyr of the struggle for independence. (The Domaine du Chapeau de Gendarme was another, becoming the Domaine Feddaoui Salah.)[13] Other estates honored figures more widely known from the war, like the Domaine Colonel Amirouche in Reghaïa or the Domaine Ramdane Abane in Dar El Beïda. An older hero was celebrated in the western Mitidja at the Domaine Emir Abdelkader, close to the town of Hadjout (formerly Marengo)—itself renamed for a tribe that had harried early European settlers in the region. A few estates generalized the language of struggle into the realm of ideology: Larbaâ now had a Domaine Révolution Socialiste.[14] There was a more tangible reminder of the war at the Domaine Bouglouf Braïek, as Léopold Morel's mansion on the estate was turned into a home for children of "martyrs of the revolution."[15]

Despite some revolutionary trappings, however, there was also continuity. This was certainly true in terms of personnel. The Domaine Kacem Ali in Ahmar El Aïn, for example—Louis Jourdan's former estate—retained a decades-old connection to an area east of El Asnam (formerly Orléansville), where many of the permanent workforce had family roots; every fall, 300 seasonal migrants would travel from this area to Kacem Ali for the grape harvest, as they had done for years.[16] In the West, Moroccan nationals were still a presence for a time, and some were even elected to the new workers' councils.[17] Assistance in some of the more technical roles also came from French people who stayed on in Algeria as so-called *coopérants*. In 1963 the management at the Domaine du Kéroulis, now under *autogestion*, appealed for help with the estate's winemaking, and obtained it from the French director of the agricultural school in Aïn-Témouchent.[18] On the business side, the chief administration and finance officer of the Domaine du Chapeau de Gendarme, Marcel Castelbou, left Algeria in July 1962, but, finding it hard to settle in France and hearing that his old job had not been filled, returned to it a few months later and remained in the position until 1971.[19]

The imprint of the state on the new self-managed farms was supposed to be relatively light, and workers tried to ensure that they got to choose the representatives they themselves wanted.[20] There is evidence nonetheless of attempts by outsiders to interfere in committee elections. In late 1963, for example, the French anarchist Daniel Guérin observed the election for the management committee at the Domaine de Sainte-Louise in Ahmar El Aïn (a property that in the colonial era had been the birthplace of the Germain family's fortune). There, Guérin witnessed an unsubtle effort by members of the army and the local prefecture first to tamper with the ballot, and then to install three ex-combatants on the committee. The workers reacted with outrage and resisted as best they could, but two of the outsiders' men still ended up "chosen."[21] Such committees became all the more vulnerable to the army's influence after Algeria's first major postindependence upheaval, when Ben Bella was overthrown in June 1965 in a military coup led by Colonel Houari Boumediène. After the coup, new cooperatives of ex-combatants (*coopératives d'anciens moudjahidine*), approved by compliant local authorities, played their own part in chipping away at the self-managing sector.[22]

Workers remained committed to self-management and the freedom it allowed them in comparison to colonial times.[23] With about 90 percent of Algeria's vines under *autogestion,* wine production was central to the broader project of self-management.[24] Nevertheless, the challenges that confronted viticulture soon became plain. Despite some post–World War II replanting, the Algerian vineyard as a whole was aging badly, hastened in many instances by neglect during the war of independence; falling yields represented the most important manifestation of this decline. Many temporary vineyard workers obtained permanent positions under self-management, but to a point that became a serious financial burden for many estates. Tractors and other machines that were now seen as integral to the practice of viticulture lacked a sufficient supply of replacement parts, or qualified mechanics to repair them: mechanics were typically the busiest workers on self-managing estates (and among the highest paid).[25]

Many of these problems—an excess of permanent workers and deteriorating vines, as well as factionalism in the workforce—are dramatized in Mouloud Achour's novella *Les dernières vendanges* (The last grape harvests, 1971). The story's central character, the director of a self-managed farm on what appears to be the Mitidja plain, regards the vines that predominate on the estate as a "parasitic plant introduced by the occupier and cultivated to his exclusive profit," and becomes obsessed with the idea that he must replace them with "a more useful crop," specifically wheat.[26] But in reality, self-managing workers in the Mitidja were cautious about the prospect of such a change. In a study led by the sociologist Claudine Chaulet between 1968 and 1970, interviewees expressed concern that replacing vines with much less labor-intensive wheat would simply put people out of work. "If we rip up the vine, the people will die of hunger," worried one worker, while another reasoned that "there is gold in the vine; cereal crops cannot earn as much."[27] Those assessments at the point of production, however, did not factor in the problems that had accumulated in selling Algeria's wine.

BREAKING DEPENDENCE?

The Evian Accords of 1962 that offered Algerians their independence also laid out a framework for the transition to a new relationship between France and Algeria. As to how the new era would relate to agricultural production, the accords offered little detail; but some general statements of economic principle envisaged cooperative relations and minimal obstacles to commercial exchange.

Though the accords did represent a reasonably effective mechanism for the transfer of power, they also drew intense criticism on both sides of the Mediterranean. Even before the accords were ratified, the FLN deemed them "neocolonialist" and a formula for Algeria's continued economic and cultural dependence. Many in France, by contrast, regarded them as one last betrayal by the French government.[28]

For a contingent of wine producers in the Midi, the betrayal consisted not so much in granting independence but rather in allowing Algerian wine to continue to enter France on favorable terms. In March 1963, militant Midi producers marked the first anniversary of the signing of the accords by smashing bottles of Algerian wine in the streets of towns like Béziers and Perpignan.[29] Unrest continued on and off throughout the year, causing particular consternation in the port of Sète, which once again did not want to see any interruption to the flow of wine into its facilities.[30]

Independent Algeria, of course, could not expect the support that colonial Algeria had received from the French metropole in the 1930s, and less so after such Evian-defying actions as Ben Bella's October 1963 nationalization of "colonial" properties. Even so, just as in the 1930s, Midi producers did not represent the whole of France, and there were French consumers who continued to appreciate Algerian wine. Jean-Baptiste Doumeng, an enterprising communist who dealt internationally in a wide variety of agricultural products and was well attuned to the working-class palate, observed that the miners of the Nord seemed to prefer Algerian wines to weaker French ones.[31] And nowhere was Algerian wine more popular than in Brittany, where it remained the drink of choice and held greater status than locally produced cider. An anthropologist who conducted research in a rural community in Finistère in 1965 found that "everyone" drank imported Algerian red, preferably with an alcohol content of at least thirteen percent, though local women liked to mix it with lemonade.[32]

A range of interests were therefore in play when French and Algerian negotiators met in late 1963 to establish more clearly what the Evian Accords should mean in relation to Algeria's wine industry. The Algerians wanted to escape economic dependency but recognized that this conspicuous relic of the colonial era remained essential for the export receipts it generated and the jobs it sustained.[33] For the French, concern over protests in the Midi had to be balanced against their desire for continued access to Algerian markets and in particular Algeria's oil and gas. The agreement signed in January 1964 by the Algerian minister for the economy, Bashir Boumaza, and the French secretary for Algerian affairs, Jean de Broglie, looked like a modest plan to wean Algeria away from its dependence on French clients while limiting its wine's impact on the French market. The agreement put a cap on how much Algerian wine could enter France over the following five years, with the quantity set to decrease gradually from 8.76 million hectoliters in 1964 to a projected 7 million hectoliters in 1968.[34]

Aside from a brief interruption in 1965, this agreement more or less held up until January 1967, when the French government announced a suspension of Algerian wine imports. This move came just after a militant Midi winegrowers' group, the Comité régional d'action viticole (CRAV), called for major protests to defend local viticulture against imported wines that they blamed for driving down prices and causing local distress.[35] Algerians believed, however, that the timing of the ban also connected closely to political campaigning ahead of the legislative elections to be held in France in March. An editorial in the FLN's newspaper, *El Moudjahid,* noted that left-wing candidates for office were targeting Algerian wine in their speeches, in ways that seemed out of step with their expressions of solidarity with recently liberated peoples.[36] By contrast, and not for the first time, defenders of Algerian wine in France were more likely to come from traditionally conservative backgrounds, as chambers of commerce with an interest in the trade, like the one in Nantes, campaigned for the bar on imports to be lifted.[37] Meanwhile, Algerians faced such problems with storage that they sought space for their unsold wine in facilities as far afield as Antwerp.[38]

The French bar on Algerian wine in 1967, though it proved only temporary, underlined Algeria's need to develop alternative outlets at a time when its wine exports and its petroleum exports remained comparable in value. Indeed, the energy minister, Belaïd Abdesselam, was a leading figure in talks with the Soviet Union to relieve the pressure by purchasing some of the country's wine output. Abdesselam later recalled telling the Soviets that the French had wanted to punish Algeria for gradually removing the influence of foreign companies over the country's oil production; Soviet negotiators, in turn, expressed their desire to support "Third World" nations. The discussions led in 1968 to an agreement with the Soviet Union's food ministry to buy five million hectoliters of Algerian wine annually for the next seven years.

Abdesselam considered this a modest victory in the broader struggle against Algeria's dependency on France, though the agreement itself posed problems on both sides. For the Algerians there was little interest in fulfilling the contract with Soviet products, with the exception of oil-prospecting equipment, some cotton, and perhaps some sugar (though Soviet sugar reputedly did not dissolve in coffee). More importantly, the contract set a price that was well below that previously paid by French importers and failed to reflect production costs. On the Soviet side, the infrastructure needed to import wine at scale—tanks and other containers for distribution, storage facilities in port, factories in which to process Algeria's blending wines—was for the time being lacking.[39] Short of workers to build a wine-processing facility in the Siberian city of

Irkutsk, the Soviet ministry of construction secured a detachment of 127 labor-camp detainees for the task—an unexpected echo of colonial uses of prisoners in Algerian vineyards.[40]

Despite such hindrances, the deal took effect and left a cultural mark. Algerian wine entered the Soviet Union either through Leningrad or via one of the Black Sea ports of Illichivsk, Tuapse, and Novorossiiysk.[41] The wine was often marketed to Soviet citizens using a type of Orientalist imagery familiar from the colonial era (see fig. 7.1). When fortified and sold under brand names like Solntsedar ("gift of the sun"), it acquired a certain notoriety: in one popular limerick the drink brings about the death of an unsuspecting grandmother. After the original agreement expired, the Soviets contracted in smaller amounts until Mikhail Gorbachev's anti-alcoholism campaign of the mid-1980s.[42]

The Soviet deal was certainly better than "throw[ing] the wine in the sea," as Abdesselam put it, but no one could pretend it resolved any of the industry's underlying problems.[43] The commercial challenges appeared even more grave after July 1970, when the European Economic Community (EEC) finally opened up the wine trade among its member states and Italian wines began to enter France in large quantities.[44] Yet Algerian policy toward wine appeared to drift until April 1971, when Boumediène announced in a speech that the time had come to reconvert much of the Algerian vineyard to other forms of production.[45]

Boumediène's declaration was linked to a broader strategy of economic disentanglement from France. His government took its most important measure toward that end in February 1971, when it nationalized French oil interests in the country.[46] It was entirely predictable that French authorities should respond to this by declaring that they could not accept any imports of Algerian wine. To Boumediène, wine—this colonial holdover that "our people do not consume" and were obliged to export—had become a card that France held in reserve to exert pressure in its dealings with Algeria. In his April 1971 speech, Boumediène stated simply that Algeria should "tear up this card."[47]

"Tearing up this card" translated in practice to tearing up vines. There had, of course, been some uprooting in the preceding years, particularly of older vines. At the Domaine Bouglouf Braïek, Léopold Morel's former property, the vineyard decreased in size from 308 hectares in 1950 to 134 hectares in 1969.[48] But after the 1971 grape harvest, the uprooting across Algeria was much more extensive. In October and

FIG. 7.1 A Soviet label for "Algerian red table wine," probably 1970s. This particular batch was marketed in the Soviet Socialist Republic of Georgia, and vaguely announced an alcohol content of "9 to 14%." Reproduced from the author's collection.

November of that year, 11,500 hectares were torn up on the Mitidja plain alone.[49] In the East, the uprooting in 1971 and 1972 on what was now called the plain of Annaba (formerly Bône) was nearly total. The old Domaine de Daroussa was almost the only vineyard that remained; others, like the former Domaine du Chapeau de Gendarme, were no more.[50]

For vineyards still in production, Boumediène's minister for agriculture and agrarian reform, Tayebi Mohamed Belhadj, urged a new focus on table wines for immediate consumption, rather than high-alcohol blending wines. Just before the 1971 *vendange*, Belhadj instructed producers to carry out the harvest more quickly than had become usual, to avoid the over-ripening that made for undrinkable wines.[51] But there is not much evidence that the quality of the wine improved as the quantity decreased. The story instead is one of declining yields along with an aging workforce and stagnant salaries. From 1965 to 1975, the size of the Algerian vineyard decreased from about 340,000 to 210,000 hectares, and the output from over fourteen million to about four million hectoliters. In the same span of time, the average annual yield approximately halved.[52]

Cereal crops were the most common replacement for torn-up vines, and represented in many instances a kind of reclamation of land that had been usurped by the vine in earlier decades. Cereal cultivation could still only supply an eighth of the workdays offered by viticulture, but new varieties did deliver higher yields. The happy ending to Mouloud Achour's novella *Les dernières vendanges* revolves around the first harvest of a strain of Canadian wheat that provides a "simply miraculous" yield on land once covered with vines.[53] By 1975, the value of cereal production in the self-managed sector outstripped that of wine.[54]

In reality, Algeria's agricultural quandaries persisted.[55] One of Boumediène's signature policies was an "agrarian revolution" launched in 1971, which aimed to redress some of the legacies of colonialism (and, a bit belatedly, reward peasants for their contribution to its demise) through land redistribution and other measures such as the abolition of sharecropping. But these reforms did not resolve a growing problem of food insufficiency. A consequence of systemic inefficiency, as well as underinvestment in agriculture as industry attracted greater attention (and rural migrants), total annual cereal production was barely higher at the end of the 1970s than it had been in the immediate postindependence period, even as the population had expanded by well over half during that time.[56] The result was increasing dependence on imports of staples like wheat. Paid for with revenues from oil and natural gas, these imports only reduced the incentive for peasants to cultivate basic crops rather than attempt more lucrative forms of production like poultry farming. At Boumediène's death in December 1978, nearly two-thirds of the flour and semolina consumed by Algerians was imported. Though the country had an overall growth rate of around 7 percent and particularly strong development in the petrochemical industry, it was far from fulfilling the agrarian revolution's goal of food self-sufficiency.[57]

WINE REPATRIATED

As independent Algeria struggled to define a consistent wine policy, the Euro-Algerians who had once dominated the industry had more personal choices to make: whether to attempt to stay involved with viticulture or find some alternative path as they assumed their new identity as *rapatriés,* "repatriated" French citizens "returning" to a country most had never previously inhabited.[58]

The choice, of course, was strongly influenced by the means at their disposal. As we have seen, some wealthy Euro-Algerians had already bought vineyards in France in the years before what turned out to be the date of Algerian independence. Thus, Nicolas Tari, from a family that had migrated to Algeria from the Spanish province of Alicante in the nineteenth century and settled to the west of Oran, in 1954 completed the purchase of Château Giscours, a prestigious domain that had fallen on hard times in the Médoc near Bordeaux.[59] The Bordeaux region continued to attract well-off Euro-Algerians at the moment of independence in 1962. In that year, for example, members of the Chanfreau family, who had owned several large vineyards in an area southwest of Sidi-Bel-Abbès, bought two estates in the Médoc: Château Fonréaud and Château Lestage.[60] The wine trader Georges Raoux followed a less conventional path, moving his company to Bordeaux in 1962 and pioneering the sale of wine by mail order. Over time, the family also acquired wineries in the region.[61]

Those of lesser means found it more difficult to replicate the standard of living wine had allowed them in Algeria, especially as the mass arrival of *rapatriés* in France (679,000 in 1962) drove up land prices.[62] One wine producer who moved to the Côte d'Azur east of Toulon could not afford the land he calculated he would need to make a living from viticulture again, so instead he opted to grow flowers commercially (and succeeded quite well).[63] Others moved away from any form of agriculture, though in some cases not definitively.[64] The former director of the *cave coopérative* of Marengo, Paul Bosc, relocated to Epinal in the Vosges, where he found a job as a traveling salesman for a textile company, while his wife, Andrée, worked in the tax office. Unhappy in their new lives, however, they decided to follow the example of two family members who had gone to Canada. Bosc's expertise earned him a position with the Quebec liquor board, and then a job with a wine producer in Ontario. By the late 1970s he was able to buy his own estate, and he became a leading figure in the development of viticulture in the Niagara region.[65]

Many *rapatriés* nevertheless managed to re-involve themselves with wine production in France, largely in the South, whether through their own means, by teaming up with other returnees, or with help from government-created agencies to manage access to agricultural land such as the Société d'aménagement foncier et d'établissement rural (known as SAFER).[66] These *pieds-noirs*, as they were now typically referred to in their postcolonial lives, stood out to local people for the techniques they applied to viticulture and the attitudes they held toward their work.

Resettled *pieds-noirs* often felt the rural regions of France they had moved to were behind the times. Wine-producing communities in colonial Algeria had often been villages, but these villages had had broad main streets, an open appearance, and a strong sense of connection to the ports that were essential to the wider trade. There was "nothing medieval" about the places they had left, one *rapatrié* who moved to an area near Nîmes told the sociologist René Domergue.[67] In the eyes of *pied-noir* wine producers, viticulture in the Midi reflected a more general air of backwardness. Midi producers seemed out of touch with their market and their competition, and slow to embrace new production techniques. In terms of wine, "it was the Middle Ages here," a *pied-noir* who bought a domain near Béziers later recalled.[68]

The suspicion that often greeted the new arrivals was not only the stereotypical response of small communities to "outsiders." More specifically, local people might look at Euro-Algerian wine producers as recent competitors, or feel resentment due to the death of young French draftees in the war of independence.[69] Added to this could be jealousy of the subsidies at the *rapatriés'* disposal.[70] This might have led some *pieds-noirs* to want to keep a low profile, but agriculture is by its nature a relatively public form of economic activity. Local people would notice, for example, if a *rapatrié* chose to work his vines into the evening by the light of his vehicle headlamps.[71] But if the new arrivals sometimes seemed to go about their work in an unusual way, there was also curiosity about what they were doing.

Pieds-noirs, it seemed to local observers, took some particular approaches to their work. They did not hesitate to clear difficult terrain, such as the shrubby *garrigue* in the Costières region near Nîmes.[72] They pursued high yields from their vines, which often meant harvesting the grapes later than was customary; they did not feel the need to respect traditions that might dictate that the *vendange* be brought in before the hunting season began. They liked to use a lot of fertilizer and chemical treatments. They also liked new machines, which connected to their desire to reduce labor costs—agricultural salaries in France coming as something of a shock after Algeria.[73] But they also often employed North Africans on their vineyards, like the producer who moved from a 140-hectare estate near Mascara to one of 30 hectares in the Var and hired three Algerians to work on it. More common still were Moroccans, some of whom had past experience in vineyards in colonial Algeria. To local residents, the *pieds-noirs* were very active landowners, frequently riding their tractors themselves, but they also *faisaient suer le burnous*— they made their workers sweat, often in ways that recalled their recent colonial past.[74]

As producers, then, they manifested the same strengths and weaknesses they had displayed in Algeria. A *pied-noir* named Pascual Monrreal bought the Domaine d'Entenepay at Saint-Cézert near Toulouse, secured loans to replant over sixty hectares of vines and renovate the château on the property, then went bust a few years later.[75] Despite skepticism about some of the newcomers' methods, however, rural people in regions like the Midi took note and often imitated, as wine producers increasingly realized that they needed to place more emphasis on a quality product.[76]

CORSICA, A NEW ALGERIA?

The region whose viticulture was most obviously affected by *rapatriés* from Algeria was Corsica. Corsicans had played no small part in ruling and peopling France's colonial empire, including Algeria, and, for some *pieds-noirs,* a move to the island was in a sense a genuine return.[77] But it was an appealing destination for more than just those with Corsican ancestry. For *pieds-noirs* angry at the loss of French Algeria, Corsica looked less blameworthy than mainland France: Corsicans, for example, had shown support for the settler uprising of May 1958. Much of Corsica's terrain evoked coastal Algeria, as did the climate. From a less sentimental standpoint, too, new arrivals stood to benefit from the Société pour la mise en valeur agricole de la Corse (known as SOMIVAC). Created in 1957, this development agency aimed to revitalize Corsica's agriculture by means of irrigation works and by supporting the clearance of new lands for cultivation. The majority of the beneficiaries of this program turned out to be returnees from North Africa, for whom SOMIVAC's focus on the eastern plain of the island held particular promise as a new site of extensive viticulture.[78]

Corsican viticulture at that time bore little similarity to what had become normal in colonial Algeria. Though viticulture was quite widely practiced, vineyards were typically no bigger than a hectare or so, there was a great diversity of grape varieties, and the vines were often old and unproductive, with the consequence that most wine was consumed by families and not much of it left the island.[79] (During the colonial period, indeed, Corsica imported Algerian wine.) This helps to explain why Corsica had been allowed to follow a set of wine regulations distinct from the mainland, and chaptalization (adding sugar to the grape juice or must to increase alcohol content) was still permitted.[80]

Pieds-noirs took to viticulture in Corsica with such vigor that in 1965 they already accounted for 88 percent of the island's wine harvest. Clearing the *maquis* scrubland on the eastern plain became, for some *rapatriés,* almost an act of commemoration of the colonial past. One *pied-noir* told the geographer Françoise Brun, "In Corsica I found lands that allowed me to create beautiful vineyards, and I rediscovered the pioneering spirit of my grandparents from Lorraine, who were exiled in 1870."[81] The parallels did not stop there. A *rapatrié* from the Mitidja who wore a colonial-style helmet and carried a switch as he oversaw thirty Moroccan workers whose lodgings resembled Algerian *gourbis* took the image almost to the point of caricature. But the scale of these vineyards (usually twenty to a hundred hectares, though quite often more than that), the use of familiar grape varieties that emphasized color and yield (Grenache, Carignan, Cinsault), the construction of family wineries, and even the tapping of commercial networks that dated back to colonial times, all helped *pied-noir* wine producers feel they had come as close as they possibly could to recreating their former lives.[82]

This was precisely why Corsicans began to object. As in parts of mainland France, *pieds-noirs* initially attracted some curiosity; local people sometimes even came to spectate as the recent arrivals used their machines to tackle the *maquis* or other difficult terrain, and some Corsicans felt inspired to borrow their techniques. As demand caused land prices to spike, however, many came to see these newcomers as unfairly favored. Though Corsicans still dominated local politics, they considered villages on the eastern plain like Ghisonaccia to be less and less culturally Corsican.[83] By the late 1960s, the Corsican autonomist movement, led by the Action régionaliste corse (ARC, Corsican Regionalist Action Group), was becoming increasingly militant. There were attacks on SOMIVAC offices, and, in 1969, demonstrations against the sale of land to a *pied-noir*. Activists began to speak of Corsica as a colony of France.[84]

Eventually, wine became a focal point of the conflict. The French state finally decided to ban chaptalization in Corsica, closing a loophole that had allowed *pied-noir* producers to boost the alcohol content of their wines. Not long afterward, in 1974, five wine traders were prosecuted for trying to evade the new rules. In the view of the ARC, the scandal was caused by newcomers but tarnished the image of Corsican producers, who traditionally had not engaged in the practice. This, however, was only a prelude to a more serious drama that centered on Henri Depeille, one of several *pieds-noirs* who simultaneously owned vineyards—his was nearly 200 hectares—and wine-trading companies. To try to manage some serious debts, Depeille concocted a murky financial arrangement with some of his *pied-noir* creditors and a wine company based in Paris. When this company got into financial trouble, it looked likely to take down a well-known Corsican trading house with it, and, in turn, hurt small Corsican producers.[85]

Members of the ARC, under the group's leader, Edmond Simeoni, had been looking for an occasion to bring their autonomist demands to greater public attention. They certainly achieved this on August 21, 1975, by occupying Henri Depeille's winery at Aléria, near Ghisonaccia on the eastern plain. Depeille and his family were allowed to leave, while the occupiers covered the main building with graffiti demanding "COLONS ESCROCS FORA"—"swindling colonists out." The next day, the authorities sent in a squadron of the riot police to end the occupation, but during the confrontation two of the police were shot dead and one of the occupiers was badly wounded. The event led to the banning of the ARC, but came to be regarded as a formative moment in the development of a militant Corsican nationalist movement.[86]

Corsica's vineyard went from about 5,550 hectares before the large-scale arrival of *rapatriés,* to 30,000 hectares in the mid-1970s, to 5,800 hectares in 2014.[87] The contraction of the late 1970s and 1980s can partly be linked to autonomist violence, as *pieds-noirs* migrated once more to the French mainland. (North African agricultural workers who had been on Corsica—especially Moroccans, who had gone to the island in greater numbers than Algerians—followed a similar path in search of work in southern France.[88]) A more important factor in the widespread uprooting of vines that took place after 1976, however, was a newly concerted emphasis on higher-quality output, backed up with subsidies from the EEC, which was trying to tackle the overproduction that had helped form a European "wine lake." As local grape varieties like Nielluccio underwent a revival, Corsican producers retrospectively criticized the *pieds-noirs* for having brought their yield-fixated habits to the island.[89]

By no means did this accusation apply to all *pied-noir* producers. The Skalli family's property near Aléria, for example, the Domaine Terra Vecchia, became known for prioritizing quality varietals.[90] But even quality producers became the target of Corsican nationalists. In July 1962, Paul Birebent had walked away from his domain near Oran after one of his Algerian workers warned him it was no longer safe for him to be there.[91] Birebent moved to Corsica instead, taking advantage of the assistance offered by SOMIVAC to clear land and develop a vineyard on the eastern coast, and working progressively over the years to improve his wines. One night in October 1990, armed intruders in masks rounded him up with his employees, and then proceeded to open the wine vats and destroy buildings and equipment on the domain with explosives and fire. Finding the local authorities unsupportive in the aftermath, Birebent chose to relocate to the Côte d'Azur on the mainland. "Twice in one lifetime, it's too much," he reflected.[92] For some *pieds-noirs,* Corsica turned out to be too much like Algeria.

ALGERIAN WINE AT THE MARGINS

Though wine production became an increasingly marginal activity in Algeria in the years that followed Boumediène's death in 1978, it did not disappear entirely from view. The brand Sidi Brahim, owned by the *pied-noir* Vigna family and bottled at their plant in Chalon-sur-Saône, helped Algerian wine to remain familiar to French consumers.[93] And while Italian wine may have become the principal focus of Midi producers' hostility, in 1981 a group of militants still felt the need to attack twenty-five wagon-tankers holding Algerian wine in the railway station at Sète, spilling 10,000 hectoliters onto the tracks.[94] But by then Algeria barely represented much competition. In 1985 the country's total production dropped below one million hectoliters, the first time it had failed to pass that threshold in exactly a century.[95]

This decline was the outcome, as we have seen, of efforts to reduce a sense of postcolonial dependence, as well as changes in the wine market. Objections to viticulture in a predominantly Muslim country, by contrast, do not seem to have been an important factor. Certainly, independence exposed alcohol's place in Algerian society to new scrutiny. In 1963, a French observer noted that most cafés in small towns across Algeria now closed early, as they did not serve alcohol.[96] Later in the 1960s, Boumediène made overtures to Islamic leaders as he went about securing his authority, and he allowed some room for them to criticize social behavior, including alcohol use. While Islamic authorities favored the program of uprooting that took place under Boumediène's watch, however, there is little reason to doubt Belaïd Abdesselam's insistence that government policy on wine was shaped according to secular considerations.[97] Indeed, Boumediène's regime was altogether too secular (and socialist) in the eyes of Muslim scholars like Sheikh Abdellatif

Soltani, who, from exile in Morocco in 1974, criticized Boumediène for allowing a wine industry to continue, among other faults.[98]

Islamic opposition to viticulture began to pose a serious threat to Algerians involved with wine production in the 1990s. By then Algeria's experiment with *autogestion* was over, and most growers of wine-producing grapes supplied the state wine company, the Office national de commercialisation des produits viti-vinicoles (ONCV).[99] But the political regime created at independence was about to come under attack. An Islamist party, the Front islamique du salut (FIS, Islamic Salvation Front), achieved widespread success in local elections held in June 1990, and then took control of well over half of Algeria's regional and communal councils. Many of these councils immediately began to clamp down on sales of alcohol.[100]

Though these measures most often targeted distributors in towns and cities, some rural cultivators made the decision to tear up their vines. The pressures became far greater as Algeria slid into civil war after the army carried out a coup in January 1992, in response to victory by the FIS in parliamentary elections. (The FIS was banned two months later.) Armed Islamist groups, known collectively as the Groupe islamique armé (GIA), tried to intimidate winegrowers into abandoning viticulture. Ahead of the 1994 grape harvest, for example, growers in the Mascara region were warned, "Cut one grape and we cut your throat"—a threat to be taken literally, as it described a favored GIA form of execution.[101] Production hit a new low of 357,000 hectoliters in 1997, but after that year the violence began to ease up, and wine output gradually increased again.[102] The war, however, had claimed tens of thousands of lives.

The ONCV played a leading role in shoring up what was left of the wine industry during the civil war, by supporting growers and planting new vineyards of its own. When I visited ONCV headquarters in Algiers in 2013, the official I met with assured me that Islamists no longer menaced the agency's operations. (I had to wonder if the absence of any identifying mark at the entrance to the ONCV offices gave the lie to that assertion. None of the uniformed men I asked in the vicinity could point me to the address, and I ended up late for my appointment.) The official looked toward new opportunities in the future. He showed me a photograph of himself standing in a field near Tlemcen with the French film star Gérard Depardieu, who had been part of a joint venture to develop new vineyards in the west of the country. The initial project had failed, as the bank financing it, the Banque Khalifa, went under amid charges of corruption against its founder, Rafik Khalifa.[103] But the ONCV had picked up the pieces and continued at the Tlemcen site to develop a quality brand named Cuvée Monica—recalling, as the label on the bottle duly noted, Saint Augustine's mother, if not also her weakness for wine. Quality wines like this, the ONCV official hoped, could help attract Chinese consumers. But with wealthy Chinese buying up vineyards in French regions like Bordeaux—something that would be impossible in Algeria due to its stringent controls on foreign ownership of land—and China itself producing more and more wine, this seemed a rather remote prospect.[104] By 2015, indeed, Algeria's wine exports had fallen so far that they were comfortably exceeded by imports.[105]

If the wine industry in the 2010s seemed to function behind closed doors, reminders of its colonial past remained out in the open. In small towns in western Algeria, for example, abandoned wineries stood dilapidated but distinct, sometimes with the name from the colonial era still visible. Stucco bunches of grapes adorned the walls of the rural development bank in Tlemcen, a flourish dating from when the building was the town's Maison du Colon and local wine producers came to secure loans and advice and socialize with their fellow colonists. Other sites revealed their connections only through local memory. Staff in Tlemcen's medieval Sidi Bellahsen mosque, now a small museum, told me that the French had for a time used the building as a wine store, which to them required no further commentary.[106]

A few of the colonial buildings had been rehabilitated. A private wine company, Grands Crus de l'Ouest, restarted production in wineries like the old *cave coopérative* in El Amria (formerly Lourmel). Machinery at the site evoked long-departed industrial manufacturers that once supplied colonial agriculture: Blachère of Hussein-Dey, Mangon of Boufarik. Less functional buildings with viticultural associations also received attention. Some Algerians believed that the châteaux built by prosperous wine producers were worth restoring and incorporating into the country's patrimony. In Sidi-Bel-Abbès, for example, while the Perrin family château remained in ruins, the one built by Léon Bastide was renovated, with plans to house a museum there.[107]

Most of the colonial vineyards, however, had long since disappeared, and Algerians had moved on to other concerns. In 2012, in the Algiers suburb of Mohammadia, which was once part of the colonial town of

Maison-Carrée, work began on a new grand mosque, designed to be the third-biggest in the world. The scale and expense of the project attracted considerable comment, but none of the coverage I saw noted that the main construction site was on land once occupied by vineyards planted under the guidance of Archbishop Lavigerie in the late 1860s.[108] Rather, commentary concentrated on the fact that the contract had been awarded to the China State Construction Engineering Corporation, which would bring 10,000 Chinese workers to Algeria to build the mosque, while employing a smaller number of Algerians.[109] China had become Algeria's biggest supplier of imports, and a broader economic shift seemed well under way.[110] But, in this land that had so much experience of empire, Algerians knew to be wary of the possibility of new imperial formations.

Epilogue
The Geometry of Colonization

The village of Oued Berkèche is situated high amid an undulating range of hills about twenty kilometers southeast of the town of Aïn-Témouchent. I was pleased to have the opportunity to visit a place that had become familiar to me in my research as Gaston-Doumergue, its name during the colonial era. Though the British sometimes named their colonial towns after prominent living politicians—Salisbury (now Harare) in what was then Southern Rhodesia is one example—to put so prosaic a statesman as Doumergue on the map struck me as somehow emblematic of the Third Republic's imprint on Algeria, at once far-reaching and mundane. Doumergue at least had a long history of support for imperial causes as well as a connection to the area, having briefly served as a justice of the peace in nearby Aïn-el-Arba at the beginning of his career.[1]

I knew that the village of Gaston-Doumergue had been one of the last new official French settlements in Algeria, planned for years but only realized after a lengthy dispute with local notables, who insisted on adequate compensation for the lands they were losing.[2] Colonists did not arrive to occupy their properties until the late 1920s, shortly before Doumergue, then president of the Third Republic (a mostly ceremonial role), returned to Algeria to mark the centenary of the French conquest. The administration had identified the area as particularly well suited for viticulture, and the settlers wasted no time in planting vines. Before long, some of them banded together to establish a cooperative winery, which in 1934 sent Doumergue himself seventy-one liters of the rosé its members had produced.[3]

My guide, an employee of a private wine company based in Oran, had known Oued Berkèche well for a long time; in the mid-1970s he had been based there for ten months of research as he trained to become an agricultural engineer. As we drove up toward the village, he pointed to slopes on which, he said, vines had once grown, but were now planted with cereal crops. It was clear even to my untrained eyes that the slopes were eroding badly.[4] Not much wine was produced from grapes grown here anymore, but the land continued to inspire my guide. Its light, chalky soil and the microclimate in the hills made for a genuine terroir, distinct from the regional appellation of which Oued Berkèche nominally formed a part. My guide seemed wistful as he described the aroma of violets that was an interesting feature of wine from this place. Talking about wine had this effect on several Algerian men I spoke to who had come of age in the 1970s, and for whom wine seemed integral to their memory of a sort of postindependence belle époque.[5] But my guide's thinking was partly commercial. He had visited the Bordeaux region and particularly admired the Petrus domain, whose reputation was built on a mere seven hectares. He liked to imagine what might be achieved with even a small output from the Berkèches at a time when rich people were willing to pay big money for high-quality wine.

Passing the old *cave coopérative*—the year 1932 still clearly inscribed above its entrance—we headed on to a smaller facility at the highest point of the village. This winery, an unusual circular structure whose design ensured the flow of liquid via gravity rather than pumps, had once belonged to a colonist named Victor Trouche. In the archives later I found that in 1928 Trouche was one of the first settlers to arrive in the village, and that he actively defended it: in 1955, along with his son, he joined one of three twelve-man self-protection units in Gaston-Doumergue, which the authorities kept supplied with guns and ammunition.[6] After discovering this piece of information, I reimagined Trouche's circular winery with its view across the hills as a defensive tower; the area around Gaston-Doumergue, after all, had seen a good deal of bloody conflict during the war for independence.[7] But now, in 2013, my guide's company maintained the facility. Sitting outside the building on this weekday afternoon was a group of bored-looking young men, and in their presence I felt too self-conscious to take the photographs I wanted.

My guide liked his job, but it came at a price: he told me he was looked on with disfavor (*mal vu*) by neighbors and even members of his own family for working in the wine industry. For him, wine functioned best as a family affair, passed down through the generations—perhaps as Victor Trouche did with his son. To no form of cultivation did the French word "culture" better apply than to the grapevine: more than just a crop, it felt like a way of being. But Algeria had no culture of wine, my guide lamented, and now children were taught in school that the vine was *la culture de Satan*—"the devil's crop." He speculated that in twenty years there would not be a single vineyard left in Algeria.[8]

If wine is a culture, however, so too is its rejection. In this book we have seen that wine was fundamental to France's colonization of Algeria. Referring to rows of grapevines became a shorthand way of capturing how colonization had remade the Algerian land and reoriented its history. In Jean Pelegri's novel *Les oliviers de la justice* (1959), the vines are "like lines of writing on a page."[9] The geographer Hildebert Isnard's assessment in the 1940s was that they "discipline the topography" in a fashion that "clearly expresses logical thought."[10] But these very associations made them an obvious target for opponents of the colonial system, especially during the war for independence. Hostility continued after the colonists departed. The protagonist of Mouloud Achour's novella *Les dernières vendanges* (1971) regards the parallel rows of vines that "devour our countryside" as "so many enemies" to be eliminated.[11]

The geometry of colonization and its cultural dimensions are encapsulated in a brief memoir written by Jean Pelegri, whose grandfather Michel-Louis, a scrappy immigrant from Majorca, got rich in the late nineteenth-century wine boom. Pelegri recalled how, as a boy on the vineyard his father, Michel, inherited on the Mitidja plain, he would watch with fascination as the Algerian workers in the fields got down on their knees to pray. The scene was startling to him, but not because of the workers' overt piety. The shock came instead from the fact that they did not align themselves with the rigid geometry established by the vines. In orienting themselves toward Mecca they followed their own geometry, an invisible axis that the young Pelegri had to ask his father to explain to him. From that moment, Pelegri began to understand that the space he inhabited was not neutral. It was informed by culture and overlaid by different mental geometries, just as different people spoke different languages.[12]

Pelegri's recollection depicts a moment of peace and religious tolerance, even as the workers he describes are being paid to produce something that does not align with their faith. What Algerians like those fieldworkers ultimately rejected, however, was not the colonizers' cultural difference. Rather, it was the inequality of a colonial system that, for well over a century, maintained its own rigid geometry, and in so doing misaligned human relations.

Abbreviations

ACCM	Archives de la Chambre de Commerce de Marseille, Marseille
ADBR	Archives Départementales des Bouches-du-Rhône, Marseille
ADG	Archives Départementales de la Gironde, Bordeaux
ADH	Archives Départementales de l'Hérault, Montpellier
ADLA	Archives Départementales de Loire-Atlantique, Nantes
ADMAE	Archives Diplomatiques du Ministère des Affaires Etrangères, La Courneuve
ADN	Archives Diplomatiques, Nantes
ADSM	Archives Départementales de la Seine-Maritime, Rouen
AGMAfr	Archives Générales de la Société des Missionnaires d'Afrique (White Fathers), Rome
ANMT	Archives Nationales du Monde du Travail, Roubaix
ANOM	Archives Nationales d'Outre-Mer, Aix-en-Provence
ANP	Archives Nationales, Paris
AS	Archives du Sénat, Paris
AWA	Archives de la Wilaya d'Alger, Algiers
AWO	Archives de la Wilaya d'Oran, Oran
BA	Banque de l'Algérie
CANA	Centre des Archives Nationales, Algiers
CC	Chamber of Commerce
CDHA	Centre de Documentation Historique sur l'Algérie, Aix-en-Provence

CMAT   Commune Mixte d'Aïn-Témouchent

FLN   Front de Libération Nationale

GARF   Gosudarstvennyi Arkhiv Rossiiskoi Federatsii, Moscow

GG   Governor-General

GGA   Gouvernement-général de l'Algérie

Min Ag Minister of Agriculture

SIAH   Société Immobilière et Agricole de l'Harrach

Notes

1 Detailed statistics can be found at the website of the International Organization of Vine and Wine, www.oiv.int. In the 2010s Italy was usually the top producer.

2 Karen Barkey, *Empire of Difference: The Ottomans in Comparative Perspective* (Cambridge: Cambridge University Press, 2008), 3–4; Ulrike von Hirschhausen and Jörn Leonhard, "Beyond Rise, Decline and Fall: Comparing Multi-Ethnic Empires in the Long Nineteenth Century," in Leonhard and von Hirschhausen, eds., *Comparing Empires: Encounters and Transfers in the Long Nineteenth Century* (Göttingen: Vandenhoech & Ruprecht, 2011), 9–11; Antoinette Burton, *The Trouble with Empire: Challenges to Modern British Imperialism* (Oxford: Oxford University Press, 2015), 4–5, 12–13. For parabolas, see Alexander J. Motyl, *Imperial Ends: The Decay, Collapse, and Revival of Empires* (New York: Columbia University Press, 2001), 41–46.

3 Albert Camus, *Le premier homme* (Paris: Gallimard, 1994), 186, from a manuscript that Camus left unfinished at his death in 1960: "Dans ce pays d'immigration, d'enrichissement rapide et de ruines spectaculaires." Translations throughout the book are the author's own unless noted.

4 Marc Côte, *L'Algérie: Espace et société* (Paris: Masson, 1996), 241.

5 For overviews on alienation of land, see André Nouschi, "La dépossession foncière et la paupérisation de la paysannerie algérienne," in Abderrahmane Bouchène, Jean-Pierre Peyroulou, Ouanassa Siari Tengour, and Sylvie Thénault, eds., *Histoire de l'Algérie à la période coloniale 1830–1962* (Paris: La Découverte, 2012), 189–194; John Ruedy, *Land Policy in Colonial Algeria: The Origins of the Rural Public Domain* (Berkeley: University of California Press, 1967), 98–105.

6 Pierre Berthault, quoted in *Oran-Matin*, 17 Feb. 1933.

7 Giovanni Federico writes that "a farm should be labeled as 'capitalist' only if wage workers account for most of its permanent labor force." That definition would encompass a great many of the vineyards of French Algeria. Giovanni Federico, "Growth, Specialization, and Organization of World Agriculture," in Larry Neal and Jeffrey G. Williamson, eds., *The Cambridge History of Capitalism*, vol. 2, *The Spread of Capitalism: From 1848 to the Present* (Cambridge: Cambridge University Press, 2014), 64.

8 For example, Madame Veuve Porcellaga and Madame Tramoy de Laubeypie (Veuve Brossette), who both owned lands around Boufarik. See Julien Franc, *La colonisation de la Mitidja* (Paris: Librairie Ancienne Honoré Champion, 1928), 590; ANOM, GGA, 1O 57, Affaire Tramoy de Laubeypie 1923–1925.

9 For example, see AGMAfr, Voillard 227, Société immobilière et agricole de l'Harrach, meeting of 16 Mar. 1925; Michel Launay, *Paysans algériens 1960–2006,* 3rd ed. (Paris: Karthala, 2007), 104–105, 137–138, 282–285.

10 For some pointers on the social history of colonial Algeria, see Emmanuel Blanchard and Sylvie Thénault, "Quel 'monde du contact'? Pour une histoire sociale de l'Algérie pendant la période coloniale," *Le mouvement social* 236 (2011): 3–7; Muriel Cohen and Annick Lacroix, "Entre Algérie et France: écrire une histoire sociale des Algériens au vingtième siècle," *French Politics, Culture and Society* 34:2 (2016): 1–10. A range of approaches to colonial Algeria is captured in Bouchène et al., *Histoire de l'Algérie à la période coloniale.* Pioneering work on colonial Algeria in English includes David Prochaska, *Making Algeria French: Colonialism in Bône, 1870–1920* (Cambridge: Cambridge University Press, 1990); and on the conquest phase, Jennifer E. Sessions, *By Sword and Plow: France and the Conquest of Algeria* (Ithaca, NY: Cornell University Press, 2011). For an innovative social history of trans-Mediterranean migration, see Julia A. Clancy-Smith, *Mediterraneans: North Africa and Europe in an Age of Migration, c. 1800–1900* (Berkeley: University of California Press, 2012).

11 Hildebert Isnard, "La vigne en Algérie: Etude géographique" (PhD diss., Université de Paris I-Sorbonne, 1947). The section of the dissertation that covers the period to 1914 was published in two volumes as *La vigne en Algérie: Etude géographique* (Gap: Ophrys, 1951 / 1954). Where possible I cite the published section. More recently, Paul Birebent's *Hommes, vignes et vins de l'Algérie française* (Nice: Editions Jacques Gandini, 2007) contains much useful material and is particularly good on the technical aspects of wine production in Algeria, though the author (who in colonial times was a vigneron near Oran) makes no secret of his allegiances.

12 In 1947 Isnard published an article in the journal *Annales: Economies-Sociétés-Civilisations,* and in 1953 contributed to a Festschrift for that journal's co-founder, Lucien Febvre. Members of the Annales school were innovators in the study of food and alimentation. Though she does not mention Isnard, see Sydney Watts, "Food and the Annales School," in Jeffrey M. Pilcher, ed., *The Oxford Handbook of Food History* (Oxford: Oxford University Press, 2012), 3–22.

13 William H. Sewell Jr., "A Strange Career: The Historical Study of Economic Life," *History and Theory* 49 (2010): 146, 157. For applications of this general approach to the study of the French Empire, see Owen White and Elizabeth Heath, "The French Empire and the History of Economic Life," *French Politics, Culture and Society* 35:2 (2017): 76–88.

14 Gerard Sasges, *Imperial Intoxication: Alcohol and the Making of Colonial Indochina* (Honolulu: University of Hawai'i Press, 2017).

15 Owen White, "Drunken States: Temperance and French Rule in Côte d'Ivoire, 1908–1916," *Journal of Social History* 40:3 (2007): 663–684; quotation at 674.

16 Romuald Dejernon, *Les vignes et les vins de l'Algérie,* 2 vols. (Paris: Librairie Agricole de la Maison Rustique, 1883–1884), 1:38–39.

17 For a useful overview of colonial Algeria's changing administrative status, see Claude Collot, *Les institutions de l'Algérie pendant la période coloniale (1830–1962)* (Paris: CNRS, 1987), 5–20.

18 Léonce de Lavergne, *Economie rurale de la France depuis 1789* (Paris: De Guillaumin, 1860).

19 For a typical example, in one standard work Algeria receives just two passing mentions: Annie Moulin, *Les paysans dans la société française de la Révolution à nos jours* (Paris: Seuil, 1988).

20 This *monopole de pavillon* made shipping goods from Algeria to France relatively expensive; Gilbert Meynier, *L'Algérie révélée: La guerre de 1914–1918 et le premier quart du XXe siècle* (Geneva: Librairie Droz, 1981), 52. On assimilationism under the early Third Republic, see Collot, *Les institutions de l'Algérie*, 10–11; Charles-Robert Ageron, *Histoire de l'Algérie contemporaine,* vol. 2, *De l'insurrection de 1871 au déclenchement de la guerre de libération (1954)* (Paris: Presses Universitaires de France, 1979), 19–38.

21 Jean Lacouture, *Mitterrand: Une histoire de Français,* vol. 1, *Les risques de l'escalade* (Paris: Editions du Seuil, 1998), 155.

22 Charles-André Julien, *L'Afrique du Nord en marche: Nationalismes musulmans et souveraineté française,* 3rd ed. (Paris: René Julliard, 1972), 97. For population figures, see Kamel Kateb, *Européens, "indigènes" et juifs en Algérie (1830–1962): Représentations et réalités des populations* (Paris: Editions de l'INED, 2001), 241.

23 Germaine Tillion, *L'Algérie bascule vers l'avenir: L'Algérie en 1957 et autres textes* (Paris: Editions de Minuit, 1961), 31–33. For a useful discussion of terminology around the time of the Algerian War, see Raphaëlle Branche, *La guerre d'Algérie: Une histoire apaisée?* (Paris: Editions du Seuil, 2005), 349–359.

24 Jacques Bouveresse, *Un parlement colonial? Les Délégations financières algériennes, 1898–1945,* 2 vols. (Mont-Saint-Aignan: Publications des Universités de Rouen et du Havre, 2008 / 2010).

25 From online searches I have found a few scattered uses of this term in writing in English, but I believe I am the first to use it in a sustained fashion.

26 For further discussion of colonial-era labels, see Guy Pervillé, "Comment appeler les habitants de l'Algérie avant la définition légale d'une nationalité algérienne?," *Cahiers de la Méditerranée* 54:1 (1997): 55–60, though I do not think the author would agree with all of my choices.

27 On this and other citizenship-related questions, see Laure Blévis, "L'invention de l' 'indigène,' Français non citoyen," in Bouchène et al., *Histoire de l'Algérie à la période coloniale,* 212–218. Also Tillion, *L'Algérie bascule vers l'avenir,* 31. "Indigeneity" is a contested topic within Algeria, where the country's Berber peoples, representing by the 2010s perhaps a quarter of the population and of whom Kabyles are the most numerous and prominent, often distinguish themselves from Algerians of Arab ethnicity. On Berbers and stereotyping in the colonial era, see Patricia M. E. Lorcin, *Imperial Identities: Stereotyping, Prejudice, and Race in Colonial Algeria* (London: I. B. Tauris, 1995).

1. ROOTS

1 Jean-Toussaint Merle, *Anecdotes historiques et politiques pour servir à l'histoire de la conquête d'Alger en 1830* (Paris: G.-A. Dentu, 1831), 25–26. On the expedition, see Charles-André Julien, *Histoire de l'Algérie contemporaine,* vol. 1, *La conquête et les débuts de la colonisation (1827–1871)* (Paris: Presses Universitaires de France, 1964), 48–58.

2 Si Abd al-Qadir, "Song about the Taking of Algiers," in Alf Andrew Heggoy, *The French Conquest of Algiers, 1830: An Algerian Oral Tradition* (Athens: Ohio University Press, 1986), 19–24.

3 Quotation from Merle, *Anecdotes historiques*, 105. Further research, especially in Arabic-language sources, may reveal more of a Muslim critique of wine throughout the colonial era.

4 From a letter reproduced in ibid., 308.

5 Jennifer E. Sessions, *By Sword and Plow: France and the Conquest of Algeria* (Ithaca, NY: Cornell University Press, 2011), 1–7.

6 Patrick E. McGovern, *Ancient Wine: The Search for the Origins of Viniculture* (Princeton, NJ: Princeton University Press, 2003), 7–15.

7 Serge Lancel, *Carthage: A History*, trans. Antonia Nevill (Oxford: Blackwell, 1995), 1–34, 273–276; Hildebert Isnard, *La vigne en Algérie: étude géographique*, 2 vols. (Gap: Ophrys, 1951 / 1954), 1:239–246; Patrick E. McGovern, *Uncorking the Past: The Quest for Wine, Beer, and Other Alcoholic Beverages* (Berkeley: University of California Press, 2009), 194–195.

8 Michael Dietler, *Archaeologies of Colonialism: Consumption, Entanglement, and Violence in Ancient Mediterranean France* (Berkeley: University of California Press, 2010), 197–203.

9 Isnard, *La vigne en Algérie*, 1:247.

10 Suetonius, quoted in Peter Garnsey, *Famine and Food Supply in the Graeco-Roman World* (Cambridge: Cambridge University Press, 1988), 225.

11 Dietler, *Archaeologies of Colonialism*, 224; Roger Dion, *Histoire de la vigne et du vin en France des origines au XIXe siècle* (Paris: Roger Dion, 1959), 134–166.

12 Isnard, *La vigne en Algérie*, 1:246–260.

13 Sabah Ferdi, *Corpus des mosaïques de Cherchel* (Paris: CNRS Editions, 2005), 15–16, 60–62, 69–70, 106–108, 114–118. On Iol's origins and eastern Mauretania, see Duane W. Roller, *The World of Juba II and Kleopatra Selene: Royal Scholarship on Rome's African Frontier* (New York: Routledge, 2003), 39–46.

14 Leslie Dossey, *Peasant and Empire in Christian North Africa* (Berkeley: University of California Press, 2010), 1.

15 Saint Augustine, *Confessions*, trans. Henry Chadwick (Oxford: Oxford University Press, 1991), 29, 166–168, 207.

16 Henry Chadwick, *Augustine of Hippo: A Life* (Oxford: Oxford University Press, 2009), 14.

17 John 15:1–5 (King James Version). On wine and the vine in the New Testament, see Tim Unwin, *Wine and the Vine: An Historical Geography of Viticulture and the Wine Trade* (London: Routledge, 1991), 139–141.

18 Augustine, *Confessions*, 20.

19 Ibid., 91–92.

20 Quran 47:15.

21 Unwin, *Wine and the Vine*, 151; Ronald A. Messier, *The Almoravids and the Meanings of Jihad* (Santa Barbara, CA: Praeger, 2010), 15, 26.

22 On drinking among Muslims, see Rudi Matthee, "Alcohol in the Islamic Middle East: Ambivalence and Ambiguity," *Past and Present* supplement 9 (2014): 100–125; Mat-

thee, "The Ambiguities of Alcohol in Iranian History: Between Excess and Abstention," in Bert G. Fragner, Ralph Kauz, and Florian Schwarz, eds., *Wine Culture in Iran and Beyond* (Vienna: Osterreichische Akademie der Wissenschaften, 2014), 137–163.

23 Some consumption and limited production did continue in Muslim North Africa. See Isnard, *La vigne en Algérie,* 1:261–262.

24 Dion, *Histoire de la vigne et du vin en France,* 181–187; Rod Phillips, *A Short History of Wine* (New York: HarperCollins, 2000), 68–74, 93–97.

25 See especially Rebecca Earle, *The Body of the Conquistador: Food, Race and the Colonial Experience in Spanish America, 1492–1700* (Cambridge: Cambridge University Press, 2012), 67–78. Also Unwin, *Wine and the Vine,* 216–220; Phillips, *A Short History of Wine,* 154–160.

26 José Gabriel Martinez-Serna, "Vineyards in the Desert: The Jesuits and the Rise and Decline of an Indian Town in Spain's Northeastern Borderlands" (PhD diss., Southern Methodist University, 2009), 4–5.

27 Andrew A. Painter, *Virginia Wine: Four Centuries of Change* (Fairfax, VA: George Mason University Press, 2018), 11–13; quotation at 11.

28 Thomas Pinney, *A History of Wine in America: From the Beginnings to Prohibition* (Berkeley: University of California Press, 1989), 31–33.

29 Owen Stanwood, "Between Eden and Empire: Huguenot Refugees and the Promise of New Worlds," *American Historical Review* 118:5 (2013), 1331–1335; Stanwood, "From the Desert to the Refuge: The Saga of New Bordeaux," *French Historical Studies* 40:1 (2017): 5–32; Bertrand Van Ruymbeke, *From Babylon to New Eden: The Huguenots and their Migration to Colonial South Carolina* (Columbia: University of South Carolina Press, 2006), 205; Johan Fourie and Dieter Von Fintel, "Settler Skills and Colonial Development: The Huguenot Wine-Makers in Eighteenth-Century Dutch South Africa," *Economic History Review* 67:4 (2014): 932–963; Unwin, *Wine and the Vine,* 250–252.

30 Amie Sexton, "The French in the Australian Wine Industry: 1788–2009," *International Journal of Wine Business Research* 23:3 (2011): 200; Unwin, *Wine and the Vine,* 296–300.

31 Léonce Jore, "Jean Louis Vignes of Bordeaux, Pioneer of California Viticulture," *Southern California Quarterly* 45:4 (1963): 289–303; Pinney, *A History of Wine in America,* 238, 246–249; Erica Hannickel, *Empire of Vines: Wine Culture in America* (Philadelphia: University of Pennsylvania Press, 2013), 157–159. I refer here to upper California; viticulture arrived earlier in Baja California.

32 Juan Cole, *Napoleon's Egypt: Invading the Middle East* (New York: Palgrave Macmillan, 2007), 146.

33 Yves Laissus, "Gaspard Monge et l'expédition d'Egypte (1798–1799)," *Revue de synthèse* 81 (1960): 320.

34 Ibid., 335.

35 Rafe Blaufarb, *Bonapartists in the Borderlands: French Exiles and Refugees on the Gulf Coast, 1815–1835* (Tuscaloosa: University of Alabama Press, 2005), xi–xii, 8–9, 57–58, 117–118, 122–123, 131–132, 160; Pinney, *A History of Wine in America,* 135–139. On Clauzel, see also Julien Franc, *La colonisation de la Mitidja* (Paris: Librairie Ancienne Honoré Champion, 1928), 81–89.

36 On imperial continuities across different early nineteenth-century French regimes, see David Todd, "A French Imperial Meridian, 1814–1870," *Past and Present* 210 (2011): 155–186.

37 Frederick H. Smith, *Caribbean Rum: A Social and Economic History* (Gainesville: University Press of Florida, 2005), 66–68, 208–209. The island colony of Réunion in the Indian Ocean did produce some wine, as well as rum; see Annie Hubert, "Drinking in La Réunion: Between Living, Dying and Forgetting," in Igor and Valerie de Garine, eds., *Drinking: Anthropological Approaches* (New York: Berghahn, 2001), 232.

38 Auguste-Théodore-Hilaire Barchou de Penhoën, *Mémoires d'un officier d'état-major* (Paris: Charpentier, 1835), 210, 316–317.

39 Isnard, *La vigne en Algerie*, 1:266–268.

40 Alexis de Tocqueville, "Notes on the Voyage to Algeria in 1841," in *Writings on Empire and Slavery*, ed. and trans. Jennifer Pitts (Baltimore: Johns Hopkins University Press, 2001), 41–43.

41 Quoted in A. Desjobert, *La question d'Alger: Politique, colonisation, commerce* (Paris: P. Dufart, 1837), 128; and in Andrew Aisenberg, "The Facts of Social Organization in the Debate over North Africa, 1834–1852: Law, Government, Critique," *French Historical Studies* 35:2 (2012), 369. See also Sessions, *By Sword and Plow*, 209–210.

42 Louis-François Trolliet, *Statistique médicale de la province d'Alger, mêlée d'observations agricoles* (Lyon: Ch. Savy Jeune, 1844), 92–94, 149–150, 152–153.

43 Antony Thrall Sullivan, *Thomas-Robert Bugeaud: France and Algeria, 1784–1849. Politics, Power, and the Good Society* (Hamden, CT: Archon, 1983), 96; M.-L.-Bonav. Urtis, *Opinion émise par M. Urtis, propriétaire à Alger, devant la Commission de colonisation de l'Algérie, à la séance du 12 mars 1842* (Paris: Paul Dupont, 1842), 17–18.

44 Tocqueville, *Writings on Empire and Slavery*, 41–42.

45 François Véron de Forbonnais, "Colony," trans. Alyssa Goldstein Sepinwall, in *The Encyclopedia of Diderot and d'Alembert Collaborative Translation Project* (Ann Arbor: University of Michigan Library, 2004). On *ancien régime* colonial trade, see, for example, Glenn J. Ames, *Colbert, Mercantilism, and the French Quest for Asian Trade* (DeKalb: Northern Illinois University Press, 1996); Paul Cheney, *Revolutionary Commerce: Globalization and the French Monarchy* (Cambridge, MA: Harvard University Press, 2010); Anoush Fraser Terjanian, *Commerce and its Discontents in Eighteenth-Century French Political Thought* (Cambridge: Cambridge University Press, 2013).

46 Jean Tarrade, *Le commerce colonial de la France à la fin de l'ancien régime: L'évolution du régime de "l'Exclusif" de 1763 à 1789*, 2 vols. (Paris: Presses Universitaires de France, 1972), 1:14–15.

47 See Pernille Røge, "A Natural Order of Empire: The Physiocratic Vision of Colonial France after the Seven Years' War," and Bertie Mandelblatt, "How Feeding Slaves Shaped the French Atlantic: Mercantilism and the Crisis of Food Provisioning in the Franco-Caribbean during the Seventeenth and Eighteenth Centuries," both in Sophus A. Reinert and Pernille Røge, eds., *The Political Economy of Empire in the Early Modern World* (Basingstoke, UK: Palgrave Macmillan, 2013), 32–52, 192–220.

48 Jennifer Pitts, *A Turn to Empire: The Rise of Liberal Imperialism in Britain and France* (Princeton, NJ: Princeton University Press, 2005), 53–54, 124; also Sessions, *By Sword and Plow*, 179–180.

49 Adolphe Blanqui, *Algérie: Rapport sur la situation économique de nos possessions dans le nord de l'Afrique* (Paris: W. Coquebert, 1840), 82. On Blanqui and Algeria, see Kay Adamson, *Political and Economic Thought and Practice in Nineteenth-Century France and the Colonization of Algeria* (Lewiston, NY: Edwin Mellen Press, 2002), 63–106.

50 Tocqueville, *Writings on Empire and Slavery,* 92.

51 Julien, *Histoire de l'Algérie contemporaine,* 1:251; David Todd, *Free Trade and its Enemies in France, 1814–1851* (Cambridge: Cambridge University Press, 2015), 178.

52 See, for example, Jacques-François Poirel, *De l'occupation et de la colonisation militaire, agricole et pénale d'Alger* (Paris: Hingray, 1837), 1–4.

53 Hélène Blais and Florence Deprest, "The Mediterranean, a Territory between France and Colonial Algeria: Imperial Constructions," *European Review of History: Revue européenne d'histoire* 19:1 (2012): 34–36, 40–42.

54 Sessions, *By Sword and Plow,* 178.

55 C.-J.-A. Mathieu de Dombasle, *De l'avenir de l'Algérie* (Paris: Dufart, 1838), 12–13. As Pernille Røge points out, eighteenth-century physiocrats had promoted colonial expansion in Africa in part for its proximity to France compared to the Americas. See Røge, "'La clef de commerce': The Changing Role of Africa in France's Atlantic Empire ca. 1760–1797," *History of European Ideas* 34:4 (2008): 431–443.

56 "Un ami de la justice et de l'humanité," *Abrégé ou aperçu de l'histoire d'Alger et des nations barbaresques* (Bordeaux: J. Lebreton, 1 July 1830), 131–132. For more on this topic, see Diana K. Davis, *Resurrecting the Granary of Rome: Environmental History and French Colonial Expansion in North Africa* (Athens: Ohio University Press, 2007).

57 Julien, *Histoire de l'Algérie contemporaine,* 1:252.

58 Desjobert, *La question d'Alger,* 133.

59 Armand-Pignel, *Conducteur ou guide du voyageur et du colon de Paris à Alger et dans l'Algérie* (Paris: Debécourt, Sept. 1836), 181–182.

60 Un habitant de l'Afrique, *Révélations sur l'Algérie, en réponse à M. Mathieu de Dombasle* (Paris: P. Baudouin, 1838), 13–14; Général Bugeaud, *L'Algérie: Des moyens de conserver et d'utiliser cette conquête* (Paris: Dentu, 1842), 45–46.

61 Général d'Hautpoul, *Du ministère de la guerre en 1850, et de l'Algérie en 1851* (Paris: J. Dumaine, 1851), 130–131.

62 Comte H . . . de B . . . , *De l'Algérie et de sa colonisation* (Paris: Crochard, 1834), 33.

63 L. Moll, *Colonisation et agriculture de l'Algérie,* 2 vols. (Paris: Librairie Agricole de la Maison Rustique, 1845), 2:273–477.

64 Ibid., 2:358. On madder production in early nineteenth-century France, see Louis Bergeron, *France under Napoleon,* trans. R. R. Palmer (Princeton, NJ: Princeton University Press, 1981), 166–167.

65 Moll, *Colonisation et agriculture,* 2:457–458.

66 Jenna Nigro, "Colonial Logics: Agricultural, Commercial, and Moral Experiments in the Making of French Senegal, 1763–1870" (PhD diss., University of Illinois at Chicago, 2014), 95–162; Boubacar Barry, *Le royaume du Waalo: le Sénégal avant la conquête* (Paris: François Maspero, 1972), 241–245; Richard L. Roberts, *Two Worlds of Cotton: Colonialism and the Regional Economy in the French Soudan, 1800–1946* (Stanford, CA: Stanford University Press, 1996), 61–65; Comte H . . . de B . . . , *De l'Algérie et de sa colonisation,* 7–8.

67 Louis-François Trolliet, *Mémoire sur la nécessité et les avantages de la colonisation d'Alger* (Lyon: J. M. Barret, 1835), 5–9. There are echoes here of the economic organization of Napoleon's European empire; see, for example, Michael Broers, *Europe under Napoleon, 1799–1815* (London: Arnold, 1996), 222–229.

68 Speech of 21 March 1832, quoted in *Histoire de l'Algérie française* (Paris: H. Morel, 1850), 302.

69 Jean-François Caze, *Notice sur Alger* (Paris: Félix Locquin, 1831), 13–14; Franc, *La colonisation de la Mitidja,* 85–88.

70 Michael A. Osborne, *Nature, the Exotic, and the Science of French Colonialism* (Bloomington: Indiana University Press, 1994), 144–171; Osborne, "The System of Colonial Gardens and the Exploitation of French Algeria, 1830–1852," *Proceedings of the Eighth Annual Meeting of the French Colonial Historical Society* (1982): 160–168; Moll, *Colonisation et agriculture,* 2:576–580.

71 Osborne, *Nature, the Exotic, and the Science of French Colonialism,* 1–13. On the earlier history of acclimatization in France, see E. C. Spary, *Utopia's Garden: French Natural History from Old Regime to Revolution* (Chicago: University of Chicago Press, 2000); Joseph Horan, "King Cotton on the Middle Sea: Acclimatization Projects and the French Links to the Early Modern Mediterranean," *French History* 29:1 (2015): 93–108.

72 Blanqui, *Algérie,* 75.

73 Victor Demontès, *Le peuple algérien: essais de démographie algérienne* (Algiers: Imprimerie Algérienne, 1906), 418; also Isnard, *La vigne en Algérie,* 2:11–13.

74 Félix Dessoliers, *L'Algérie libre: étude économique sur l'Algérie* (Algiers: Gojosso, 1895), 113.

75 Pétrus Borel, "Algérie. Colonisation. Des travaux exécutés à la Reghaïa, province d'Alger, de septembre 1846 à avril 1847," and Th. Fortin d'Ivry, "Résultats des cultures et essais de cultures faits à la Reghaïa, 1847," in *Revue de l'Orient et de l'Algérie* 2 (1847): 112–136. See also Franc, *La colonisation de la Mitidja,* 173–175, 312–316.

76 John Laffey, "Roots of French Imperialism in the Nineteenth Century: The Case of Lyon," *French Historical Studies* 6:1 (1969), 80–83; Junko Thérèse Takeda, "Global Insects: Silkworms, Sericulture, and Statecraft in Napoleonic France and Tokugawa Japan," *French History* 28:2 (2014): 207–225.

77 Lucette Valensi, *Tunisian Peasants in the Eighteenth and Nineteenth Centuries* (Cambridge: Cambridge University Press, 1985), 113.

78 Afaf Lutfi al-Sayyid Marsot, *Egypt in the Reign of Muhammad Ali* (Cambridge: Cambridge University Press, 1984), 152–157; Cole, *Napoleon's Egypt,* 12, 20, 28.

79 Nigro, "Colonial Logics," 147–148; E. R. J. Owen, *Cotton and the Egyptian Economy, 1820–1914* (Oxford: Oxford University Press, 1969), 28–33.

80 F. Ribourt, *Le gouvernement de l'Algérie de 1852 à 1858* (Paris: E. Panckoucke, 1859), 75.

81 In 1833, France imported 70 percent of its cotton from the United States. See Roberts, *Two Worlds of Cotton,* 66. On the global cotton market, see Sven Beckert, *Empire of Cotton: A Global History* (New York: Alfred A. Knopf, 2014).

82 On resistance, see, for example, John Ruedy, *Modern Algeria: The Origins and Development of a Nation* (Bloomington: Indiana University Press, 1992), 55–68.

83 Sullivan, *Thomas-Robert Bugeaud,* 88–89.

84 On the Rhine situation, see James M. Brophy, "The Rhine Crisis of 1840 and German Nationalism: Chauvinism, Skepticism, and Regional Reception," *Journal of Modern History* 85:1 (2013): 1–3.

85 Sullivan, *Thomas-Robert Bugeaud,* 88.

86 Benjamin Claude Brower, *A Desert Named Peace: The Violence of France's Empire in the Algerian Sahara, 1844–1902* (New York: Columbia University Press, 2009), 22–23; William Gallois, *A History of Violence in the Early Algerian Colony* (Basingstoke, UK: Palgrave Macmillan, 2013), 100–121.

87 Letter dated 26 April 1843 in *Campagnes d'Afrique 1835–1848: Lettres adressées au Maréchal de Castellane* (Paris: Plon, 1898), 309–312; see also Brower, *A Desert Named Peace,* 50; Sullivan, *Thomas-Robert Bugeaud,* 124–125.

88 P. Henrichs, *Guide du colon et de l'ouvrier en Algérie* (Paris: Garnier frères, 1843), 3, 6.

89 For example, Bugeaud, *L'Algérie,* 98–99. The themes in this paragraph are well explored in Sessions, *By Sword and Plow,* 232–245.

90 Blanqui, *Algérie,* 73.

91 Tocqueville, *Writings on Empire and Slavery,* 37; Philip D. Curtin, *Death by Migration: Europe's Encounter with the Tropical World in the Nineteenth Century* (Cambridge: Cambridge University Press, 1989), 37, 62–68.

92 Thomas Dodman, "Un pays pour la colonie: Mourir de nostalgie en Algérie française, 1830–1880," *Annales HSS* 3 (July–Sept. 2011), 761–762.

93 Tocqueville, *Writings on Empire and Slavery,* 179.

94 Sessions, *By Sword and Plow,* 216.

95 Moll, *Colonisation et agriculture,* 1:155–157; 2:441–444.

96 Léroy de Béthune, *Une lettre de M. le Maréchal Bugeaud au sujet du rapport de M. Ch. Dupin sur l'Algérie* (Douai: A. d'Aubers, 1850), 6–7.

97 A. Noirot, "La culture de la vigne en Algérie," *L'Algérie agricole, commerciale, industrielle* 1 (1859), 34; Isnard, *La vigne en Algérie,* 2:30; Julien, *Histoire de l'Algérie contemporaine,* 1:382–383.

98 Quotation from de Béthune, *Une lettre de M. le Maréchal Bugeaud,* 8.

99 ANOM, Préfecture d'Oran (henceforth Oran), 1H 11, Commissaire civil of Mascara to Prefect of Oran, 13 Dec. 1854.

100 ANOM, Oran, 1H 11, Mayor of Aïn el-Turck to Prefect of Oran, 25 Apr. 1854.

101 A. Villacrose, *Vingt ans en Algérie ou tribulations d'un colon racontées par lui-même* (Paris: Challamel aîné, 1875), 250–251. On the 1866 swarms, see J. Künckel d'Herculais, *Invasions des acridiens vulgo sauterelles en Algérie,* 2 vols. (Algiers: Giralt, 1893), 1:162–182.

102 ANOM, Oran, 1H 11, Commissaire civil of Sidi-Bel-Abbès to Prefect of Oran, 11 Jan. 1858; Inspecteur de colonisation to Commissaire civil of Sidi-Bel-Abbès, 8 May 1859.

103 Noirot, "La culture de la vigne en Algérie," 126.

104 ANOM, Oran, 1H 11, Commissaire civil of Sidi-Bel-Abbès to Prefect of Oran, 11 Jan. 1858; Narcisse Faucon, *Le livre d'or de l'Algérie* (Paris: Augustin Challamel, 1890), 39–40.

105 ANOM, Oran, 1H 11, Inspecteur de colonisation to Commissaire civil of Tlemcen, 28 Jan. 1858; Inspecteur de colonisation to sub-prefect of Mostaganem, 4 Dec. 1860.

106 Société impériale et centrale d'horticulture, *Rapport sur les produits de l'Algérie qui ont figuré à l'exposition du mois de mai 1858* (Paris: Imprimerie horticole de J.-B. Gros et Donnaud, 1858), 33–35.

107 Société impériale et centrale d'horticulture, *Rapport sur les produits de l'Algérie*, 34, 36; C. T. de Fallon, *Archives mitidjéennes: Une page de l'histoire de la colonisation algérienne: Bou-Farik et son marché* (Blida: A. Mauguin, 1869), 262.

108 Peter J. Howland, "From 'Civilizing' Māori to Fruit-Driven Exuberance: An Introduction to Wine in New Zealand," in Howland, ed., *Social, Cultural and Economic Impacts of Wine in New Zealand* (New York: Routledge, 2014), 11–12; Li Zhengping, *Chinese Wine* (Cambridge: Cambridge University Press, 2011), 56; Jean-Pierre Bel, *Les paysages viticoles de la Bekaa (Liban)* (Paris: Edition Books on Demand, 2009), 42–44; Michael Karam, *Wines of Lebanon* (London: SAQI, 2005), 73–75.

109 Bernard Delpal, *Le silence des moines: Les Trappistes au XIXe siècle: France-Algérie-Syrie* (Paris: Beauchesne, 1998), 149–158; Hippolyte Lecq, *L'exploitation agricole de La Trappe de Staouëli* (Algiers: Adolphe Jourdan, 1882), 5–7; Gabriel Verge, *Monographie du Domaine de la Trappe de Staouëli* (Algiers: V. Heintz, 1930), 1–4.

110 Delpal, *Le silence des moines,* 158–192.

111 Ibid., 170; Isnard, *La vigne en Algérie*, 2:90.

112 Octave Teissier, *Napoléon III en Algérie* (Paris: Challamel, 1865), 51–61, quotation at 55.

113 Pastoral letter dated 5 May 1867, in *Recueil de lettres publiées par Mgr. l'archevêque d'Alger sur les oeuvres et missions africaines* (Paris: Plon, 1869), 7–25, quotation at 14.

114 Letters from early 1868, in ibid., 26–36.

115 Kamel Kateb, *Européens, "indigènes" et juifs en Algérie (1830–1962): Représentations et réalités des populations* (Paris: Editions de l'INED, 2001), 58–68; Brock Cutler, "'Water Mania!' Drought and the Rhetoric of Rule in Nineteenth-Century Algeria," *Journal of North African Studies* 19:3 (2014), 320–321.

116 Bertrand Taithe, "Algerian Orphans and Colonial Christianity in Algeria, 1866–1939," *French History* 20:3 (2006): 240–259. The fathers baptized a few hundred of the orphans.

117 AGMAfr, Maison Mère et Annexes I, "Le domaine d'Ouali-Dadda à Maison-Carrée."

118 François Renault, *Cardinal Lavigerie: Churchman, Prophet and Missionary,* trans. John O'Donohue (London: Athlone Press, 1994), 89, 102.

119 Lavigerie, quoted in Charles Bertin, "S. E. le Cardinal Lavigerie: la vigne, le vin," *Bulletin de l'Institut Oenologique d'Algérie* 117 (Dec. 1937): 267.

120 Ibid., 267, 273–275, 277.

121 Monseigneur Lavigerie, "Essais d'acclimatation en Algérie," *Bulletin de la Société Impériale Zoologique d'Acclimatation,* series 2, vol. 4 (1869): 506–508; AGMAfr, Lavigerie Casier B8 / 310, President of the Société impériale zoologique d'acclimatation (Edouard Drouyn de Lhuys) to Lavigerie, 25 Oct. 1869. See also Osborne, *Nature, the Exotic, and the Science of French Colonialism,* 101.

122 Bertin, "S. E. le Cardinal Lavigerie," 268–269.

123 The quotation in French reads, "Il suffit d'une plante pour faire la richesse d'une nation." See A. Rastoul, *Le maréchal Randon (1795–1871) d'après ses mémoires et des doc-*

uments inédits: étude militaire et politique (Paris: Firmin-Didot, 1890), 102–103; Ribourt, *Le gouvernement de l'Algérie*, 76.

124 Ribourt, *Le gouvernement de l'Algérie*, 74.

125 Davis, *Resurrecting the Granary of Rome*, 47.

126 On tobacco, see Blanqui, *Algérie*, 76; Moll, *Colonisation et agriculture*, 2:364–381; Isnard, *La vigne en Algérie*, 2:19–21.

127 Ribourt, *Le gouvernement de l'Algérie*, 75–76.

128 See, for example, R. E. Elson, "Sugar Factory Workers and the Emergence of 'Free Labour' in Nineteenth-Century Java," *Modern Asian Studies* 20:1 (1986): 139–174; Jan Breman, *Mobilizing Labour for the Global Coffee Market: Profits from an Unfree Work Regime in Colonial Java* (Amsterdam: Amsterdam University Press, 2015), 211–254.

129 P. Clergeaud, *De la culture du coton en Algérie* (Paris: Dentu, 1862), 8–13. See also Beckert, *Empire of Cotton*, 249–251.

130 Osborne, *Nature, the Exotic, and the Science of French Colonialism*, 168; Isnard, *La vigne en Algérie*, 2:14–17.

131 Teissier, *Napoléon III en Algérie*, 86, 93, 98, 102, 155.

132 Gustave Mercier-Lacombe, Directeur général des Services civils (the governor-general's deputy), quoted in Isnard, *La vigne en Algérie*, 2:32.

133 Teissier, *Napoléon III en Algérie*, 46.

134 Isnard, *La vigne en Algérie*, 2:47; James Simpson, *Creating Wine: The Emergence of a World Industry, 1840–1914* (Princeton, NJ: Princeton University Press, 2011), 66.

135 Isnard, *La vigne en Algérie*, 2:33. The 1867 agreement was superseded by a full customs union in December 1884. See Albert Révillon, "Le régime douanier de l'Algérie et ses conséquences économiques," *Journal des économistes*, series 6, vol. 6 (May–June 1905): 321–345.

2. PHYLLOXERA AND THE MAKING OF THE ALGERIAN VINEYARD

1 See especially James Simpson, *Creating Wine: The Emergence of a World Industry, 1840–1914* (Princeton, NJ: Princeton University Press, 2011), 191–262; and on individual countries, Kym Anderson and Vicente Pinilla, eds., *Wine Globalization: A New Comparative History* (Cambridge: Cambridge University Press, 2018). For a useful study of wine producers in a "New World" territory in a period similar to the one covered in this chapter, see Uttam Bajwa, "Frontier Enterprise: Immigrant Winemaking in Mendoza, Argentina (1884–1914)" (PhD diss., Johns Hopkins University, 2012).

2 Statistics from Hildebert Isnard, *La vigne en Algérie: étude géographique*, 2 vols. (Gap: Ophrys, 1951 / 1954), 2:47, 58, 443; Louis Jacquet, *L'Alcool, étude économique générale* (Paris: Masson et Cie, 1912), 64, 75; Octave Audebert, *Les exportations des vins français à l'étranger et le transit des vins exotiques en France* (Bordeaux: F. Pech, 1916), 5–7. For population data, see Kamel Kateb, *Européens, "indigènes" et juifs en Algérie (1830–1962): Représentations et réalités des populations* (Paris: Editions de l'INED, 2001), 187.

3 David Blackbourn, *The Conquest of Nature: Water, Landscape, and the Making of Modern Germany* (New York: W. W. Norton, 2006), 66.

4 AS, 124 S 1907, Commission de l'Algérie, meeting of 15 June 1892.

5 Leo Loubère, *The Red and the White: A History of Wine in France and Italy in the Nineteenth Century* (Albany: State University of New York Press, 1978), 155.

6 Quoted in George Gale, *Dying on the Vine: How Phylloxera Transformed Wine* (Berkeley: University of California Press, 2011), 14.

7 Michael P. M. Finch, *A Progressive Occupation? The Gallieni-Lyautey Method and Colonial Pacification in Tonkin and Madagascar, 1885–1900* (Oxford: Oxford University Press, 2013), 2–3.

8 Figures from Jacquet, *L'Alcool*, 62–63.

9 For estimates of numbers involved in French viticulture, see, for example, Gale, *Dying on the Vine*, 15–16; Harry W. Paul, *Science, Vine, and Wine in Modern France* (Cambridge: Cambridge University Press, 1996), 9–11.

10 Ministère de l'Agriculture, du Commerce et des Travaux Publics, *Enquête agricole. Algérie. Alger—Oran—Constantine* (Paris: Imprimerie Impériale, 1870), 40, 48, 50–51, 134–136, 167, 225, 235, 299–300, 357, 385.

11 John Ruedy, *Modern Algeria: The Origins and Development of a Nation* (Bloomington: Indiana University Press, 1992), 81–84.

12 Some examples of these posters are in ADSM, 8M 358.

13 ANOM, GGA, 1O 55, GG Chanzy speech to Conseil supérieur du gouvernement, 15 Nov. 1877.

14 Speech of July 1878, quoted in Isnard, *La vigne en Algérie*, 2:109.

15 Isnard, *La vigne en Algérie*, 2:32, 61, 86, 105; Simpson, *Creating Wine*, 41.

16 Paul Leroy-Beaulieu, *L'Algérie et la Tunisie* (Paris: Guillaumin, 1887), 111.

17 Mohamed Lazhar Gharbi, *Crédit et discrédit de la Banque d'Algérie (seconde moitié du XIXème siècle)* (Paris: L'Harmattan, 2005), 20–21, 62, 118, 138–140; Isnard, *La vigne en Algérie*, 2:86–87; René Passeron, "Les grandes Sociétés et la colonisation dans l'Afrique du Nord," in *Congrès de la colonisation rurale, Alger 26–29 mai 1930, 2ᵉ partie: Les problèmes économiques et sociaux posés par la colonisation* (Algiers: Victor Heintz, 1930), 50–52.

18 Gharbi, *Crédit et discrédit*, 165–173, 202–205; Maurice Jaïs, *La Banque de l'Algérie et le crédit agricole* (Paris: Arthur Rousseau, 1902), 79–86; Isnard, *La vigne en Algérie*, 2:111–117; Hubert Bonin, *Un outre-mer bancaire méditerranéen: Histoire du Crédit foncier d'Algérie et de Tunisie (1880–1997)* (Paris: Société Française d'Histoire d'Outre-Mer, 2004), 25–44.

19 Loubère, *The Red and the White*, 274. Something similar is asserted or implied in George Ordish, *The Great Wine Blight* (New York: Charles Scribner's Sons, 1972), 159; Gale, *Dying on the Vine*, 58, 264; Laura Levine Frader, *Peasants and Protest: Agricultural Workers, Politics, and Unions in the Aude, 1850–1914* (Berkeley: University of California Press, 1991), 62. Sources like L. Trabut and R. Marès, *L'Algérie agricole en 1906* (Algiers: Imprimerie Algérienne, 1906), 69, may have helped to establish the image.

20 ANOM, GGA, L5 dossier 8, correspondence from April to October 1878. A few individual requests appear in ADH, 6M 854 and 855.

21 Paul Bourde, *A travers l'Algérie: Souvenirs de l'excursion parlementaire (septembre-octobre 1879)* (Paris: G. Charpentier, 1880), 35. The Midi proper consists of the de-

partments of the Hérault, the Gard, the Aude, and Pyrénées-Orientales, though the term is often used to refer to the South of France in general.

22 Jean-Jacques Jordi, *Espagnol en Oranie: Histoire d'une migration, 1830–1914* (Calvisson: Editions Jacques Gandini, 1996), 216; Henri de Peyerimhoff, *Enquête sur les résultats de la colonisation officielle de 1871 à 1895*, 2 vols. (Algiers: Imprimerie Torrent, 1906), 2:207–208. Another solid example of southern relocation is in ANOM, GGA, L5 dossier 8, correspondence from the prefect of Constantine, Feb. 1877 and May 1878.

23 Colonization statistics are from Peyerimhoff, *Enquête sur les résultats de la colonisation officielle*, 1:108–109; departmental wine production statistics are from *Annuaire statistique de la France*, 1878–1890.

24 Isnard, *La vigne en Algérie*, 2:88. Peyerimhoff, *Enquête sur les résultats de la colonisation officielle*, 1:143–144, also shows that over half of the land made available for colonization between 1871 and 1895 ended up in the hands of Europeans who were already in Algeria.

25 Robert Tinthoin, *Colonisation et évolution des genres de vie dans la région ouest d'Oran de 1830 à 1885* (Oran: L. Fouque, 1947), 264–265; ADH, 6M 854, concessions de terre en Algérie, 1874. One source suggests that by 1888 the vignoble of Hammam-Bou-Hadjar was at four hundred hectares: L. Berniard, *L'Algérie et ses vins. Première partie: Oran* (Paris: G. Masson, 1888), 78.

26 On the politics of Frenchness in late nineteenth-century Algeria, and the impact of the 1889 law that naturalized the children of non-French settlers, see, for example, Andrea L. Smith, *Colonial Memory and Postcolonial Europe: Maltese Settlers in Algeria and France* (Bloomington: Indiana University Press, 2006), 98–118; David Prochaska, *Making Algeria French: Colonialism in Bône, 1870–1920* (Cambridge: Cambridge University Press, 1990), 135–178.

27 ANOM, BA, 80CX 131 and 132; Ernest Mallebay, *Cinquante ans de journalisme*, 3 vols. (Algiers: F. Fontana, 1937), 2:153–163; ANOM, état civil, marriage certificate for Charles Debono [*sic*] and Eugénie Martin, 1871; Colonel C. Trumelet, *Bou-Farik* (Algiers: Adolphe Jourdan, 1887), 484–487, 499–500, 530–537; Jules Maistre, *L'Algérie en 1899. Deuxième Partie: Agriculture* (Clermont-l'Hérault: S. Léotard, 1899), 3–4.

28 J. Angelini, *Le livre d'or des colons algériens* (Algiers: Joseph Angelini, 1903), 142–147; Julien Franc, *La colonisation de la Mitidja* (Paris: Librairie Ancienne Honoré Champion, 1928), 595–596; Isnard, *La vigne en Algérie*, 2:490.

29 Mallebay, *Cinquante ans de journalisme*, 2:159.

30 Trumelet, *Bou-Farik*, 490; ANP, F10 1588.

31 "Nécrologie: Claude Grellet," *Revue de viticulture* 36 (1911): 286–287; L. Berniard, *L'Algérie et ses vins. Deuxième partie: Alger* (Paris: G. Masson, 1890), 20–21; ANOM, état civil, birth of Louise Grellet, 1871. On French merchants in mid-century California, see Malcolm J. Rohrbough, *Rush to Gold: The French and the California Gold Rush, 1848–1854* (New Haven, CT: Yale University Press, 2013), 177–180; on "wintering" in Algiers, see Rebecca Rogers, *A Frenchwoman's Imperial Story: Madame Luce in Nineteenth-Century Algeria* (Stanford, CA: Stanford University Press, 2013), 146–147.

32 H. Lecq, *Le Domaine des Sources (Oued-el-Halleg). Exploitation agricole de M. A. Arlès-Dufour* (Algiers: Imprimerie Lavagne, 1882), esp. 11, 42–48, 61; Berniard, *L'Algérie*

et ses vins. Deuxième partie: Alger, 94–96; Narcisse Faucon, *Le livre d'or de l'Algérie* (Paris: Augustin Challamel, 1890), 17–18; Franc, *La colonisation de la Mitidja,* 582–586. On Lecq, see Omar Bessaoud, "Hippolyte Lecq (1856–1922): Un agronome colonial ou la défense d'une agrologie nord-africaine," *Insaniyat: revue algérienne d'anthropologie et de sciences sociales* 19–20 (2003): 177–197; on the Arlès-Dufour family and Algeria, see Jean-François Klein, "Une culture impériale consulaire? L'exemple de la Chambre de Commerce de Lyon (1830–1920)," in Hubert Bonin, Catherine Hodeir, and Jean-François Klein, eds., *L'esprit économique impérial (1830–1970): Groupes de pression et réseaux du patronat colonial en France et dans l'empire* (Paris: Publications de la SFHOM, 2008), 355–357; Pamela Pilbeam, *Saint-Simonians in Nineteenth-Century France: From Free Love to Algeria* (Basingstoke, UK: Palgrave Macmillan, 2014), 175.

33 L. Bastide, *Bel-Abbès et son arrondissement* (Oran: Ad. Perrier, 1881), 145.

34 Faucon, *Le livre d'or de l'Algérie,* 39–41; V. Pulliat, *Les vignobles d'Algérie* (Montpellier: Camille Coulet, 1898), 57–58; Angelini, *Le livre d'or des colons algériens,* 101–103.

35 Pulliat, *Les vignobles d'Algérie,* 104.

36 Comité départemental du Rhône, *Exposition Universelle de 1900: La colonisation lyonnaise* (Lyon: A. Rey, 1900), 28–55; Association française pour l'avancement des sciences, *Lyon et la région lyonnaise en 1906* (Lyon: A. Rey, 1906), 263–265.

37 Charles Pourcher, *Souvenirs et impressions recueillies au cours d'une période d'action coloniale de cinquante-cinq ans (1867–1922)* (Paris: R. Chiberre, 1924), 67–82. On the Dollfus family, see Nicolas Stoskopf, "La culture impériale du patronat textile mulhousien," in Bonin, Hodeir, and Klein, *L'esprit économique impérial,* 398–401.

38 "A Model Farm in Algeria," *The Times* (London), 22 May 1891; "Obituary: Jonathan Holden," *The Times,* 17 Feb. 1906; ANOM, état civil, death of John Holden, 1891; "Mélanges," *Revue de Champagne et de Brie* 5 (1893), 398–399; Franc, *La colonisation de la Mitidja,* 590; Katrina Honeyman and Jordan Goodman, *Technology and Enterprise: Isaac Holden and the Mechanisation of Woolcombing in France, 1848–1914* (Aldershot, UK: Scolar Press, 1986).

39 Franc, *La colonisation de la Mitidja,* 573; *Station balnéaire de Fort de l'Eau. Fort de l'Eau et son avenir comme station balnéaire maritime d'été* (Algiers: Imprimerie de la Revue Algérienne, 1893), 14, 16; Berniard, *L'Algérie et ses vins. Deuxième partie: Alger,* 110; Gilbert Bresson, *Histoire d'un centre rural algérien: Fort de l'Eau* (Algiers: Vve. J. Bringau, 1957); Gérard Crespo and Jean-Jacques Jordi, *Les Espagnols dans l'Algérois, 1830–1914: Histoire d'une migration* (Versailles: Editions de l'Atlanthrope, 1991), 134–135.

40 ADBR, private papers of Louis Gastine, 127 J 17, Département d'Oran: Syndicat de défense contre le phylloxéra, 14 Nov. 1885; Le citoyen Bézy, "Taxe sur la vigne," *Le Petit Fanal Oranais,* 28 Oct. 1885; *Notice sur un projet de Société agricole, viticole et industrielle de la Safia, domaine de 3,200 hectares en Algérie, arrondissement de Philippeville, département de Constantine* (Mâcon: Protat frères, 1883), 7.

41 ANP, F10 1621, Min Ag to GG, 10 Feb. 1885.

42 ANP, F10 1621, miscellaneous correspondence from 1884 and early 1885. Relevant laws and decrees are in Robert Estoublon and Adolphe Lefébure, *Code de l'Algérie annoté: recueil chronologique des lois, ordonnances, décrets, arrêtés, circulaires, etc., formant la législation algérienne actuellement en vigueur* (Algiers: Adolphe Jourdan, 1896), 530–531, 604–606, 637.

43 Law of 21 Mar. 1883, in Estoublon and Lefébure, *Code de l'Algérie annoté*, 604–606.

44 AS, 124 S 430, Commission chargé de l'examen du projet de loi sur les mesures à prendre contre l'invasion et la propagation du phylloxéra en Algérie, meeting of 5 Mar. 1883.

45 Quotation from ADBR, 127 J 17, report by Louis Gastine to Min Ag, 10 Dec. 1884.

46 ANP, F10 1621, GG to Min Ag, 3 Mar. 1886, list of experts and their districts.

47 Biographical information from ANOM, état civil, marriage of Onésime Havard and Anne Robin, 1874; marriage of Marie Mollier, 1881; death of Calixte Spenon, 1896; marriage of Fernando Alberto and Francisca Seguí, 1882; Angelini, *Le livre d'or des colons algériens*, 238–240; Jacques Bouveresse, *Un parlement colonial? Les Délégations financières algériennes, 1898–1945*, 2 vols. (Mont-Saint-Aignan: Publications des Universités de Rouen et du Havre, 2008/2010), 1:372. See also Léon Mathiss, *La lutte contre le phylloxéra en Algérie* (Mostaganem: Imprimerie de "L'Aïn-Sefra," 1904), 18.

48 ADBR, 127 J 17, misc. correspondence from July 1885.

49 P. Cardonne and J. Rabot, *La colonisation dans l'ouest-Oranais* (Algiers: V. Heintz, 1930), 228.

50 A. Drot, "Phylloxéra," *L'Insurgé*, 19 July 1885.

51 ADBR, 127 J 17, documents in folder marked "Parquet de Tlemcen—enquêtes."

52 Ibid., Procès-verbal dated 16 July 1885. Compensation under the 1883 law was calculated on the basis of three average harvests.

53 Mathiss, *La lutte contre le phylloxéra en Algérie*, 19–20; Isnard, *La vigne en Algérie*, 2:280–281.

54 ADBR, 127 J 17, Louis Gastine to Gabriel Gastine, 27 Oct. 1885.

55 Law of 28 July 1886 in Estoublon and Lefébure, *Code de l'Algérie annoté*, 689–691; Isnard, *La vigne en Algérie*, 2:248–251; ADBR, 127 J 17, Département d'Oran: Syndicat de défense contre le phylloxéra, 14 Nov. 1885; ANP, F10 1621, GG to Min Ag, 23 Apr. 1887, composition of syndicates in Algiers and Oran.

56 Mathiss, *La lutte contre le phylloxéra en Algérie*, 21.

57 For example ANP, F10 1621, Syndicat des viticulteurs du département d'Alger, assemblée générale, 7 Oct. 1887.

58 Gale, *Dying on the Vine*, 57, 76; Alan R. H. Baker, *Fraternity among the French Peasantry: Sociability and Voluntary Associations in the Loire Valley, 1815–1914* (Cambridge: Cambridge University Press, 1999), 227–228; Kolleen M. Guy, *When Champagne Became French: Wine and the Making of a National Identity* (Baltimore: Johns Hopkins University Press, 2003), 108–112.

59 Another method used in parts of France—drowning the bug by flooding the vines—does not seem to have been considered for the few parts of Algeria where it might have been possible, perhaps because of an aversion to standing water in low-lying areas.

60 Gale, *Dying on the Vine*, 144–145.

61 ADBR, 127 J 17, Louis Gastine to Gabriel Gastine, 28 Aug. 1885; ANOM, Oran, 1H 11, L. Gastine to Couanon, 4 Sept. 1885; Helga Tietz, "One Centennium of Soil Fumigation: Its First Years," in T. A. Toussoun, Robert V. Bega, and Paul E. Nelson, eds., *Root Diseases and Soil-Borne Pathogens* (Berkeley: University of California Press, 1970), 203–207.

62 On *marchands de plantes*, see Gale, *Dying on the Vine*, 100; Le citoyen Bézy, "Taxe sur la vigne," *Le Petit Fanal Oranais*, 28 Oct. 1885.

63 On the French dismantling of Russicada, see Michael Greenhalgh, *The Military and Colonial Destruction of the Roman Landscape of North Africa, 1830–1900* (Leiden: Brill, 2014), 145–150.

64 ANP, F10 1621, Georges Couanon to Min Ag, 10 June 1887.

65 On politics in Constantine at this time, see, for example, Bouveresse, *Un parlement colonial,* 1:481–484.

66 ANP, F10 1621, Lecq to GG, 19 Nov. 1886; GG to Min Ag, 3 Oct. 1887; Lecq to GG, 24 June 1889; GG to Min Ag, 13 Sept. 1890; Couanon to Min Ag, 26 Feb. 1891; Isnard, *La vigne en Algérie,* 2:266–272.

67 Berniard, *L'Algérie et ses vins. Première partie: Oran,* 115–116.

68 ANP, F10 1621, Lecq to GG, 24 Jan. 1889 and 10 Apr. 1889.

69 ANP, F10 1621, Département d'Oran: Syndicat de défense des vignobles, assemblée du 9 Oct. 1893, and H. Viénot to Min Ag, no date; Mathiss, *La lutte contre le phylloxéra en Algérie,* 25–33. On the conflict in the Champagne, see Guy, *When Champagne Became French,* 86–127.

70 ANP, F10 1621, petitions dated Oct. 1886 and GG to Min Ag, 5 Nov. 1886, 2 Dec. 1886, and 10 Aug. 1887; Isnard, *La vigne en Algérie,* 2:265–266.

71 ANP, F10 1621, decree of 28 Jan. 1892; L. Berniard, *L'Algérie et ses vins. Troisième partie: Constantine* (Paris: G. Masson, 1892), 60–63, listing vignerons in Philippeville and their annual production (quotation at 61).

72 ANP, F12 4703, Syndicat professionnel viticole de la région de Jemmapes, 1896–1900.

73 Isnard, *La vigne en Algérie,* 2:285–286.

74 Law of 23 Mar. 1899, in Robert Estoublon and Adolphe Lefébure, *Code de l'Algérie annoté: recueil chronologique des lois, ordonnances, décrets, arrêtés, circulaires, etc., formant la législation algérienne actuellement en vigueur, 1896–1905* (Algiers: Adolphe Jourdan, 1907), 14–16, supplement 1899; Isnard, *La vigne en Algérie,* 2:295–301.

75 Isnard, *La vigne en Algérie,* 2:284, 320, 329–331, 337–338; Mathiss, *La lutte contre le phylloxéra en Algérie,* 22–23, 32–33; Henri Pensa, *L'Algérie: Voyage de la délégation de la commission sénatoriale d'études des questions algériennes* (Paris: J. Rothschild, 1894), 328–329.

76 P. Viala, *Mission viticole pour la reconstitution du vignoble algérien* (Algiers: Giralt, 1900), 1–7. On Viala, see Paul, *Science, Vine, and Wine,* 25–28.

77 Quoted in Mathiss, *La lutte contre le phylloxéra en Algérie,* 58.

78 Isnard, *La vigne en Algérie,* 2:134–135, 273, 303.

79 André Nouschi, *Enquête sur le niveau de vie des populations rurales constantinoises, de la conquête jusqu'en 1919: Essai d'histoire économique et sociale* (Paris: Presses Universitaires de France, 1961), 746.

80 Isnard, *La vigne en Algérie,* 2:277. Isnard was echoing the earlier judgment of Léon Mathiss in *La lutte contre le phylloxéra en Algérie,* 79–82.

81 Guy, *When Champagne Became French,* 88.

82 Loubère, *The Red and the White,* 173.

83 Charles-Robert Ageron documents numerous examples in *Les Algériens musulmans et la France (1871–1919)* (Paris: Presses Universitaires de France, 1968).

84 Donald Denoon points to the importance of governmental support for the economic ventures of other settler societies in his *Settler Capitalism: The Dynamics of Dependent Development in the Southern Hemisphere* (Oxford: Oxford University Press, 1983), 122. For early agricultural associations in Algeria, see, for example, *Statuts du Comice agricole de la province d'Alger* (Algiers: A. Bourget, 1849). Bugeaud had advocated the formation of agricultural societies as governor-general.

85 On the commission, see Charles-Robert Ageron, "Jules Ferry et la question algérienne en 1892 (d'après quelques inédits)," in Ageron, *De l'Algérie française à l'Algérie algérienne* (Paris: Editions Bouchène, 2005), 161–182; Ageron, *Les Algériens musulmans et la France*, 447–458.

86 AS, 124 S 1907, Commission de l'Algérie, meeting of 15 June 1892.

87 Ageron, "Jules Ferry," 167.

88 Jules Ferry, *Le gouvernement de l'Algérie* (Paris: Armand Colin, 1892), 8.

89 Berniard, *L'Algérie et ses vins. Deuxième partie: Alger*, 20–21. The Sahel algérois is a zone of hills and coastland to the west of the city of Algiers between the Mediterranean and the Mitidja plain (the word "sahel" is from the Arabic for "coast" or "shore"). It is not to be confused with the ecological zone called the Sahel that stretches across Africa along the southern edge of the Sahara.

90 The building was described admiringly in P. Ferrouillat and M. Charvet, *Les celliers. Construction et matériel vinicole avec la description des principaux celliers du Midi, du Bordelais, de la Bourgogne et de l'Algérie* (Montpellier: Camille Coulet, 1896), 460–465.

91 See also Erica Hannickel's analysis of pictures of American and Australian vineyards in "Cultivation and Control: Grape Growing as Expansion in Nineteenth-Century United States and Australia," *Comparative American Studies* 8:4 (2010): 283–299; and John Zarobell, *Empire of Landscape: Space and Ideology in French Colonial Algeria* (University Park: Pennsylvania State University Press, 2010), 6.

92 Comité départemental du Rhône, *Exposition Universelle de 1900*, 32–48; ANOM, BA, 80 ES 329, Société anonyme des vignobles algériens, property map in annual report, 31 Mar. 1931. On eucalyptus, see Diana K. Davis, *Resurrecting the Granary of Rome: Environmental History and French Colonial Expansion in North Africa* (Athens: Ohio University Press, 2007), 102–108.

93 Isnard, *La vigne en Algérie*, 2:149.

94 Loubère, *The Red and the White*, 183–184; Guy, *When Champagne Became French*, 113–114.

95 Romuald Dejernon, *Les vignes et les vins de l'Algérie*, 2 vols. (Paris: Librairie Agricole de la Maison Rustique, 1883–1884), 2:94.

96 Lucette Valensi, *On the Eve of Colonialism: North Africa before the French Conquest*, trans. Kenneth J. Perkins (New York: Africana, 1977), 26; Nouschi, *Enquête sur le niveau de vie des populations rurales constantinoises*, 161–162, 191, 241.

97 Michael J. Heffernan and Keith Sutton, "The Landscape of Colonialism: The Impact of French Colonial Rule on the Algerian Rural Settlement Pattern, 1830–1987," in Christopher Dixon and Michael Heffernan, eds., *Colonialism and Development in the Contemporary World* (London: Mansell, 1991), 146.

98 For the phrase "vignes géométriques," see Cardonne and Rabot, *La colonisation dans l'ouest-Oranais*, 12.

99 On Montparnasse cemetery (with its "geometrical rigor" and its graves "in orderly rows"), see Richard A. Etlin, *The Architecture of Death: The Transformation of the Cemetery in Eighteenth-Century Paris* (Cambridge, MA: MIT Press, 1984), 240–243.

100 AS, 124 S 1907, Commission de l'Algérie, meeting of 15 June 1892.

101 ANOM, CMAT, F2, Garde champêtre d'Aboubellil to administrateur de la commune mixte d'Aïn-Témouchent, 22 July and 20 Dec. 1897.

102 S. Leroux, *Traité pratique sur la vigne et le vin en Algérie et en Tunisie* (Blida: A. Mauguin, 1894), 562; ANOM, GGA, 1O 34, Prefect of Algiers to GG, 2 Aug. 1893.

103 Pourcher, *Souvenirs et impressions*, 80; Bouveresse, *Un parlement colonial*, 2:187–188; "L'Assurance mutuelle agricole contre la grêle en Algérie," *Le Musée social* 13:5 (1908): 150–152; Alan R. H. Baker, "Hail as Hazard: Changing Attitudes to Crop Protection against Hail Damage in France, 1815–1914," *Agricultural History Review* 60:1 (2012): 19–36; Isnard, *La vigne en Algérie*, 2:171–179. For the full array of viticultural foes, see Leroux, *Traité pratique sur la vigne*.

104 "Sur le zinc: Comment sont fabriqués les petits vins," *Le Matin*, 3 Sept. 1893.

105 CANA, Chambre de Commerce 179, Jules Ricome to President of Algiers CC, 3 Sept. 1893; ANP, F10 1621, President of Algiers CC to Minister of Commerce, 17 Sept. 1893.

106 Isnard, *La vigne en Algérie*, 2:180–184; ANP, F10 1621, GG to Min Ag, 25 Feb. 1894.

107 A good summary is in Simpson, *Creating Wine*, 65–70.

108 The language of crisis is to some extent reproduced in Kolleen Cross, "The Evolution of Colonial Agriculture: The Creation of the Algerian 'Vignoble,' 1870–1892," *Proceedings of the Sixteenth Meeting of the French Colonial Historical Society*, ed. Patricia Galloway (Lanham, MD: University Press of America, 1992), 57–72; and John Strachan, "The Colonial Identity of Wine: The Leakey Affair and the Franco-Algerian Order of Things," *Social History of Alcohol and Drugs* 21:2 (2007): 118–137. Ageron, *Les Algériens musulmans et la France*, 567–568, is skeptical of the *colons*' crisis talk in this period, as is Didier Guignard, "Les crises en trompe l'œil de l'Algérie française des années 1890," in Abderrahmane Bouchène, Jean-Pierre Peyroulou, Ouanassa Siari Tengour, and Sylvie Thénault, eds., *Histoire de l'Algérie à la période coloniale 1830–1962* (Paris: La Découverte, 2012), 218–223.

109 Bourde, *A travers l'Algérie*, 36; Leroux, *Traité pratique sur la vigne*, 68–69.

110 Georges Viollier, *Les deux Algérie* (Paris: Paul Dupont, 1898), 253.

111 AGMAfr, Livinhac 7, 007329, P. Burtin to P. Livinhac, 2 Dec. 1905.

112 ANP, F10 1621, M. Malbot, "Les vins d'Algérie," in *Bulletin officiel du Syndicat départemental de défense contre le phylloxéra*, no. 48, 1893, 3–4.

113 Quotation in ANP, F10 1621, *Département d'Alger: Bulletin official du Syndicat de défense contre le phylloxéra*, no. 16, 1888, 319.

114 ANMT, 9 AQ 263, Faillite de la maison Joly et Pertus, négociants en vins d'Alger, 1890–1893.

115 ANOM, CMAT, F2, prefect of Oran to mayors and administrators, 20 May and 5 Sept. 1890 and 30 Jan. 1892.

116 Angelini, *Le livre d'or des colons algériens*, 73–76; Isnard, *La vigne en Algérie*, 2:189–194; Charles Naylies, *Monographie de la commune de Koléa (Algérie)* (Nevers: G. Vallière, 1905), 57.

117 Gabriel Simian, *Notes pratiques sur la vinification en Algérie* (Algiers: Typographie Adolphe Jourdan, 1900), 3–5.

118 Gaston Galtier, *Le vignoble du Languedoc et du Roussillon, étude comparative d'un vignoble de masse,* 3 vols. (Montpellier: Editions Causse, 1960), 1:9.

119 Edmond Théry, *Les progrès économiques de la France: Bilan du régime douanier de 1892* (Paris: Economiste Européen, 1908), 142–143; Charles K. Warner, *The Winegrowers of France and the Government since 1875* (New York: Columbia University Press, 1960), 9–14.

120 Warner, *The Winegrowers of France,* 14. On adulteration, see also Alessandro Stanziani, *Rules of Exchange: French Capitalism in Comparative Perspective, Eighteenth to Twentieth Centuries* (Cambridge: Cambridge University Press, 2012), 128–135.

121 ANOM, GGA, 1O 290, CC of Carcassonne to Minister of Commerce, no date and CC of Algiers, minutes of 23 Aug. 1899 meeting; CANA, Chambre de Commerce 179, L. Altairac and J. Bertrand to Pres. of CC of Carcassonne, 11 Aug. 1899.

122 Ageron, *Les Algériens musulmans et la France,* 569–573.

123 Dessoliers's *L'Algérie libre* from 1895 provides the most complete statement of this line of thought.

124 See, for example, Patricia M. E. Lorcin, *Imperial Identities: Stereotyping, Prejudice, and Race in Colonial Algeria* (London: I. B. Tauris, 1995), 196–213.

125 See Bouveresse, *Un parlement colonial,* esp. 1:359–429. On anti-Semitism in this period, see Sophie B. Roberts, *Citizenship and Antisemitism in French Colonial Algeria, 1870–1962* (Cambridge: Cambridge University Press, 2017), 48–110.

126 Isnard, *La vigne en Algérie,* 2:441–442, and figures in Vicente Pinilla and Maria-Isabel Ayuda, "The Political Economy of the Wine Trade: Spanish Exports and the International Market, 1890–1935," *European Review of Economic History* 6 (2002): 65; Théry, *Les progrès économiques de la France,* 144. On protectionism, see Eugene O. Golob, *The Méline Tariff: French Agriculture and Nationalist Economic Policy* (New York: Columbia University Press, 1944); and Michael Stephen Smith, *Tariff Reform in France, 1860–1900: The Politics of Economic Interest* (Ithaca, NY: Cornell University Press, 1980).

127 ANOM, GGA, 1O 288, for example, Mission économique en Allemagne, Nov.–Dec. 1901.

128 Multiple documents in ANP, F12 7443, for example, GG to Minister of Commerce, 11 Nov. 1905, and in ANOM, GGA, 1O 289. The "dietetic" quotation appeared in *The Times,* 6 Nov. 1907; "the Bordeaux market" in *Ridley's Wine & Spirit Trade Circular,* 8 Sept. 1905. See also Strachan, "The Colonial Identity of Wine."

129 ANOM, GGA, 1O 289.

130 AWO, H 824, minutes of municipal council of Mascara, 8 Dec. 1905.

131 ANP, F12 7443, GG to Minister of Commerce, 21 Nov. 1905.

132 Warner, *The Winegrowers of France,* 18; Frader, *Peasants and Protest,* 65–66.

133 Geneviève Gavignaud-Fontaine, *Le Languedoc viticole, la Méditerranée et l'Europe au siècle dernier (XXe)* (Montpellier: Publications de l'Université Paul-Valéry, 2000), 68.

134 Isnard, *La vigne en Algérie,* II:449; Jean Sagnes, ed., *Histoire de Sète* (Toulouse: Editions Privat, 1987), 216–217. Cette was renamed Sète in 1928.

135 James Simpson, "Cooperation and Conflicts: Institutional Innovation in France's Wine Markets, 1870–1911," *Business History Review* 79:3 (2005), 541. The commission visited Algeria in May 1907; AWO, H 824.

136 AWO, H 824, Commune de Palissy, municipal council meeting of 21 Apr. 1907, and Commissaire chef de service to sous-préfet de Mascara, 3 June 1907; Frader, *Peasants and Protest*, 141.

137 Warner, *The Winegrowers of France*, 41–42. These rules applied equally to Algeria.

138 For example, in a system of advances for smaller growers. See the GG's circular of 15 Nov. 1901 in Estoublon and Lefébure, *Code de l'Algérie annoté (1896–1905)*, 56, supplement 1901; ANOM, CMAT, F2, GG to mayor of Aïn-Témouchent, 22 Nov. 1901.

139 Xavier Yacono, *La colonisation des plaines du Chélif (de Lavigerie au confluent de la Mina)*, 2 vols. (Algiers: Imprimerie E. Imbert, 1955), 2:153–154; Isnard, *La vigne en Algérie*, 2:362, 529–530; Nouschi, *Enquête sur le niveau de vie des populations rurales constantinoises*, 613–614.

140 Pourcher, *Souvenirs et impressions*, 211–220, 225–234; Bonin, *Un outre-mer bancaire*, 17.

141 AS, 124 S 1907, Commission de l'Algérie, meeting of 25 Feb. 1892; Peyerimhoff, *Enquête sur les résultats de la colonisation officielle*, 2:329–330, 420–421; Isnard, *La vigne en Algérie*, 2:368–372; Gharbi, *Crédit et discrédit de la Banque d'Algérie*, 234–237; Bonin, *Un outre-mer bancaire*, 40–43. For an overview of the bank's activities, see Samir Saul, "Colonial Banking in French North Africa: Banque de l'Algérie et de la Tunisie (1851–1963)," in Hubert Bonin and Nuno Valério, eds., *Colonial and Imperial Banking History* (Florence: Taylor and Francis, 2015), 131–164.

142 Henri Hauser, *Esquisses Algériennes* (Paris: Société de l'Annuaire Colonial, 1905), 10. See also Ferrouillat and Charvet, *Les celliers*, 475–480.

143 ANOM, BA, 80CX 132, Sous-directeur to directeur of Bank of Algeria, 10 Apr. 1902. See also Alain Sainte-Marie, "La crise de 1900–1902 en Algérie: simple crise viticole?," *Cahiers de la Méditerranée* 2 (1976): 176.

144 Based on multiple documents in ANOM, BA, 80CX 131 and 132; and, on his death, BA, 11CX 20. See also Banque de l'Algérie, report to shareholders dated 28 Nov. 1907, in *L'économiste français*, 28 Dec. 1907, 946; Mallebay, *Cinquante ans de journalisme*, 2:172; Isnard, *La vigne en Algérie*, 2:399–401.

145 See Mallebay, *Cinquante ans de journalisme*, 2:163; press coverage in ANOM, BA, 80CX 131 and 132; E. F. Gautier, *Un siècle de colonisation: Etudes au microscope* (Paris: Félix Alcan, 1930), 76.

146 AGMAfr, Casier B19, Livinhac 28, "Court historique des biens de la Société," 14 June 1940; Birraux 336, various confidential notes, 1907–1911.

147 Bernard Delpal, *Le silence des moines: Les Trappistes au XIXe siècle: France-Algérie-Syrie* (Paris: Beauchesne, 1998), 10, 149, 452–454; Gabriel Verge, *Monographie du Domaine de la Trappe de Staouëli* (Algiers: V. Heintz, 1930), 29–30.

148 Pourcher, *Souvenirs et impressions*, 247–248.

149 ANOM, BA, 11CX 20, 80CX 131, and 11ES 211; Mallebay, *Cinquante ans de journalisme*, 2:166; Trumelet, *Bou-Farik*, 536; Franc, *La colonisation de la Mitidja*, 670–671, 689; Eliane Perrin, *L'âge d'or de la parfumerie à Grasse d'après les archives Chiris (1768–1967)* (Aix-en-Provence: Edisud, 1996), 45–63.

150 Pinilla and Ayuda, "The Political Economy of the Wine Trade," 58.

151 Bouveresse, *Un parlement colonial,* 2:103.

152 For lists of mayors and *conseillers généraux,* see *Almanach national: Annuaire officiel de la République Française pour 1906–1907* (Paris: Berger-Levrault, 1907), 1246–1248, 1255–1256, 1261–1263. On Bertagna (whose brother Dominique also owned vineyards), see Prochaska, *Making Algeria French,* xvii–xviii, 192–201; Pensa, *L'Algérie: Voyage de la délégation de la commission sénatoriale,* 299–300; Albert Meunier, *Voyage en Algérie* (Paris: Alcide Picard, 1909), 34–39.

153 "Vinelords" is my own term. For context on "Randlords," see Stanley Trapido, "Imperialism, Settler Identities, and Colonial Capitalism: The Hundred-Year Origins of the 1899 South African War," in Robert Ross, Anne Kelk Mager, and Bill Nasson, eds., *The Cambridge History of South Africa,* vol. 2, *1885–1994* (Cambridge: Cambridge University Press, 2011), 66–101; and, for a popular history that usefully highlights their social world, Geoffrey Wheatcroft, *The Randlords: The Exploits and Exploitations of South Africa's Mining Magnates* (New York: Atheneum, 1986).

3. COMPANIES AND COOPERATIVES, WORK AND WEALTH

1 On Muriel, see ANOM, état civil, marriage of Antonio Muriel and Maria Fuster, 1886, and birth of Joseph Muriel, 1889; GGA, 1O 52, Feuilles d'attachements des journées d'ouvriers, 1914; 1O 137, Ministre de Guerre to GG, 13 Sept. 1916, and Directeur des services financiers to Directeur de l'agriculture, 12 Oct. 1916. On Lucien Camus, see Olivier Todd, *Albert Camus: Une vie* (Paris: Gallimard, 1996), 13–23; and Albert Camus, *Le premier homme* (Paris: Gallimard, 1994). On Borgeaud, see Michèle Barbier, *Le mythe Borgeaud: Henri Borgeaud (1895–1964). Trente ans d'histoire de l'Algérie française à travers un symbole* (Châteauneuf-les-Martigues: Editions Wallâda, 1995), 23; and Jean-Maurice di Costanzo, *Allemands et Suisses en Algérie 1830–1918* (Nice: Editions Jacques Gandini, 2001), 182–183.

2 For the "enemy" quotation, see AGMAfr, Livinhac 28, report on annual meeting of the SIAH, 31 Mar. 1916.

3 He was exonerated in 1920 by a military tribunal. Barbier, *Le mythe Borgeaud,* 233; Ernest Mallebay, *Cinquante ans de journalisme,* 3 vols. (Algiers: F. Fontana, 1937), 3:135–153; Jean-Pierre Borgeaud, *Jules Borgeaud: Consul de la confédération suisse,* typescript held at the CDHA.

4 On some of these issues, see Hildebert Isnard, "La vigne en Algérie: étude géographique" (PhD diss., Université de Paris I-Sorbonne, 1947), 760–775.

5 Todd, *Albert Camus,* 28–29.

6 ADBR, 127 J 17, Liste des visiteurs des vignes phylloxérées de Mansourah du 6 au 31 juillet 1885; 127 J 18, "Le phylloxéra à Tlemcen," *Le Petit Colon,* 15 July 1885.

7 Namely, Draria, Birmandreis, El Biar, El Achour, and Dély Ibrahim.

8 ANOM, GGA, 1O 58, Gouvernement-Général de l'Algérie, *Commission technique du phylloxéra, séance du 28 Dec. 1909* (Algiers: Victor Heintz, 1910), 12–13; Hildebert Isnard, *La vigne en Algérie: Etude géographique,* 2 vols. (Gap: Ophrys, 1951 / 1954), 2:306; AGMAfr, Livinhac 28.

9 *Les vins algériens: Annuaire de la viticulture algérienne* 13 (1931), 9; Isnard, *La vigne en Algérie,* 2:491. I have rounded down these numbers, which in any case should always be taken as approximate.

10 Charles-Robert Ageron, *Histoire de l'Algérie contemporaine*, vol. 2, *De l'insurrection de 1871 au déclenchement de la guerre de libération (1954)* (Paris: Presses Universitaires de France, 1979), 116; Isnard, *La vigne en Algérie*, 2:491; Julien Franc, *La colonisation de la Mitidja* (Paris: Librairie Ancienne Honoré Champion, 1928), 655.

11 Georges Bailly, *A la mémoire des agriculteurs de la plaine de Bône* (Nice: Self-published, 2009), 37. Details about Jacques Germain are sparse, and there are some discrepancies in John Franklin, "La famille Germain," *Mémoire vive* 31 (2005): 3–4. See also ANOM, état civil, death of Jacques Germain, 1864.

12 Obituary of Pierre Germain, in *La Dépêche algérienne*, 30 July 1905; ANOM, état civil, deaths of Anne Françoise Cazes, Marie Germain, Louise Germain, all 1857.

13 ANOM, BA, 11ES 287, director of Algiers branch office to BA director, 15 Feb. 1908.

14 ANOM, BA, 11ES 287, Chef du bureau auxiliaire de Blida to sous-directeur de la Banque de l'Algérie, 28 Dec. 1910 and 27 Mar. 1911; Proposition de crédit de campagne en faveur de M. Pierre Germain, 7 Oct. 1918.

15 ANOM, BA, 11ES 332, Demande d'admission à l'escompte en faveur de la Société anonyme des Domaines du Kéroulis, 5 Jan. 1920.

16 ANOM, BA, 11ES 287, bank documents on Auguste Germain-Branthomme (1916), Jean Germain (1908, 1910), Maurice Germain (1911, 1914, 1918). On Maurice, see also Bailly, *A la mémoire des agriculteurs de la plaine de Bône*, 38; ANMT, 2001 026 3056 CFAT, bank report on Domaine de Sidi-Salem, 1932.

17 Geneviève Gavignaud-Fontaine, *Le Languedoc viticole, la Méditerranée et l'Europe au siècle dernier (XXe)* (Montpellier: Publications de l'Université Paul-Valéry, 2000), 48–49.

18 AGMAfr, Livinhac 28, for example, annual reports from the 1910s; Livinhac 29, Rapport du chef de l'exploitation viticole to Conseil d'administration, 23 Dec. 1913; Birraux 34, "Note sur le domaine d'Oulid Adda."

19 For the decree and the debate, see ANOM, GGA, 1O 58; also Isnard, *La vigne en Algérie*, 2:311–312.

20 AWA, 1H 76, Prefect of Algiers to GG, 12 Oct. 1912.

21 ANOM, GGA, 1O 58, Délégué régional du Service du phylloxéra to GG, 16 May 1913. The growers were Pelegri and Welter.

22 ANOM, GGA, 1O 58, esp. Prefect of Algiers to GG, 6 Sept. 1913. On Averseng, see ANOM, BA, 11ES 137.

23 ANOM, GGA, 1O 58, Gt-Gl de l'Algérie, *Commission technique du phylloxéra, séance du 28 décembre 1909*, 17.

24 Un vieil colon de la région, *Médéa et son vignoble* (Algiers: Imprimerie Moderne, 1930), 5–6; ANOM, GGA, 5X 8, report by Conseiller Boulogne to Conseil de gouvernement, 11 Aug. 1916; AWA, 1H 79, Rapport sur les opérations effectués par le syndicat au cours de l'année 1918; P. Cardonne and J. Rabot, *La colonisation dans l'ouest Oranais* (Algiers: V. Heintz, 1930), 231–232.

25 AWA, 1H 24, Germain-Branthomme to GG, 8 Nov. 1917, and to Prefect of Algiers, 27 Nov. 1917; see also 1H 76 and 1H 78.

26 Advertisement in *Agenda P.L.M.* for 1921; Paul Borg, *Report on a Tour of Inspection in the Wine-Growing Districts of Western Europe and Algeria* (Malta: Government Printing Office, 1922), 12; ANOM, GGA, 1O 36, Pépinières de vignes américaines,

1927; AS, 69S 190, Commission des douanes, meeting of 21 June 1921; Isnard, "La vigne en Algérie," 776.

27 ANOM, BA, 11ES 337 and 11ES 332; "M. Jaime Sabaté," *L'Afrique du Nord illustrée,* 22 June 1929. Despite this flush of success, Sabaté went bankrupt in 1932 (ANOM, BA, 80CX 103).

28 On the wartime requisitioning of Algerian wine, see esp. ANOM, GGA, 1O 150 and 1O 283; Gilbert Meynier, *L'Algérie révélée: La guerre de 1914–1918 et le premier quart du XXe siècle* (Geneva: Librairie Droz, 1981), 312–313.

29 AGMAfr, Livinhac 28, annual reports to shareholders, 1914–1921; AWA, 1H 76.

30 See, esp., ANOM, GGA, 1O 280, Charles Welter, "L'Algérie et le port de Rouen," 17 Feb. 1915. Also Isnard, *La vigne en Algérie,* 2:446–448.

31 Isnard, "La vigne en Algérie," 769.

32 Sapiens, "La crise des transports," *L'Echo d'Alger,* 4 Feb. 1917. On wartime shipping, see Meynier, *L'Algérie révélée,* 293–300; Augustin Bernard, *L'Afrique du Nord pendant la guerre* (Paris: Presses Universitaires de France, 1926), 29–33; Olivier Boudot, *Les Schiaffino, une dynastie d'armateurs* (Saint-Malo: Pascal Galodé, 2008), 84–103.

33 Sapiens, "La crise des transports."

34 ANOM, GGA, 1O 283, founding documents, membership list, and misc. correspondence, May–Sept. 1917. See also Meynier, *L'Algérie révélée,* 298; and ANP, C 7754, dossier 122.

35 See, for example, Gaston Marguet, "La flotte algérienne," *L'Echo d'Alger,* 21 Mar. 1917; "A l'Union des viticulteurs d'Algérie," *L'Echo d'Alger,* 17 Aug. 1917.

36 L. Pasquier-Bronde, *Les associations agricoles en Algérie* (Algiers: Baldachino-Laronde-Viguier, 1911), 209–286; Robert Estoublon and Adolphe Lefébure, *Code de l'Algérie annoté: recueil chronologique des lois, ordonnances, décrets, arrêtés, circulaires, etc., formant la législation algérienne actuellement en vigueur, 1896–1905* (Algiers: Adolphe Jourdan, 1907), 37–40, supplement 1901; Jacques Bouveresse, *Un parlement colonial? Les Délégations financières algériennes, 1898–1945,* 2 vols. (Mont-Saint-Aignan: Publications des Universités de Rouen et du Havre, 2008 / 2010), 2:158–163; Cardonne and Rabot, *La colonisation dans l'ouest-Oranais,* 265–272.

37 On early attempts at viticultural cooperation, see esp. Adrien Berget, *La coopération dans la viticulture européenne: Etude d'économie rurale et d'histoire agronomique* (Lille: A. Devos, 1902).

38 For brief overviews of the emergence of cooperatives in France, see James Simpson, *Creating Wine: The Emergence of a World Industry, 1840–1914* (Princeton, NJ: Princeton University Press, 2011), 71–75; and Leo Loubère, *The Red and the White: A History of Wine in France and Italy in the Nineteenth Century* (Albany: State University of New York Press, 1978), 346–351.

39 Dominique Ganibenc, "L'architecture des caves coopératives héraultaises: L'exemple de Paul Brès (1901–1995)," in Sophie Delbrel and Bernard Gallinato-Contino, eds., *Les hommes de la vigne et du vin: Figures célèbres et acteurs méconnus* (Paris: Eds. du Comité des travaux historiques et scientifiques, 2011), 130.

40 Comte de Rocquigny, *La coopération dans l'agriculture algérienne* (Paris: Arthur Rousseau, 1906), 288–291; L. Trabut and R. Marès, *L'Algérie agricole en 1906* (Algiers: Imprimerie Algérienne, 1906), 471–476; Isnard, *La vigne en Algérie,* 2:389–392.

41 Pasquier-Bronde, *Les associations agricoles,* 321.

42 CANA, 10E 516, J. Foussat to Directeur de l'Ecole d'Agriculture, 11 Nov. 1909 and 16 Nov. 1910.

43 L. Boyer-Banse, "Le crédit agricole et la colonisation de l'Algérie," in *Congrès de la colonisation rurale, Alger 26–29 mai 1930, 2ᵉ partie: Les problèmes économiques et sociaux posés par la colonisation* (Algiers: Victor Heintz, 1930), 357.

44 *Annuaire de la viticulture algérienne* 13 (1931), consulted at the CDHA.

45 Princesse Nhu May d'Annam, "La mutualité et la coopération agricoles en Algérie," *Annales de l'Institut national agronomique* 22 (1929): 239–303 (the author was daughter of the deposed emperor of Annam, Hàm Nghi, who lived in exile in Algiers); see also Cardonne and Rabot, *La colonisation dans l'ouest-Oranais,* 275–297.

46 Quoted in Gavignaud-Fontaine, *Le Languedoc viticole,* 79.

47 On the politics of agricultural mutualism, see esp. M. C. Cleary, *Peasants, Politicians and Producers: The Organization of Agriculture in France since 1918* (Cambridge: Cambridge University Press, 1989), 48–70. On interwar Catholic critiques of individualism, see Philip Nord, "Catholic Culture in Interwar France," *French Politics, Culture and Society* 21:3 (2003): 6–7.

48 Nhu May d'Annam, "La mutualité et la coopération agricoles," 167–168.

49 ANOM, BA, 11ES 137; Louis Pasquier-Bronde, "Les associations agricoles d'El-Affroun," *L'Algérie agricole et viticole,* 6 Mar. 1924; "La population de la Mitidja et du Sahel ont fêté hier, avec M. Averseng, l'œuvre sociale d'une famille et la mutualité agricole," *L'Echo d'Alger,* 6 Jan. 1930. Other Catholic mutualists included Pasquier-Bronde, who had close connections to the White Fathers, as did Alexandre Vanoni, who founded the cooperative winery at Rivet in the Mitidja.

50 CANA, 10E 516, Pres. of Chekfa cooperative to Directeur de l'agriculture, 14 Jan. 1916; ANOM, Préfecture de Constantine (henceforth Constantine), 1H 31, coopérative vinicole de Chekfa-Taher.

51 *Les vins algériens: Annuaire de la viticulture algérienne* 13 (1931): 86–87; Nhu May d'Annam, "La mutualité et la coopération agricoles," 245–246. The topography of much of the Sahel tended to limit larger landholdings.

52 *Les grands vins d'Oranie: Numéro spécial de l'Afrique du Nord illustrée* (Oran: L. Fouque, 1934), 82–85; L. Abadie, *Aïn-Témouchent de ma jeunesse* (Nice: Jacques Gandini, 2004), 5, 122.

53 L. Bastide, *L'agriculture dans le département d'Oran: Rapport sur le concours des exploitations pour la prime d'honneur en 1877* (Oran: J. Gérard, 1878), 38.

54 ANMT, 65 AQ J479, Société de viticulture algérienne, report of conseil d'administration to assemblée générale, 29 May 1882; Bastide, *L'agriculture dans le département d'Oran,* 38.

55 US Department of Commerce, *Seasonal Trends of Rubber Production* (Washington, DC: Government Printing Office, 1932).

56 G.-J. Stotz, *Questions actuelles d'agriculture et de colonisation algérienne: La main-d'œuvre* (Algiers: Imprimerie Algéroise, 1931), 35–36; Isnard, *La vigne en Algérie,* 2:72.

57 Gilbert Bresson, *Histoire d'un centre rural algérien: Fort de l'Eau* (Algiers: Vve. J. Bringau, 1957), 63–68; Gérard Crespo and Jean-Jacques Jordi, *Les Espagnols dans l'Algérois, 1830–1914: Histoire d'une migration* (Versailles: Editions de l'Atlanthrope, 1991), 115–118.

58 ANOM, GGA, L5, Prefect of Algiers to minister of war, 9 May 1857.

59 See, for example, A. Villacrose, *Vingt ans en Algérie ou tribulations d'un colon racontées par lui-même* (Paris: Challamel aîné, 1875), 267–268. Also Charles-Robert Ageron, *Les Algériens musulmans et la France (1871–1919)* (Paris: Presses Universitaires de France, 1968), 387; Isnard, *La vigne en Algérie*, 2:96.

60 Robert Tinthoin, *Colonisation et évolution des genres de vie dans la région ouest d'Oran de 1830 à 1885* (Oran: L. Fouque, 1947), 295–296; Gabriel Tortella, *The Development of Modern Spain: An Economic History of the Nineteenth and Twentieth Centuries* (Cambridge, MA: Harvard University Press, 2000), 71; Isnard, *La vigne en Algérie*, 2:214.

61 Mallebay, *Cinquante ans de journalisme*, 2:159–160; also Charles Naylies, *Monographie de la commune de Koléa (Algérie)* (Nevers: G. Vallière, 1905), 77–78. More generally on Spanish migration, see Jean-Jacques Jordi, *Espagnol en Oranie: Histoire d'une migration, 1830–1914* (Calvisson: Editions Jacques Gandini, 1996); and Crespo and Jordi, *Les Espagnols dans l'Algérois.*

62 Ministère de l'Agriculture, du Commerce et des Travaux Publics, *Enquête agricole. Algérie. Alger—Oran—Constantine* (Paris: Imprimerie Impériale, 1870), 99.

63 John Ruedy, *Modern Algeria: The Origins and Development of a Nation* (Bloomington: Indiana University Press, 1992), 74–76.

64 André Nouschi, *Enquête sur le niveau de vie des populations rurales constantinoises, de la conquête jusqu'en 1919: Essai d'histoire économique et sociale* (Paris: Presses Universitaires de France, 1961), 306–453; quotation at 402.

65 For example, Mahfoud Bennoune, *The Making of Contemporary Algeria, 1830–1987* (Cambridge: Cambridge University Press, 1988), 44.

66 AGMAfr, Casier B10, and Casier D19–16, Journal Caisse, 1882–1891; Charles Pourcher, *Souvenirs et impressions recueillies au cours d'une période d'action coloniale de cinquante-cinq ans (1867–1922)* (Paris: R. Chiberre, 1924), 307. On Lavigerie and the Kabyles, see Patricia M. E. Lorcin, *Imperial Identities: Stereotyping, Prejudice, and Race in Colonial Algeria* (London: I. B. Tauris, 1995), 177–181.

67 ANOM, Oran, 1H 11, L. Gastine to G. Couanon, 4 Sept. 1885, and Couanon to GG, 9 Sept. 1885; ADBR, 127 J 17, L. Gastine to G. Gastine, 28 Aug. 1885. Also L. Bastide, *Bel-Abbès et son arrondissement* (Oran: Ad. Perrier, 1881), 401.

68 Gérard Crespo, *Les Italiens en Algérie 1830–1960: Histoire et sociologie d'une migration* (Calvisson: Eds. Jacques Gandini, 1994), 87–88; David Prochaska, *Making Algeria French: Colonialism in Bône, 1870–1920* (Cambridge: Cambridge University Press, 1990), 168.

69 Comité départemental du Rhône, *Exposition Universelle de 1900: La colonisation lyonnaise* (Lyon: A. Rey, 1900), 28–55; Association française pour l'avancement des sciences, *Lyon et la région lyonnaise en 1906* (Lyon: A. Rey, 1906), 34.

70 Exceptions include ANMT, 65AQ J479, reports of the Société de viticulture algérienne, 1881–1889; ANP, F10 1621, *Département d'Alger: Bulletin official du Syndicat de défense contre le phylloxéra* 18 (Oct. 1888), 372–374.

71 Quotation from Henri Pensa, *L'Algérie: Voyage de la délégation de la commission sénatoriale d'études des questions algériennes* (Paris: J. Rothschild, 1894), 320. See also Stotz, *Questions actuelles d'agriculture,* 49–50; Nouschi, *Enquête sur le niveau de vie des populations rurales constantinoises,* 542–556. On forest laws at this time, see

Diana K. Davis, *Resurrecting the Granary of Rome: Environmental History and French Colonial Expansion in North Africa* (Athens: Ohio University Press, 2007), 81–82.

72 Isnard, *La vigne en Algérie,* 2:216–217.

73 ADN, Madrid Ambassade B12, French Consul of Cartagena to French Ambassador in Madrid, 26 July 1897. See also ADMAE, Séries de l'Administration Centrale, Conventions administratives et contentieux 1808–1950, no. 428: Algérie, travailleurs espagnols 1897–1908.

74 Tortella, *The Development of Modern Spain,* 41, 412–413; Isnard, *La vigne en Algérie,* 2:215.

75 For an example of rates of pay, see "Note de M. Thesmar sur la main-d'œuvre employée dans le domaine de Lismara (propriété Dollfus)," *Bulletin agricole de l'Algérie et de la Tunisie* 9:12 (15 June 1903): 284–285, about a ninety-hectare vineyard near Tlemcen.

76 Marcel Larnaude, "Déplacements des travailleurs indigènes en Algérie," *Revue Africaine* 368–369 (1936): 207–215; Louis Milliot, "L'exode saisonnier des Rifains vers l'Algérie," *Bulletin économique du Maroc* 1:5 (1934): 313–315; Neil MacMaster, *Colonial Migrants and Racism: Algerians in France, 1900–62* (Basingstoke, UK: Macmillan, 1997), 39–41.

77 ANOM, GGA, 1O 106, for example, GG to prefect of Algiers, 2 Sept. 1913; Oran, série continue 83, lists of seasonal Spanish workers for 1932 and 1933. The Spanish Civil War finally disrupted this pattern: see Oran, 1H 12, "Situation du vignoble algérien," survey of 1942.

78 Henri de Peyerimhoff, *Enquête sur les résultats de la colonisation officielle de 1871 à 1895,* 2 vols. (Algiers: Imprimerie Torrent, 1906), 1:178, 188; similarly, see Maurice Pouyanne, "La main-d'œuvre indigène," *Bulletin agricole de l'Algérie et de la Tunisie* 9:12 (15 June 1903): 282. For a more pessimistic view, see Joost van Vollenhoven, *Essai sur le fellah algérien* (Paris: Arthur Rousseau, 1903), 242–260.

79 Peyerimhoff, *Enquête sur les résultats de la colonisation officielle,* 2:17.

80 Christian Phéline, *L'aube d'une révolution: Margueritte, Algérie, 26 avril 1901* (Toulouse: Editions Privat, 2012), 11–20, 27.

81 Peyerimhoff, *Enquête sur les résultats de la colonisation officielle,* 2:73–74.

82 Quoted in Phéline, *L'aube d'une révolution,* 148.

83 See, for example, "Vendanges algériennes," *L'Afrique du Nord illustrée,* 2 Oct. 1909, 6–7; ANOM, Constantine, 1H 72, Prefect of Algiers to Prefect of Constantine, 30 Aug. 1914.

84 Naylies, *Monographie de Koléa,* 77; see also Jean du Nador, *A travers l'Algérie: Vue d'ensemble, colons, indigènes, le vignoble* (Algiers: J. Angelini, 1903), 18.

85 ANOM, GGA, 8L 1, Main-d'œuvre pénitentiaire 1892–1907; AGMAfr, Lavigerie Casier B8 / 319, General Wolff to Lavigerie, 16 Nov. 1871; Emile Larcher and Jean Olier, *Les institutions pénitentiaires de l'Algérie* (Paris: Art. Rousseau, 1899), 201–203, 209, 243–244. See also Dominique Kalifa, *Biribi: Les bagnes coloniaux de l'armée française* (Paris: Perrin, 2009), 124–130. Convict labor was, of course, a feature of many colonial projects: see, for example, Anand A. Yang, "Indian Convict Workers in Southeast Asia in the Late Eighteenth and Early Nineteenth Centuries," *Journal of World History* 14:2 (2003): 179–208.

86 AGMAfr, Livinhac 29, SIAH conseil d'administration, meeting of Oct. 1921. On the 1921 famine, see Kamel Kateb, *Européens, "indigènes" et juifs en Algérie (1830–1962): Représentations et réalités des populations* (Paris: Editions de l'INED, 2001), 67; Meynier, *L'Algérie révélée*, 649.

87 See, especially, Rémi Adam, *Histoire des soldats russes en France (1915–1920): Les damnés de la guerre* (Paris: L'Harmattan, 1996); also Jamie H. Cockfield, *With Snow on Their Boots: The Tragic Odyssey of the Russian Expeditionary Force in France during World War One* (New York: St. Martin's Press, 1998).

88 ANOM, Constantine, 1H 72, M. Dalaise to prefect of Constantine, 4 Jan. 1919.

89 Ibid., Dalaise to prefect of Constantine, 13 Oct. 1918.

90 A. B. Letnev, "Soldaty Rossii v Alzhire (1918–1920 GG)" [Russian soldiers in Algeria, 1918–1920], *Voprosy istorii* 5 (1998): 131–132. I am grateful to David Shearer for his help with this source. See also Adam, *Histoire des soldats russes en France*, 246–247, 317–318.

91 Isnard, "La vigne en Algérie," 777–778; ANMT, 65AQ J296, report on annual meeting of the Compagnie des vignobles de la Méditerranée, 29 May 1926. For context, see MacMaster, *Colonial Migrants and Racism*, 68–69; and Johan H. Meuleman, *Le Constantinois entre les deux guerres mondiales: L'évolution économique et sociale de la population rurale* (Assen: Van Gorcum, 1985), 104–106; Daniel Lefeuvre, *Chère Algérie: La France et sa colonie 1930–1962* (Paris: Flammarion, 2005), 35–41.

92 ANOM, BA, 11ES 332, Société anonyme des domaines du Kéroulis, report of annual meeting, 25 May 1922.

93 ANOM, BA, 11ES 201 bis, report on annual meeting, 18 Apr. 1931; *Vignobles et vins d'Algérie: Etude spéciale de Grands Crus et Vins de France, octobre 1934* (Lyon: Publications Pierre Argence, 1934), 20–21. The president of the company at this time was Lucien Borgeaud, who also used convicts at his vineyard in Staouëli: ANOM, BA, 11ES 176; Gabriel Verge, *Monographie du Domaine de la Trappe de Staouëli* (Algiers: V. Heintz, 1930), 51–52.

94 ANOM, BA, 11ES 201 bis, report on annual meeting, 30 Mar. 1929.

95 Stotz calculated in 1931 that Algerian vineyards required 255,000 workers per year, of whom two-thirds could expect work for only four to five months. *Questions actuelles d'agriculture*, 71.

96 Louis Bertrand, *Sur les routes du Sud* (Paris: Arthème Fayard, 1936), 278.

97 Augustin Bernard, "Le recensement de 1921 dans l'Afrique du Nord," *Annales de Géographie* 31:169 (1922): 54.

98 René Lespès, *Alger: Etude de géographie et d'histoire urbaines* (Paris: Félix Alcan, 1930), 608–613; Crespo, *Les Italiens en Algérie*, 22–24. Roughly a third of the 6,221 people of European origin counted in Hussein-Dey in 1921 retained a foreign nationality (1,232 Spanish and 991 Italian).

99 ANOM, GGA, 1O 18; Algiers Chamber of Commerce, *General Information on the Products of Algeria: Wools, Skins and Industrial Products* (Algiers: Imprimerie Algérienne, 1908); Eugène Battistini, *Les forêts de chêne-liège de l'Algérie* (Algiers: Victor Heintz, 1937), 111 and table listing forest concessions.

100 Paulin Borgeaud, *Mission remplie* (Paris: Editions Mazarine, 1971), 63; Di Costanzo, *Allemands et Suisses en Algérie*, 182–183.

101 For a sense of the scale of the phylloxera bureaucracy, see ANOM, GGA, 1O 24 to 32, records of the phylloxera service, 1905–1921.

102 AGMAfr, Birraux 333, M. Roig to Mgr. Birraux, 14 Dec. 1940, and Birraux 336, curriculum vitae of M. Roig, 1944; ANOM, état civil, marriage of Michel Joseph Roig and Catherine Torrès, 1894 and birth of Michel Roig, 1895; ANOM, BA, 11ES 316, SIAH annual report, 2 June 1956.

103 For an idea of the range of businesses that served viticulture at this time, see the advertisements in publications like the *Annuaire de la Viticulture Algérienne*.

104 See, for example, Meynier, *L'Algérie révélée*, 146–156, and for a good local study, David Prochaska, "Approaches to the Economy of Colonial Annaba, 1870–1920," *Africa* 60:4 (1990): 497–523.

105 Pourcher, *Souvenirs et impressions*, 261, 397–398.

106 See, especially, Jean-Louis Escudier, "Entre marché et régulation étatique: L'industrie du soufre (1850–1940)," in Pierre Lamard and Nicolas Stoskopf, eds., *L'industrie chimique en question* (Paris: Editions A. et J. Picard, 2010), 161–180. See also Federal Trade Commission, *Report on Cooperation in American Export Trade, Part II: Exhibits* (Washington, DC: Government Printing Office, 1916), 108–109; advertisement for the Société Française des Minerais de Soufre d'Apt, in Charles Gervais, *Indicateur des Vignobles Méridionaux* (Montpellier: Gustave Firmin et Montane, 1896); and Meynier, *L'Algérie révélée*, 152.

107 ANMT, 65AQ J296, annual report of Compagnie des vignobles de la Méditerranée, June 1910; Les Raffineries de soufre réunies, *Les emplois agricoles du soufre et leurs perfectionnements* (Marseille: Société d'Edition Ars, ca. 1925).

108 On the CVM, see ANMT, 65AQ J296; and ANOM, BA, 80ES 329; on Francalfûts, see ANOM, BA, 11ES 273 bis; on Jean and Guy Roubaud, see AGMAfr, Durrieu 552.

109 ANOM, BA, 11ES 211, Chef du bureau d'encaissement de Boufarik to director of Algiers branch, 27 Apr. 1923. Chiris himself lived in Paris.

110 ANOM, BA, 11ES 332.

111 ANOM, BA, 11ES 201 bis.

112 ANOM, BA, 11ES 176 bis, Proposition de crédit de campagne en faveur de Lucien Borgeaud, 1933–1934; see also lists of shares in this folder and in 11ES 176; and Barbier, *Le mythe Borgeaud*, 54, 233–234. The Borgeauds had significant interests in Morocco too.

113 Bouveresse, *Un parlement colonial*, both volumes, especially 2:754–755. See also Maurice Viollette, *L'Algérie vivra-t-elle?* (Paris: Félix Alcan, 1931), 297–303.

114 "Notre banquet anniversaire," *L'Echo d'Alger*, 18 Mar. 1913; Idir Bouaboud, *L'Echo d'Alger: Cinquante ans de vie politique française en Algérie, 1912–1961* (Villeneuve d'Ascq: Presses Universitaires du Septentrion, 1999), 33; ANOM, état civil, marriages of Jean Manent to Victorine Pelegri and Pierre (known as Michel) Germain to Clémentine Pelegri, both 1889. The other key investors in the *Echo* were Alphonse and Alfred Blachette, a family whose wealth stemmed mainly from esparto grass (used to make paper) and construction.

115 Bouaboud, *L'Echo d'Alger*, 65–66; Bouveresse, *Un parlement colonial*, 1:422; Jean-Marc Valentin, *Les parlementaires des départements d'Algérie sous la IIIe République* (Paris: L'Harmattan, 2010), 131, 179; Franc, *La colonisation de la Mitidja*, 686; Boudot, *Les Schiaffino*, 183.

116 Viollette, *L'Algérie vivra-t-elle*, 7. On Viollette as governor-general, see Jacques Cantier, "Les gouverneurs Viollette et Bordes et la politique algérienne de la France à la fin des années vingt," *Revue française d'histoire d'outre-mer* 84:314 (1997): 25–49.

117 ANOM, BA, 11ES 332, Société anonyme des domaines du Kéroulis, annual reports, 1925–1927.

118 Jacques Marseille, *Empire colonial et capitalisme français: Histoire d'un divorce* (Paris: Albin Michel, 1984), 131. "French Empire" in this reckoning excludes metropolitan France.

119 ANOM, BA, 11ES 332, Société anonyme des domaines du Kéroulis, annual report, 30 Mar. 1929.

120 "Les sociétés anonymes: force de l'expansion coloniale," *L'Afrique du Nord illustrée*, 18 May 1929, 12–14.

121 "Une automobile incendiée," *L'Echo d'Alger*, 31 Oct. 1917; and death notice in same, 8 Nov. 1917.

122 "Mort de M. Bertrand," *L'Echo d'Alger*, 16 May 1925.

123 Pierre Jarrige, *L'aviation légère en Algérie (1909–1939)* (Revel: P. Jarrige, 1992), 66–68.

124 Augustin Bernard, "Le recensement de 1926 dans l'Afrique du Nord," *Annales de Géographie* 36:200 (1927): 138.

125 Nabila Oulebsir, *Les usages du patrimoine: Monuments, musées et politique coloniale en Algérie, 1830–1930* (Paris: Fondation de la Maison des Sciences de l'Homme, 2004), 266–267; on Boufarik, see E. F. Gautier, *Un siècle de colonisation: Etudes au microscope* (Paris: Félix Alcan, 1930), 13–87.

126 Augustin Bernard, *L'Algérie* (Paris: Félix Alcan, 1929), 446.

4. ALGERIA AND THE MIDI

1 Henri de Peyerimhoff, *Enquête sur les résultats de la colonisation officielle de 1871 à 1895*, 2 vols. (Algiers: Imprimerie Torrent, 1906), 1:8.

2 Gordon T. Stewart, *Jute and Empire: The Calcutta Jute Wallahs and the Landscapes of Empire* (Manchester: Manchester University Press, 1998); Jim Tomlinson, *Dundee and the Empire: 'Juteopolis' 1850–1939* (Edinburgh: Edinburgh University Press, 2014); Tariq Omar Ali, *A Local History of Global Capital: Jute and Peasant Life in the Bengal Delta* (Princeton, NJ: Princeton University Press, 2018).

3 Yujiro Hayami, *A Century of Agricultural Growth in Japan: Its Relevance to Asian Development* (Minneapolis: University of Minnesota Press, 1975), 61–63; Thomas R. H. Havens, *Farm and Nation in Modern Japan: Agrarian Nationalism, 1870–1940* (Princeton, NJ: Princeton University Press, 1974), 90–91, 142–143; Mitsuhiko Kimura, "The Economics of Japanese Imperialism in Korea, 1910–1939," *Economic History Review* 48 (1995): 558–559.

4 Hayami, *A Century of Agricultural Growth*, 61–62; W. G. Beasley, *Japanese Imperialism 1894–1945* (Oxford: Oxford University Press, 1987), 152–153.

5 Elizabeth Heath, *Wine, Sugar, and the Making of Modern France: Global Economic Crisis and the Racialization of French Citizenship, 1870–1910* (Cambridge: Cambridge University Press, 2014), 235–239.

6 "Marcellin Albert," *L'Afrique du Nord illustrée,* 1 Nov. 1910; ANOM, état civil, birth in Oran of Etienne Albert (son of Pierre-Etienne Albert, Marcellin's brother), 27 Sept. 1883; Guy Bechtel, *1907: La grande révolte du Midi* (Paris: Robert Laffont, 1976), 30–31.

7 Bechtel, *1907,* 277–308.

8 Though the term "the Midi" is sometimes used to refer broadly to the South of France, the CGV's "Midi" corresponded more specifically to the Languedoc-Roussillon region, especially the four departments of the Aude, the Hérault, the Gard, and Pyrénées-Orientales. That demarcation of the Midi is the one I employ in this chapter.

9 Elizabeth Heath, "The Color of French Wine: Southern Wine Producers Respond to Competition from the Algerian Wine Industry in the Early Third Republic," *French Politics, Culture and Society* 35:2 (2017): 89–110 (quotation at 99); Hildebert Isnard, *La vigne en Algérie: Etude géographique,* 2 vols. (Gap: Ophrys, 1951 / 1954), 2:411–412; ANOM, Constantine, 1H 142, Commission administrative de défense contre le phylloxéra, meeting of 22 Oct. 1908.

10 "Marcellin Albert," *L'Afrique du Nord illustrée,* 15 Dec. 1910, and, in the same newspaper, "Chronique du Quinzaine," 3 Sept. 1910; and "Marcellin Albert à Alger," 15 Nov. 1910.

11 ANOM, GGA, 1O 291, R. Berthault, "La crainte du Maroc et la limitation des vins d'Algérie," *Le Libéral,* 29 Nov. 1911; GGA, 1O 149, prefect of Oran to GG, 24 May 1912 and prefect of Constantine to GG, 10 Oct. 1912. On prices at this time, see Charles K. Warner, *The Winegrowers of France and the Government since 1875* (New York: Columbia University Press, 1960), 48–49.

12 Isnard, *La vigne en Algérie,* 2:412–417.

13 On the supply of Algerian goods to the metropole during the war, see Augustin Bernard, *L'Afrique du Nord pendant la guerre* (Paris: Presses Universitaires de France, 1926), 52–60.

14 On the culture of wine-drinking among French troops in World War I and the particular associations of *pinard,* see Adam Derek Zientek, "Wine and Blood: Alcohol, Morale, and Discipline in the French Army on the Western Front, 1914–1918" (PhD diss., Stanford University, 2012).

15 Gilbert Meynier, *L'Algérie révélée: La guerre de 1914–1918 et le premier quart du XXe siècle* (Geneva: Librairie Droz, 1981), 734–736; Samir Saul, "Les pouvoirs publics métropolitains face à la Dépression: La Conférence économique de la France métropolitaine et d'Outre-Mer (1934–1935)," *French Colonial History* 12 (2011): 170–171.

16 Albert Sarraut, *La mise en valeur des colonies françaises* (Paris: Payot, 1923), 339–341. For another influential voice, see Charles Régismanset, *L'Exposition nationale coloniale de Marseille, 1922* (Paris: Imprimeries françaises réunies, 1921), 7–17. On Sarraut, see also Martin Thomas, "Albert Sarraut, French Colonial Development, and the Communist Threat, 1919–1930," *Journal of Modern History* 77 (2005): 917–955.

17 Christopher M. Andrew and A. S. Kanya-Forstner, *France Overseas: The Great War and the Climax of French Imperial Expansion* (London: Thames and Hudson, 1981), 226–227.

18 See, for example, Gouvernement-Général de l'Algérie: Direction de l'Agriculture, du Commerce, et de la Colonisation, *Les produits algériens: Les vins d'Algérie* (Algiers: Imprimerie Algérienne, 1923), 1. Algeria fell outside the remit of the colonial ministry, as did the protectorates of Morocco and Tunisia.

19 On Barthe and the *groupe viticole,* see Jean-Marc Bagnol, *Le Midi viticole au parlement: Edouard Barthe et les députés du vin de l'Hérault (années 1920–1930)* (Montpellier: Presses Universitaires de la Méditerranée, 2011).

20 Gouvernement-Général de l'Algérie, *Voyage en Algérie du Groupe Viticole de la Chambre des Députés, 18 mars–10 avril 1923* (Paris: A. Tournon, 1924), quotations at 30, 41, 43, 45. Steeg, like Sarraut, was a Radical from the Gironde. In 1920 he had been minister for the interior while Sarraut ran the colonial ministry.

21 Ibid., 30; compare the 1834 text by Comte H . . . de B . . . , *De l'Algérie et de sa colonisation* (Paris: Crochard, 1834), 33 (cited in Chapter 1).

22 "Les cultures complémentaires de celles de la Métropole," *Les Annales Coloniales,* 23 Mar. 1927, 9–10.

23 M. Guillon, "Le voyage en Algérie de la délégation du Groupe Viticole de la Chambre des Députés (mars-avril 1923)," *Les Annales Coloniales,* 22 Dec. 1923, 5–6.

24 For one use of this phrase, see V. Demontès, ed., "L'Algérie," special edition of *La Vie Technique, Industrielle, Agricole et Coloniale* (1922), 97.

25 See Edouard Lynch, "Interwar France and the Rural Exodus: The National Myth in Peril," *Rural History* 21:2 (2010): 169.

26 Jean-Marie Moine, "La sidérurgie, le Comité des forges et l'empire colonial: Mythes et réalités," in Hubert Bonin, Catherine Hodeir, and Jean-François Klein, eds., *L'esprit économique impérial (1830–1970): Groupes de pression et réseaux du patronat colonial en France et dans l'empire* (Paris: Publications de la SFHOM, 2008), 492–493; Charles-Robert Ageron, *Histoire de l'Algérie contemporaine,* vol. 2, *De l'insurrection de 1871 au déclenchement de la guerre de libération (1954)* (Paris: Presses Universitaires de France, 1979), 500–501; Meynier, *L'Algérie révélée,* 150, 153, 354–355; Daniel Lefeuvre, *Chère Algérie: La France et sa colonie 1930–1962* (Paris: Flammarion, 2005), 43–45. More generally on industrialization, see Jacques Bouveresse, *Un parlement colonial? Les Délégations financières algériennes, 1898–1945,* 2 vols. (Mont-Saint-Aignan: Publications des Universités de Rouen et du Havre, 2008/2010), 2:691–692.

27 Henri Pello, ed., *Algérie: Histoire et souvenirs d'un canton de la Mitidja, 1830 à 1962. L'Arba, Rivet, Rovigo, Sidi-Moussa et Baraki* (Saint-Estève: Presses Littéraires, 1998), 81–82.

28 Gouvernement-Général de l'Algérie, *Voyage en Algérie du Groupe Viticole,* 39–40.

29 ANOM, GGA, 1O 59, "Les vignerons du Midi contre les vins de l'Algérie," *La Dépêche Algérienne,* 2 Nov. 1925.

30 R. Peyronnet, "Viticulteurs du Midi et viticulteurs d'Algérie," *Bulletin de la Société de Géographie d'Algérie et de l'Afrique du Nord* 120:4 (1929): 682–683; Hildebert Isnard, "La vigne en Algérie: Etude géographique" (PhD diss., Université de Paris I-Sorbonne, 1947), 810.

31 See Assemblées financières algériennes, *Session extraordinaire de 1925* (Algiers: Victor Heintz, 1925), session of 3 Nov. 1925, 16–17.

32 Quoted in Bagnol, *Le Midi viticole au parlement,* 69.

33 Gustave Pelegri, "Les arbres fruitiers et la colonisation," in *Congrès de la colonisation rurale, Alger 26–29 mai 1930, 2ᵉ partie: Les problèmes économiques et sociaux posés par la colonisation* (Algiers: Victor Heintz, 1930), 223–229; Isnard, "La vigne en Algérie," 813. See also Victor Demontès, *L'Algérie économique,* tome 4, *Cultures et productions alimentaires* (Algiers: Imprimerie Algérienne, 1930), 488–538.

34 Will D. Swearingen, *Moroccan Mirages: Agrarian Dreams and Deceptions, 1912–1986* (Princeton, NJ: Princeton University Press, 1987), 18–25; Sarraut, *La mise en valeur,* 156–158; Robert O. Paxton, *French Peasant Fascism: Henry Dorgères's Greenshirts and the Crises of French Agriculture, 1929–1939* (New York: Oxford University Press, 1997), 12–14. For the global context, see Dietmar Rothermund, *The Global Impact of the Great Depression, 1929–1939* (London: Routledge, 1996), 39–40.

35 Statistics from ANOM, BA, série continue 455, supplemented by *Annuaire de la viticulture algérienne* 13 (1931).

36 Assemblées financières algériennes, *Session extraordinaire de 1928* (Algiers: Victor Heintz, 1928), 243–244 (session of 12 Nov. 1928).

37 Isnard, "La vigne en Algérie," 813–815.

38 Bagnol, *Le Midi viticole au parlement,* 266.

39 ADG, 8M 13, contains sixteen such statements from June to August 1929.

40 ANOM, Commune mixte de Remchi 1, report by Chambre d'agriculture d'Oran, 25 Apr. 1929; ANOM, Oran, 1H 63, report by the same, 17 Jan. 1930.

41 Pierre Roux-Freissineng, quoted in Pierre Berthault, *L'Algérie et la production des vins* (Algiers: Société des agriculteurs d'Algérie, 1929), 7–8.

42 Peyronnet, "Viticulteurs du Midi et viticulteurs d'Algérie," 684. For a comparable argument, see Maurice Viollette, *L'Algérie vivra-t-elle?* (Paris: Félix Alcan, 1931), 42.

43 ANOM, Commune mixte de Remchi 1, report by Chambre d'agriculture d'Oran, 25 Apr. 1929; Bouveresse, *Un parlement colonial,* 2:281–282.

44 George Orwell, *Down and Out in Paris and London* (New York: Harcourt Brace Jovanovich, 1961), 95. First published in 1933, this book was partly based on the author's experiences in Paris in 1928–1929.

45 On North African product trademarks, see Dana S. Hale, *Races on Display: French Representations of Colonized Peoples, 1886–1940* (Bloomington: Indiana University Press, 2008), 46–53, 118–124. On alcohol marketing in this period, see Sarah Howard, "The Advertising Industry and Alcohol in Interwar France," *Historical Journal* 51:2 (2008): 421–455.

46 *Le Livre d'or du centenaire de l'Algérie française. Réimpression de l'édition d'Alger (1930)* (Nice: Jacques Gandini, 2003), 275.

47 Lauren Janes, *Colonial Food in Interwar Paris: The Taste of Empire* (London: Bloomsbury, 2016), 137–140.

48 Louis Bertrand, *Sur les routes du Sud* (Paris: Arthème Fayard, 1936), 181.

49 Quoted in Janes, *Colonial Food in Interwar Paris,* 138.

50 Useful presentations of this debate and legislation include Warner, *The Winegrowers of France,* 93–109; and Bagnol, *Le Midi viticole au parlement,* 289–320.

51 A. Volck, *Le problème viticole franco-algérien* (Paris: Domat-Montchrestien, 1934), 33.

52 ANOM, BA, série continue 457, debate in the Senate, 3 July 1931, p. 1505. On Tardieu's politics, see Marjorie M. Farrar, "Leaders without Parties: The Essential Role of Moderate Republicanism in France, 1899–1929," in William B. Cohen, ed., *The Transformation of France* (Boston: Houghton Mifflin, 1997), 157–158. Later in the 1930s Tardieu took a more authoritarian turn.

53 ANOM, GGA, 1O 55, debate in the Chamber of Deputies, 12 June 1931, p. 2955.

54 ANOM, GGA, 1O 55, debate in the Chamber of Deputies, 18 June 1931, p. 3082.

55 ANOM, GGA, 1O 55, Rapport supplémentaire fait au nom de la Commission des boissons chargée d'examiner le projet de loi sur la viticulture et le commerce des vins, p. 50.

56 Ibid, p. 7, and ANOM, BA, 11ES 332, Société des domaines du Kéroulis, annual reports dated 30 March 1929, 16 April 1930, 16 April 1931.

57 ANOM, GGA, 1O 55, debate in the Chamber of Deputies, 17 June 1931, p. 3075.

58 ANOM, GGA, 1O 55, debate in the Chamber of Deputies, 24 June 1931, p. 3280.

59 ANOM, GGA, 1O 55, debate in the Chamber of Deputies, 12 June 1931, p. 2955.

60 ANOM, GGA, 1O 55, debate in the Chamber of Deputies, 24 June 1931, p. 3282, quoting Henri Maupoil.

61 ANOM, GGA, 1O 55, debate in the Chamber of Deputies, 17 June 1931, p. 3078; also GG to Min Ag, 11 June 1931, reporting the views of the Délégations financières algériennes concerning the bill.

62 For details, see Bagnol, *Le Midi viticole au parlement*, 316–320.

63 ANOM, GGA, 1O 55, debate in the Chamber of Deputies, 24 June 1931, p. 3320.

64 ANOM, GGA, 1O 55, "Les colons du centre de colonisation de Gaston-Doumergue" [thirty-six signatories] to GG, President Doumergue, and others, 30 July 1931 [seemingly unknown to the authors, Doumergue's term as president had ended on June 13]; Oran, 1M 62, Enquête sur la situation des détenteurs de propriétés de colonisation au point de vue des plantations de vignes: Gaston-Doumergue, 1931; Isnard, "La vigne en Algérie," 820–821. The Algiers deputy André Mallarmé proposed the exception for new colonists in the Chamber.

65 Isnard, "La vigne en Algérie," 822–823.

66 Quoted in Volck, *Le problème viticole franco-algérien*, 10.

67 For example, ANOM, Oran, 1H 12, administrator of the *commune mixte* of Sebdou to prefect of Oran, 12 Apr. 1934.

68 On the Benchiha family, see ANOM, Oran, 2M 73A / B, and 1H 12, administrator of the *commune mixte* of Aïn-Témouchent to prefect of Oran, 7 May 1942; Michel Launay, *Paysans algériens 1960–2006*, 3rd ed. (Paris: Karthala, 2007), 263–264; Bouveresse, *Un parlement colonial*, 1:945–946. El-Hadj Benchiha was the *qaid* (local leader) in the *commune mixte* where Gaston-Doumergue was created. He was also a member of the permanent commission of the Chambre d'Agriculture of Oran.

69 Ahmed Henni, "La naissance d'une classe moyenne paysanne musulmane après la Première Guerre mondiale," *Revue française d'histoire d'outre-mer* 83:311 (1996): 47–63; Isnard, "La vigne en Algérie," 821, 847–848; ANOM, Oran, 1H 12, responses to inquiry on indigenous Algerian viticulture, 1942. See also Charles-Robert Ageron, "Les classes moyennes dans l'Algérie coloniale," in Ageron, *Genèse de l'Algérie algérienne* (Paris: Editions Bouchène, 2005), 380–386.

70 On this committee, see Sarah Howard, "Selling Wine to the French: Official Attempts to Increase French Wine Consumption, 1931–1936," *Food and Foodways* 12 (2004): 197–224; Bagnol, *Le Midi viticole au parlement*, 178–180.

71 On the onset of the Depression in France, see Kenneth Mouré, *Managing the Franc Poincaré: Economic Understanding and Political Constraint in French Monetary Policy, 1928–1936* (Cambridge: Cambridge University Press, 1991), 10–45.

72 Isnard, "La vigne en Algérie," 825–826.

73 Confédération Général des Vignerons Algériens, *Le problème viticole. L'aménagement du marché intérieur et la viticulture algérienne* (Algiers: La Typo-Litho, 1932).

74 Ribalte, "La réunion de la Commission interministérielle: Le danger algérien," *L'Eclair,* 12 July 1932. On *L'Eclair,* see Bagnol, *Le Midi viticole au parlement,* 209–211.

75 *La vérité sur le différend économique Métropole-Algérie* (Paris: Imprimerie Artistique, 1932 or 1933).

76 *Le différend Métropole-Algérie: Les 59 départements vinicoles métropolitains vous demandent d'ouvrir les yeux, voici des faits,* brochure at CDHA.

77 ANOM, GGA, IO 55, Commission des boissons, minutes of meeting of 23–24 Mar. 1933, 35–36.

78 "Un mouvement de protestation des vignerons et des élus de l'Hérault contre 'l'envahissement des vins algériens,'" *L'Echo d'Alger,* 23 May 1933. See also Jean Vigneron, "Les réflexions du vigneron: Les provocateurs de la surproduction," *L'Eclair,* 6 June 1933.

79 Eugène Gross, *Est-il vrai de dire que l'Algérie c'est la France? demande la C.G.V. du Midi. Elle dit: non; nous disons: oui, et nous le prouvons* (Oran: Heintz, 1933).

80 ANOM, Oran, série continue 96, report by Commissaire de police, 20 Jan. 1933.

81 ANOM, Constantine, B3 332, report by Commissaire Central de Police of Bône, 23 June 1933; "Vingt-cinq mille personnes ont assisté, hier, à Alger, au meeting de protestation contre le contingentement des produits algériens," *L'Echo d'Alger,* 21 June 1933.

82 Lucien Bellat (mayor of Sidi-Bel-Abbès and a wine producer), "Notre vin," in *Catalogue Guide: Foire du Vin d'Algérie. Sidi-bel-Abbès, 29 avril–16 mai 1933,* brochure at CDHA.

83 "Le Grand Meeting du Gallia: 50,000 Algériens appartenant à toutes les classes et professions, affirment leur volonté de rester français," *Oran-Matin,* 11 June 1933; ANOM, Oran, série continue 2493, Chef de sûreté départementale to Prefect, 10 June 1933; Augustin Bernard, "Le recensement de 1931 dans l'Afrique du Nord," *Annales de Géographie* 41:230 (1932): 213. Crowd estimates should, of course, be treated with caution.

84 "La guerre du vin. Une manœuvre de la dernière heure. Les méridionaux placardent dans Paris une affiche absurde," *Oran-Matin,* 25 June 1933.

85 Bagnol, *Le Midi viticole au parlement,* 333–335; for the Tardieu quotation, ANOM, BA, série continue 457, debate in the Senate, 3 July 1931, p. 1186.

86 Full details about the law are in Volck, *Le problème viticole franco-algérien,* 133–147.

87 "Un mouvement de protestation des vignerons," *L'Echo d'Alger,* 23 May 1933. On the CVA's tour, see ADSM, 8M 22, Commissaire Central de Police to Prefect of Seine-Inférieure, 16 Feb. 1933; ANOM, BA, série continue 455, *Le Courrier Nord-Africain,* 7 Feb. 1933. Also ANP, F10 2023, Director of Association des Grands Ports Français to Min Ag, 11 May 1933.

88 "La question du vin: Deux vœux en faveur des viticulteurs algériens," *L'Echo d'Alger,* 24 Aug. 1932; Isnard, "La vigne en Algérie," 831.

89 ANOM, GGA, IO 55, minutes of Conseil général of Constantine, 27 Apr. 1934; roll call of votes after debate in Chamber of Deputies, 24 June 1931. In one respect this

was incongruous: though the likes of Morinaud decried "big firms," in 1932 a much higher percentage of Constantine's wine output was produced by companies (32.9%) than in Algiers (15.8%) or Oran (2.8%). Calculated from ANOM, BA, série continue 455, Ministry of Finance statistics regarding company-owned vineyards, 1932.

90 Bagnol, *Le Midi viticole au parlement*, 197–203.

91 "Groupement amical des petits viticulteurs du département d'Alger," *Le Courrier Nord-Africain*, 17–18 July 1932; "Pressant appel aux petits et moyens viticulteurs," *La Dépêche Algérienne*, 29 July 1932.

92 Bagnol, *Le Midi viticole au parlement*, 202.

93 Gilles Laferté, *La Bourgogne et ses vins: Image d'origine contrôlée* (Paris: Belin, 2006), 55–57; Olivier Jacquet, "Territoire politique socialiste et terroir viticole," *Cahiers d'histoire: Revue d'histoire critique* 103 (2008): 24–36; Paxton, *French Peasant Fascism*, 27–36.

94 For example ANOM, GGA, 1O 55, Commission des boissons, meeting of 23–24 Mar. 1933.

95 "A la Chambre: La viticulture et le commerce des vins," *Le Matin*, 1 July 1933.

96 For a brief overview of the development of the concept of *appellation d'origine* up to the codification of the category of *appellation d'origine contrôlée* (AOC) in 1935, see Leo A. Loubère, *The Wine Revolution in France: The Twentieth Century* (Princeton, NJ: Princeton University Press, 1990), 119–123. In theory, Algeria was covered by the laws regulating *appellations,* but, in practice, none of its wines were given a "quality" label until after the introduction in the 1940s of the classification *vins délimités de qualité supérieure* (VDQS), a ranking below that of AOC. See Joseph Bohling, *The Sober Revolution: Appellation Wine and the Transformation of France* (Ithaca, NY: Cornell University Press, 2018), 42, 58.

97 ANOM, GGA, 1O 55, minutes of Conseil général of Constantine, meeting of 28 Oct. 1934. For a metropolitan example, see Philip Whalen, "'Insofar as the Ruby Wine Seduces Them': Cultural Strategies for Selling Wine in Inter-war Burgundy," *Contemporary European History* 18:1 (2009): 67–98.

98 ANOM, GGA, 1O 55, statement of Confédération Générale des Vignerons du Centre et de l'Ouest, 31 Jan. 1933.

99 "Groupement amical des petits viticulteurs du département d'Alger," *Le Courrier Nord-Africain*, 17–18 July 1932.

100 Bouveresse, *Un parlement colonial,* 2:260–261.

101 Quotation from "Un mouvement de protestation des vignerons," *L'Echo d'Alger,* 23 May 1933; also ANOM, GGA, 1O 55, Gustave Coste to Min Ag, 5 Oct. 1932.

102 Edouard Kruger, *Les bienfaits de l'Union douanière Métropole-Algérie et la question vinicole* (Oran: Syndicat du commerce des vins en gros du département d'Oran, 1933), 7; Volck, *Le problème viticole franco-algérien,* 44–45; Blum quoted in Bagnol, *Le Midi viticole au parlement,* 335. Blum's view was anticipated by Viollette, *L'Algérie vivra-t-elle,* 149–150.

103 ANOM, GGA, 1O 55, Commission des boissons, minutes of meeting of 23–24 Mar. 1933, 37–41.

104 Gustave Coste, "Aux vignerons," *L'Eclair,* 9 July 1933. See also Alfred Cazes, "La croisade antialgérienne," *Oran-Matin,* 17 Feb. 1933.

105 See the price indices in Lefeuvre, *Chère Algérie,* 56.

106 Isnard, "La vigne en Algérie," 855, 860–865, 870–873; AS, 69S 286, Commission de l'Algérie, meeting of 20 Feb. 1936.

107 On the law of 24 Dec. 1934 and decree-law of 30 July 1935, see Bagnol, *Le Midi viticole au parlement,* 338–367; Warner, *The Winegrowers of France,* 112–115; Bouveresse, *Un parlement colonial,* 2:256–258. For Algerian opposition to proposals in this period, see, for example, ANOM, Oran, série continue 2394.

108 Statistics in Sully Ledermann, *Alcool, alcoolisme, alcoolisation: Données scientifiques de caractère physiologique, économique et social* (Paris: Presses Universitaires de France, 1956), 22–25. In 1935 the surface covered by vines in the Midi was 490,111 hectares; Geneviève Gavignaud-Fontaine, *Le Languedoc viticole, la Méditerranée et l'Europe au siècle dernier (XXe)* (Montpellier: Publications de l'Université Paul-Valéry, 2000), 106.

109 ANOM, BA, 11ES 332, annual reports from 1933 to 1939; quotations from 1934 and 1935.

110 See, for example, ANOM, BA, 80ES 329, Compagnie des vignobles de la Méditerranée, report to shareholders, 7 May 1937.

111 ANOM, BA, 11CX 31, miscellaneous documents on Pierre *dit* Michel Germain.

112 Chambre de Commerce d'Alger, *Débouchés offerts aux vins d'Algérie à l'étranger et dans les colonies* (Algiers: Imprimerie Solal, 1935); "Le Transsaharien et l'avenir de la viticulture," *Revue générale des transports,* 10 Dec. 1937 (I am grateful to John Perry for this reference).

113 AGMAfr, Birraux 338, reports to shareholders from 1930s.

114 Vicente Pinilla and Maria-Isabel Ayuda, "The Political Economy of the Wine Trade: Spanish Exports and the International Market, 1890–1935," *European Review of Economic History* 6 (2002): 71; Isnard, "La vigne en Algérie," 890.

115 See, for example, J.-L. Gheerbrandt, *L'expérience française et l'empire: Rapport moral présenté à l'Assemblée Générale de l'Association, le 16 juin 1936* (Paris: Institut Colonial Français, 1936).

116 ANOM, BA, 11ES 458, Société des Domaines de Sidi-Salem, report to shareholders, 26 June 1936.

117 Jean Watin-Augouard, "Orangina, la petite boisson secouée," *Histoire d'entreprises* 7 (July 2009): 28–29. The drink did not take off in popularity until after World War II.

118 ANP, F10 2023, GG to Min Ag, 21 July 1936; Xavier Yacono, *La colonisation des plaines du Chélif (de Lavigerie au confluent de la Mina),* 2 vols. (Algiers: Imprimerie E. Imbert, 1955), 2:202–205; Bouveresse, *Un parlement colonial,* 2:276.

119 ANP, F60 737, Chef des Services d'OFALAC to Albert Sarraut, Ministre d'Etat, 21 Dec. 1937; "L'Algérie, Californie française," *La Dépêche de Constantine,* 12 Jan. 1938. In some ways Algeria was following a lead set by Morocco; see Swearingen, *Moroccan Mirages,* 59–77.

120 ANOM, GGA, 1O 55, Senate report from Commission de l'agriculture, annexe au procès-verbal de la séance du 4 juillet 1933.

121 CANA, 2F 16, Chambre de Commerce de Brest to President of Région économique d'Algérie, 2 July 1937; ANP, F10 2023, Louis L'Hédéver to Min Ag, 30 June 1939.

122 The Algiers senator Jacques Duroux rejected the dominion idea in ANOM, GGA, 1O 55, Commission des boissons, minutes of meeting of 23–24 Mar. 1933, 52. For a dis-

senting view, see the radical rightist Jean Paillard's *Faut-il faire de l'Algérie un dominion?* (Paris: Fernand Sorlot, 1938). See also Jonathan K. Gosnell, *The Politics of Frenchness in Colonial Algeria, 1930–1954* (Rochester, NY: University of Rochester Press, 2002), 84–89.

123 Saul, "Les pouvoirs publics métropolitains face à la Dépression," 172–174.

124 ANP, F60 231, Ligue des Petits et Moyens Viticulteurs d'Oranie to President du Conseil des ministres, 3 July 1935; ANOM, GGA, 1O 55, J. Laumet (vice-president of the Union des Ligues des Petits et Moyens Viticulteurs d'Algérie) to President du Conseil des ministres, 11 June 1936.

5. LABOR QUESTIONS

1 Jean Mélia, *Le triste sort des indigènes musulmans d'Algérie* (Paris: Mercure de France, 1935), 16.

2 Jacques Berque, *French North Africa: The Maghrib between Two Wars*, trans. Jean Stewart (New York: Praeger, 1967 [1962]), 261.

3 Charles-Robert Ageron, "1936: L'Algérie entre le Front populaire et le Congrès musulman," in Ageron, *De l'Algérie française à l'Algérie algérienne* (Paris: Editions Bouchène, 2005), 387. Ageron wrote this article in 1979.

4 Mahfoud Kaddache, *La vie politique à Alger de 1919 à 1939* (Algiers: SNED, 1970), 301–304.

5 James McDougall, *History and the Culture of Nationalism in Algeria* (Cambridge: Cambridge University Press, 2006). McDougall also calls 1936 a "watershed year" (97).

6 Charles-Robert Ageron, *Histoire de l'Algérie contemporaine*, vol. 2, *De l'insurrection de 1871 au déclenchement de la guerre de libération (1954)* (Paris: Presses Universitaires de France, 1979), 438–439, 449–466. Mélia opposed the Blum-Viollette plan as insufficiently assimilationist.

7 Kaddache, *La vie politique à Alger de 1919 à 1939,* 369.

8 See, for example, the narrative of frustrated hopes in Ferhat Abbas, *Guerre et révolution d'Algérie,* vol. 1, *La nuit coloniale* (Paris: René Julliard, 1962), 106–133.

9 For a sense of the mixed employee rosters of barrel-company workshops, see the lists from 1939 in ANOM, Préfecture d'Alger (henceforth Alger), 1K 3.

10 In some ways my approach here echoes Frederick Cooper, *Decolonization and African Society: The Labor Question in French and British Africa* (Cambridge: Cambridge University Press, 1996), 5–9.

11 David Prochaska, "Fire on the Mountain: Resisting Colonialism in Algeria," in Donald Crummey, ed., *Banditry, Rebellion and Social Protest in Africa* (London: James Currey, 1986), 229–252. For more on rural resistance, see, for example, Neil MacMaster, "The Roots of Insurrection: The Role of the Algerian Village Assembly (*Djemâa*) in Peasant Resistance, 1863–1962," *Comparative Studies in Society and History* 52:2 (2013): 419–447; Peter Von Sivers, "Rural Uprisings as Political Movements in Colonial Algeria, 1851–1914," in Edmund Burke III and Ira M. Lapidus, eds., *Islam, Politics, and Social Movements* (Berkeley: University of California Press, 1988), 39–59.

12 On the Constantine uprising, see Gilbert Meynier, *L'Algérie révélée: La guerre de 1914–1918 et le premier quart du XXe siècle* (Geneva: Librairie Droz, 1981), 567–598.

13 Charles-Robert Ageron, *Les Algériens musulmans et la France (1871–1919)* (Paris: Presses Universitaires de France, 1968), 552–561. See also Michel Launay, *Paysans algériens 1960–2006,* 3rd ed. (Paris: Karthala, 2007), 138–139.

14 ANOM, GGA, 1O 33, Pres. of Syndicat professionnel agricole et viticole de Mostaganem to GG, Nov. 1913; 1O 150, Chambre d'agriculture d'Oran, *Procès-verbaux des séances, Mars 1915* (Oran: D. Heintz et fils, 1915), 242–243.

15 Jean du Nador, *A travers l'Algérie: Vue d'ensemble, colons, indigènes, le vignoble* (Algiers: J. Angelini, 1903), 16–19. The horseman rumor evokes the story of Muhammad's night flight to Jerusalem on a winged horse. On rumors (of which a new crop appeared during the Great War), see also Sylvie Thénault, *Violence ordinaire dans l'Algérie coloniale: Camps, internements, assignations à résidence* (Paris: Odile Jacob, 2012), 58–59; Abdelkader Djeghloul, "Hors-la-loi, violence rurale et pouvoir colonial en Algérie au début du XXe siècle: Les frères Boutouizerat," *Revue de l'Occident musulman et de la Méditerranée* 38 (1984): 41–42; Arthur Asseraf, "La société coloniale face à l'actualité internationale: Diffusion, contrôle, usages (1881–1899)," *Revue d'histoire moderne et contemporaine* 63:2 (2016): 110–132. On India, see Kim Wagner, "'Treading upon Fires': The 'Mutiny' Motif and Colonial Anxieties in British India," *Past and Present* 218 (2013): 159–197.

16 ANOM, F80 / 1838, for example, Note à l'appui du projet de décret portant révocation de maire de Sidi Moussa and GG to Minister of Interior, 23 Oct. 1897. See also Didier Guignard, *L'abus de pouvoir dans l'Algérie coloniale (1880–1914): Visibilité et singularité* (Nanterre: Presses Universitaires de Paris Ouest, 2014), 372; Ageron, *Les Algériens musulmans et la France,* 505; *Recueil des arrêts du Conseil d'Etat statuant au contentieux des décisions du tribunal des conflits et de la Cour des comptes,* vol. 68, series 2 (1898), 566; "Indigènes séquestrés," *La Croix,* 20–21 Nov. 1898; Victor Spielmann, *Les grands domaines nord-africains: Comment et pourquoi l'on colonise* (Algiers: Editions du "Trait-d'Union," 1928), 89–90. Pelegri's son Michel was also implicated but eventually let off.

17 "Vendanges algériennes," *L'Afrique du Nord illustrée,* 2 Oct. 1909.

18 See, for example, Stuart D. Brandes, *American Welfare Capitalism, 1880–1940* (Chicago: University of Chicago Press, 1976).

19 Xavier Daumalin, *Le patronat marseillais et la deuxième industrialisation 1880–1930* (Aix-en-Provence: Presses Universitaires de Provence, 2014), 225–234.

20 Shakila Yacob, "Model of Welfare Capitalism? The United States Rubber Company in Southeast Asia, 1910–1942," *Enterprise and Society* 8:1 (2007): 136–174; Jean-Louis Moreau, "The Genesis of Paternalism in the Colonial Territories: The Union Minière du Haut-Katanga's Social Policy in the 1920s," in Hubert Bonin and Paul Thomes, eds., *Old Paternalism, New Paternalism, Post-Paternalism (19th–21st Centuries)* (Brussels: Peter Lang, 2013), 127–142. See also Ann Laura Stoler, *Capitalism and Confrontation in Sumatra's Plantation Belt, 1870–1979* (Ann Arbor: University of Michigan Press, 1985), 36–43.

21 Liew Kai Khiun, "Planters, Estate Health and Malaria in British Malaya (1900–1940)," *Journal of the Malay Branch of the Royal Asiatic Society* 83:1 (2010): 91–115; Randall M. Packard, "The Invention of the 'Tropical Worker': Medical Research and the Quest for Central African Labor on the South African Gold Mines, 1903–1936," *Journal of African History* 34:2 (1993): 271–292.

22 Pierre Brocheux, "Le prolétariat des plantations d'hévéas au Vietnam méridional: Aspects sociaux et politiques (1927–1937)," *Le mouvement social* 90 (1975): 70–71.

23 Michel Hau, "Industrial Paternalism and Social Development: The Commitment of the Community of Businessmen in Alsace," in Bonin and Thomes, eds., *Old Paternalism, New Paternalism,* 36–37.

24 P. Cardonne and J. Rabot, *La colonisation dans l'ouest-Oranais* (Algiers: V. Heintz, 1930), 38. For some similar examples, see Hildebert Isnard, "La vigne en Algérie: Etude géographique" (PhD diss., Université de Paris I-Sorbonne, 1947) 932–933.

25 Johan H. Meuleman, *Le Constantinois entre les deux guerres mondiales: L'évolution économique et sociale de la population rurale* (Assen: Van Gorcum, 1985), 104–106; Isnard, "La vigne en Algérie," 798–799; see also Claude Liauzu, *Salariat et mouvement ouvrier en Tunisie: Crises et mutations, 1931–1939* (Paris: Editions du CNRS, 1978), 17.

26 ANOM, BA, 11ES 332, reports to shareholders, 20 May 1926 and 16 May 1927.

27 AGMAfr, Voillard 231, Père Clément to Comte de Richemont, 5 Dec. 1930; Clément, "Maisons ouvrières," 8 Aug. 1931; *Le Petit Echo* 216, 25 Aug. 1931, 89–90.

28 On this company, a strong promoter of European colonization in Tunisia that also owned some properties in Algeria, see Jules Saurin (the company's founder), *Vingt-cinq ans de colonisation nord-africaine* (Paris: Société d'éditions géographiques, maritimes et coloniales, 1925).

29 ANOM, BA, 11ES 201 bis, annual reports dated 24 Apr. 1928, 18 Apr. 1931; Augustin Bernard, *Enquête sur l'habitation rurale des indigènes d'Algérie, faite par ordre de M. le Gouverneur Général* (Algiers: Fontana Frères, 1921), 114. A study conducted in the 1910s found 152 Algerian families living in rented rooms in Mondovi.

30 Launay, *Paysans algériens,* 56–57. For more on housing, see Neil MacMaster, "From Tent to Village Regroupement: The Colonial State and Social Engineering of Rural Space, 1843–1962," in Ed Naylor, ed., *France's Modernizing Mission: Citizenship, Welfare and the Ends of Empire* (London: Palgrave Macmillan, 2018), 113–117.

31 Georges Bardelli, *Mémoires ultramarines: La Trappe de Staouëli, ferme modèle (1843–1963)* (Castelnaudary: Imprimerie du Lauragais, 2001), 77–78; ANOM, BA, 11ES 332, Kéroulis annual report, 19 June 1933.

32 See, for example, Spielmann, *Les grands domaines nord-africains,* 89.

33 Gabriel Verge, *Monographie du Domaine de la Trappe de Staouëli* (Algiers: V. Heintz, 1930), 51–52.

34 AGMAfr, Voillard 228, meetings of Conseil d'administration, 22 Mar. 1926, 21 Nov. 1928; ANOM, Oran, 5Q 12, Etat des tracteurs existant dans le département d'Oran, 22 Apr. 1939. See also Julien Franc, *La colonisation de la Mitidja* (Paris: Librairie Ancienne Honoré Champion, 1928), 642–644.

35 The poem appears in French translation in Liauzu, *Salariat et mouvement ouvrier en Tunisie,* 165–167.

36 Isnard, "La vigne en Algérie," 880–882, 901.

37 Jean Bordes, "Le transport des vins en vrac par voie fluviale," *Journal de la Marine Marchande* 1649 (26 July 1951): 1605. For more detail on the events and trends discussed in this section, see Owen White, "Roll Out the Barrel: French and Algerian Ports and the Birth of the Wine Tanker," *French Politics, Culture and Society* 35:2 (2017): 111–132.

38 ADH, 10M 266, Commissaire spécial de Sète to prefect of Hérault, 5 and 7 Mar. 1934. Tunisian production peaked in the 1930s and was typically less than a tenth of Algeria's. See Francis-Raymond Peyronnet, *Le vignoble nord-africain* (Paris: J. Peyronnet,

1950), 102; also Nessim Znaien, "Le vin et la viticulture en Tunisie coloniale (1881–1956): Entre synapse et apartheid," *French Cultural Studies* 26:2 (2015): 140–151.

39 Kaddache, *La vie politique à Alger de 1919 à 1939,* 209.

40 On urban demographic trends and shanty towns, see Kamel Kateb, *Européens, "indigènes" et juifs en Algérie (1830–1962): Représentations et réalités des populations* (Paris: Editions de l'INED, 2001), 270–273, 276–277; and Jim House, "Shantytowns and Rehousing in Late Colonial Algiers and Casablanca," in Naylor, ed., *France's Modernizing Mission,* 133–163; on migration to France at this time, see Neil MacMaster, *Colonial Migrants and Racism: Algerians in France, 1900–62* (Basingstoke, UK: Macmillan, 1997), 178–179; on rural immiseration, see André Nouschi, *L'Algérie amère, 1914–1994* (Paris: Editions de la Maison des sciences de l'homme, 1995), 56–61.

41 Houari Touati, *Dictionnaire biographique du mouvement ouvrier de l'Oranie* (Oran: Centre de Documentation des Sciences Humaines, 1981), 39.

42 ANOM, Alger, 1K 75, report by Chef du Service de la Police des Chemins de Fer et Ports, 10 Jan. 1935; ANP, F60 328, "Quelques précisions sur le transport des vins par navires-citernes," 19 Feb. 1935; ADSM, 10M 398, Prefect of Seine-Inférieure to Minister of Commerce and Industry, 29 Jan. 1935.

43 ANOM, Alger, 1K 75, report by Chef de la Sûreté Départementale, 26 Feb. 1935; report by Pierre Renaud, Ingénieur en Chef, Directeur du Port d'Alger to Police des Ports Maritimes et Commerce, 26 Feb. 1935; ADH, 10M 266, Commissaire spécial de Sète to Prefect of Hérault, 26 Feb. 1935.

44 "Les transports des vins en cargos-citernes: Le *Bacchus* est arrivé la nuit dernière," *Le Journal de Rouen,* 11 Mar. 1935.

45 ANP, F60 328, Deputy for the Hérault to Minister of Merchant Marine, 12 Mar. 1935; ANOM, Alger, 1K 75, Chef de Sureté départementale, report of 23 Mar. 1935.

46 ANOM, Alger, 1K 75, SOFLUMAR and Société Franco-Algérienne de Stockage to GG, 8 June 1935; "Le *Bacchus* sera désarmé à son retour," *La Dépêche de Rouen,* 9 June 1935; ANP, F60 328, Ministre de la Marine Marchande to Président du Conseil, 29 June 1935.

47 ACCM, MP 3181 / 07, President of Sète Chamber of Commerce to Union des Chambres de Commerce Maritimes, 29 June 1934; CANA, Chambre de Commerce d'Alger 1935, boîte 87, dossier 18, minutes of meeting of Assemblée des présidents des chambres de commerce d'Algérie, 26 Oct. 1934; ANP, F60 328, Rouen Chamber of Commerce to Président du Conseil des Ministres, 21 Feb. 1935; ACCM, MP 3181 / 07, Marseille Chamber of Commerce to various government ministers, 16 Feb. 1935.

48 ANOM, Alger, 1K 75, motion of Conseil municipal of the commune of Hussein-Dey, meeting of 8 Mar. 1935.

49 ANOM, Alger, 1K 75, report by Chef de la Sûreté Départementale, 16 Feb. 1935.

50 L. D. Trotsky, "The 'Third Period' of the Comintern's Mistakes," *The Militant* 3:4 (25 Jan. 1930): 4–5.

51 "Le Grand Meeting du Gallia: 50,000 Algériens appartenant à toutes les classes et professions, affirment leur volonté de rester français," *Oran-Matin,* 11 June 1933; on Benchiha, see Jacques Bouveresse, *Un parlement colonial? Les Délégations financières algériennes, 1898–1945,* 2 vols. (Mont-Saint-Aignan: Publications des Universités de Rouen et du Havre, 2008 / 2010), 1:945.

52 "Dans une manifestation digne et calme la population Bônoise a unanimement protesté contre les menaces de contingentement de la production algérienne," *Dépêche de Constantine,* 23 June 1933; on Benyacoub, see Bouveresse, *Un parlement colonial,* 1:948–949.

53 G.-J. Stotz, *Questions actuelles d'agriculture et de colonisation algérienne: La main-d'œuvre* (Algiers: Imprimerie Algéroise, 1931), 49; ANOM, 1O 122, GG to General de Gaulle, 31 Aug. 1943.

54 Quoted in Mélia, *Le triste sort des indigènes musulmans d'Algérie,* 111–112.

55 Nouschi, *L'Algérie amère,* 64–65; Augustin Bernard, "Le recensement de 1936 dans l'Afrique du Nord," *Annales de Géographie* 46:259 (1937): 84–85. For more detailed demographic data from 1920 to independence, see Kateb, *Européens, "indigènes" et juifs en Algérie,* 215–320.

56 Louis Milliot, "L'exode saisonnier des Rifains vers l'Algérie," *Bulletin économique du Maroc* 1:5 (1934): 315. See also Meuleman, *Le Constantinois entre les deux guerres mondiales,* 262.

57 For example, Edouard Kruger, *Les bienfaits de l'Union douanière Métropole-Algérie et la question vinicole* (Oran: Syndicat du commerce des vins en gros du département d'Oran, 1933), 6–9; R. Peyronnet, "Viticulteurs du Midi et viticulteurs d'Algérie," *Bulletin de la Société de Géographie d'Algérie et de l'Afrique du Nord* 120:4 (1929): 686.

58 Quoted in Mélia, *Le triste sort des indigènes musulmans d'Algérie,* 126.

59 Fromentin, "La situation agricole en Algérie: état des cultures et des récoltes," *L'Echo d'Alger,* 17 Mar. 1936. See also Idir Bouaboud, *L'Echo d'Alger: Cinquante ans de vie politique française en Algérie, 1912–1961* (Villeneuve d'Ascq: Presses Universitaires du Septentrion, 1999), 193–209, 503.

60 Laird Boswell, *Rural Communism in France, 1920–1939* (Ithaca, NY: Cornell University Press, 1998), 242; Robert O. Paxton, *French Peasant Fascism: Henry Dorgères's Greenshirts and the Crises of French Agriculture, 1929–1939* (New York: Oxford University Press, 1997), 11–50; M. C. Cleary, *Peasants, Politicians and Producers: The Organization of Agriculture in France since 1918* (Cambridge: Cambridge University Press, 1989), 71.

61 Paxton, *French Peasant Fascism,* 51–67. For a good overview of the FP in Algeria, see Samuel Kalman, *French Colonial Fascism: The Extreme Right in Algeria, 1919–1939* (Basingstoke, UK: Palgrave Macmillan, 2013), 81–93.

62 ANOM, Oran, série continue 2493, Chef de sûreté départementale to prefect of Oran, 23 Aug. 1935.

63 Ibid., Chef de sûreté départementale to prefect of Oran, 5 Sept. 1935.

64 Quoted in Mélia, *Le triste sort des indigènes musulmans d'Algérie,* 127. A kindred far-right organization, the more urban Croix de Feu (Crosses of Fire), similarly tried to attract Algerian Muslims around the same time. See Caroline Campbell, *Political Belief in France, 1927–1945: Gender, Empire, and Fascism in the Croix de Feu and Parti Social Français* (Baton Rouge: Louisiana State University Press, 2015), 157–160; Kalman, *French Colonial Fascism,* 64–69.

65 ANOM, Oran, série continue 2493, Chef de sûreté départementale to prefect of Oran, 20 Sept. 1935.

66 Robert Paxton similarly notes the failure of Dorgères to attract support in wine-producing regions of France, with the partial exception of the Loire Valley. Paxton, *French Peasant Fascism,* 21–22, 122, 161–162.

67 Charles Vergobbi, "Lettre à M. Corbières, président de la Ligue des petits et moyens viticulteurs," *Oran-Matin,* 24 July 1935, in ANOM, Oran, série continue 2493.

68 ANOM, Oran, série continue 2493, Chef de sûreté départementale to prefect, 5 Sept. 1935.

69 ANP, F60 231, Ligue des Petits et Moyens Viticulteurs d'Oranie to Président du Conseil des ministres, 3 July 1935; ANOM, BA, série continue 454, "Chronique des Ligues," *Courrier agricole et viticole de l'Algérie,* 9 Feb. 1936.

70 E. Gilbert, "Dorgères à Montpellier, Pitollet à Bannalec," *L'Echo d'Oran,* 28 Jan. 1936.

71 Kalman, *French Colonial Fascism,* 90–91; for membership estimates, Bouaboud, *L'Echo d'Alger,* 216.

72 Allison Drew, *We Are No Longer in France: Communists in Colonial Algeria* (Manchester, UK: Manchester University Press, 2014), 26–56.

73 René Gallissot, ed., *Algérie: Engagements sociaux et question nationale. De la colonisation à l'indépendance de 1830 à 1962* (Paris: Les Editions de l'Atelier, 2006), 598–599.

74 Ibid., 484.

75 Drew, *We Are No Longer in France,* 56–76; quotation at 70.

76 Thomas-Adrian Schweitzer, "Le Parti communiste français, le Comintern et l'Algérie dans les années 1930," *Le Mouvement social* 78 (Jan.-Mar. 1972), 124.

77 ANOM, Oran, série continue 2394, Rayon d'Oran du Parti Communiste, "La crise viticole: Notre position," flyer, 20 June 1933.

78 Drew, *We Are No Longer in France,* 86–88. An Algerian Communist Party, separate from the Parti communiste français, was eventually founded in October 1936.

79 McDougall, *History and the Culture of Nationalism in Algeria,* 84–86.

80 "Un jeune cultivateur qui tua un maraudeur est acquitté," *L'Echo d'Alger,* 21 June 1936; ANOM, état civil, birth of Charles Jauvion, Blida 1904.

81 For example, in a case where an eleven-year-old boy was shot in the back: "Boufarik: Coup de fusil," *L'Echo d'Alger,* 14 Aug. 1937. See also "Tizi-Ouzou: Cour criminelle," *L'Echo d'Alger,* 29 Apr. 1937; "Un maraudeur surprise est tué par un garde," *L'Echo d'Alger,* 9 Sept. 1937.

82 For an overview of this moment, see Ageron, *Histoire de l'Algérie contemporaine,* 2:443–448.

83 Julian Jackson, *The Popular Front in France: Defending Democracy, 1934–1938* (Cambridge: Cambridge University Press, 1988), 85.

84 Jean-Louis Planche, "Une tentative de rupture anticolonialiste: Les grèves de l'été 1936 en Algérie," *Cahiers du GREMAMO* 4 (1986–1987): 86–120; René Gallissot, *La République française et les indigènes: Algérie colonisée, Algérie algérienne (1870–1962)* (Paris: Les Editions de l'Atelier, 2006), 105–114.

85 "Le projet de contrat adopté par les tonneliers et les ouvriers des chais," *L'Echo d'Alger,* 16 June 1936; "La situation pour Alger" and "Le conflit des établissements de liège Alfred Borgeaud," *L'Echo d'Alger,* 21 June 1936.

86 Bouaboud, *L'Echo d'Alger*, 268–269; Jonathan K. Gosnell, *The Politics of Frenchness in Colonial Algeria, 1930–1954* (Rochester, NY: University of Rochester Press, 2002), 87–89; Kaddache, *La vie politique à Alger*, 285.

87 Nora Benallègue-Chaouia, *Algérie: Mouvement ouvrier et question nationale, 1919–1954* (Algiers: Office des Publications Universitaires, 2005), 179–182; Planche, "Une tentative de rupture anticolonialiste." Firm conclusions about the 1936 rural conflicts are made more difficult by a scarcity of archival sources.

88 ANOM, Alger, 1K 5, Mayor of Sidi Moussa to Prefect of Algiers (telegram), 13 June 1936; "Les propriétaires de Sidi-Moussa demandent au préfet de les protéger," *L'Echo d'Alger*, 15 June 1936.

89 "La protection des campagnes," *L'Echo d'Alger*, 13 June 1936; ANOM, Alger, 1K 5, Mayor of L'Arba to Prefect of Algiers, 13 June 1936, and Prefect to GG, 8 July 1936.

90 ANOM, Alger, 1K 75, Rapport du Capt. Demoyen, commandant la section de la Corps d'Armée Gendarmerie Nationale, 4 June 1935; ADSM, 10M 398, Prefect of Seine-Inférieure to Minister of Interior, 29 Jan. 1935. On the gendarmerie in Algeria, see Martin Thomas, *Violence and Colonial Order: Police, Workers and Protest in the European Colonial Empires, 1918–1940* (Cambridge: Cambridge University Press, 2012), 89–111.

91 Thomas, *Violence and Colonial Order*, 109.

92 ANOM, Alger, 1K 6, Prefect of Algiers to GG, 13 June and 17 June 1936; "Contre le débauchage des ouvriers agricoles," "M. Bourrat, préfet d'Alger, fait une longue tournée dans le Sahel," "Quinze indigènes arrêtés à Fort-de-l'Eau," *L'Echo d'Alger*, 16 June 1936; "Quarante-huit manifestants à l'instruction," *L'Echo d'Alger*, 18 June 1936.

93 "Le docteur Bendjelloul adresse aux musulmans un appel au calme," *L'Echo d'Alger*, 17 June 1936; ANOM, Alger, 1K 5, Commissaire de police de Maison-Carrée to Prefect of Algiers, 18 June 1936; "Une proclamation de M. Si Salah," *L'Echo d'Alger*, 18 June 1936.

94 ANOM, Alger, 1K 6, Prefect of Algiers to GG, 17 June 1936; "Quarante-huit manifestants à l'instruction," *L'Echo d'Alger*, 18 June 1936.

95 "La discussion générale du budget aux Délégations financières," *L'Echo d'Alger*, 23 June 1936; Bouveresse, *Un parlement colonial*, 1:907–908, 976.

96 Gordon Wright, *Rural Revolution in France: The Peasantry in the Twentieth Century* (Stanford, CA: Stanford University Press, 1964), 68. On the strikes, see, especially, John Bulaitis, *Communism in Rural France: French Agricultural Workers and the Popular Front* (London: I. B. Tauris, 2008), 89–155; also Edouard Lynch, *Moissons rouges: Les socialistes français et la société paysanne durant l'entre-deux-guerres (1918–1940)* (Villeneuve d'Ascq: Presses universitaires du Septentrion, 2002), 333–345; Jean-Claude Farcy, "Les grèves agricoles de 1936–1937 dans le bassin parisien," in Ronald Hubscher and Farcy, eds., *La moisson des autres: Les salariés agricoles aux XIXe et XXe siècles* (Paris: Créaphis, 1996), 303–324.

97 Bulaitis, *Communism in Rural France*, 100–106.

98 "Marengo: Syndicat des ouvriers agricoles," *L'Echo d'Alger*, 9 July 1936. For statistics on agricultural unionization in the department of Oran, see Ahmed Abid, "Les grèves agricoles en Oranie à l'approche du 1er novembre 1954," *Cahiers du GREMAMO* 4 (1986–1987): 124.

99 Bulaitis, *Communism in Rural France,* 105–109.

100 ANOM, Alger, 1K 5 and Oran, 1H 113, Min Ag to prefects of Algiers and Oran, 2 July 1936.

101 "Salaires moyens normaux des travailleurs agricoles en Algérie," *L'Echo d'Alger,* 3 Aug. 1936.

102 ANOM, Oran, 1H 113, Union départemental des syndicats de l'Oranie / Fédération des ouvriers agricoles de l'Oranie, Première région d'Oranie, viticulture: Cahier des revendications des ouvriers agricoles (vendanges), 20 Aug. 1936; Annexe à l'arrêté préfectoral du 22 août 1936, Commission des salaires normaux des travailleurs agricoles: Tableau des salaires, 1ère région.

103 "Damiette: Salaires agricoles de la 3e région (Médéa)," *L'Echo d'Alger,* 13 Sept. 1936. For the Burgundy comparison, Un vieil colon de la région, *Médéa et son vignoble* (Algiers: Imprimerie Moderne, 1930), 7. In the Midi that year, male *vendangeurs* received thirty-five francs per day plus three liters of wine; women got twenty-two francs and two liters. "L'accord pour le paiement des vendanges dans le Midi," *L'Echo d'Alger,* 16 Aug. 1936.

104 "Le kilo de pain coûte 2 francs 15," *L'Echo d'Alger,* 15 Sept. 1936; ANOM, Oran, 1H 113, Salaire minima des travailleurs des entreprises agricoles, 1ère region: Oran, meeting of 10 May 1937.

105 ANOM, Alger, 1K 5, Mayor of Boufarik (Amédée Froger) to Prefect of Algiers, 12 Aug. 1936, and 1K 6, Prefect to GG, 27 Aug. 1936; "La situation agricole en Algérie: Vignes," *L'Echo d'Alger,* 1 Sept. 1936; Planche, "Une tentative de rupture anticolonialiste," 99–100.

106 ANOM, Oran, 5I 39, "Main d'oeuvre indigène," *Oran-Matin,* 26 Oct. 1936; "La main d'oeuvre indigène," *Oran-Matin,* 9 Nov. 1936. For other examples of underpayment in 1936, see "Une grève de vendangeurs à Sonis," *L'Echo d'Alger,* 25 Sept. 1936; "Lamoricière: Main-d'oeuvre indigène," *L'Echo d'Alger,* 11 Nov. 1936.

107 AWO, 1F 289, multiple documents including report for Chef de la brigade mobile de Mostaganem, 16 Apr. 1937; report by Chef de la brigade mobile de Mostaganem, 12 May 1937.

108 AWO, 1F 289, report by Chef de la brigade mobile de Mostaganem, 12 May 1937.

109 ANOM, Oran, 5I 39, Edmond Arnaud, "Au sujet des troubles de Belle-Côte et de la région Mostaganémoise," *Oran-Matin,* 29 Apr.'1937.

110 AWO, 1F 289, report by Commandant de la section de Tlemcen, 16 Apr. 1937.

111 Ibid., Commissaire central de police (Tlemcen) to Prefect of Oran, 15 Apr. 1937; President of Chambre du syndicat agricole de Tlemcen (Havard) to Minister of Interior, 19 Apr. 1937. On Badsi, see Gallissot, ed., *Algérie: Engagements sociaux et question nationale,* 78. One Bahi Ahmed ould Miloud was later sentenced to five years in prison for killing Belahcene; ANOM, Oran, 5I 39, "Cour criminel de Tlemcen," *Oran-Matin,* 19 Feb. 1938.

112 AWO, 1F 289, Administrateur détaché à la sous-préfecture de Mostaganem to prefect of Oran, 8 Apr. 1937; sous-préfet of Mostaganem to prefect of Oran, 12 May 1937; report by gendarmerie Captain Bobillon, 3 Apr. 1937.

113 ANOM, Oran, 1H 113, Union départemental des syndicats de l'Oranie / Fédération des ouvriers agricoles de l'Oranie, Première région d'Oranie, viticulture: Cahier des revendications des ouvriers agricoles (vendanges), 20 Aug. 1936.

114 "Des indigènes armés de matraques et de revolvers attaquent à deux reprises des groupes de vendangeurs," *L'Echo d'Alger,* 28 Aug. 1936; "Après les incidents des vendangeurs de Mostaganem: Trente-deux arrestations ont été opérées," *L'Echo d'Alger,* 29 Aug. 1936.

115 AWO, 1F 289, message to gendarmerie about Gaston-Doumergue, early Apr. 1937; reports on disturbances at Aïn-Kial, 5 Apr. and 8 Apr. 1937; report from town hall of *commune* of Saint-Maur, 13 Apr. 1937.

116 Bulaitis, *Communism in Rural France,* 148–155; Lynch, *Moissons rouges,* 371–375. Immigrant workers were also present in numbers in the Midi vineyards, especially from Spain. See, for example, Jean Sagnes, "Le syndicalisme des ouvriers agricoles du Languedoc méditerranéen-Roussillon," in Hubscher and Farcy, eds., *La moisson des autres,* 339–340; Leo A. Loubère, Jean Sagnes, Laura Frader, and Rémy Pech, *The Vine Remembers: French Vignerons Recall Their Past* (Albany: State University of New York Press, 1985), 49–54.

117 Pierre Fromont and François Bourgeois, "Les grèves agricoles de Tremblay-lès-Gonesse en 1936," *Revue d'économie politique* 51 (1937): 1425.

118 ANOM, Alger, 1K 75, report by Commissaire de la sûreté départementale chargé du service des chemins de fer et ports, 6 June 1935.

119 David Montgomery Hart, *The Aith Waryaghar of the Moroccan Rif: An Ethnography and History* (Tucson: University of Arizona Press, 1976), 90. For a *fait divers* involving a Moroccan guard, see "Un gardien de vigne est tué à Kherba d'un coup de matraque," *L'Echo d'Alger,* 28 Aug. 1937. On Algerian-Moroccan tensions prior to 1936, see Louis Milliot, "L'exode saisonnier des Rifains vers l'Algérie" (part 2), *Bulletin économique du Maroc* 1:6 (1934): 401–402.

120 ANP, F60 713, GG Le Beau to Président du Conseil des ministres, 12 May 1937; ANOM, GGA, 3 CAB 71, dossier on seasonal migration of Moroccan agricultural workers to Algeria, Feb. 1938; David Seddon, *Moroccan Peasants: A Century of Change in the Eastern Rif, 1870–1970* (Folkestone, UK: Wm Dawson and Sons, 1981), 129, 131–132.

121 AWO, 1F 289, gendarmerie report on CGT meeting in Sidi-Bel-Abbès, 1 June 1937; ANOM, GGA, 3 CAB 71, GG Le Beau to Resident-General Noguès of Morocco, 24 Aug. 1937.

122 ANOM, Alger, 1K 6, Commandant de l'air en Algérie, compte-rendu de missions de sécurité intérieure, 17 June 1936; also Launay, *Paysans algériens,* 141–142.

123 AWO, 1F 289, Syndicat agricole de Mostaganem to Senator Roux-Freissineng, 10 Apr. 1937; President of Chambre du syndicat agricole de Tlemcen to Minister of Interior, 19 Apr. 1937.

124 Drew, *We Are No Longer in France,* 104.

125 On the French context, see Jackson, *The Popular Front in France,* 264–268.

126 AWO, 1F 289, Syndicat agricole de Mostaganem to parliamentary commission on Algeria, 20 Apr. 1937.

127 Laure Blévis, "Quelle citoyenneté pour les Algériens?," in Abderrahmane Bouchène, Jean-Pierre Peyroulou, Ouanassa Siari Tengour, and Sylvie Thénault, eds., *Histoire de l'Algérie à la période coloniale 1830–1962* (Paris: La Découverte, 2012), 357.

128 ANOM, Oran, 1H 113, meeting of salary commission for the Tlemcen region, 12 Sept. 1938.

129 ANOM, Oran, 5I 39, Prefect of Oran to GG, 18 June 1938; GGA, 3 CAB 71, dossier on seasonal migration of Moroccan agricultural workers to Algeria, Feb. 1938.

130 For a good example of expanded machine usage after 1936–1937, see Launay, *Paysans algériens,* 88–89.

131 ANOM, Alger, 1K 3, police interview dated 23 Aug. 1937; White, "Roll Out the Barrel," 123–124.

132 Quoted in "La population indigène a plus que triplé depuis que les Français sont installés en Algérie," *L'Echo d'Oran,* 16 May 1939.

6. WINE IN THE WARS

1 Quoted in Kim Munholland, "'Mon docteur le vin': Wine and Health in France, 1900–1950," in Mack P. Holt, ed., *Alcohol: A Social and Cultural History* (Oxford: Berg, 2006), 83–84.

2 ANP, F60 231, Barthe to Marshal Pétain, chef de l'état, 15 July and 15 Aug. 1940; Jacques Cantier, *L'Algérie sous le régime de Vichy* (Paris: Odile Jacob, 2002), 33. Of the 215,000 *mobilisés* in 1939, 123,000 were Algerian and 92,000 Euro-Algerian.

3 Idir Bouaboud, *L'Echo d'Alger: Cinquante ans de vie politique française en Algérie, 1912–1961* (Villeneuve d'Ascq: Presses Universitaires du Septentrion, 1999), 299, 303.

4 Annie Rey-Goldzeiguer, *Aux origines de la guerre d'Algérie, 1940–1945: De Mers-el-Kébir aux massacres du Nord-Constantinois* (Paris: La Découverte, 2006), 29; René Gallissot, ed., *Algérie: Engagements sociaux et question nationale. De la colonisation à l'indépendance de 1830 à 1962* (Paris: Les Editions de l'Atelier, 2006), 78. See also Mahfoud Kaddache, "L'opinion politique musulmane en Algérie et l'administration française (1939–1942)," *Revue d'histoire de la Deuxième Guerre mondiale* 29:114 (1979): 95–115.

5 AGMAfr, Birraux 327, Fêtes 1941; Allocution prononcée à Maison-Carrée pour la fête du RP Carrière, 29 Dec. 1941.

6 Martin Thomas, "Resource War, Civil War, Rights War: Factoring Empire into French North Africa's Second World War," *War in History* 18:2 (2011): 225–248.

7 Cantier, *L'Algérie sous le régime de Vichy,* 28, 72–73, 90; for "Little Berlin," see Amar Ouzegane, *Le meilleur combat* (Paris: René Julliard, 1962), 87; Sophie B. Roberts, *Citizenship and Antisemitism in French Colonial Algeria, 1870–1962* (Cambridge: Cambridge University Press, 2017), 222–242.

8 "La population de la Mitidja et du Sahel ont fêté hier, avec M. Averseng, l'œuvre sociale d'une famille et la mutualité agricole," *L'Echo d'Alger,* 6 Jan. 1930; Maurice Viollette, *L'Algérie vivra-t-elle?* (Paris: Félix Alcan, 1931), 62; ANOM, GGA, 1O 118, speech by Averseng, 6 July 1942.

9 Cantier, *L'Algérie sous le régime de Vichy,* 90.

10 ANOM, GGA, 1O 122, President of Fédération des vignerons du département d'Alger to GG, 17 July 1942; Oran, 1H 12; Hildebert Isnard, "La vigne en Algérie: Etude géographique" (PhD diss., Université de Paris I-Sorbonne, 1947), 1014; Christine Levisse-Touzé, *L'Afrique du Nord dans la guerre 1939–1945* (Paris: Albin Michel, 1998), 189.

11 Owen White, "Roll Out the Barrel: French and Algerian Ports and the Birth of the Wine Tanker," *French Politics, Culture and Society* 35:2 (2017): 124; AWA, 4H 215; Isnard, "La vigne en Algérie," 1016–1017; Olivier Boudot, *Les Schiaffino, une dynastie d'armateurs* (Saint-Malo: Pascal Galodé, 2008), 346.

12 ACCM, MP 3181 / 08, Syndicat des négociants en gros en vins, note on importation of Algerian wine via Marseille, 23 July 1940; Secrétaire d'état au ravitaillement to president of Marseille chamber of commerce, 9 Jan. 1941.

13 Based on figures from Edouard Kruger, "La viticulture en Algérie: Ses possibilités d'exportation," *Journal de la Marine Marchande,* no. 1649 (26 July 1951): 1593.

14 ANP, F60 789, Vice-Admiral Fenard to Secrétaire d'état à la production industrielle (Direction des carburants), 9 May 1942; see also ANOM, GGA, 1O 122 and 1O 147.

15 ANP, F60 789, President of Union des syndicats des vignerons d'Algérie to Pierre Laval, président du conseil, 16 Sept. 1942; minutes on Conférence des vins et alcools, Algiers, 10 and 11 Sept. 1941. For more on the Vichy regime and Algerian wine, see Joseph Bohling, *The Sober Revolution: Appellation Wine and the Transformation of France* (Ithaca, NY: Cornell University Press, 2018), 42–43.

16 Daniel Lefeuvre, *Chère Algérie: La France et sa colonie 1930–1962* (Paris: Flammarion, 2005), 212–214. For a few months in 1941 Weygand was also Algeria's governor-general.

17 On the plans considered and attempted by the Vichy government, see ibid., 208–239.

18 Charles-Robert Ageron, *Histoire de l'Algérie contemporaine,* vol. 2, *De l'insurrection de 1871 au déclenchement de la guerre de libération (1954)* (Paris: Presses Universitaires de France, 1979), 553–554.

19 Cantier, *L'Algérie sous le régime de Vichy,* 121–123; Lefeuvre, *Chère Algérie,* 219–220; Viollette, *L'Algérie vivra-t-elle,* 87–92. The land reallocation measure passed into law in March 1942 but never resulted in any of the expropriation it envisaged.

20 ANOM, BA, 11ES 332, Société anonyme des domaines du Kéroulis, report to shareholders, 30 June 1942, referring to a property belonging to its related company La Mitidja s.a.

21 ANOM, BA, 11ES 201 bis, Société du domaine du Chapeau de Gendarme, report to shareholders, 21 Apr. 1942.

22 Levisse-Touzé, *L'Afrique du nord dans la guerre,* 157–158.

23 ANOM, Oran, 5I 39, Note dated 5 Mar. 1941; Centre d'Information et d'Etudes (henceforth CIE), prefecture of Algiers, 17 Oct. 1941; CIE, prefecture of Oran, 12 Feb. 1942 and 1 July 1942; Prefect of Oran to GG, 24 Nov. 1941. See also Cantier, *L'Algérie sous le régime de Vichy,* 173–179; Rey-Goldzeiguer, *Aux origines de la guerre d'Algérie,* 57.

24 Cantier, *L'Algérie sous le régime de Vichy,* poster following p. 41.

25 AGMAfr, Birraux 323, Rapport d'activité, 26 June 1941.

26 ANOM, Oran, 5I 39, CIE, prefecture of Oran, 3 Apr. 1942 and 1 July 1942; "Salaire des travailleurs agricoles," *L'Echo d'Oran,* 28 Apr. 1942. On accusations of idleness at this time, see also Cantier, *L'Algérie sous le régime de Vichy,* 180–183.

27 ANOM, BA, 11ES 316, Rapport d'activité (SIAH), 1 June 1942.

28 David J. Smith, "'French Like the Others': Colonial Migrants in Wartime France, 1939–1947" (PhD diss., University of Toronto, 2013), 251–269; Cantier, *L'Algérie sous le régime de Vichy,* 166–169; ANOM, GGA, 1O 122, President of Fédération des syndicats agricoles de l'Oranie to GG, 27 Aug. 1942.

29 ANOM, GGA, 1O 122, President of Fédération des syndicats agricoles de l'Oranie to GG, 27 Aug. 1942. See also Jean-Louis Planche, "Violence et nationalismes en Algérie (1942–1945)," *Les temps modernes* 590 (Oct.-Nov. 1996): 116–117, 121.

30 AGMAfr, Birraux 334, Proposition d'augmentation générale des appointements du personnel de la SIAH, 30 Dec. 1942. On Operation Torch, see, for example, Levisse-Touzé, *L'Afrique du Nord dans la guerre,* 233–277.

31 On Vichy and Algerian Jews, see Michel Abitbol, *The Jews of North Africa during the Second World War* (Detroit, MI: Wayne State University Press, 1989), 56–101; Cantier, *L'Algérie sous le régime de Vichy,* 315–336; Roberts, *Citizenship and Antisemitism in French Colonial Algeria,* 250–296. For a sense of Algerian Jewish economic activity around the beginning of the war, see André N. Chouraqui, *Between East and West: A History of the Jews of North Africa* (Philadelphia: Jewish Publication Society of America, 1968), 217–220.

32 CANA, 10E 659, Demandes d'autorisation d'exportation des vins.

33 On Moatti, see ANOM, GGA, 30G 16; and Emile Moatti, *Les crus d'Algérie: Rapport présenté au Congrès National de la Vigne et du Vin à Oran, le 24 Mai 1930* (Algiers: Imprimerie Algérienne, 1931). On the decree, see Abitbol, *The Jews of North Africa,* 71–73.

34 "Domaines de MM. Douïeb frères," in *Vignobles et vins d'Algérie. Etude spéciale de Grands Crus et Vins de France, octobre 1934* (Lyon: Publications Pierre Argence, 1934), 28.

35 ANOM, GGA, 30G 2, Raymond Laquière to Auguste Schnetzler (administrateur provisoire des biens de MM Douïeb), 19 June 1942; miscellaneous documents in 30G 2, 3, 7, and 9; Henri Pello, ed., *Algérie: Histoire et souvenirs d'un canton de la Mitidja, 1830 à 1962. L'Arba, Rivet, Rovigo, Sidi-Moussa et Baraki* (Saint-Estève: Presses Littéraires, 1998), 100. On Laquière, see Jean-Marc Valentin, *Les parlementaires des départements d'Algérie sous la IIIe République* (Paris: L'Harmattan, 2010), 182.

36 Jay Winter and Antoine Prost, *René Cassin and Human Rights: From the Great War to the Universal Declaration* (Cambridge: Cambridge University Press, 2013), 8, 304.

37 Abitbol, *The Jews of North Africa,* 141–165.

38 Charles-Robert Ageron, "Ferhat Abbas et l'évolution politique de l'Algérie musulmane pendant la Seconde guerre mondiale," in Ageron, *Genèse de l'Algérie algérienne* (Paris: Editions Bouchène, 2005), 259–284; André Nouschi, *L'Algérie amère, 1914–1994* (Paris: Editions de la Maison des sciences de l'homme, 1995), 163–168, including text from the Manifesto.

39 ANOM, BA, 11ES 332, Société des domaines du Kéroulis, report to shareholders, 30 June 1944; 11ES 201 bis, Société du Domaine du Chapeau de Gendarme, report to shareholders, 26 May 1944.

40 CANA, 10E 659, Demandes d'autorisation d'exportation des vins, 1943; Isnard, "La vigne en Algérie," 1017–1018.

41 ANOM, GGA, 1O 127, Réquisitions agricoles, Société du Domaine de l'Etoile to president of Syndicat des vignerons d'Algérie, 29 Mar. 1943, and Général d'armée aéri-

enne Bouscat to GG, 27 Nov. 1943; AGMAfr, Birraux 322, conseils d'exploitation, July and Aug. 1943.

42 Christophe Campos, *Fleurus en Oranie 1848–1962: Monographie communale* (Paris: Riveneuve Editions, 2016), 520.

43 *Instructions for British Servicemen in France 1944*, reprint (Oxford: Bodleian Library, 2005), 44.

44 ANOM, GGA, 1O 128, Secrétaire à la production to général d'armée (service de prisonniers de guerre), 19 May 1943.

45 ANOM, GGA, 1O 118, Directeur de l'économie algérienne, situation agricole de l'Algérie au 30 juin 1943; on salaries, see Oran, série continue 3011 / 1, circulars from prefect of Oran on use of Italian prisoners of war in agriculture, 10 June and 3 Aug. 1943; AGMAfr, Birraux 322, conseils d'exploitation, May and June 1943. A living wage at this time was more in the range of twenty francs per day.

46 AGMAfr, Birraux 334, reports on exploitation de Mirabeau, May–July and Aug.–Sept. 1943; Aug.–Sept. 1944; Aug.–Sept. 1945 (quoted).

47 ANOM, GGA, 1O 118, miscellaneous reports on Algeria (May 1945), department of Constantine (1 Feb., 8 Mar., 4 Apr. 1945), department of Oran (26 Feb., 20 Mar. [quoted], 26 Apr. 1945); AGMAfr, Birraux 325, rapport de direction générale, 4 June 1945 and 30 Oct. 1945.

48 AGMAfr, Birraux 334, questions du personnel, 28 Mar. 1945; ANOM, GGA, 1O 118, situation agricole mensuelle (Constantine), 4 Apr. 1945.

49 Martin Thomas, *The French Empire at War 1940–1945* (Manchester, UK: Manchester University Press, 1998), 184.

50 Rey-Goldzeiguer, *Aux origines de la guerre d'Algérie*, 226–232; John Ruedy, *Modern Algeria: The Origins and Development of a Nation* (Bloomington: Indiana University Press, 1992), 147–148.

51 Examples include Michael Goebel, *Anti-Imperial Metropolis: Interwar Paris and the Seeds of Third World Nationalism* (New York: Cambridge University Press, 2015); Martin Thomas, *The French Empire between the Wars: Imperialism, Politics, and Society* (Manchester, UK: Manchester University Press, 2005).

52 David G. Marr examines the complexities of this moment in two books: *Vietnam 1945: The Quest for Power* (Berkeley: University of California Press, 1995); and *Vietnam: State, War, and Revolution (1945–1946)* (Berkeley: University of California Press, 2013).

53 See Rey-Goldzeiguer, *Aux origines de la guerre d'Algérie*, 257–307 (quotation at 294); Jean-Louis Planche, *Sétif 1945: Chronique d'un massacre annoncé*, 2nd ed. (Paris: Perrin, 2010).

54 Rey-Goldzeiguer, *Aux origines de la guerre d'Algérie*, 271, 278, 280, 303; on the demographics of Sétif, see André Prenant, "Facteurs du peuplement d'une ville de l'Algérie intérieure: Sétif," *Annales de géographie* 62:334 (1953): 434–451.

55 For one compelling example, see Hamou Amirouche, *Memoirs of a Mujahed: Algeria's Struggle for Freedom, 1945–1962* (San Diego: Amirouche Publishing, 2014), 24–28.

56 ANOM, Oran, 5Q 18, sous-préfet d'Oran, note on isolated farms in *arrondissement* of Oran, 1 June 1945.

57 On the need to reconstitute, see G. Charles, *Le vignoble algérien et sa reconstitution* (Algiers: La Typo-Litho & Jules Carbonel, 1946).

58 Don and Petie Kladstrup, *Wine and War: The French, the Nazis, and the Battle for France's Greatest Treasure* (New York: Broadway Books, 2001), 115–118.

59 Paul Reboux, *L'Algérie et ses vins* (Algiers: L'Agence Française de Librairie, 1945), 16–20; quotation at 20. See also ANOM, GGA, 1O 150, Chambre d'agriculture du département d'Alger, meeting of 9 May 1945.

60 Maud S. Mandel, *Muslims and Jews in France: History of a Conflict* (Princeton, NJ: Princeton University Press, 2014), 25; Winter and Prost, *René Cassin and Human Rights*. On SAPVIN, which until 1941 had been called Fédia Cassin & Cie, see ANOM, BA, 80ES 288; ACCM, MP 3181 / 08, Fédia Cassin & Cie to Chambre de Commerce de Marseille, 11 July 1941.

61 R. Caralp, "Trafic et moyens de transport entre la France et l'Algérie," *L'information géographique* 16:5 (1952): 198; Max Daumas, "L'essor du port de Sète," *L'information géographique* 24:4 (1960): 148–156.

62 White, "Roll Out the Barrel," 124–126; see also Boudot, *Les Schiaffino*, 413–419.

63 Though I have not been able to quantify the decline in the workforce, its proportions might be deduced from Francalfûts' barrel stocks, which went from 67,725 in 1935, to 34,756 in 1948, to 9,279 in 1954 (ANOM, BA, 11ES 273 bis).

64 Michel-François Auquebon, *La mécanisation de l'agriculture algérienne: Aspects agricoles, démographiques et économiques* (Constantine: Attali, 1953), 147; Campos, *Fleurus en Oranie*, 233; *Rapport de l'Algérie à la XXVIIe session officielle plénière du Comité de l'Office International du Vin* (Algiers: Imprimerie Officielle, 1948), 15–30. See also Céline Pessis, "The Tractor as a Tool of Development? The Mythologies and Legacies of Mechanised Tropical Agriculture in French Africa, 1944–1956," in Joseph M. Hodge, Gerald Hödl, and Martina Kopf, eds., *Developing Africa: Concepts and Practices in Twentieth-Century Colonialism* (Manchester: Manchester University Press, 2014), 179–203.

65 Auquebon, *La mécanisation de l'agriculture algérienne*, 135; AGMAfr, Durrieu 551, Rapport de Direction Générale pour le 4e trimestre 1952.

66 AGMAfr, Durrieu 550, Rapport de Direction Générale, Nov. 1947–June 1948; Durrieu 551, Rapport de Direction Générale, Oct. 1950–Sept. 1951.

67 Pessis, "The Tractor as a Tool of Development." For another view of machines, see Laura Ann Twagira, "'Robot Farmers' and Cosmopolitan Workers: Technological Masculinity and Agricultural Development in the French Soudan (Mali), 1945–68," *Gender and History* 26:3 (2014): 459–477.

68 Auquebon, *La mécanisation de l'agriculture algérienne*, 188. See also Gouvernement-Général de l'Algérie, *Le recensement de l'agriculture 1950–1951 en Algérie*, 5 vols. (Algiers: Imprimerie Officielle, 1956).

69 Paul Birebent, *Hommes, vignes, et vins de l'Algérie française* (Nice: Editions Gandini, 2007), 154–155. On the increasing use of machines in French vineyards at the same time, see Leo A. Loubère, *The Wine Revolution in France: The Twentieth Century* (Princeton, NJ: Princeton University Press, 1990), 44–60.

70 Michel Launay, *Paysans algériens 1960–2006*, 3rd ed. (Paris: Karthala, 2007), 89 (Launay refers to the brothers only as "Hubert" and "Lucien," but their true identity can be deduced from annual lists of wine producers); Auquebon, *La mécanisation de l'agriculture algérienne*, 131–133.

71 Mohammed Dib, *L'incendie* (Paris: Editions du Seuil, 1954), 74–79.

72 Paul Messerschmitt, *Vignes et vignerons* (Algiers: Editions du "Messager," 1944), 11.

73 Lefeuvre, *Chère Algérie*, 240–324; Samir Saul, *Intérêts économiques français et décolonisation de l'Afrique du Nord (1945–1962)* (Geneva: Droz, 2016), 35–37.

74 Catherine Hodeir, *Stratégies d'empire: Le grand patronat colonial face à la décolonisation* (Paris: Editions Belin, 2003), 173; William A. Hoisington Jr., *The Assassination of Jacques Lemaigre Dubreuil: A Frenchman between France and North Africa* (London: RoutledgeCurzon, 2005), 56–58.

75 ANOM, BA, 11ES 377, La Mitidja s.a., report to shareholders, 30 June 1942; proposition de crédit de campagne 1948–49. Pierre Germain had bought the property in 1919.

76 AGMAfr, Birraux 324, "Situation de la SIAH," 24 Feb. 1944; Birraux 331, documents on domaine d'El-Alia, 1938–1941.

77 AGMAfr, Durrieu 550, rapports de direction générale, Nov. 1947–June 1948 and July 1948–Sept. 1949; Durrieu 551, miscellaneous documents, including publicity materials. On housing in postwar Algiers, primarily for Algerians, see Zeynep Çelik, *Urban Forms and Colonial Confrontations: Algiers under French Rule* (Berkeley: University of California Press, 1997).

78 Paulin Borgeaud, *Mission remplie* (Paris: Editions Mazarine, 1971), 70.

79 Bouaboud, *L'Echo d'Alger*, 66.

80 Birebent, *Hommes, vignes et vins*, 204–206.

81 Isnard, "La vigne en Algérie," 943, 1012.

82 See the website of the Château Marquis de Terme (still owned by the Sénéclauze family) at www.chateau-marquis-de-terme.com; see also Grands vins de Provence de la famille Sénéclauze, press dossier, 2009.

83 ANOM, BA, 11ES 332, "Situation immobilière de M. Robert Germain," Apr. 1949; http://chateaudenolet.overblog.com, "La famille Germain (1941–1996)"; Jean-Paul Ernst, "Les agriculteurs rapatriés d'Afrique du Nord dans le Gers et le Lauragais," in Anne-Marie Magnou, Julien Martinez, and Jean-Paul Ernst, *Trois études sur le sud-ouest* (Paris: Pédone, 1968), 284. Eventually Robert Germain moved to the estate definitively and lived there until his death in 1986. He founded a successful fruit company, Vergers d'Aquitaine, whose fruit-conservation techniques were widely imitated.

84 Georges Bailly, *A la mémoire des agriculteurs de la plaine de Bône* (Nice: Self-published, 2009), 38–40. On the relatively backward state of the region in which Robert and Maurice Germain made their purchases, see Peter H. Amann, *The Corncribs of Buzet: Modernizing Agriculture in the French Southwest* (Princeton, NJ: Princeton University Press, 1990).

85 Bailly, *A la mémoire des agriculteurs de la plaine de Bône*, 60–62; "Etablissements Bertagna," *Le Temps*, 17 June 1929; www.domainebertagna.com. Claude Bertagna's father, Roland, was mayor of Mondovi and maintained the Bertagna vineyards on the plain until his death in 1958. The family of Maurice Germain kept its huge vineyards in the same area.

86 André Prenant, "Questions de structure urbaine dans trois faubourgs de Sidi-Bel-Abbès," *Bulletin de l'Association de géographes français* 257–258 (Mar.–Apr. 1956): 62–72. The neighborhood's population was 96 percent Muslim.

87 Emmanuel Sivan, *Communisme et nationalisme en Algérie, 1920–1962* (Paris: Presses de la Fondation Nationale des Sciences Politiques, 1976), 169–170. For more indicators on rural migrants and rural poverty in this period, see André Prenant, "La marginalisation sociale des Algériens, du 'Manifeste' à l'insurrection, aboutissement du système colonial," *Insaniyat* 12 (2001): 139–153; Pierre Bourdieu and Abdelmalek Sayad, *Le déracinement: La crise de l'agriculture traditionnelle en Algérie* (Paris: Les Editions du Minuit, 1964), 17–21; H. Isnard, "Structures de l'agriculture musulmane en Algérie à la veille de l'insurrection" (two parts), *Méditerranée* 1:2–3 (1960): 49–59, and 1:4 (1960): 43–57.

88 On the Statute, see Nouschi, *L'Algérie amère*, 180–188.

89 AGMAfr, Birraux 326, rapport de direction générale, May-Oct. 1947. For more on protests in 1947 and 1948, see ANOM, Oran, série continue 105 and Oran, 5I 162; Nora Benallègue-Chaouia, *Algérie: Mouvement ouvrier et question nationale, 1919–1954* (Algiers: Office des Publications Universitaires, 2005), 303–305, 310–312; Ahmed Abid, "Les grèves agricoles en Oranie à l'approche du 1er novembre 1954," *Cahiers du GREMAMO* 4 (1986–1987): 126–127.

90 ANOM, BA, 11ES 332, report to shareholders, 30 June 1950.

91 ANOM, BA, 11ES 377, report to shareholders, 12 June 1953; Oran, 5I 162, "Les 50 ouvriers agricoles du domaine de la Mitidja à Bou Zadjar (Oranie) remportent une victoire," *Alger républicain*, 11 Oct. 1951.

92 Allison Drew, *We Are No Longer in France: Communists in Colonial Algeria* (Manchester, UK: Manchester University Press, 2014),164–165; Launay, *Paysans algériens*, 64. The 1951 *Annuaire de la viticulture algérienne* shows that in the preceding year about one hundred individuals, none of them Algerian, declared a wine harvest in Descartes. In twenty-one cases, more than one member of the same family registered a declaration, and there were eight declarations by companies.

93 "Lamoricière: Main d'oeuvre indigene," *L'Echo d'Alger*, 11 Nov. 1936; ANOM, Oran, 1H 113, gendarmerie reports, 21 and 22 Sept. 1937; Oran, 5I 39, prefect of Oran to GG, 18 June 1938.

94 AMOM, Oran, 5I 162, sub-prefect of Tlemcen *arrondissement* to prefect of Oran, 14 Sept. 1951.

95 ANOM, Oran, 5I 162, Rapport sur les incidents de Descartes du 13 septembre 1951, plus other documents and press cuttings. See also Abid, "Les grèves agricoles en Oranie à l'approche du 1er novembre 1954," 127–132, though I cannot verify some of the details in his account.

96 On Boumédiène, see Houari Touati, *Dictionnaire biographique du mouvement ouvrier de l'Oranie* (Oran: Centre de Documentation des Sciences Humaines, 1981),106–107; on Berrahou, see Gallissot, *Algérie: Engagements sociaux et question nationale*, 136. Berrahou was first inspired to take up the cause by Mohamed Badsi.

97 For details on the trials and protests, see ANOM, Oran, 5I 162, including flyers from Apr. 1952 and report by Oran police, 25 Apr. 1952. On the faubourg Victor-Hugo, see M. Coquéry, "L'extension récente des quartiers musulmans d'Oran," *Bulletin de l'Association de géographes français* 39:307 (1962): 169–187; on the UFA, see Drew, *We Are No Longer in France*, 129, 157.

98 Abid, "Les grèves agricoles en Oranie à l'approche du 1er novembre 1954," 128; Benallègue-Chaouia, *Algérie: Mouvement ouvrier et question nationale*, 364.

99 Sivan, *Communisme et nationalisme en Algérie*, 187–189; Drew, *We Are No Longer in France*, 168.

100 ANOM, Oran, 5I 162, flyer, Apr. 1952. On Dien, see Alain Ruscio, *Les communistes français et la guerre d'Indochine (1944–1954)* (Paris: L'Harmattan, 1986), 253–255. On the ship protests in Oran, see Drew, *We Are No Longer in France*, 165–166; ANOM, Oran, série continue 2479, Chargement des navires en partance pour l'Indochine.

101 This strike seems to have originated more with followers of Messali Hadj. ANOM, Oran, 5I 162, Police des renseignements généraux, Oran, report on strike at Er-Rahel, 23 Aug. 1952. For more on Moroccan labor in Algeria at this time, see Oran, 5I 190, "Main d'oeuvre marocaine en Algérie," 5 Apr. 1954, and Mohamed Choukri's semi-autobiographical 1973 novel, *For Bread Alone*, trans. Paul Bowles (London: Telegram Books, 2006), 53–68. In general on Moroccan nationalism, see Susan Gilson Miller, *A History of Modern Morocco* (Cambridge: Cambridge University Press, 2013), 146–153.

102 Jean Vaujour, *De la révolte à la révolution: Aux premiers jours de la guerre d'Algérie* (Paris: Albin Michel, 1985), 203, 207.

103 Drew, *We Are No Longer in France*, 198–199; Gallissot, *Algérie: Engagements sociaux et question nationale*, 136.

104 From a collection of menus held at the CDHA.

105 On rigged elections, see Ageron, *Histoire de l'Algérie contemporaine*, 2:610–616; Nouschi, *L'Algérie amère*, 188–189; Ferhat Abbas, *Guerre et révolution d'Algérie*, vol. 1, *La nuit coloniale* (Paris: René Julliard, 1962), 182–183.

106 Quoted in Vaujour, *De la révolte à la révolution*, 149.

107 Jean Lacouture, *Mitterrand: Une histoire de Français*, vol. 1, *Les risques de l'escalade* (Paris: Editions du Seuil, 1998), 152–153. See also François Malye and Benjamin Stora, *François Mitterrand et la guerre d'Algérie* (Paris: Calmann-Lévy, 2010).

108 Abbas, *Guerre et révolution d'Algérie*, 1:188; Vaujour, *De la révolte à la révolution*, 147.

109 Vaujour, *De la révolte à la révolution*, 190; Jules Ferry, *Le gouvernement de l'Algérie* (Paris: Armand Colin, 1892), 8. On Ferry and Algerian vineyards, see Chapter 2 in this volume.

110 Michèle Barbier, *Le mythe Borgeaud: Henri Borgeaud (1895–1964). Trente ans d'histoire de l'Algérie française à travers un symbole* (Châteauneuf-les-Martigues: Editions Wallâda, 1995),134; Bernard Delpal, *Le silence des moines: Les Trappistes au XIXe siècle: France-Algérie-Syrie* (Paris: Beauchesne, 1998), 149; also Hodeir, *Stratégies d'empire*, 191–192.

111 Jules Roy, "Celui qui n'est pas parti," *L'Express*, 31 Jan. 1963, 11. Photos of the events can be found in Barbier, *Le mythe Borgeaud*, following 192.

112 Quoted in Michael K. Clark, *Algeria in Turmoil. The Rebellion: Its Causes, Its Effects, Its Future* (New York: Grosset & Dunlap, 1960), 117.

113 On the attacks and their toll, see Henri Alleg, ed., *La Guerre d'Algérie*, 3 vols. (Paris: Editions Messidor, 1981), 1:429–431; Vaujour, *De la révolte à la révolution*, 240–244. The military wing of the FLN was called the Armée de Libération Nationale (ALN); I elide the two in the account that follows.

114 Lacouture, *Mitterrand: Une histoire de Français*, 1:155; Vaujour, *De la révolte à la révolution*, 309–313.

115 Vaujour, *De la révolte à la révolution,* 200–202.

116 ANOM, BA, série continue 338, director of Mostaganem branch to governor of Banque de l'Algérie, 26 Nov. 1954; Vaujour, *De la révolte à la révolution,* 207–209. A Monsonégo property had been attacked in 1937, too: AWO, 1F 289.

117 General histories of the war include Sylvie Thénault, *Histoire de la guerre d'indépendance algérienne* (Paris: Flammarion, 2012); and Martin Evans, *Algeria: France's Undeclared War* (Oxford: Oxford University Press, 2012).

118 ANOM, Constantine, 4Q 74, dossier 3, gendarmerie report for mayor of Philippeville, 24 June 1955.

119 On the night of May 6–7, 1956, for example, there was a coordinated attack on over fifty farms in the Aïn-Témouchent region. See Launay, *Paysans algériens,* 172–178; "47 fermes incendiées et pillées dans les régions d'Aïn-Témouchent et de Béni-Saf," *L'Echo d'Oran,* 8 May 1956.

120 Quoted in Abbas, *Guerre et révolution d'Algérie,* 1:69.

121 For an example of crop destruction from Grande Kabylie, see Alleg, *La guerre d'Algérie,* 2:156; for napalm, see, for example, Launay, *Paysans algériens,* 182.

122 ANOM, BA, 80ES 329, report to shareholders, 18 Sept. 1957.

123 See Claire Mauss-Copeaux, *Algérie, 20 août 1955: Insurrection, répression, massacres* (Paris: Payot, 2011); Charles-Robert Ageron, "L'insurrection du 20 août 1955 dans le Nord-Constantinois," in *Genèse de l'Algérie algérienne,* 535–553.

124 ANOM, Constantine, 4Q 95, dossier 17, multiple documents.

125 ANOM, Constantine, 4Q 76, dossier 4, multiple documents. As economic targets themselves, countless farm animals were killed during the war.

126 ANOM, Oran, série continue 554, administrator of commune mixte de Ténès to prefect of Algiers, 7 June 1955, and police report of 10 June 1955.

127 On the French side, see Pierre-Alfred-Hippolyte-André-René Pinaud, *L'alcoolisme chez les Arabes en Algérie* (Bordeaux: Imprimerie-Librairie de l'Université, 1933); on the Algerian side, see ANOM, Alger, 4I 186, documents on the Ligue anti-alcoolique musulmane, 1933–1935. For Tunisian critiques, see Nessim Znaien, "Le vin et la viticulture en Tunisie coloniale (1881–1956): Entre synapse et apartheid," *French Cultural Studies* 26:2 (2015): 146.

128 ANOM, 81F 1622, decree of 25 Oct. 1941 and letters of thanks from Nov. and Dec. On Vichy's anti-alcohol campaigns in France, see Patricia E. Prestwich, *Drink and the Politics of Social Reform: Antialcoholism in France since 1870* (Palo Alto, CA: Society for the Promotion of Science and Scholarship, 1988), 246–256.

129 ANMT, 2001 026 3096 CFAT, multiple documents, including Expertise effectuée dans la région de Palestro, 8 Apr. 1958. On Palestro in 1956, see Raphaëlle Branche, *L'embuscade de Palestro: Algérie 1956* (Paris: Le Grand Livre du Mois, 2010), 15–40.

130 Neil MacMaster, "The 'Silent Native': *Attentisme,* Being Compromised, and Banal Terror during the Algerian War of Independence, 1954–1962," in Martin Thomas, ed., *The French Colonial Mind,* vol. 2, *Violence, Military Encounters, and Colonialism* (Lincoln: University of Nebraska Press, 2011), 286–288.

131 Launay, *Paysans algériens,* 179. The example is from Aïn-el-Arba in the department of Oran.

132 "Assassinat près de Cherchell," *L'Echo d'Oran*, 8 Sept. 1956; Alleg, *La guerre d'Algérie*, 2:135. On the war in this area, see Kamel Kateb, Nacer Melhani, and M'hamed Rebah, *Les déracinés de Cherchell: Camps de regroupement dans la guerre d'Algérie (1954–1962)* (Paris: INED, 2018).

133 ANOM, Oran, série continue 5237, Marcel Petit to prefect of Tlemcen, 7 and 22 Apr. 1957. Launay discusses similar incidents in summer 1956 as well as foot-dragging in *Paysans algériens*, 90, 178–180.

134 ANOM, BA, 11ES 201 bis, report to shareholders, 26 Apr. 1956.

135 For example, see photos at https://sites.google.com/site/117erienalgeriephototheque /home/fondouk.

136 See, for example, ANOM, GGA, 14CAB 75, note à l'attention du directeur du Cabinet Militaire, 7 Sept. 1959, on a property at Les Issers.

137 ANOM, Oran, série continue 5237, miscellaneous documents on surveillance and protection of farms; Launay, *Paysans algériens*, 180.

138 See, for example, ANOM, Constantine, 5Q 413, Sous-préfet de Mila to Inspecteur général de l'administration en mission extraordinaire, 9 Aug. 1957.

139 ANOM, Oran, série continue 5237, Général de division Dodelier to Général d'armée, 28 Aug. 1958.

140 David Montgomery Hart, *The Aith Waryaghar of the Moroccan Rif: An Ethnography and History* (Tucson: University of Arizona Press, 1976), 92–93; Guy Pervillé and Cécile Marin, *Atlas de la guerre d'Algérie* (Paris: Autrement, 2003), 34–35.

141 See ANOM, BA, 11ES 332, especially reports to shareholders dated 19 June 1957, 3 May 1958, 8 June 1959. (In 1958 a Muslim worker was murdered, there was an act of arson, and ten hectares of vines were sabotaged.) See also Launay, *Paysans algériens*, 80–81, 184–188. Colonists in other parts of Algeria also benefited from having *camps de regroupement* near their properties. See Michel Cornaton, *Les camps de regroupement de la guerre d'Algérie*, 2nd ed. (Paris: L'Harmattan, 1998), 94–95, 156–157; Bourdieu and Sayad, *Le déracinement*, 38–40.

142 For troop numbers, see Pervillé and Marin, *Atlas de la guerre d'Algérie*, 30.

143 William B. Cohen, ed., *Robert Delavignette on the French Empire* (Chicago: University of Chicago Press, 1977), 119–123; Raphaëlle Branche, *La torture et l'armée pendant la Guerre d'Algérie, 1954–1962* (Paris: Gallimard, 2001), 157–160, quotation at 159; and Hafid Keramane, *La pacification: Livre noir de six années de guerre en Algérie* (Lausanne: La Cité Editeur, 1960), 62–63, a book that also documents torture at certain vineyards in the vicinity of Algiers.

144 The documentary aired on Canal Algérie.

145 ANOM, Constantine, 4Q 76, dossier 4, report dated 12 Feb. 1958; CDHA, 737 BRU, "79 armoiries des communes de l'Algérie."

146 Alain Darbel, Jean-Paul Rivet, Claude Seibel, Pierre Bourdieu, *Travail et travailleurs en Algérie* (Paris: Mouton, 1963), 145–149; Jean Despois, "La population algérienne au 31 octobre 1954," *Annales de géographie* 65:347 (1956): 55–56. See also François Tomas, *Annaba et sa région: Organisation de l'espace dans l'extrême-Est algérien* (Saint-Etienne: F. Tomas, 1977), 311–313.

147 Société des Fermes Françaises de Tunisie, *Vingt-cinq ans de colonisation nord-africaine* (Paris: Société d'éditions géographiques, maritimes et coloniales, 1925),

preface by Saurin dated 1920, xx; Ageron, *Histoire de l'Algérie contemporaine,* 2:474–477; Claude Collot, *Les institutions de l'Algérie pendant la période coloniale (1830–1962)* (Paris: CNRS, 1987), 119. For a suggestive example, see Christine Mussard, "Une 'décolonisation' par défaut? Le cas de Lacroix, centre de colonisation de la commune mixte de La Calle (1920–1950)," *French Colonial History* 13 (2012): 55–72.

148 L. Boyer-Banse, "Le crédit agricole et la colonisation en Algérie," in *Congrès de la colonisation rurale, Alger 26–29 mai 1930, 2ᵉ partie: Les problèmes économiques et sociaux posés par la colonisation* (Algiers: Victor Heintz, 1930), 366–370.

149 Isnard, "La vigne en Algérie," 950. This was a familiar refrain in other parts of the empire in the period after World War I; see, for example, Albert Londres, *Terre d'ébène* (Paris: Albin Michel, 1929), 13.

150 Reboux, *L'Algérie et ses vins,* 31–33.

151 ANOM, BA, 11ES 137, multiple documents, esp. director of Algiers branch to director of Bank of Algeria, 15 Mar. 1937; *Annuaire de la viticulture algérienne,* 1951.

152 See the street plans of Sidi-Bel-Abbès at www.mekerra.fr.

153 Gordon Wright, *Rural Revolution in France: The Peasantry in the Twentieth Century* (Stanford, CA: Stanford University Press, 1964), 114–115.

154 Jean Pelegri, *Les oliviers de la justice* (Paris: Gallimard, 1959), 124.

155 Jules Roy, *The War in Algeria,* trans. Richard Howard (New York: Grove Press, 1961), 120.

156 Ibid., 29–30.

157 Hélène Brun-Puginier and Philippe Roudié, *Château Carbonnieux: Sept siècles dans les Graves* (Paris: Stock, 1999), 140–145.

158 See Pierre Laffont, "Rendez-vous au Mexique," *L'Echo d'Oran,* 7 Mar. 1956, and the restatement of the newspaper's policy in the *petites annonces classées,* 1 June 1956. I am grateful to Christophe Campos for pointing this out to me. Also see Campos, *Fleurus en Oranie,* 620; on absenteeism, see Launay, *Paysans algériens,* 84.

159 Campos, *Fleurus en Oranie,* 250; *Annuaire de la viticulture algérienne,* 1951.

160 Campos, *Fleurus en Oranie,* 250–254, 618. More small-scale studies like the one by Campos would be invaluable. For an example of what such studies might achieve, see Kathleen Neils Conzen, "Peasant Pioneers: Generational Succession among German Farmers in Frontier Minnesota," in Steven Hahn and Jonathan Prude, eds., *The Countryside in the Age of Capitalist Transformation* (Chapel Hill: University of North Carolina Press, 1985), 259–292.

161 ANOM, Constantine, 4Q 47, dossier 8 (concerning a widow who owned property in Jemmapes but lived in Constantine); 4Q 46, dossiers 8 and 9; 4Q 74, dossier 5. It is unfortunate that Constantine appears to be the only department for which compensation dossiers survive or are available.

162 See, for example, *Annuaire de la viticulture algérienne,* 1951, communes of Jemmapes and Jemmapes *mixte.*

163 Hildebert Isnard, "Vineyards and Social Structure in Algeria," *Diogenes* 27 (1959): 80. For other plans to partition Algeria, see Alain Peyrefitte, *Faut-il partager l'Algérie?* (Paris: Plon, 1962); and Arthur Asseraf, "'A New Israel': Colonial Comparisons and the Algerian Partition That Never Happened," *French Historical Studies* 41:1 (2018):

95–120. An 18:1 population imbalance was still more favorable to Europeans than in other colonies of settlement like Southern Rhodesia (Zimbabwe), where the ratio in 1939 was 25:1. Dane Kennedy, *Islands of White: Settler Society and Culture in Kenya and Southern Rhodesia, 1890–1939* (Durham, NC: Duke University Press, 1987), 1.

164 Geneviève Gavignaud-Fontaine, *Le Languedoc viticole, la Méditerranée et l'Europe au siècle dernier (XXe)* (Montpellier: Publications de l'Université Paul-Valéry, 2000), 149–173; Charles K. Warner, *The Winegrowers of France and the Government since 1875* (New York: Columbia University Press, 1960), 180–189; Andrew W. M. Smith, *Terror and Terroir: The Winegrowers of the Languedoc and Modern France* (Manchester, UK: Manchester University Press, 2016), 63–67. For an unfriendly view of the Midi from Algeria, see Paul Bellat, *Cent ans d'Algérie* (Paris: Editions Debresse, 1955), 154–162.

165 ANOM, GGA, 10 CAB 247, GG Léonard to Minister of Interior and Min Ag, 1 June 1954. On the drive for quality in France, see Bohling, *The Sober Revolution*.

166 For the broader context, see Herrick Chapman, *France's Long Reconstruction: In Search of the Modern Republic* (Cambridge, MA: Harvard University Press, 2018).

167 Maurice Dupont, "Les intérêts français contre l'intérêt de la France en Afrique du Nord," *Esprit* 192 and 193–194 (July and Aug.–Sept. 1952): 45–65, 321–352.

168 Claude Bourdet, "Les maîtres de l'Afrique du Nord," *Les Temps Modernes,* June 1952, 2259.

169 "Les maîtres de l'Algérie," *L'Express,* 22 Jan. 1955. This view was not rejected by all colonists, even conservative ones. For the militant royalist (and Mitidja wine producer) Robert Martel, for example, the likes of Borgeaud and the Germain family had caused trouble by "monopolizing the wealth" of Algeria. Claude Mouton, *La contre-révolution en Algérie,* 2nd ed. (Chiré-en-Montreuil: Diffusion de la Pensée Française, 1972), 119–120.

170 Quoted in Christopher Harrison, "French Attitudes to Empire and the Algerian War," *African Affairs* 82:326 (1983): 80. See also Bohling, *The Sober Revolution,* 104–105.

171 On integrationism, see Todd Shepard, *The Invention of Decolonization: The Algerian War and the Remaking of France* (Ithaca, NY: Cornell University Press, 2006).

172 Barbier, *Le mythe Borgeaud,* 171–172; Jacques Bouveresse, *Un parlement colonial? Les Délégations financières algériennes, 1898–1945,* 2 vols. (Mont-Saint-Aignan: Publications des Universités de Rouen et du Havre, 2008 / 2010), 1:363; ANOM, BA, 11ES 201 bis, especially eulogy in report to shareholders, 30 Apr. 1957. On Virgile Froger, see Ecole de droit d'Alger, *Revue algérienne et tunisienne de législation et jurisprudence 2e partie* (1887): 55–58.

173 See Marta Musso, "'Oil Will Set Us Free': The Hydrocarbon Industry and the Algerian Decolonization Process," in Andrew W. M. Smith and Chris Jeppesen, eds., *Britain, France and the Decolonization of Africa: Future Imperfect?* (London: UCL Press, 2017), 62–84.

174 ANOM, 81F 731, L'agriculture algérienne et le marché commun, Oct. 1958; 81F 2363, Organisation du marché des vins et spiritueux, 28 Mar. 1958. See also Peo Hansen and Stefan Jonsson, *Eurafrica: The Untold History of European Integration and Colonialism* (London: Bloomsbury, 2014), 226–234; Megan Brown, "Drawing Algeria into Europe: Shifting French Policy and the Treaty of Rome (1951–1964)," *Modern and Contemporary France* 25:2 (2017): 191–208; Bohling, *The Sober Revolution,* 109–110.

175 Newsreel accessed at https://www.youtube.com/watch?v=t6dNsyzDDsI. On Berliet in Algeria, see Saul, *Intérêts économiques français et décolonisation de l'Afrique du Nord*, 351–360; Lefeuvre, *Chère Algérie*, 476–482.

176 Muriam Haleh Davis, "Restaging mise en valeur: 'Postwar Imperialism' and the Plan de Constantine," *Review of Middle East Studies* 44:2 (2010): 176–186; Chapman, *France's Long Reconstruction*, 278–290; and, for a good sense of the plan's ambitions, Présidence du Conseil—Délégation générale en Algérie, *Documents algériens 1959* (Paris: Editions arts et métiers graphiques, 1959).

177 Barbier, *Le mythe Borgeaud*, 197.

178 Interview with Paul Bosc, Niagara-on-the-Lake, Ontario, 5 June 2011. On Bosc's career, see Linda Bramble, *Niagara's Wine Visionaries: Profiles of the Pioneering Winemakers* (Toronto: J. Lorimer, 2009), 82–101.

179 The winery was in the district of Souf-el-Tell, and as of 2013 was still being used for its intended purpose.

180 AWA, 4H 214, decree of 3 Sept. 1958.

181 Jacques Vigna, "Le vin en Algérie: L'histoire de 'Sidi Brahim'," *Mémoire vive* 49:3–4 (2011).

182 Marc Coppin, "Les ports de la Côte d'Opale pendant la guerre d'Algérie," *Outre-Mers* 99:374–375 (2012), 306–309.

183 Quoted in Boudot, *Les Schiaffino*, 521. See also Thierry Fillaut, *Les Bretons et l'alcool (XIXe-XXe siècle)* (Rennes: Editions ENSP, 1991).

184 H. Isnard, "Le commerce extérieur de l'Algérie en 1960," *Méditerranée* 2:3 (1961): 94. See also Roger Lequy, "L'agriculture algérienne de 1954 à 1962," *Revue de l'Occident musulman et de la Méditerranée* 8 (1970): 78–79.

185 ANMT, 2001 026 3096 CFAT, report on Domaine d'El-Faroun, 7 May 1957; AGMAfr, Durrieu 549, report of Conseil d'administration, 10 Dec. 1957; Birraux 335, "La main-d'oeuvre agricole d'un domaine agricole," Dec. 1945. The CAPER did not have much success, not least because the FLN did not want it to; Algerians who acquired land by that route became instant targets. See Abdellatif Benachenhou, *Formation du sous-développement en Algérie*, 6th ed. (Algiers: Office des Publications Universitaires, 2009), 376–381; Lequy, "L'agriculture algérienne de 1954 à 1962," 66; Lefeuvre, *Chère Algérie*, 375–376.

186 AGMAfr, Durrieu 549, Pierre de Roux to Père Tiquet, 31 July 1958; ANOM, BA, 11ES 316, reports to shareholders, 8 June 1959 and 10 June 1960. On the airport and other economic developments, see Jean-François Troin and R. Laurent, "Aspects de l'infrastructure économique de l'Algérie," *Méditerranée* 3:3 (1962): 53–68.

187 AGMAfr, Durrieu 552 bis, report to shareholders, 3 June 1961.

188 ANOM, BA, 11ES 332, reports to shareholders, 9 June 1960 and 19 June 1961.

189 ANOM, BA, 80ES 329, report to shareholders, 25 Sept. 1959, and ANMT, 65AQ J296, report dated 28 Sept. 1961. Evidence like this supports the argument made by Samir Saul in *Intérêts économiques français et décolonisation de l'Afrique du Nord* that capitalists had far from given up on Algeria even late into the war of independence, in contrast to what the work of scholars like Jacques Marseille and Daniel Lefeuvre might lead one to believe.

190 On the diplomatic dimensions of the war, see Matthew Connelly, *A Diplomatic Revolution: Algeria's Fight for Independence and the Origins of the Post-Cold War Era* (Oxford: Oxford University Press, 2002).

191 Roy, *The War in Algeria*, 25, 30; Launay, *Paysans algériens*, 171.

192 Roger Mas, *Sous-préfet d'Aïn-Témouchent (La source des chacals) 1962–1963: Témoignage* (Paris: L'Harmattan, 2001), 139; Mouton, *La contre-révolution en Algérie*, 204–205.

193 Roy, "Celui qui n'est pas parti," 11.

194 Françoise Brun, *Les Français d'Algérie dans l'agriculture du Midi méditerranéen: Etude géographique* (Gap: Editions Ophrys, 1976), 40.

195 Roy, *The War in Algeria*, 123–124.

196 Quoted in Antony Thrall Sullivan, *Thomas-Robert Bugeaud: France and Algeria, 1784–1849. Politics, Power, and the Good Society* (Hamden, CT: Archon, 1983), 75; on this period, see Charles-André Julien, *Histoire de l'Algérie contemporaine,* vol. 1, *La conquête et les débuts de la colonisation (1827–1871)* (Paris: Presses Universitaires de France, 1964), 106–163.

7. PULLING UP ROOTS

1 Michèle Barbier, *Le mythe Borgeaud: Henri Borgeaud (1895–1964). Trente ans d'histoire de l'Algérie française à travers un symbole* (Châteauneuf-les-Martigues: Editions Wallâda, 1995), 226–228, 230–231; Peter Braestrup, "Algerians Seize Big French Farm," *New York Times,* 1 Apr. 1963. These two accounts differ somewhat on the sequence of events. See also Jules Roy, "Celui qui n'est pas parti," *L'Express,* 31 Jan. 1963; "Chronologie 1963: Vie économique, sociale et culturelle," *Annuaire de l'Afrique du Nord* 2 (1963): 689; on the Chapeau de Gendarme, "Manager Bitter as Algerians Seize a Rich Farm," *New York Times,* 12 Apr. 1963. Borgeaud moved to Normandy but died in May 1964.

2 Barbier, *Le mythe Borgeaud,* 69, 145, 191–192; AWA, 1H 75. On Nasser's time in Algeria, see Jeffrey James Byrne, *Mecca of Revolution: Algeria, Decolonization, and the Third World Order* (New York: Oxford University Press, 2016), 183–184.

3 There is an extensive sociological literature from the 1960s and 1970s on Algerian *autogestion.* Ian Clegg, *Workers' Self-Management in Algeria* (New York: Monthly Review Press, 1971) provides a clear account; and Serge Koulytchizky, *L'autogestion, l'homme et l'état: L'expérience algérienne* (Paris: Mouton, 1974) much useful data.

4 H. Isnard, "La viticulture algérienne: colonisation et décolonisation," *Méditerranée* 4 (1975): 5.

5 Koulytchizky, *L'autogestion, l'homme et l'état,* 36. For a valuable study of the practicalities involved in the transition from French Algeria to independent Algeria, see Andrew Harold Bellisari, "Colonial Remainders: France, Algeria, and the Culture of Decolonization (1958–1970)" (PhD diss, Harvard University, 2018).

6 Thomas L. Blair, *"The Land to Those That Work It": Algeria's Experiment in Workers' Management* (New York: Doubleday, 1969), 41 (Blair misrenders the name as Malevalle); *Annuaire de la viticulture algérienne,* 1955; Clegg, *Workers' Self-Management in Algeria,* 44–52.

7 Clegg, *Workers' Self-Management in Algeria,* 61–65; Annie Krieger, "Les prémices d'une réforme agraire an Algérie," in François d'Arcy, Annie Krieger, and Alain Marill, *Essais sur l'économie de l'Algérie nouvelle* (Paris: Presses Universitaires de France, 1965), 115–117.

8 Translation of section 1, article 1 of 22 Mar. 1963 decree in Clegg, *Workers' Self-Management in Algeria*, 201. See also Koulytchizky, *L'autogestion, l'homme et l'état*, 87–91.

9 "Chronologie 1963: Vie économique, sociale et culturelle," *Annuaire de l'Afrique du Nord* 2 (1963): 689. See also Michel Launay, "Dialogue avec Amar Ouzegane" [Algeria's first minister of agriculture], *Esprit* 319:7–8 (July–Aug. 1963): 27–28. It is worth noting that in the early decades of the French conquest the state had taken control of much land it declared "vacant." John Ruedy, *Land Policy in Colonial Algeria: The Origins of the Rural Public Domain* (Berkeley: University of California Press, 1967), 99.

10 On the Jourdan estate, see Kazuo Miyaji, *Kacem Ali: Monographie d'un domaine autogéré de la plaine de Mitidja (Algérie)* (Tokyo: Institute for the Study of Languages and Cultures of Asia and Africa, 1976), 33 (Miyaji refers to Jourdan only as "J.," but I have deduced his identity from other sources); "Chronologie 1963: Vie économique, sociale et culturelle," *Annuaire de l'Afrique du Nord* 2 (1963): 743; Ben Bella quoted in Blair, *"The Land to Those That Work It,"* 56–57; AGMAfr, Durrieu 552 bis, A. de Sèze to Père Fisset, 6 Jan. and 18 Mar. 1964. (The SIAH had by then changed its name to the Société Immobilière et Agricole France-Méditerranée.) For other departures in late 1963, see, for example, Campos, *Fleurus en Oranie*, 624–625.

11 Grigori Lazarev, "Remarques sur l'autogestion agricole en Algérie," in Lazarev and Jacques Dubois, *Institutions et développement agricole du Maghreb* (Paris: Presses universitaires de France, 1965), 28–30.

12 Marc Côte, "Un bel exemple de reconversion du vignoble: Le domaine 'Bouglouf Braïek' (Bassin de Skikda)," *Annales algériennes de géographie* 4:8 (1969–1970): 74. Morel's father, Louis, founded the newspaper in 1908 and bought the estate after World War I.

13 On domains named after local "martyrs," see Claudine Chaulet, *La Mitidja autogérée: Enquête sur les exploitations autogérées agricoles d'une region d'Algérie, 1968–1970* (Algiers: SNED, 1971), 47.

14 Names from the Algiers region in AWA, 1H 72 and 73, *vendange* declarations 1967–1968; Georges Mutin, *La Mitidja: Décolonisation et espace géographique* (Paris: Editions du CNRS, 1977), 185.

15 Côte, "Un bel exemple de reconversion," 76.

16 Miyaji, *Kacem Ali*, 30, 51; see also Mutin, *La Mitidja*, 317. In 1980 El Asnam was renamed again and became Chlef.

17 Hamid Temmar, "Le choix des organes de l'autogestion dans l'Algérie de l'ouest," *Revue algérienne des sciences juridiques, politiques et économiques* 4 (Dec. 1964): 28.

18 Roger Mas, *Sous-préfet d'Aïn-Témouchent (La source des chacals) 1962–1963: Témoignage* (Paris: L'Harmattan, 2001), 58. On technical cooperation, see Bellisari, "Colonial Remainders," 258–260; Phillip C. Naylor, *France and Algeria: A History of Decolonization and Transformation* (Gainesville: University Press of Florida, 2000), 62–63.

19 Georges Bailly, *A la mémoire des agriculteurs de la plaine de Bône* (Nice: Self-published, 2009), 105. For more names of *coopérants* involved with winemaking, see AWA, 1H 73, Direction départementale de l'agriculture d'Alger, meeting of 19 July 1968; 1H

75, Répartition du personnel technique ONCV-IVV-DAW pour la campagne vendange-vinification 1971.

20 Mas, *Sous-préfet d'Aïn-Témouchent,* 105.

21 Daniel Guérin, *L'Algérie qui se cherche* (Paris: Présence Africaine, 1964), 38–39. On the importance of this domain to the Germain family, see ANOM, BA, 11ES 287, director of Algiers branch to director of Banque de l'Algérie, 15 Feb. 1908. On anarchists and Algerian *autogestion,* see David Porter, *Eyes to the South: French Anarchists and Algeria* (Oakland, CA: AK Press, 2011), 90–136.

22 Koulytchizky, *L'autogestion, l'homme et l'état,* 171–176; Mutin, *La Mitidja,* 176–177; Clegg, *Workers' Self-Management in Algeria,* 151–153. On the coup, see Naylor, *France and Algeria,* 72–73. As of 1969, for example, there was a ninety-three-hectare vineyard in El Harrach controlled by a cooperative of ex-combatants; AWA, 1H 74, harvest declarations, El Harrach, 27 Nov. 1969.

23 See, for example, Blair, *"The Land to Those That Work It,"* 77–78; Chaulet, *La Mitidja autogérée,* 258–282.

24 Isnard, "La viticulture algérienne," 6.

25 For good case studies, see Côte, "Un bel exemple de reconversion"; and Miyaji, *Kacem Ali.* On the problem of broken-down tractors and machines, see Lazarev, "Remarques sur l'autogestion agricole en Algérie," 56–58; Ahmed Mahsas, *L'autogestion en Algérie: Données politiques de ses premières étapes et de son application* (Paris: Editions Anthropos, 1975), 180–182, 288–289.

26 Mouloud Achour, *Les dernières vendanges* (Algiers: SNED, 1975), quotations at 44, 45.

27 Chaulet, *La Mitidja autogérée,* 258–282, quotations at 281.

28 For a brief overview, see Naylor, *France and Algeria,* 36–41; and for more detail, René Gallissot, ed., *Les accords d'Evian: En conjoncture et en longue durée* (Paris: Karthala, 1987); Guy Pervillé, *Les accords d'Evian (1962): Succès ou échec de la réconciliation franco-algérienne (1954–2012)* (Paris: Armand Colin, 2012).

29 Geneviève Gavignaud-Fontaine, *Le Languedoc viticole, la Méditerranée et l'Europe au siècle dernier (XXe)* (Montpellier: Publications de l'Université Paul-Valéry, 2000), 213–214; Andrew W. M. Smith, *Terror and Terroir: The Winegrowers of the Languedoc and Modern France* (Manchester, UK: Manchester University Press, 2016), 96. Smith shows how service in the Algerian War helped to radicalize many young Midi vignerons.

30 ADH, 6ETP 1198, miscellaneous documents on 1963 wine protests; F.-H. de Virieu, "Les viticulteurs de l'Hérault annoncent qu'ils 'ne capituleront pas devant le gouvernement,'" *Le Monde,* 29 Oct. 1963.

31 Jacques Lamalle, *Jean-Baptiste Doumeng: Le milliardaire rouge* (Paris: Editions Jean-Claude Lattès, 1980), 58–62; see also "Les vins algériens sur les marchés français," *El-Moudjahid,* 12 Apr. 1967, reprinted in *Annuaire de l'Afrique du Nord* 6 (1967): 792–793. Doumeng managed to profit from helping Algerians deal with French wine merchants.

32 Charles Pelras, "Goulien, commune rurale du Cap Sizun (Finistère): Etude d'ethnologie globale," *Bulletins et mémoires de la Société d'anthropologie de Paris,* series 11, 10:3–4 (1966): 385.

33 On this dilemma, see Ahmed Akkache, *Capitaux étrangers et libération économique: L'expérience algérienne* (Paris: François Maspero, 1971), 68.

34 Maurice Parodi, "Chronique économique: Algérie," *Annuaire de l'Afrique du Nord* 3 (1964): 253–254; Mouloud Sloughi, "Agriculture et coopération algéro-française," in Gallissot, *Les accords d'Evian*, 174–177; H. Isnard, "La viticulture nord-africaine," *Annuaire de l'Afrique du Nord* 4 (1965), 43–47; Keith Sutton, "Algeria's Vineyards: An Islamic Dilemma and a Problem of Decolonization," *Journal of Wine Research* 1:2 (1990): 107. For some broader context, see Muriam Haleh Davis, "North Africa and the Common Agricultural Policy: From Colonial Pact to European Integration," in Davis and Thomas Serres, eds., *North Africa and the Making of Europe: Governance Institutions and Culture* (London: Bloomsbury Academic, 2018), 43–65.

35 Gavignaud-Fontaine, *Le Languedoc viticole*, 225–229. On the CRAV, see Smith, *Terror and Terroir*.

36 "La cooperation algéro-française: Les vins algériens au dossier des prochaines négociations," *El-Moudjahid*, 14 Apr. 1967, reprinted in *Annuaire de l'Afrique du Nord* 6 (1967): 794–795.

37 ADLA, 1ET H 238, Nantes chamber of commerce to ministers of industry and agriculture, 8 May 1967.

38 Mahfoud Bennoune and Ali El-Kenz, *Le hasard et l'histoire: Entretiens avec Belaïd Abdesselam*, 2 vols. (Algiers: Editions ENAG, 1990), 1:387.

39 Bennoune and El-Kenz, *Le hasard et l'histoire*, 1:387–391; Belaïd Abdesselam, *Le pétrole et le gaz naturel en Algérie* (Rouïba: Editions ANEP, 2012), 532–533; Pierre Judet, "Chronique économique," *Annuaire de l'Afrique du Nord* 8 (1969): 527–528; Koulytchizky, *L'autogestion, l'homme et l'état*, 221–222; Mutin, *La Mitidja*, 248; Sutton, "Algeria's Vineyards," 107–108; GARF, fond 5446, opis 103, delo 913, list 27, 37–38.

40 GARF, fond 5446, opis 103, delo 913, list 63–64, 68.

41 GARF, fond 5446, opis 103, delo 913, list 12. The Ukrainian port of Illichivsk is now called Chornomorsk.

42 I am very grateful to Marina Dobronovskaya for her recollections and assistance with this section.

43 Bennoune and El-Kenz, *Le hasard et l'histoire*, 1:389.

44 Gavignaud-Fontaine, *Le Languedoc viticole*, 252–262; see also Joseph Bohling, *The Sober Revolution: Appellation Wine and the Transformation of France* (Ithaca, NY: Cornell University Press, 2018), 169–171, which shows how the EEC's position against Algerian wine hardened in October 1971.

45 Speech of 13 Apr. 1971 reproduced in Chaulet, *La Mitidja autogérée*, 339–346.

46 See Abdesselam, *Le pétrole et le gaz naturel en Algérie*, 387–433; André Nouschi, *L'Algérie amère, 1914–1994* (Paris: Editions de la Maison des sciences de l'homme, 1995), 250–253.

47 Chaulet, *La Mitidja autogérée*, 345–346.

48 Côte, "Un bel exemple de reconversion," 76. On uprooting before 1971, see also Mutin, *La Mitidja*, 246; Adrien Zeller, "Le problème du vin: Une solution de coopération Algéro-Française," *Développement et civilisations* 33 (Mar. 1968): 26; Mohamed Boudjellal Aouf, "La conversion-reconstitution du vignoble algérien," *Options Méditerranéennes* 12 (Apr. 1972): 65–67.

49 Mutin, *La Mitidja*, 212.

50   François Tomas, *Annaba et sa région: Organisation de l'espace dans l'extrême-Est al-gérien* (Saint-Etienne: F. Tomas, 1977), 376.

51   AWA, 1H 75, circular from minister of agriculture and agrarian reform, 27 Aug. 1971: "Directive concernant le déroulement de la campagne vendange-vinification." The French market for *vins de coupage* had tightened up since 1967: see Gavignaud-Fontaine, *Le Languedoc viticole*, 228–229; Zeller, "Le problème du vin," 26.

52   Statistics from D. Boubals, "Le problème de la reconversion du vignoble algérien," *Bulletin de l'Office international de la vigne et du vin* 578 (Apr. 1979): 310; Sutton, "Algeria's Vineyards," 105. (The figures in these sources do not entirely align.) On the workforce, see Abdellatif Benachenhou, *L'exode rural en Algérie* (Algiers: SNED, no date), 67–68, 72–76; Mahfoud Bennoune, *The Making of Contemporary Algeria, 1830–1987* (Cambridge: Cambridge University Press, 1988), 209. For a case study of yields, see Miyaji, *Kacem Ali*, 90.

53   Achour, *Les dernières vendanges*, 98. See also Mutin, *La Mitidja*, 271–276, 297.

54   Giovanni Balcet and Michel Nancy, "Chronique économique: Algérie," *Annuaire de l'Afrique du Nord* 14 (1975): 514.

55   The following paragraph is based largely on Will D. Swearingen, "Agricultural Poli-cies and the Growing Food Security Crisis," in John P. Entelis and Phillip C. Naylor, eds., *State and Society in Algeria* (Boulder, CO: Westview Press, 1992), 117–149; John P. Entelis, *Algeria: The Revolution Institutionalized* (Boulder, CO: Westview Press, 1986), 131–154; Karen Pfeifer, *Agrarian Reform under State Capitalism in Al-geria* (Boulder, CO: Westview Press, 1985); Nouschi, *L'Algérie amère*, 253–262; Bennoune, *The Making of Contemporary Algeria*, 176–217; Benachenhou, *L'exode rural en Algérie*.

56   I base this on figures in Pfeifer, *Agrarian Reform under State Capitalism in Algeria*, 32–33, not Nouschi, *L'Algérie amère*, 260, which suggests a decline in total production.

57   Bennoune, *The Making of Contemporary Algeria*, 212; Michel Nancy, "Algérie: Chro-nique économique," *Annuaire de l'Afrique du Nord* 16 (1977): 558; Luis Martinez, *The Violence of Petro-Dollar Regimes: Algeria, Iraq and Libya*, trans. Cynthia Schoch (New York: Columbia University Press, 2012), 24–28. For a useful overview of agri-cultural production at the time of Boumediène's death, see Marc Côte, "Le produit agricole algérien," *L'Espace géographique* 8:2 (Apr.–June 1979): 143–152.

58   On "repatriation," see Yann Scioldo-Zurcher, *Devenir métropolitain: Politique d'intégration et parcours de rapatriés d'Algérie en métropole (1954–2005)* (Paris: Edi-tions de l'Ecole des hautes études en sciences sociales, 2010); Sung-Eun Choi, *Decolo-nization and the French of Algeria: Bringing the Settler Colony Home* (Basingstoke, UK: Palgrave Macmillan, 2016).

59   David Peppercorn, *Bordeaux* (London: Mitchell Beazley, 2003), 75–77; information on the Tari family is found in ANOM, lists of *état civil*.

60   Peppercorn, *Bordeaux*, 235, 239; *Annuaire de la viticulture algérienne*, 1951; www .chateau-fonreaud.com; www.chateau-lestage.com.

61   George M. Taber, *In Search of Bacchus: Wanderings in the Wonderful World of Wine Tourism* (New York: Scribner, 2009), 221–222; www.chateau-arsac.com/raoux.php; http://pr-ws.com/fr/histoire. The Raoux family is related to the Sénéclauze family (see Chapter 6 in this volume).

62 Statistic in Scioldo-Zurcher, *Devenir métropolitain,* 15.

63 Françoise Brun, *Les Français d'Algérie dans l'agriculture du Midi méditerranéen: Etude géographique* (Gap: Editions Ophrys, 1976), 207.

64 Ibid., 24–30.

65 Interview with Paul Bosc, Niagara-on-the-Lake, Ontario, 5 June 2011; www .fromtheboscfamily.com/chateau-des-charmes.

66 Brun, *Les Français d'Algérie dans l'agriculture du Midi méditerranéen,* 96; Peter H. Amann, *The Corncribs of Buzet: Modernizing Agriculture in the French Southwest* (Princeton, NJ: Princeton University Press, 1990), 108–109; Scioldo-Zurcher, *Devenir métropolitain,* 253–255; René Domergue, *L'intégration des pieds-noirs dans les villages du Midi* (Paris: L'Harmattan, 2005), 124–125.

67 Domergue, *L'intégration des pieds-noirs dans les villages du Midi,* 74–75.

68 Brun, *Les Français d'Algérie dans l'agriculture du Midi méditerranéen,* 96–97, 328; quotation in Rosemary George, *The Wines of the South of France: From Banyuls to St. Raphaël* (London: Mitchell Beazley, 2003), 457.

69 Domergue, *L'intégration des pieds-noirs dans les villages du Midi,* 61–62, 98–100.

70 Emile Chabal, "Managing the Postcolony: Minority Politics in Montpellier, c.1960– 2012," *Contemporary European History* 23:2 (2014): 243.

71 Brun, *Les Français d'Algérie dans l'agriculture du Midi méditerranéen,* 287.

72 Domergue, *L'intégration des pieds-noirs dans les villages du Midi,* 106–107.

73 Brun, *Les Français d'Algérie dans l'agriculture du Midi méditerranéen,* 122–123, 290–293, 306; Domergue, *L'intégration des pieds-noirs dans les villages du Midi,* 15, 111.

74 René Domergue, *L'intégration des Maghrébins dans les villages du Midi* (Montpézat: René Domergue, 2011), 23–29, 32; Domergue, *L'intégration des pieds-noirs dans les villages du Midi,* 28–29; Brun, *Les Français d'Algérie dans l'agriculture du Midi méditerranéen,* 122–124, 192.

75 Amann, *The Corncribs of Buzet,* 107–108, and information supplied by the town hall of Saint-Cézert.

76 Brun, *Les Français d'Algérie dans l'agriculture du Midi méditerranéen,* 123.

77 See Robert Aldrich, "France's Colonial Island: Corsica and the Empire," *French History and Civilization: Papers from the George Rudé Seminar* 3 (2009): 112–125.

78 Jean Hermitte, "Conditions et traits généraux de l'implantation des 'pieds-noirs' en Corse," in Hermitte, ed., *L'implantation en Corse des Français d'Afrique du Nord* (Nice: Institut d'études et de recherches interethniques et interculturelles, 1971), 1–9; Brun, *Les Français d'Algérie dans l'agriculture du Midi méditerranéen,* 232–233; on 1958, see Paul Silvani, *Corse des années ardentes (1939–1976)* (Paris: Editions Albatros, 1976), 81–96; and Robert Ramsay, *The Corsican Time-Bomb* (Manchester, UK: Manchester University Press, 1983), 27–30.

79 H. Isnard, "Structures des vignobles méditerranéens français: La Corse," *Méditerranée* 4:3 (1963): 79–87.

80 Brun, *Les Français d'Algérie dans l'agriculture du Midi méditerranéen,* 234–235, 255, 318.

81 Ibid., 251; statistic at 247. On *pieds-noirs* and memory, see Claire Eldridge, *From Empire to Exile: History and Memory within the Pied-Noir and Harki Communities,*

1962–2012 (Manchester, UK: Manchester University Press, 2016); Andrea L. Smith, *Colonial Memory and Postcolonial Europe: Maltese Settlers in Algeria and France* (Bloomington: Indiana University Press, 2006).

82 Brun, *Les Français d'Algérie dans l'agriculture du Midi méditerranéen*, 240–254, 322; Jean-Claude Baysang, "Les Français d'Afrique du Nord dans la plaine orientale corse," in Hermitte, ed., *L'implantation en Corse des Français d'Afrique du Nord*, 37–48.

83 Brun, *Les Français d'Algérie dans l'agriculture du Midi méditerranéen*, 257, 287, 329–331.

84 Ramsay, *The Corsican Time-Bomb*, 56–57, 60. Anti-colonial language was also a feature of other autonomist movements, like the one in Brittany. See, for example, Maryon McDonald, *"We Are Not French!" Language, Culture and Identity in Brittany* (London: Routledge, 1989), 84–85.

85 Ramsay, *The Corsican Time-Bomb*, 83–84, 99–100.

86 Ibid., 100–104; Silvani, *Corse des années ardentes*, 228–236. The graffiti is seen in a photograph of the occupied Depeille winery in Paul Silvani, "Aléria: una storia d'oghje," http://www.interromania.com/corsu-cismuntincu/impara-u-corsu/documentu/aleria-una-storia-doghje-2-10440.html.

87 Figures from Isnard, "Structures des vignobles méditerranéens français"; François-Noël Mercury, *Vignes, vins et vignerons de Corse* (Ajaccio: Editions Alain Piazzola, 1991), 218; Conseil interprofessionnel des Vins de Corse, press kit, 2014.

88 Domergue, *L'intégration des Maghrébins dans les villages du Midi*, 28. Four North African workers were briefly held hostage during the Aléria occupation. See Silvani, *Corse des années ardentes*, 230–231.

89 Mercury, *Vignes, vins et vignerons de Corse*, 90–95, 219; George, *The Wines of the South of France*, 684; "Corsica," in Jancis Robinson, ed., *The Oxford Companion to Wine*, 3rd ed. (Oxford: Oxford University Press, 2006), 203–204.

90 Francis Skalli bought this property in 1961; his son Robert sold it in 2011. See www.fortant-de-france.com/fr/l-histoire-d-un-pionnier.r-226/notre-histoire.r-230/; www.clospoggiale.fr/histoire.html; George, *The Wines of the South of France*, 680–681. Robert Skalli is also known for developing the very successful St. Supéry estate in California's Napa Valley. See www.stsupery.com/inside/#timeline; and Michaela Kane Rodeno (former CEO at St. Supéry), *From Bubbles to Boardrooms: Serendipitous Stories from inside the Wine Business* (Oakville, CA: Villa Ragazzi Press, 2015). Of a Jewish family from Oranie, Skalli experimented at St. Supéry with producing Passover wine. See Roger Horowitz, *Kosher USA: How Coke Became Kosher and Other Tales of Modern Food* (New York: Columbia University Press, 2016), 153–154. In 2015 the family sold St. Supéry to Chanel, Inc.

91 Paul Birebent, *Hommes, vignes et vins de l'Algérie Française* (Nice: Editions Gandini, 2007), 197.

92 Personal communication, 19 July 2013. Two of Birebent's sons found work in the wine industry, one of them in the Napa Valley as chief winemaker at the Signorello Estate, whose winery was destroyed by wildfires in October 2017.

93 Jacques Vigna, "Le vin en Algérie: L'histoire de 'Sidi Brahim,'" *Mémoire vive* 49:3–4 (2011). The Vigna family eventually sold the brand; as of 2018 it was owned by Groupe Castel, using wine from Tunisian rather than Algerian vineyards (www.sidi-brahim.fr).

94 Roger Bécriaux, "18000 hectolitres de vin détruits," *Le Monde*, 12 Aug. 1981; Gavignaud-Fontaine, *Le Languedoc viticole*, 394–395.

95　The 1985 statistic is from Sutton, "Algeria's vineyards," 105; the 1885 statistic from *Annuaire de la viticulture algérienne,* 1931.

96　Guérin, *L'Algérie qui se cherche,* 24.

97　Bennoune and El-Kenz, *Le hasard et l'histoire,* 1:394; Martin Evans and John Phillips, *Algeria: Anger of the Dispossessed* (New Haven, CT: Yale University Press, 2007), 85–86.

98　Michael Willis, *The Islamist Challenge in Algeria: A Political History* (Reading, UK: Garnet Publishing, 1996), 65; Martin Stone, *The Agony of Algeria* (New York: Columbia University Press, 1997), 153–154.

99　Founded in 1968, the ONCV monopolized the supply of Algerian wine until 1988, when a program of economic liberalization allowed a few private production companies to form. ONCV, *Vins d'Algérie* (brochure); and interview with Omar Fodil, ONCV head office, Algiers, 25 June 2013. On the reduction of state control over Algerian agriculture in the 1980s, see Nouschi, *L'Algérie amère,* 294–298.

100　Stone, *The Agony of Algeria,* 167–168; Evans and Phillips, *Algeria,* 160. On the elections, see Willis, *The Islamist Challenge in Algeria,* 132–137.

101　John and Erica Platter, *Africa Uncorked: Travels in Extreme Wine Territory* (San Francisco: Wine Appreciation Guild, 2002), 40–42. Key studies of the civil war include Luis Martinez, *The Algerian Civil War 1990–1998* (New York: Columbia University Press, 2000); Hugh Roberts, *The Battlefield: Algeria, 1988–2002. Studies in a Broken Polity* (London: Verso, 2003).

102　Official statistics since 1995 at www.oiv.int/en/databases-and-statistics/statistics. By the mid-2010s, total annual output was typically around 500,000 hectoliters, most of it consumed in Algeria.

103　Gilles Fontaine, "Les sulfureux business de Gérard Depardieu," *L'Express,* 1 Jan. 2003; Chawki Amari, "Le projet Depardieu," *El Watan,* 17 June 2013; on Khalifa, see Amel Boubekeur, "Rolling Either Way? Algerian Entrepreneurs as Both Agents of Change and Means of Preservation of the System," *Journal of North African Studies* 18:3 (2013): 475–476. In 2017 the ONCV was renamed Société de transformation des produits viticoles (SOTRAVIT).

104　Isabelle Fraser, "Red, Red Wine: China Snaps up French Vineyards to Quench its Newfound Thirst," *Daily Telegraph* (London), 12 June 2017; L. Curran and M. Thorpe, "Chinese Foreign Investment in Wine Production: A Comparative Study of the Bordeaux Region in France and Western Australia," in Roberta Capitello, Steve Charters, David Menival, and Jingxue Yuan, eds., *The Wine Value Chain in China: Consumers, Marketing and the Wider World* (Cambridge, MA: Chandos Publishing, 2017), 209–227. See also Andrew Trotman, "China's Vineyards Dwarf the French," *Daily Telegraph,* 28 Apr. 2015.

105　Fahim Djebara, "En Algérie, les autorités encouragent la production locale . . . sauf celle du vin," *Le Monde Afrique,* 14 June 2017; www.oiv.int/en/databases-and-statistics/statistics.

106　I was unable to verify this claim.

107　"Vestiges et édifices anciens, sauver l'histoire de la ville," *Bel Abbès info* (online), 11 May 2014; "Le château de Bastide Léon, ressuscité," *Bel Abbès info,* 20 Sept. 2016. Some examples in this section resonate with material in Ann Laura Stoler, ed., *Imperial Debris: On Ruins and Ruination* (Durham, NC: Duke University Press, 2013).

108 The White Fathers' motherhouse, which once stood about 150 meters away, no longer existed.

109 Benjamin Roger, "Algérie: La grande mosquée d'Alger, les raisons de la colère," www .jeuneafrique.com, 22 Aug. 2012; "Les gros œuvres du minaret de la Grande mosquée d'Alger achevés," www.huffpostmaghreb.com, 11 Nov. 2017.

110 Import statistics from 2016 at https://tradingeconomics.com/algeria/imports-by -country. On Chinese-Algerian relations and other construction projects, see Muhamad S. Olimat, *China and North Africa since World War II: A Bilateral Approach* (Lanham, MD: Lexington Books, 2014), 33–48.

EPILOGUE

1 Jean Rives, *Gaston Doumergue: Du modèle républicain au Sauveur Suprême* (Toulouse: Presses de l'Institut d'études politiques de Toulouse, 1999), 27. Doumergue was in Aïn-el-Arba in 1891.

2 See ANOM, Oran, 2M 73A and 73B.

3 Letter to Doumergue reproduced in L. Abadie, *Aïn-Témouchent de ma jeunesse* (Nice: Jacques Gandini, 2004), 91; ANOM, Oran, 1M 34.

4 The susceptibility of soils to erosion in this area was already a concern in colonial times. See ANOM, Oran, 2M 73A, Chef du Service départementale de la défense et de la restauration des sols to prefect of Oran, "Gaston-Doumergue: protection des terres contre l'érosion," 25 Nov. 1948.

5 Ed McAllister explores this image of the period in "Algeria's 'Belle Époque': Memories of the 1970s as a Window on the Present," in Patrick Crowley, ed., *Algeria: Nation, Culture and Transnationalism* (Liverpool: Liverpool University Press, 2017), 46–62.

6 ANOM, Oran, 1M 62, Enquête sur la situation des détenteurs de propriétés de colonisation Oran au point de vue de plantation des vignes: centre de Gaston-Doumergue (1931 survey); Oran, 5Q 18, sub-prefect of Oran to lieutenant commandant of gendarmerie of Aïn-Témouchent, "Défense des centres et des fermes isolées," 20 Oct. 1955.

7 Some of this is documented in Michel Launay, *Paysans algériens 1960–2006,* 3rd ed. (Paris: Karthala, 2007).

8 On Islamist calls for a "wine-free Algeria" in the mid-2010s, see, for example, Amer Ouali, "Algérie: La vente d'alcool échauffe les esprits salafistes," *Le Point,* 30 Apr. 2015.

9 Jean Pelegri, *Les oliviers de la justice* (Paris: Gallimard, 1959), 142.

10 Hildebert Isnard, "La vigne en Algérie: Etude géographique" (PhD diss., Université de Paris I-Sorbonne, 1947), 952.

11 Mouloud Achour, *Les dernières vendanges* (Algiers: SNED, 1975), 98, 103.

12 Jean Pelegri, *Ma mère l'Algérie* (Arles: Actes Sud, 1990), 22–23.

Acknowledgments

I am very pleased to acknowledge the financial assistance I received in the making of this book from the University of Delaware's Department of History, College of Arts and Sciences, Institute for Global Studies, and Center for Global and Area Studies. I am fortunate to work in a department that is committed to supporting original research. I will not list all of my excellent colleagues, but must give special thanks to John Hurt and Arwen Mohun, who each as department chair provided help at crucial moments; to David Shearer, who, with Marina Dobronovskaya, enabled me to explore Algerian wine's Russian / Soviet connections; and to Anne Boylan and Peter Kolchin, who remain as generous and supportive in their retirement as on the day I arrived in Delaware twenty years ago. Angela Hoseth helped in countless ways with images and other technical matters and, like all of my department's wonderful staff—Deborah Hartnett, Doug Tobias, Diane Clark, and Amy Dolbow—often made a day working on the manuscript feel less lonely. Robert Schultz was a pleasure to work with on the maps.

Chapters 5 and 6 build on ideas first presented in "Roll Out the Barrel: French and Algerian Ports and the Birth of the Wine Tanker," *French Politics, Culture and Society* 35:2 (2017): 111–132. I thank Herrick Chapman for overseeing that publication.

Across the Atlantic I benefited from the help of Daniel Hick at the Archives Nationales d'Outre-Mer in Aix-en-Provence; Hervé Noël at the Centre de Documentation Historique sur l'Algérie, also in Aix; and Father Stefaan Minnaert, formerly at the White Fathers' archives in Rome. My research in Algeria was facilitated by Robert Parks, Karim Ouaras, and Rachid Hammamouche; while there, I was privileged to learn from Lahcene Amirouche, Hafif Bousahba, Fouad Soufi, and Zohra Kheddar. I hope I have represented the past of their extraordinary country in a way that feels real.

I had many occasions during this project to be grateful for the advice and friendship of Alice Conklin, J. P. Daughton, Eric Jennings, and Elizabeth Foster. I also enjoyed the camaraderie of Elizabeth Heath and Joe Bohling, excellent scholars whose research interests paralleled and sometimes intersected with my own. Looking back further, it is a pleasure finally to acknowledge a long-standing debt to my undergraduate history teachers at the University of Exeter. It was there that Colin Jones first got me interested in studying things French and messily social, and encouraged me to take the interest further. Undoubtedly it was my father, B. T. White (1927–2012), however, whose enthusiasm for history first kindled my own. I am sad that he will not see this book.

Historians like to warn against making predictions, then often prove their own point by misjudging how long it will take to complete a piece of work. I didn't anticipate that my daughter, Stella, would be at university by the time I finished a project that was in the background of so much of her childhood, but I'm happy that she wasn't put off the study of history and hope that the book preserves some memories for her. (Stella, the wild boar reference is for you.) As for my other beloved fellow traveler, Patricia Sloane-White, my words feel inadequate. Her work as an anthropologist on economic lives in Southeast Asia has inspired me and expanded my horizons, and she is always the reader I have most in mind when I write. I don't know whom to thank for the fact she survived what happened as we walked to work together one November morning in 2018. I only know that I am more grateful than ever for the strength and love she has brought me in our years together. I dedicate this book to her.

Index

Abbas, Ferhat, 176, 178–179, 191, 194
Abdelkader, Emir, 27–29, 58, 213
Abdesselam, Belaïd, 217, 227
Absenteeism, 48, 202–203
Acclimatization, 25–26, 34, 37
Achour, Mouloud, 214–215, 220, 233
Action régionaliste corse (ARC), 225
Ageron, Charles-Robert, 72, 142
Agricultural capitalism, 77–79, 108–109, 135, 144, 161, 163, 186, 239n7
Agricultural societies, 46, 55, 62, 74, 77
Ahmar El Aïn, 214. *See also* Ameur-el-Aïn
Aïn-el-Arba, 182, 231
Aïn el-Turck, 30
Aïn-Isser, 199
Aïn-Kial, 167
Aïn-Tédélès, 165, 176
Aïn-Témouchent, 42, 167, 198, 213; viticulture in region, 68, 84, 109, 126, 128, 154, 206, 231
Alabama, 18, 25
Albert, Marcellin, 114–115
Alberto, Fernando, 52–55
Aléria, 226
Alfa. See Esparto grass
Algerian Assembly, 187, 190–191
Algerian Communist Party, 165–166, 189, 280n78. *See also* Communists
Algerian nationalism, 142, 159, 176–180, 192, 195
Algerians as wine producers, 128–129, 154

Algerian War (for independence), 190–209
Alger républicain, 189
Algiers (city), 26, 131, 190–192, 202, 228–229; industries serving viticulture in, 103–108, 181; land use in, 174, 183, 207; port of, 50–51, 150–154, 207
Algiers (department), 7, 55, 60, 122; phylloxera in, 81–82, 84–87
Alibert, René, 157
Alicante (region), 52, 95, 221
Allard, Jacques, 199
Alsace, 122
Alvernhe, René, 165–166
Ameur-el-Aïn, 85. *See also* Ahmar El Aïn
Amis du Manifeste et de la Liberté (AML), 178–179
Annaba, 14. *See also* Bône
Anti-alcoholism, 6, 196–197, 218, 228
Anti-Semitism. *See* Jews in Algeria
Antwerp, 217
Apt, 108
Aramon (grape variety), 71
Ardèche (department), 44, 52
Argentina, 16, 38–39, 84
Arlès-Dufour family: Armand, 47, 55, 59, 75–76; Alphonse, 76
Armée roulante, 95
Arzew, 80, 106
Association des ulama musulmans algériens, 142, 159–160, 195
Aube (department), 52
Aucamville, 186